DATE DUE

AUG 2 9 1982		
DEC 1 7 1982		

DEMCO NO. 38-298

THE THIRD CENTURY

THE THIRD CENTURY

America as a Post-Industrial Society

Edited by
SEYMOUR MARTIN LIPSET

HOOVER INSTITUTION PRESS
Stanford University, Stanford, California

The Hoover Institution on War, Revolution and Peace, founded at Stanford University in 1919 by the late President Herbert Hoover, is an interdisciplinary research center for advanced study on domestic and international affairs in the twentieth century. The views expressed in its publications are entirely those of the authors and do not necessarily reflect the views of the staff, officers, or Board of Overseers of the Hoover Institution.

Hoover Institution Publication 203

Designed by Elizabeth Gehman

Contents

Seymour Martin Lipset

Predicting the future of post-industrial society:

Can we do it?

1 The title of this book, an outgrowth of a lecture series under the same heading, suggests an effort to predict the future of the United States in its third century. As the reader will note, the essays presented here have not done so. Rather, for the most part they constitute analyses of what has happened to different institutions and groups, particularly in the recent past, and suggest scenarios for the immediate future that largely form a projection of present trends.

This refusal to engage in long-range futurology represents a deliberate conclusion: social scientists are not in a position to make such predictions with any degree of certainty that their anticipations are likely to be accurate. The reasons for this are simple. It has become increasingly evident that for good methodological reasons we are still in a situation comparable to that of the meteorologists—they can describe what is happening to produce a cold wave or a drought; they can look at yesterday's weather and predict tomorrow's; but they do not understand enough about the complex relations among the many forces that produce diverse weather to make reliable long-term predictions.

It seems clear that social scientists also can explain only a small part of the variance, of the causal factors, involved in dealing with the major societal or worldwide issues that concern them. To a considerable degree, scholars, like other people, tend to react to what are often short-term changes in mood when defining the major problems that require analysis and understanding. Many changes, initially perceived as secular, structural ones, occur in waves that ebb and flow, though not necessarily in any regular cycle. In this introductory chapter I would like, therefore, to point up some of the problems faced by the different social sciences in predicting major developments, and to look in more detail at the discussions of possible sources of limits to growth, or of continued growth.

THE LIMITS TO FUTUROLOGY AND
SOCIAL SCIENCE ANALYSIS

Awareness of the difficulties in making projections is evident in the writings of the futurologists themselves. Rudolf Klein has noted that the dominant concerns of the young field of futurology, itself, have changed dramatically. "Indeed, just to glance at some recent products is to realize how quickly intellectual fashions now oscillate: man's future (if one is to believe the professional social prophets) is changing almost on a year to year basis." In the 1960s, futurologists were concerned with the ways to secure growth, with the negative implications of automation, with the problems of nuclear destruction:

> Now . . . it appears that the world's long-term future has suddenly changed. We no longer live under the shadow of nuclear war. We are no longer faced by the threat of enforced idleness brought on by automation. We are no longer faced by the danger of domination by an all-knowing because all-computerized bureaucracy or by a military-industrial elite (to quote some other prophetic visions of the past). Instead we are told that we are living in the the shadow of an overpopulated, overexploited, overproducing, and overconsuming world.[1]

Social scientists, working on more specialized topics, cannot boast of a better record. Our standard operative procedure seems to be to account for a current trend, or current definition of the mess that we are in, by looking for other concomitant structural trends. Since the structural tendencies associated with the trend we are trying to explain or find solutions for generally continue, while more often than not the trend or problem that concerns us disappears or ebbs away, much of our interpretive analysis turns out to be inadequate. This can be seen by looking back at some of the kinds of analyses and predictions made by social scientists and economists over the past three decades, that is, since World War II. An examination of this record suggests that we should be exceedingly modest about using our status as experts to draw conclusions that call for major policy changes. I would like to briefly mention some of these.

The first misprediction is the depression that never arrived. As we all know, the Great Depression of the 1930s was not ended by the natural play of economic forces or, in most countries, by deliberate government action. Rather, mass unemployment and low prices were eliminated by World War II. Many economists generally assumed, therefore, that once the war ended, large-scale unemployment would recur, particularly in those industries and areas that had concentrated heavily on defense work.

Scholars were so certain of this development that a number of research projects were planned that involved studying the impact of unemployment on people who had been employed during the war. Detailed interviews were made with people whose jobs were certain to disappear with the end of the war. The call by Henry Wallace and others for government planning to guarantee 60 million jobs was dismissed as utopian. In fact, as we know, there was no postwar depression of any major consequence. The developed world has sustained three decades of relatively high levels of employment. Most of the recessions resulted in lower rates of unemployment than were experienced in some prewar periods, such as the 1920s, which had been considered times of prosperity.

It is now almost forgotten that continued depression consciousness in the late 1950s and early 1960s led many economists to pay considerable attention to finding ways to speed up growth both within the United States and on a world scale. As Henry Wallich has noted:

> There can be little doubt that, particularly following the recession of 1957–58, economists began to go overboard in their glorification of growth. In part this was a political response to the slow growth of the late 1950s, in part a reflection of the impact of Sputnik. The interest of less-developed countries in catching up helped to cast growth in the role of an all-absorbing goal at that time.[2]

The record of economists in anticipating major developments during the 1970s does not lend support to any argument that their theory adequately accounts for the working of the economy. For example, they did not anticipate the postwar recessions of 1973–75. Brookings economist Arthur Okun has pointed out that "most economic forecasters, including me, saw. . . a strong but well-balanced expansion in 1973 accompanied by an imperfect but hardly alarming record of price performance. Rarely has such a broad, bi-partisan professional consensus been so wrong."[3]

Economists, on the whole, also failed to anticipate the change in relationship between unemployment and inflation. It had always been assumed that inflation was negatively related to increases in unemployment. This assumption has not held up for various periods in the postwar epoch, particularly the recession of the seventies, from which we are just emerging. As George Katona indicates:

> Before 1973, the doctrine embodied by the Philips curve was generally accepted, and inflation and unemployment were viewed as opposites. When the one increased or accelerated, the other was expected to decline or slow down. Economic policy was based on that doctrine and inflation was fought by attempting to slow down economic activity and reduce employment. But in 1974–75, at a time of unprecedented two-digit inflation, unemployment rose sharply. In 1976–77 unemployment remained high in spite of sizable inflation.[4]

Norman Macrae has also pointed to the inadequacies of economic forecasts. He notes:

> Over the first 20 postwar years, a majority of important decision-influencing people at one time or another forecast coming famines in six main particular products. The world then progressively created unsaleable and unprofitable surpluses in every one of them: temperate foodstuffs after 1947, raw materials after 1951, more "manufactured goods than could conceivably ever be sold to the United States and bridge the dollar gap" after about 1954, fuels (especially coal after 1945, and oil after Suez), orthodoxly trained university students (especially in the science faculties) after 1960.[5]

It is with good reason that Robert Heilbroner has emphasized the difficulties faced by economists in predicting the future of a national economy, saying that "the maze of interconnections in modern society is so vast and complex that it requires a Laplacean intelligence to predict the consequence of any action. An industrial economy utilizes and creates volumes of data that are beyond the capacity of the vastest computer. It is an information-generating system that can only be controlled by its interior cybernetic devices—the crude stimuli of the price mechanism—which, alas, give rise to the very problems that require policy in order to be corrected."[6]

Wassily Leontief is even more pessimistic about the ability of economics to formulate generalizations that withstand change. As he put it in his presidential address to the American Economic Association in 1971:

> In contrast to most physical sciences, we study a system that is not only exceedingly complex but also in a state of constant flux. I have in mind not the obvious changes in the variables . . . that our equations are supposed to explain, but the basic structural relationships described by the form and the parameters of these equations. In order to know what the shape of the structural relationships actually are at any given time, we have to keep them under continuous surveillance.[7]

Monetarist economists may be in no better shape. I was present at a meeting in which Allen Greenspan, then head of the Council of Economic Advisors and sympathetic to the approach, discussed inflationary pressures, and in so doing failed to mention the money supply. When asked why not by a monetarist present, Greenspan replied that unfortunately for his and the questioner's theory, the available data simply did not show a relationship.

In citing these problems of economic analysis, I am not suggesting that economics is not able to explain or understand what has happened since 1945. Economists, like the rest of us, are good historians. That is, they are able to find the factors that explain and retrospectively predict what occurred. Somehow, however, they have not been very good forecasters. Robert Solow has emphasized the problem that economists' "predictions are often wrong" poses for their role as policy advisors: "Why should anyone who forecasts so badly be expected to have worthwhile opinions on other questions?"[8]

Demography, a borderline discipline falling between sociology and economics, also cannot boast of its record. Extrapolating from the history of Western countries, demographers formulated the "theory of the demographic transition," which projected a steady decline in the rate of population growth in advanced societies characterized by "the achievement of general literacy, urbanization, and industrialization" and the diffusion of knowledge of birth control methods. But as Dudley Kirk noted in the mid-1960s, the theory seemed to break down around World War II:

It is ironic that demographers developed the techniques for projecting certain long-standing trends in the components of population growth, especially in natality, just at a time when these trends were about to dissolve. New attitudes favoring earlier marriage and more children appeared in the very societies where the great majority of families had been practicing birth control. The recovery of the birthrate in Western countries just before, during, and especially after World War II violated the projection of previous trends and those formulations of the demographic transition that considered Western countries to be approaching a stationary or declining population.[9]

As we all know, this period did not last either. Kenneth Boulding concludes that "fertility seems to be subject to quite unpredictable shifts. Thus, in the United States we had a period of high fertility (1947–1961) which was quite unpredicted, now we are in a phase of low fertility which was equally unpredicted. . . . It would be a rash prophet, however, who would assert that there could not be an equally unexpected rise in the future, or even a further unexpected drop, to the point where one country or another would exhibit the 'fertility shock' which Rumania went into in 1969, when it apparently hit the Rumanian government that Rumanians might simply die out."[10]

The same concern has recently been voiced in Australia, which has reached the zero population growth level. The slogan "populate or perish" has been revived, as students of demographic trends warn Australians that "they may be a dying race." A television program in West Germany presented in 1978 was titled: "Are the Germans Dying Out?" since Germany now has more deaths than births annually. The French began a major campaign designed to increase the birthrate and avert a population decline in 1979.

This decline in the birth rate has affected both developed and underdeveloped countries. Demographers Donald J. Bogue and Amy Ong Tsui note this "worldwide fertility decline comes as a major surprise to many demographers, who anticipated no change or only very gradual declines in fertility. For example, the United Nations population projections made in 1973 predicted levels of fertility for 1975 that were, for almost all nations, substantially above that actual fertility of these countries in 1975. Indeed, the decline seems to have been two and a half times greater than these projections!"[11]

As Charles Westoff has effectively noted:

> I must now admit that the record of population projections has not been a happy one. A 1947 projection of the 1970 U.S. population fell 65 million short of the 205 million actually enumerated. . . . The major variable determining such estimates is fertility, and fertility has changed considerably since the early 1960s. . . . To develop more accurate population forecasts, demographers would have to know a lot more than they now do about the social and economic determinants of fertility. Even assuming such theoretical understanding, one would then have to predict the future course of the appropriate social and economic indexes, and there is no evidence that the relevant social-science disciplines have developed any such capacity.[12]

Economists and demographers, of course, do not have the worst record. Other social scientists are equally inefficient. Problems, anticipated by a considerable amount of social science literature, that society would face in reabsorbing the veterans of World War II simply did not occur, for the most part, either on the level of collective or individual behavior. The sociological literature of the 1950s addressed itself in some part to explaining what seemed to be major basic changes in the American national character. Those who agreed that the conservative fifties reflected increased secular pressures for conformism in American society ranged in political point of view from Erich Fromm and C. Wright Mills to William White and David Riesman. They sought to explain structurally the increased prevalence of other-directed or market-oriented personalities, which had replaced the once dominant inner-directed or producer-oriented types. The change was related to the shift from an economy of small producers, a labor force a major segment of which was self-employed in agriculture or business, to one in which the majority worked within large-scale bureaucracies. The analyses suggested that the latter environment tended to produce conformists, for people within bureaucracies advanced by selling themselves, by impressing superiors and colleagues. In the earlier society people succeeded by working hard and intensively, with much less concern for the opinions of others. The logically predictable conformist decade of the fifties was followed, as we know, by the nonconformism of the late sixties and early seventies. Yet, the same structural environment, the factors that allegedly produced conformist trends were present in a more intensive fashion in the late 1960s.

Sociologists also erred in their anticipations about the class structure of American society. Leftist students of stratification such as

Robert Lynd and C. Wright Mills and conservative sociologists such as August Hollingshead and W. Lloyd Warner suggested the high level of social mobility that characterized American society was a consequence of economic growth and geographical expansion, trends that could not continue indefinitely. The growth of large-scale corporations, the decline of self-employment, were also logically expected to reduce opportunity. Many anticipated the emergence of hard, fixed class lines and conflict as a result. Such assumptions also turned out to be erroneous. What the experts failed to evaluate properly was the change in the occupational structure. The proportion of lowly, unskilled positions has steadily declined—it is now under 10 percent, while middle- and upper-level jobs, requiring more education, have increased. Where we once had a pyramidal structure with many menial jobs at the bottom, we now have shifted to a diamond one, which bulges at the middle. Social mobility on a mass level remains as high or higher than ever.

The analysts of stratification also failed to anticipate that the combination of a rapid expansion of higher education facilities, which permitted persons from relatively deprived backgrounds to go to universities, and the end of family capitalism, the concomitant growth of large-scale corporate bureaucracies, together with the increase in government, would create new possibilities for the lowly to rise within the corporate ladder of industry and the bureaucratic hierarchy of government. A much larger proportion of the heads of major companies now come from poor social origins than ever before in American history.[13]

As a result of these developments, there appears to be less rather than more emphasis on status (family class) background, more social egalitarianism. The technological revolution, computerization, and increased automation have reduced the proportion of people in the lower class. Increased mechanization has led to greater equality. Comparable structural trends may be found throughout the developed world.

The most striking example of a generalized failure of sociologists to anticipate developments may be found in the area of ethnicity. Until recently, Marxist and non-Marxist scholars agreed on a standardized set of generalizations about ethnic and national minorities. These assumed that ethnicity reflected the conditions of traditional society, in which people lived in small communities isolated from one another, and in which mass communications and transportation were limited. Most scholars anticipated that industrialization, urbanization, and the mass spread of education would operate to reduce ethnic consciousness, that universalism would replace particularism. Marxists were certain that socialism would mean the end of ethnic tension and consciousness on the levels that existed in presocialist societies. Non-Marxist sociologists in Western countries assumed that the processes of industrialization and modernization would do the same. Assimilation of minorities into a larger integrated whole was viewed as the inevitable future. As two scholars of the subject, Nathan Glazer and Daniel P. Moynihan note, it was generally believed that "divisions of culture, religion, language," and race:

> would inevitably lose their weight and sharpness in modern and modernizing societies, that there would be increasing emphasis on achievement rather than ascription, that common systems of education and communication would level differences, that nationally uniform economic and political systems would have the same effect. Under these circumstances the "primordial" (or in any case antecedent) differences between groups would be expected to become of lesser significance. The "liberal expectancy" flows into the "radical expectancy"—that class circumstances would become the main line of division between people, erasing the earlier lines of tribe, language, religion, national origin, and that thereafter these *class* divisions would themselves, after revolution, disappear. Thus Karl Marx and his followers reacted with impatience to the heritage of the past, as they saw it, in the form of ethnic attachments.[14]

As we all know, the opposite has occurred, both in the Western and Communist worlds, and in the less developed world as well. The Achilles' heel of Communism has turned out to be nationalism, not only the consciousness of Poles and Czechs vis-à-vis the Soviet Union, but also of the various national groupings within Yugoslavia and the Soviet Union. Most of the multilingual, binational or bi-religious states that have persisted for many decades, if not centuries, have faced turmoil in recent years. Canada, Belgium, Malaysia, and Lebanon all face crises of national existence in which minorities press for autonomy if not independence. Pakistan and Cyprus have divided. Nigeria suppressed an ethnic rebellion. In the classic Swiss case, tension has risen within multilinguistic cantons. France faces difficulties with its Basques, Bretons, and Corsicans. In Spain, Basques and Catalans have demanded linguistic rights and greater autonomy.

In seeking to explain, after the fact, the disintegration of previously united societies, some social scientists have in characteristic fashion inverted the causal process, that is, they identify the processes that once were supposed to be leading to a decline in differences as the cause of their increase. As Eugene Skolnikoff notes:

> The old belief that growing *interdependence* among nations would breed at least a sense of common purpose, and more hopefully a genuine community of values, has proved a weak reed at best. Unexpectedly rapid growth in the relations and dependencies across national borders has not reduced strife but rather has sharpened division and distinctions. Much of the change can be traced to the more rapid development and application of technology than was or could have been predicted, a phenomenon that still appears to be accelerating. . . .[I]ncreased openness and interconnectedness has led to new areas of dispute, breakdown of concerns within nations. . . .[15]

Sociological generalizations about the necessary functional requirements for the stability of family relationships, which supposedly affected relationships between men and women, also have turned out to be contradicted by developments. One may find many references, including in my own writings, to the proposition that sex cannot be a source of major political difference, that the members of the same family unit must have similar social-political attitudes. Role differentiation between men and women, husbands and wives, fathers and mothers, was perceived as fulfilling functional needs. Affective, that is emotional, relationships and instrumental ones were seen as being dealt with by different sexes because they could not be handled well by the same persons. Biological sex differences led to sex being used as a way of differentiating roles within families and societies. Once again, the events of recent years require some serious modification of these standard assumptions and predictions.

Political analysis is in no better shape. During the early fifties in the United States, I was one of a group of scholars who attempted to explain the phenomenon of McCarthyism.[16] Most of us linked it to the tensions of a prosperous society, which produced heightened status concerns and anxieties, increased competition among groups and individuals who were rising or falling in status. Status politics, rather than class politics, seemingly characterized such periods. The underlying

trends that supposedly produced increased status tensions have continued, but McCarthyism disappeared with the end of the Korean War.
There are, of course, other continuing forms of group tension, such as
the rise of white racist movements, which may be properly linked to
status threats. It is clear, however, that the broad predictive power of
the theory of status politics is nowhere near as strong as was suggested
in the early fifties.[17]

The post-McCarthy era found many people analyzing "the end of
ideology," or as in my own case, the "decline."[18] The reduction in
ideological tensions within advanced industrial societies was related in
large measure to growing affluence, to the incorporation of previously
excluded strata into the body politic, to the spread of education, and to
the seeming reduction of many of the extreme morbidities of industrial
society through the institutionalization of the planning and welfare
state. Although many of the analysts of the end of ideology excluded
intellectuals and young people from their generalizations about the
decline of ideology, it is generally true that few anticipated the
emergence of the forms of protest that have characterized the growth of
the New Left and minority movements in the late sixties and early
seventies.

The New Left and the New Politics of the sixties and seventies,
which drew their strength heavily from the universities and from the
ranks of the intelligentsia, the educated professional strata, were in turn
subjected to scholarly analysis. In this country and elsewhere, the student revolt was explained in part by changes in the situation of the
students, particularly within the university. It was argued that the
growth of large massive bureaucratic universities, of a mass student and
faculty population, all made the experience of being a student much less
pleasant, and offered fewer prospects for the future than ever before.
The Berkeley Revolt and its successors were seen in some considerable
degree to reflect a protest against bureaucracy and impersonality, and
the pressures on students to prepare for materialistic careers.[19] The
seventies, however, are characterized by a "calm," a period of political
quiescence on campus, although the structural conditions that supposedly produced student protest still continue, and if anything, have
intensified. Pressures on students to conform to educational authority,
to devote their education to preparing themselves for a niche in the
economy are stronger than ever, yet few protest.

Two political scientists, Gabriel Almond and Stephen Genco, after citing many other comparable failures, conclude about political science:

> The regularities we discover are soft. They are soft because they are the outcomes of processes that exhibit plastic rather than cast-iron control. They are imbedded in history and involve recurrent "passings-through" of large numbers of human memories, learning processes, human goal-seeking impulses, and choices among alternatives. The regularities we discover appear to have a short half-life. They decay quickly because of the memory, creative searching, and learning that underlie them. Indeed, social science itself may contribute to this decay, since learning increasingly includes not only learning from experience, but from scientific research itself.[20]

Speaking more generally to the effort to apply engineering concepts of systems analysis to "a vast array of social problems," Berkeley sociologist Ida Hoos points out that what works in the controlled system of the engineer is not applicable to society. As she states: "Although the term 'system' can be applied to both space hardware and social problems, the inputs are vastly different, as are the controls and objectives. In the engineered system, the components are tangible, the variables controlled, and the outputs identifiable. In the social sphere, the crucial elements often defy definition and control and do not behave according to a set of rules."[21]

Some who adhere to Marxism or other revolutionary doctrines may react to this brief survey of the inadequacy of social science analysis by concluding that it demonstrates the failure of bourgeois or nonradical social science. But if one looks at Marxism, it is certainly in no better shape. Marxist economists and sociologists made the same errors as non-Marxists in evaluating economic developments, ethnicity, and the prospects for political tensions in Western industrialized societies. A major figure in radical sociology, Alvin Gouldner, has pointed out that the record of "academic sociology" has been superior to that of the Marxist sociologists in anticipating various recent changes, that the non-Marxists were more sensitive than the Marxists.[22] Marxist economists also have been repeatedly disconfirmed in their anticipations of economic breakdown in the West and lack of growth in less developed societies.

On a broader scale, however, it may be said that Marxism's major assumptions and predictions about the transition to socialism bear little or no relationship to actual developments. Capitalism's progressive role, according to Marx, is to create a level of production that would enable people to live in genuine freedom for the first time in history, that would permit everyone to have enough and thus make possible a much more egalitarian if not a totally egalitarian society. Marxists, until World War I, assumed that the United States would be the first socialist country because it was the most advanced capitalist country. Marx wrote categorically that the most developed society presents to others the image of their future. Social superstructures, political systems, were supposed to follow in the train of economic development.[23]

The Russian Bolsheviks regarded their seizure of power in a less developed country as an historic anomaly, which could not and would not last. They anticipated that the only possibility for a progressive advance in the Soviet Union lay in its being tied up to advanced socialist industrial countries in the West. They looked forward eagerly to the outbreak of the revolution in Western countries. No crueler joke has been played by history than the phenomenon of Marxism becoming the banner of the revolutionary movements to totally non-industrial societies, of Communism holding power in China, Cambodia, Albania, and many other poor, largely agrarian, nations. Conversely, of course, revolutionary Marxism is weakest in the countries with the highest level of industrial development, those which have the largest working class, which have the highest standard of living. Literally, no relationship exists between Marx's anticipations about the links between economic structure, technological development, and social and political development, and what has actually happened. Marxism as a system of sociological, economic, and political analysis has been negated, not only by events in the Western industrial countries that have seemingly overcome the anticipation that their contradictions would produce massive economic crises, but even more fundamentally by the coming to power of socialist statist movements in less developed countries. Socialism in a total sense seems to be a phenomenon of less developed, non-industrial societies, the precise opposite of Marx's forecast.

In citing the failures or, more accurately, inadequate predictions of the assorted social sciences, it is not my intention to suggest that social science is unable to deal with social and economic phenomena. Clearly, all the disciplines have done much to explain the ways in which economy, society, and individuals behave. Social science, however, is still at its best in advancing what Robert Merton has called middle-level theories and in explaining specific time- and place-limited developments.[24] It can best handle interrelationships between two or more variables within specific delimited structures. As social science moves out to deal with macroscopic systemic trends and tendencies, it accounts for smaller and smaller parts of the variance. Economists escape some of this problem theoretically by dealing with analytically closed systems, based on limited sets of assumptions. They, however, are no more able than other social analysts to fully comprehend total system behavior. Our enduring analyses tend to be historical. There is nothing wrong with this. In many ways our best work resembles that of physicians who analyze the behavior of specific individuals rather than of biologists specifying the characteristics of a total system.

A leading psychologist, Lee Cronbach, discusses precisely the same difficulties faced by his supposedly more experimental and scientific field. Cronbach cites many examples of experimentally validated generalizations that no longer hold up. He notes:

> Generalizations decay. At one time a conclusion describes the existing situation well, at a later time it accounts for rather little variance, and ultimately it is valid only as history. The half-life of an empirical proposition may be great or small. The more open a system, the shorter the half-life of relations within are likely to be. . . .
>
> Though enduring systemic theories about man in society are not likely to be achieved, systematic inquiry can realistically hope to make two contributions. One reasonable aspiration is to assess local events accurately, to improve short-run control. The other reasonable aspiration is to develop explanatory concepts that will help people use their heads.[25]

This emphasis on middle-range theory and on historical case studies does not mean that we should not try to deal with macroscopic developments or predict future trends. Sociologists analyze consequences of changes in the proportion of the population who reach varying levels of education, differences in the distribution of occupations, e.g., the decline in the number of manual or skilled positions and the increase in professional or technical employment discussed earlier. We know that higher education is associated with certain kinds of values and behavior, while different occupations are conducive to varying life-styles and patterns of social organization and have specific orientations to competition, work, and the like, associated with them. Presumably, then, a systematic change in the composition of the work force or of the age levels of the population should have determinate though not necessarily predictable effects on the body politic.

Yet it should be noted that we cannot predict secular changes on a system level, or the probability of events resulting from changes in the composition of a population, or the relative weight of the same factor in different systems. Thus, there is abundant evidence that the more education people have the more tolerance they have for ambiguity, the more likely they are to be free of bigotry, to support civil liberties and civil rights. From this fact, it ought to follow that as the population of a country becomes better educated, it should be more protective of minority rights. In fact, as we know, this is not true. The McCarthyite America of the 1950s was the best educated America up to that time. Periods of massive intolerance have recurred frequently over the two centuries of American history although education and wealth have increased secularly. On a comparative scale, we may point to the fact that some of the best educated nations have fallen victim to persecution manias, such as Germany in 1933. Clearly unpredictable combinations of specific events or factors frequently negate the weight of the most powerful structural factors.[26]

An interesting example of such a reversal upsetting a structural prediction may be taken from political science. In 1965, Robert Lane published two articles in the *American Political Science Review* and the *American Sociological Review* reporting on evidence from opinion polls and other sources that indicated a steadily growing degree of satisfaction with the body politic and economic among the population from 1938 until 1965.[27] The changes included an increase in commitment to values and norms sustaining tolerance, free speech, and participation in the democratic political system. Lane attributed such changes to the steady growth in affluence and in education of every stratum in the population. The opinion polls showed that the better educated and the more well to do a person is, the more tolerant he is of others, and the more satisfied he is with his own situation and the body politic. Yet, as we all know, 1965 was the end of an epoch. From 1965 to the early seventies almost every indicator that Lane used of satisfaction, tolerance, and participation declined rapidly. The reaction to the Vietnam War followed by Watergate and the revelations about activities of various American security agencies plus, in the latter years of the period, economic recession, brought about a steady reduction in confidence in the American polity and increased intolerance.[28] Yet, until 1972 all the structural trends that Lane had identified as concomitants of the growth in positive attitudes in behavior continued.

The relationship between education, affluence, occupation, and political participation presents a somewhat similar phenomenon. All studies agree higher education, higher economic position, and wealth correlate with increased participation.[29] And it would appear that as education, wealth, and occupations of Americans improve, participation should increase; but as we know, the biggest percentage of voting occurred in the late nineteenth century. We are better educated than ever before, a higher percentage of college graduates are in professional jobs, yet in 1972, 1974, 1976, and 1978 we had the lowest turnout rate ever.

The recent low turnout figures occur in the context of a situation in which the politicians had listened to the political scientists' recommendations for increasing participation. President Kennedy had appointed a commission under an important elections expert, Richard Scammon, to inquire why the United States voting rate, then 63 percent, was so low compared to other countries and lower than in the nineteenth century. The Scammon Commission reported that much of the problem was caused by electoral registration laws, which were much more rigorous than in other countries, or in our past, i.e., the need to personally register to vote months before an election, residential requirements, and so on.[30] As a result, registration was made easier, permanent registration was extended, residency requirements were reduced sharply. But the percentage voting declined further so that a decade later it hit a low of 53 percent in a presidential contest: with increased education and easier registration, still fewer voted.

I am not suggesting that the research on which the Scammon recommendations were based was faulty. The problem is that education, class background, and ease of voting are only some of the factors that determine propensity to vote, that other factors and event effects are seemingly more important.

To repeat, this discussion is not meant to imply that we should not try to analyze and predict. Quite obviously in economic, as in political or other forms of social behavior more knowledge and systematic thinking are better than less knowledge. But when one is involved in making major policy recommendations and decisions for the future of nations, or, in the case of the Club of Rome, for the world, it is necessary to be humble, to be cautious, to know much more than we do, before being able to state conclusively, as the Club of Rome did, that humankind's commitment to growth should stop. Clearly, the less precision in an analysis or prediction, the more unexplained variance, the more likely the conclusions that people reach from the available data reflect what they want to find, whether the "what" stems from political ideology, an academic or intellectual theoretical commitment, self-interest, or something else.

As political scientist James Q. Wilson has stressed, social science can test (predict) the relationship among factors only when it can isolate them from other variables, and when the factors and their effects are unambiguous and easily measurable. But the most significant effects on a societal level rarely meet these criteria:

> Either the effects to be studied are hard to measure (as with educational attainment or true crime rates) or the possible effects are hard to define and detect (as with most habits of mind and of personality), or the possible explanatory factors are hard to disentangle (as with race, class, and education), or the act of studying the situation alters it. . . .[31]

This means that with almost any complex problem, people who disagree about the consequences of a given policy will rarely resolve their disagreement by reference to research. The improvement in research techniques—made possible by use of the computer, for example—has not increased the likelihood of reliable, unambiguous results.

In raising these questions about the ability of social scientists to predict macroscopic trends, to systematically understand contemporary problems so that they can recommend specific solutions, i.e., a change in a causally relevant variable to deal with a complex problem, I am not simply engaged in a purely academic exercise irrelevant to policy. The assumptions politicians derive from scholarly analysis can have consequences for good or ill.

THE LIMITS TO GROWTH DISCUSSION: A CASE STUDY

Currently, many politicians, such as Governor Jerry Brown of California and many New Politics Democrats, believe that there must be an end to growth. They accept the assumptions of E.P. Schumacher and of the Club of Rome report, *The Limits of Growth,* of the neo-Malthusians, that the pattern of steady growth that characterized the Western world since the Industrial Revolution began must come to an end.[32] This approach also assumes that the dreams or aspirations underlying the efforts of less developed countries to dramatically increase their productive systems are utopian. They cannot aspire to become wealthy industrialized societies. The underlying assumptions for these pessimistic conclusions are fairly simple. The neo-Malthusians point to the considerable increase in the population of the world, one that will continue to the point where we will inevitably have many more billions than we now have. Second, they note that the resources that have sustained industrial development in the West, particularly those that have contributed energy and raw materials for industry and transportation, are not inexhaustible.

Western industrialized countries, the principal claimants for such materials until recently, absorb an inordinate proportion of them. Immediately after World War II it was estimated that the 6 percent of the world's population living in the United States consumed about 50 percent of the raw materials used for industrial purposes. With the postwar growth of other Western economies and also of demands from less developed countries, the proportion of an increased world supply now used by the United States is one-third. In any case, the developed countries of North America, Europe, Japan, and Australasia clearly consume considerably over half of these resources, while they have less than a quarter of the world's population. Beyond these two main structural considerations, some advocate the cessation of growth in the foreseeable future because of value judgments that insist that growth has brought with it various negative or dysfunctional consequences for humankind. These negative effects lie mainly in the area of ecology. Industrial growth has dirtied the world in a variety of ways, which make conditions of life less good, or less healthful. It has also adversely affected social relations—as a consequence of the fact that the pace of life in large-scale industrial society is highly competitive, ultramaterialistic, and bureaucratic. The critics argue that the advanced industrial societies have not produced human happiness but rather a variety of social and psychological and biological morbidities. Thus, it is argued on one hand that growth will have to stop because of the changing ratio of available resources to the population, and on the other that it should stop because it produces a bad world.

These pessimistic views are countered by other economists and social thinkers who believe that a Malthusian perspective today is as erroneous as it was when Malthus first contended that the inevitable growth in population would prevent an increase in wealth. The counter-view holds that just as Malthus underestimated the resources that could be located and the inventive ingenuity of the human race, his contemporary disciples make the same error, and the scarcity-bound trends they emphasize will not continue.

The most optimistic version of this position has been argued by the deputy editor of the *Economist*, Norman Macrae, one that is about as diametrically opposite to the views assumed by the report of the Club of Rome as is conceivable. Macrae anticipated in 1972 that within the next 80 years the poorer "two-thirds of mankind should be raised from intolerable indigence to something better than the comfortable affluence which the other one-third of us already enjoy." In fact, he contends that much of the needed increase in the less developed countries will occur by 2012. Among other reasons for such optimism is his belief that scientific knowledge and technological development have been proceeding exponentially and that continuing even more rapid advances will solve the problems of pollution and limited resources. He suggests that it is "probable that during at least our children's lifetimes the eventual breakthrough to widespread and intelligent use of computers will add totally new dimensions to all of man's traditional powers of deduction and induction and serendipity. . . that this will drive human invention and innovation through a growing ability to put together matter molecule by molecule, through extraordinary new abilities to control natural phenomena (the weather, drawing all the energy we need from the fusion process that will utilize the waters of the oceans as their limitless reservoir of fuel). . . ."[33]

An equally optimistic view is contained in *The Next 200 Years,* written by Herman Kahn, William Brown, and Leon Martel of the Hudson Institute. Their thesis "can be summarized with the general statement that 200 years ago almost everywhere human beings were comparatively few, poor, and at the mercy of the forces of nature, and 200 years from now, we expect, almost everywhere they will be numerous, rich, and in control of the forces of nature."[34]

The Next 200 Years points to a number of factors that make this scenario plausible. These include evidence that the birthrates are declining in many less developed countries, and that a variety of population experts agree that the maximum rate of growth will soon be reached. Kahn et al. point to the fact that those who are pessimistic about the potentiality for growth in less developed countries have been wrong, since the UN's original goal for the decade of development, 5 percent growth, has not only been met but has been considerably exceeded. Further, they agree with Macrae that long-term energy prospects are good, that these rest in fact on "sources that are inexhaustible." Sources of raw materials are great and are continuing to grow, e.g., there are various sources such as ocean nodules, which will in fact increase the supplies of many materials needed by industry. As the world moves to post-industrial economies, it will become increasingly less dependent on many metals. Recycling as an economic factor has only begun to play a role that will contribute much to the raw material potential in the future. Kahn et al. argue that the anxiety about the availability of food to feed whatever size population of the world comes into existence is much exaggerated, that at the moment the problem is not production but inadequate distribution systems. This clearly can be remedied. In addition, agricultural technology can increase food production enormously in countries that today are not food surplus countries.

Here we see two diametrically opposed views as to what the actual structural trends are by reputable scholars. And, as in the past, some of the conditions defining the problem are beginning to change.

A survey dealing with *World Population Trends* by Lester Brown issued in October 1976 reported that worldwide "the rate of growth has slowed so dramatically over the past five years that a long-predicted doubling of the population may not occur." Brown stated: "I would not be surprised if the world population never again doubled. . . ." The worldwide population growth rate dropped from 1.9 percent to 1.64 between 1970 and 1975, the first such decline in world history. In the most populous country, China, the birthrate declined sharply from 32 to 19 births per thousand people. And in 1979, two demographers, Bogue and Tsui, whose work was discussed earlier, have extrapolated recent trends as suggesting that the effectiveness of international family-planning efforts may result in "zero world population growth" in the foreseeable future.[35]

A number of research publications point to sharp declines in population growth rates in developed countries, many of which are below the fertility rate for zero growth. It is anticipated that the rate for Europe will reach 1.5 by 1986, while the United States will stop growing by 2015. The Chinese growth rate, according to R.T. Havenholt, has dropped from 2.05 percent in 1971 to 0.95 in 1978. In Mexico, which has had one of the highest growth patterns, according to the Population Reference Bureau, the rate fell from 3.5 percent in 1973 to 2.9 in 1978. In the fifth most populous nation, Indonesia, it dropped from 2.9 percent in 1969 to 2.1 percent ten years later.[36]

An international group of economists headed by Nobel Laureate Wassily Leontief, who had been commissioned by the United Nations Department of Economic and Social Affairs to investigate the problems of growth, reported in 1976 after three years of research that "world resources will be sufficient to support a growing population and higher living standards, without inevitable environmental damage." The existing limits to growth, according to them, are not scarce resources, but political and institutional deficiencies. They call for accelerated rates of development in the less developed countries.[37]

Concerns about Growth

The recent increase in the number of people writing about the negative consequences of growth, of affluence, of industrialization, of urbanization, revives to some degree recurrent intellectual and political concerns. Periodically Americans have voiced anxieties comparable to the present. As literary historian Daniel Aaron has pointed out, throughout American history:

> preaching of lay or secular jeremiads feared what the phenomenon of growth (wealth, progress, power) might do to unregenerate America. Had not this surfeit of success, this obsession with progress, induced them to connive with the devil in stealing land from Mexico, condoning slavery, cheating Indians, exploiting workers, tolerating slums?
> In recent years the critique of growth has not altered much although it has taken a different tack. American literature is full of statements rating quality over quantity. . . . Most important of all . . . for writers and artists is the identification of size and growth with pollution in all of its forms—economic, political, moral.[38]

In the political arena one of the steady syndromes has been the "Mr. Clean" one. Since the late nineteenth century, groups of Americans, usually affluent reformers, have seized on some aspect of American society as dirty and have sought to clean it up and reform it. The government, the civil service, was one of the first such areas to be cleansed. Civil service reform secured its main support base from the "Mugwumps," from members of educated old families and academe, who saw in corrupt politics a destructive force in American life. The concern with corrupt politics was followed by the criticisms of the pre-World War I Progressives, recruited heavily from the same sources as the Mugwumps, who, seeking to clean up the environment, fostered the conservation movement. They also were disturbed by the destructive effect on American cultural values and way of life of the vulgar materialism fostered by the *nouveaux riches* of the decades about the turn of the century. These Mr. Clean elements have revived in our time in the form of concerns about pollution, ecology, and the influence of money on politics. Organizations like Common Cause, Nader's Raiders, the Sierra Club, and the Urban Coalition reflect this tendency. These groups have constituted the reform movement of the affluent in an affluent society. Dirt, ugliness, corruption, vulgarity, disturb those dedicated to the higher life, involved in intellectual activities or coming from privileged families, who have not had to dirty themselves in order to become well to do or get a good education.

Other advocates of an end to growth argue that advanced technological society with its emphasis on division of labor has also led, in the words of E. J. Mishan, to "a decline. . . in the satisfactions that men once derived from their daily tasks, [and] who is to say that the loss has been fully compensated by the constant proliferation of goods and gadgetry and the transformation to a mechanized environment. . . . Economic growth depends, among other things, on extreme specialization that dulls the spirit, narrows the sympathies, and cuts one off from the largeness of life."[39] But black political scientist Willard Johnson contends that Mishan "is guilty of debating the issues in terms of values that, for all their humaneness, ignore the concerns of the poor. . . . No doubt his concerns feed on a genuine consideration for the quality of life, but they seem to me mistaken about the contribution material goods can make to it."[40] Or, as the late Anthony Crosland, Cabinet member in various British Labour governments, argued, those who seek to limit growth to protect the environment are "kindly and dedicated people. But they are affluent; and fundamentally, though of course not consciously, they want to kick the ladder down behind them."[41]

Conversely, the advocates of growth, those who would down-play the consequences of pollution, those who are less concerned about beauty in the environment, tend to come from groups involved in the productive process who want to get more for themselves through material advancement. They include well-to-do businessmen, together with workers and poor people who are more interested in increasing their economic circumstances, enhancing chances for mobility for their children, getting more education, securing access to leisure facilities, and so on.

Defining or locating the groups supporting varying points of view does not, of course, say anything about the validity of a given proposition or opinion. Growth may be good or bad, possible or impossible, in the long run, regardless of who likes it or dislikes it, or benefits or is harmed by it. Since I am not an economist and I have not done first-hand research on the conditions of growth or on the limits to growth, I do not intend to take a position based on the evaluation of the evidence. Rather, I would like to spend the remainder of this chapter discussing some of the consequences of the no-growth scenario. It is possible to bring together some of the evaluations or hunches that have been advanced to describe what will happen to the human race as a result. I should note, however, that like Herman Kahn, I tend to be an optimist about growth and innovation. I believe—or perhaps more accurately I should say I hope—that we will be able to find substitutes for resources that are being depleted, to recycle or, more probably, to innovate in various ways that will enable the race to continue toward a more affluent and I hope more egalitarian and freer future. I favor the growth scenario in part because, as I shall indicate, I think the possibilites for much of what I would like to see occur, namely, the expansion of freedom and greater equality, are linked to abundance and to growth. I believe that a no-growth society would be a more authoritarian and more intensely stratified social system.

The Consequences of Growth and No-Growth

Abundance, as David Potter has told us in his brilliant book, *The People of Plenty,* lies at the center of efforts to explain American exceptionalism.[42] Countless European observers of the American national scene, such as Tocqueville and Carlyle, stressed the extent to which the richness of the American continent with a limited population made possible a new social structure, a new man, a new set of social relationships that emphasized equality. Most of the articles and books written to explain the absence of socialism as a political force and class-consciousness in the European sense in the United States have also stressed abundance. Werner Sombart put it well in his classic work, *Why Is There No Socialism in the United States of America?*: "All Socialist Utopias come to nothing on roast beef and apple pie."[43]

Historians and sociologists have agreed that abundance reduces the potential for class tensions. As David Potter stated, compared with the class societies in other countries and other times, the United States has a "new kind of social structure in which the strata may be fully demarked but where the bases of demarcation are relatively intangible. The factor of abundance has exercised a vital influence in producing this kind of structure, for it has constantly operated to equalize the overt differences between the various classes and to eliminate the physical distance between them, without, however, destroying the barriers which separate them."[44]

It is obvious, of course, that the United States is not an egalitarian country, if by egalitarianism one means anything that approaches equality of results. In fact, the most recent comparative studies completed under the auspices of the Organization for Economic Cooperation and Development indicate that income distribution is more skewed, more unequal, in the United States than in the Netherlands, Sweden, Norway, Japan, the United Kingdom, and Australia, although the differences among these relatively affluent countries are not very great.[45] It may be argued, however, that the way in which people *perceive* the distribution of income linked to the distribution of different kinds of consumer goods they use for immediate gratification is more important in affecting their feelings about equity than the actual distribution of income as such. The distribution of consumer goods has tended to become more equitable as the size of national income has increased. This relationship between wealth and the distribution of consumer goods has been commented on by Gunnar Myrdal: "It is, indeed, a regular occurrence that the poorer the country, the greater the difference between the poor and the rich."[46]

This, of course, does not mean that an increase in GNP automatically results in a narrowing of the income gap among the classes. In less developed countries, such an increase initially may largely go to increasing the wealth of the affluent and the standard of living of the middle class, without improving the lot of the large mass of the poor. The extent of income inequality in these countries also varies greatly with the policies followed by their governments, e.g., the variation in spread of education, land distribution, population control, production, and regional sectors emphasized, and the like.[47] In addition, it should be noted that a number of recent studies of income distribution find relatively little change in income inequality accompanying growth since World War II in the wealthy non-Communist countries.[48] Yet, a conclusion that the proportion of the national income received by different segments of the population does not change much in a given period does not imply that the standards of living of the less privileged may not rise considerably, enabling the *consumption gap* among the classes to decline.

In the United States, the average per capita income has increased eight times during the course of the century, and this dramatic growth has brought about a wide distribution of various social and economic benefits, greater than that which exists in almost all other countries except for a few of the wealthiest ones in Europe. Thus, in America a much larger proportion of the population graduates from high school (over 80 percent), or enters college (close to 45 percent) than in any other country. The greater wealth of the United States also means that consumer goods such as automobiles and telephones are more evenly distributed here than elsewhere. An evaluation by the (London) *Economist,* using twelve social indicators to assess the relative advantages of different countries as places to live, placed the United States far in the lead over eight other industrialized non-Communist states.[49]

Sociologist Gideon Sjoberg has traced the implications of such developments historically in America. He suggests that the emergence of mass production during the twentieth century has caused such a redistribution of highly valued prestige symbols that the distinctions between social classes are much less visible now than they were in nineteenth-century America, or in most other less affluent countries. Sjoberg argues that the status differences between many blue-collar workers and middle-class professionals have become less well defined, since working-class families, like the middle-class ones, have been able to buy goods that confer prestige on the purchaser—clothing, cars, television sets, and so on. Such improvements in style of life help to preserve a belief in the reality of the promise of equality.[50]

Economic growth is also associated, of course, with the upgrading of the occupational structure, discussed earlier. Where Western societies once had many menial jobs at the bottom, a pattern that still characterizes less developed nations, including most Communist ones, they have now changed and the proportion of reasonably well-rewarded positions has increased so that, like the United States, they bulge at the middle. One of the conditions for an increased sense of equality and greater opportunity is increased mechanization. The most advanced technological societies, such as the United States, Sweden, and Germany, have reduced onerous work to a greater degree than others. It should be evident that those who foresee or advocate no growth, who oppose technological expansion either because they do not believe available resources will sustain growth or because they feel that a more mechanized system will be a dirtier society, in a variety of meanings of that term, must anticipate a future in which the possibilities for progress toward greater equality will also decline. If we have to stop technological development, if we have to move into a no-growth age, then instead of moving toward greater equality, toward upgrading the situation of the poor, we will experience intense struggles in which those who control power resources, whether through ownership or capital or control of the state, will be at a considerable advantage.

As Kenneth Boulding has pointed out:

> One reason why the progressive [steady growth] state is "cheerful" is that social conflict is diminished by it. In a progressive state, the poor can become richer without the rich becoming poorer. In the stationary state, there is no escape from the rigors of scarcity. If one person or group becomes richer, then the rest of society must become poorer. Unfortunately, this increases the payoffs for successful exploitation—that is, the use of organized threat in order to redistribute income. In progressive societies exploitation pays badly, for almost everybody, increasing their productivity pays better. . . . One can get ten dollars out of nature for every dollar one can squeeze out of a fellow man. In the stationary state, unfortunately, investment in exploitation may pay better than in progress. Stationary states, therefore, are frequently mafia-type societies in which the government is primarily an instrument for redistributing income toward the powerful and away from the weak.[51]

Robert Heilbroner, who agrees with Boulding that growth must cease, notes that a no-growth America will not simply involve increased conflict with the upper class and the rich, for "the top 5 percent get only 15 percent of all income." The working class and the poor cannot improve their situation without coming into conflict with the middle class. Thus, he says, "when growth slows down, we must expect a struggle of redistribution on a vast scale—a confrontation not just between a few rich and many poor, but between a relatively better-off upper third of the nation and a relatively less well-off slightly larger working class. And fighting against both will be the bottom 20 percent—the group with most to gain, the least to lose."[52] This intensification of the class struggle, of course, will go on everywhere.

In the United States, rising demands for quotas, for affirmative action, with special advantages for underprivileged groups like blacks, Chicanos, and women, may be portents of the future that Boulding and Heilbroner anticipate. The premise of the argument for such quotas, in part, is that the only way these hitherto deprived groups can move up is at the expense of other groups, that they cannot take advantage of the economic expansion of society in the way in which white male and Oriental immigrant groups did in the past. But the more privileged, who are more powerful, will seek to resist such demands in a non-expanding economy.

Richard Zeckhauser also emphasizes that a "no-growth society would work most severely against the interests of the poorer members of society. . . . If zero economic growth were imposed on the current structure of the American economy, Lester Thurow has calculated 'the distribution of family income would gradually become more unequal, blacks would fall farther behind whites, and the share going to female earnings would fall below what it would otherwise be.' "[53]

For those who believe that the good society is a democratic and free one, it is also necessary to recognize that democracy requires abundance, or at least that nations in which opposition parties, contested elections, and a free press exist are largely well to do. Currently, with the exception of a limited group of poor countries, the only democratic regimes are located in the prosperous regions of Europe, North America, Australasia, and Japan. Those nations that have maintained stable democratic regimes longest, and in which antidemocratic parties are very weak, are the cluster of countries that are the wealthiest by far.

Classic democratic theory stemming from Aristotle suggests that free societies are most likely to be found in nations with a preponderant middle class. Societies with a large lower-impoverished stratum tend either to be oligarchies (ruled by a self-perpetuating traditional elite) or tyrannies (popular-based dictatorships).

Sometime ago, in discussing the conditions of the democratic order in *Political Man,* I elaborated on some of the ways in which affluence is related to democracy, noting that increased wealth changes the stratification structure, particularly by increasing the size and role of the middle class:

> A large middle class tempers conflict by rewarding moderate and democratic parties and penalizing extremist groups.
>
> The political values and style of the upper class, too, are related to national income. The poorer a country and the lower the absolute standard of living of the lower classes, the greater the pressure on the upper strata to treat the lower as vulgar, innately inferior, a lower caste beyond the pale of human society. The sharp difference in the style of living between those at the top and those at the bottom makes this psychologically necessary. Consequently, the upper strata in such a situation tend to regard political rights for the lower strata, particularly the right to share power, as essentially absurd and immoral. The upper strata not only resist democracy themselves; their often arrogant political behavior serves to intensify extremist reactions on the part of the lower classes.
>
> The general income level of a nation also affects its receptivity to democratic norms. If there is enough wealth in the country so that it does not make too much difference whether some redistribution takes place, it is easier to accept the idea that it does not matter greatly which side is in power. But if loss of office means serious losses for major power groups, they will seek to retain or secure office by any means available. A certain amount of national wealth is likewise necessary to ensure a competent civil service. The poorer the country, the greater the emphasis on nepotism—support of kin and friends. And this in turn reduces the opportunity to develop the efficient bureaucracy which a modern democratic state requires.
>
> Intermediary organizations which act as sources of countervailing power seem to be similarly associated with national wealth. Tocqueville and other exponents of what has come to be known as the theory of the "mass society" have argued that a country without a

multitude of organizations relatively independent of the central state power has a high dictatorial as well as revolutionary potential. Such organizations serve a number of functions: they inhibit the state or any single source of private power from dominating all political resources; they are a source of new opinions; they can be the means of communicating ideas, particularly opposition ideas, to a large section of the citizenry; they train men in political skills and so help to increase the level of interest and participation in politics. Although there are no reliable data on the relationship between national patterns of voluntary organization and national political systems, evidence from studies of individual behavior demonstrates that, regardless of other factors, men who belong to associations are more likely than others to give the democratic answer to questions concerning tolerance and party systems, to vote, or to participate actively in politics. Since the more well-to-do and better educated a man is, the more likely he is to belong to voluntary organizations, the propensity to form such groups seems to be a function of level of income and opportunities for leisure within given nations.[54]

The assumption that abundance is a necessary condition for a good society is not limited to the example, or the writing, of people who prefer the kinds of societies that have emerged in the so-called Western world. At the root of the Marxist theories of progress and of the condition required for a free socialist society is a similar assumption. Marx fervently believed and sought to demonstrate that inequality, the exploitation of people by each other, reflected the necessary social conditions imposed on societies by scarcity. As I noted earlier, the one major precondition for socialism is abundance. Socialism, according to Marx and Engels, must be a highly prosperous, what we now call post-industrial, society. They assumed that as long as there are not sufficient goods available to enable all people to live in comparative luxury, inequality of income and power is necessary. They believed, as Trotsky pointed out, that efforts to create socialism, a more egalitarian society, before an era of overwhelming abundance would inevitably fail, that intense stratification must recur.[55]

Marxist theory places an even greater emphasis on the relationship between abundance and political and social structure than does democratic theory. For according to the Marxist fathers, coercive social systems, that is, stratified ones, are a product of the division of labor inherent in the need to produce goods and services in societies characterized by scarcity. For people to become totally free and equal, they must have complete control of their own destiny. They must be able to choose and control their own work and their conditions of life. Economies based on the division of labor also require power relationships. Engels, in his essay "On Authority," wrote that over the entrance of every factory should be written, "He who enters here gives up his freedom."[56] It is clear from reading the essay that Engels was not just talking about factories in capitalist society, that he meant this generalization to hold under all conditions in which factories and the division of labor existed. Marx, on one of the few occasions in which he described socialist societies, portrayed them as societies in which men would be free to hunt in the morning, fish in the afternoon, and criticize or read poetry in the evening.[57] It seems evident that Marx and Engels looked forward to a society in which all the onerous, menial work is done by machines.[58] Socialism would be a free society because work would be handled by inanimate slaves, in which no one lacked for what he required in the way of food, clothing, or shelter, and in which people enjoyed the luxuries that only the well to do have in a pre-Communist world.

Marx strongly rejected Malthusian arguments that abundance is not possible, that the relationship among productivity, raw materials, and the growth of population would prevent continued increases in the per capita income, not only because these arguments seemed wrong to him, but clearly because if they were true, then socialism is impossible. Communist theorists, like Lenin, Trotsky, and Gramsci, all wrote in exuberant terms about American mass production because they believed that advanced techniques made socialism possible. Henry Ford, in spite of his reactionary political views and industrial practices, was a hero to the Russian Communists of the 1920s because of his development of the assembly line and mass production. Soviet factories contained pictures of Lenin and Ford.[59] And, of course, this worship of the god of productivity and abundance continues in the Soviet Union and China today. Authoritarianism and inequality are justified as leading to increased productivity, which will ultimately make an egalitarian Communist society possible.[60]

The revival in different ways of doctrines of neo-Malthusianism, the "limits to growth" thesis, the concern for the relationship of limited natural resources to growing populations, must be seen, therefore, not only as matter of analytic and policy concerns with respect to deciding whether there are effective limits to growth and, if so, what the social consequences of a world in which productivity will no longer increase would be. It is also necessary to recognize that the end of the dream of universal abundance, of a world in which all nations will be richer than contemporary America or northern Europe, is an end also to the dream of a democratic world, or of an egalitarian socialist world, at least in terms of the assumptions of the classic theorists of democracy and of socialism. This does not mean, of course, in terms of these theories and of our own experience, that a socialist or Communist world, as exemplified by countries that now describe themselves by these labels, is impossible. State-dominated societies, total government economies, are possible at any level of productivity or abundance. Communism exists in countries that range in economic levels from totally agrarian societies like Cambodia to industrialized ones like East Germany.

From a Marxian perspective, Trotsky argued that low productivity systems must be authoritarian and inegalitarian, that they would be failures from the point of the Communist objectives.[61] The argument, in fact, has been made by Karl Wittfogel and others that the statist Communist societies of today are actually forms of the type of social system that Marx called Asiatic. Asiatic societies in the Marxist framework existed in the ancient world, mainly in Asia and North Africa. They were characterized by state-dominated economies. The state was the central economic and power institution because of the need to control elaborate systems of irrigation and waterworks over large territories. They were statist, highly inegalitarian, and tyrannical. Wittfogel in his book *Oriental Despotism* contends that contemporary Communism is a revival of Asiatic society in the Marxian sense, that it is an intensely stratified one and cannot lead to any social order that might resemble Communism in the Marxist sense.[62] Leninism-Stalinism-Maoism have collectivized scarcity, and inequality and tyranny are necessary concomitants of such a system.

The dangers involved in increased state power are not limited to less developed Communist societies. As Mancur Olson has noted:

> Another characteristic that no-growth societies have is an extraordinary degree of governmental or other collective action. This would be true whether growth ceased through ZEG and ZPG policies now or because growth had someday proceeded to the point where it was obviously and immediately impossible to grow any further.

Whether it became so by choice or by necessity, a no-growth society would presumably have stringent regulations and wide-ranging prohibitions against pollution and other external diseconomies, and thus more government control over individual behavior than is now customary in the Western democracies. . . . Thus there is reason to ask how well democracy as we know it would fare amidst the ubiquitous controls that would be involved either in stopping growth now or in adjusting ultimately to the inescapable environmental contraint.[63]

Those who support "no growth" in order to secure a more moral and cleaner society, of course, reject these pessimistic scenarios on value grounds. They, too, favor a more egalitarian and freer society. It is not possible for any of us to categorically say that our preferences are unattainable under either conditions of growth or no growth. Obviously, growth societies like the United States have not avoided major dysfunctions, severe inequality, poverty, racial tensions, and the like. But conversely, the best single example of a developed no-growth economy, albeit involuntarily, Great Britain, which has been governed by humane social democrats who believe in planning to advance egalitarianism and the quality of life, suggests problems even greater than those that accompany growth and affluence. The British people have shown in a variety of ways that they want the kinds of changes that are dependent on growth. As British political scientist Rudolf Klein notes, they want more:

Resentment of continuing inequalities is compounded by resentment of unemployment and of the failure of living standards to rise. For poverty is not just relative. Rising standards can and do mean better food, better housing, and better clothes for people. And at the current British standard of living—the "standard" for the future, let it be remembered—these sorts of improvements still matter very much. Although Britain probably has better housing conditions than most Western European countries, 13 percent of households still lack private bathrooms and 12 percent still live in houses or flats officially classified as unfit for human habitation. More than a third of households have no refrigeration or cooling machine, 55 percent have no car, 65 percent have no telephone, and 70 percent have no central heating.[64]

Most of those who believe that we must or should move into a no-growth era do not want consciously to condemn those living in abysmal poverty, particularly in the less developed nations, to remain at that level. Rather, they see the need to reduce the standard of living of the affluent nations, to transfer access to resources to the less well-to-do so that they can at least partially catch up. Ignoring the question of how this can be done politically, it is unfortunately necessary to point out that the wealth of the former is not primarily a function of their control of resources. Nathan Keyfitz has noted that "natural resources account for only 5 percent of the value of goods and services produced in the U.S. and other developed countries." Thus, cutting back on American consumption will not enable other non-industrialized nations to sharply increase their level of productivity. As he also points out: "The trouble is that goods, as well as jobs that require materials, fit into other social activities in an interlocking scheme that is hard to change; social configurations are as solid a reality as raw materials."[65]

These disagreements among eminent economists and social scientists concerning the constraints or lack of constraints that affect the potential for growth and increased affluence on a national as well as on a world scale are not, of course, unique to that discussion. The academic's easy out is to say that they point up the need for further research to test the validity of the different assumptions made by advocates on each side. It is not likely, however, that this debate will be resolved in the foreseeable future by more data, better theory, or more sophisticated arguments.

Who is right in these sharply divergent anticipations? If we run out of resources, fuel, energy, etc., the world will suffer major social upheavals, to put it mildly. But if we sharply reduce growth, we will condemn most of the world to continued poverty, we will probably curtail movements toward greater equality within nations, we will probably see more severe class struggle over division of the general economic pie and as Robert Heilbroner and others anticipate, a greater prospect for dictatorships. The assumption that necessity is the mother of invention, that demand will provide the impetus for new discovery in the future as in the past, made by Kahn, Macrae, and many others offers a more beneficent prospect for the future of both the developed and underdeveloped worlds.

If we ask what determines the conclusions of different "experts," at least some of the factors are political. Well-to-do leftists, many intellectuals, the oppositionist intelligentsia tend to favor no growth, to think small. Trade unionists, workers, businessmen, social democrats, communists, conservatives are more likely to still see growth as both possible and desirable.

Is all this a counsel of despair, a confession of failure or inadequacy by a social scientist? I do not mean it to be. Rather, it may be viewed as a declaration of independence, of autonomy, of insistence that people can still feel free to make their own history, that the future is not so determined that we should feel helpless about our ability to affect it. We are still far from having a Calvinist social science, from having to accept predestination. Social science can help us, can trace relations, but the future still remains an uncharted sea waiting for the venturesome. I hope the essays in this volume will help us understand where we are heading as we move into America's third century.

Kingsley Davis

The Continuing Demographic Revolution in Industrial Societies

M'GUINNESS

2 It is my purpose here to analyze the demographic changes accompanying advanced industrialization and to peek into the future to see where these changes may lead. In many ways the advanced societies are the more interesting, because we can only guess what is in store for them. With respect to less developed countries, we can get some idea of where they are headed by looking at the history of industrial nations, but there is no analogy for the industrial nations themselves.

This is another way of saying that the industrial nations are traveling blindly. Although they nourish the illusion that the policies and plans they talk so much about determine the future, the truth is that whatever influence their policies have, it is almost always unanticipated and frequently undesired. For every problem these nations solve by further elaboration of their advanced technology, they unwittingly create several new ones. The industrial societies are thus speeding down a highway without knowing where it leads, pausing only when some crisis blocks their progress. There is no overall vision, no plan, but simply headlong change. Any order or regularity in the change is that of an uncontrolled process—an order in which human minds participate but which they do not govern.

In traditional societies the social order was so stable that it hardly changed in a lifetime. The question of planning hardly arose, because the changes came from outside, frequently in the form of calamities, and were forced on communities that intended no changes in their structure. In industrial societies, however, the calamities are often produced by the changes the societies themselves inaugurate. The lack of foresight as to where the changes will lead is probably inevitable, given the nature

I wish to acknowledge with thanks the valuable research assistance of Nelly Van den Oever in the preparation of this chapter. The research was partially supported by two contracts between the National Institute for Child Health and Human Development, Center for Population Research, and the University of California, Berkeley, International Population and Urban Research (NIH-NO1-HD-62825 and NIH-NO1-HD-62857).

of human societies in general and these in particular. If so, nobody is to blame. The actors are lost in a complex process they do not fully understand and cannot control.

Nowhere is the unguided character of industrial societies more evident than in their demography. In demonstrating this, one can start anywhere one wishes, because the aspects of demography are closely interlinked. Let us start with a demographic change that not only occurred quite early in modern development but also is widely regarded as the finest fruit of modern technology—the unprecedented reduction in human mortality.

THE POSTPONEMENT OF DEATH

Although the drop in mortality in Western Europe probably started before the Industrial Revolution, its progress was so slow and poorly documented that proof of its occurrence is difficult. However, after industrialism started (around 1800, depending on the country), the decline began to be indisputable. In the diocese of Norway, for example, the crude death rate was incipiently declining in the eighteenth century, clearly declining in the nineteenth century.[1]

	Mean Crude Death Rate
1735–54	26.1
1755–74	25.3
1775–94	23.9
1795–1804	25.8
1805–24	21.7
1825–44	19.3
1845–64	17.9

Even so, it is significant (as Table 1 shows) that the fastest decline did not come in the early stages—when a proportional fall would have been easier to make, because the level was so high to start with—but in the later stages, around the turn of the twentieth century. I have elsewhere explained this acceleration as due to the fact that in the first phases of the Industrial Revolution gains in health were mainly attributable to advances in *productive* technology, whereas in the later phases (after about 1870) they were also attributable to advances in *medical* technology.[2]

TABLE 1

CHANGE IN AGE-SPECIFIC DEATH RATES IN SWEDEN, FOR SELECTED AGES

	Percentage Change in Death Rates by Age					
Period	0	0–4	25–29	40–44	50–54	60–64
From 1751–1800 to 1801–50	–15.4	–21.9	–12.5	– 5.3	+ 4.8	+ 4.3
From 1801–50 to 1851–1900	–27.5	–24.8	–21.4	–33.3	–36.1	–32.6
From 1851–1900 to 1901–50	–53.1	–64.2	–36.5	–46.4	–37.2	–31.3
Average	–32.0	–37.0	–24.4	–28.3	–22.8	–19.9

SOURCE: Calculated from data given in *Historisk Statistik för Sverige*, vol. 1, *Befolkning, 1720–1967* (Stockholm: Statistiska Centralbyrån, 1969), p. 111. It will be noticed that infant mortality did not show the fastest decline. This is typical: the fastest decline normally comes in ages 1–9.

Table 1 also demonstrates that the decline of mortality occurred at all ages. Although the youngest ages generally experienced the most rapid decline, this was not true in all periods. It tended to be most true in the very beginning of the decline, less so thereafter.

A third feature of the mortality decline was the fact that it was greater for females than for males. This has produced a growing hiatus in longevity between the sexes. In Japan, for example, as Table 2 shows, the difference in life-expentancy was less than half a year in 1902–13 when mortality was still high, but by 1971–72 it had widened to 5.4 years. In the white population of the United States, according to 1975 data, the difference was 7.8 years. The social impact of this change will be discussed later.

A fourth feature of the decline in mortality is that it has not stopped. If we compute the annual rate of change in life-expectancy for Japan, for example, we find (from Table 2) that the rate between 1950–54 and

TABLE 2

LIFE EXPECTANCY AT BIRTH IN JAPAN, FOR MALES AND FEMALES, SELECTED DATES

	Life Expectancy			Percent
Period	Males	Females	Difference*	Difference*
1902–13	44.2	44.7	0.48	1.10
1921–25	42.1	43.2	1.14	2.71
1935–36	46.9	49.6	2.71	5.78
1950–54	61.2	65.1	3.86	6.31
1960–64	66.7	71.5	4.78	7.17
1971–72	70.3	75.8	5.42	7.71

SOURCE: Institute of Population Problems, *The 22nd Abridged Life Tables* (Research Series No. 194, July 15, 1970), Appendix Tables. United Nations, *Demographic Yearbook 1973*, pp. 1022–3.
*Calculated from less-rounded figures than those shown in first two columns.

1971–72 was almost identical with the rate between 1902–13 and 1950–54. In the United States and some European countries, the rate of improvement in life-expectancy slowed down noticeably in the 1950s and 1960s, particularly among males, and there was talk of a cessation of progress in this regard; however, more recent data show that rapid improvement has been resumed. In the United States white population, the rate of gain in life expectancy between 1970 and 1975 was almost identical with that made between 1900 and 1910.*

Concerning the future, one thing is certain: if the industrial nations are to make further gains in longevity, these will have to be made at older ages, because nearly everybody already survives to a fairly advanced age. In the life-table for the United States in 1975, for example, 93.4 percent of males and 96.4 percent of females reach age 40, and 78.5 and 88.1 percent respectively reach age 60. To show how little can be gained at younger ages, I have made a life-table of the United States white population in which nobody dies before age 40, but the mortality after that age is the same as it actually was in 1975. The resulting gain in life-expectancy at birth is only three years.[3]

Some experts doubt that great improvements in older ages are likely, because they believe that the lengthening of life is approaching a genetically determined upper asymptote. The assumption is that there is an aging process that causes the organism to wear out and die even when it is protected from infectious diseases, parasites, and accidents. Such an idea may be applicable to other mammals, but not to *Homo sapiens*. There is no inherent reason why medical technology cannot eventually control the aging process itself, or alter the genetic constitution of man so as to reduce or banish the aging process. I am not suggesting that human beings can be made immortal, but only that the causes of death can be altered and life prolonged to many.more years. People would still die, but more from accidents and violence than from aging. The average length of life might be 100, or 150.

In general, as noted earlier, the older ages have participated strongly in the trend toward greater survival. In Table 3 are shown life-

---

*Throughout this chapter, reference will mainly be made to the *white* population of the United States. This is done for two reasons—first, the white population is better enumerated than the black; second, the white population is more "developed" (more educated, with higher per capita income and longer life expectancy) than the black population and hence more representative of the most advanced industrial type of society. Reference to the white population implies no lack of interest in the black population on the part of the author.

TABLE 3

LIFE EXPECTANCY AFTER AGES 40 AND 60, UNITED STATES WHITE POPULATION

| | *Mean Length of Life* | | | |
| | After Age 40 | | After Age 60 | |
	Males	Females	Males	Females
1900	27.7	29.2	14.4	15.2
1940	30.0	33.2	15.0	17.0
1975	33.0	39.4	16.8	21.9
	Average Years Gained per Decade*			
1900–40	0.57	1.02	0.15	0.44
1940–75	0.85	1.76	0.50	1.40
	Average Percent Gain per Decade*			
1900–40	2.00	3.33	1.20	2.79
1940–75	2.73	4.83	3.19	7.50

SOURCE: National Center for Health Statistics, *Vital Statistics of the United States, 1974,* vol. II, section 5, p. 14; and *Monthly Vital Statistics Report,* vol. 25, no. 11 (Supplement February 11, 1977), p. 8.
*Calculated on basis of figures less rounded than those shown in the top panel.

expectancies beyond age 40 and 60 for the American white population. The surprising thing is the very large percentage increase in the recent period, especially at age 60. If the 1940–75 trend were to continue, by the year 2000 the average man reaching age 40 would live to be 75.3 years old, the average female, 84.5; and for those reaching age 60, the figures would be 78.2 and 86.3 years old, respectively. The sex difference in life-expectancy at birth would be 9.2 years for those reaching age 40, and 8.1 years for those reaching age 60.

Consequences of the Mortality Changes

Whatever the future, there have been important consequences of the mortality decline. Prominent among these have been explosive population growth and downward pressure on fertility, both of which we shall consider in a moment. Less often noted, but also important, have been the increased efficiency of labor force dynamics and the enhanced potential durability of social relationships. A word about each of these two effects is in order.

Mortality Decline and Labor Force Recruitment   The process of industrialization would have been, and is now, impossible without highly skilled workers. To give workers the skills they need, a costly process of training is required, and this is necessarily more efficient the higher the rate of survival of those trained. The gain in efficiency can be seen from Table 4. Overall, the mortality of 1783–87 would allow only

TABLE 4

Survival Rates for Sweden

	Percent Surviving (Males)	
	1783–87*	1973†
From birth to school age (age 0 to 5)	65.6	97.3
From school age to working age (5 to 20)	85.3	99.2
From working age to middle age (20 to 40)	79.9	97.3
From middle age to old age (40 to 60)	63.4	88.3

*Calculated from Nathan Keyfitz and Wilhelm Flieger, *World Population* (Chicago: University of Chicago Press, 1968), p. 464.
†Calculated from United Nations, *Demographic Yearbook 1974*, pp. 1080–81.

28 percent of males born to live through the labor-force span to age 60, while the mortality of 1973 would allow more than 84 percent to do so.

There have been other effects of mortality decline on the labor force, some advantageous and some not, but these have been mostly indirect and therefore will be discussed later. Of course, the process of training is another matter. Some industrial nations have been more successful than others in the invention and borrowing of new skills and the transmission of these to workers, but they have all had the advantage of wasting less effort on young people who die before they can use the skills transmitted.

Mortality Decline and Durable Social Relationships   A similar boon from mortality control has been the much greater potential for durable social relationships. For example, a white couple married about 1860 in the United States had approximately a 42-percent risk of being separated by death before their last child reached 18, but the risk today is only 9.8 percent. As for the children themselves, the risk to each one of dying before age 18 was about 36 percent for those born in 1840 as compared to 2.3 percent for those born recently. If three births are assumed in a family, the chance of one or more deaths occurring within the family before the children reach 18 has dropped from 85 percent around the middle of the nineteenth century to 16 percent today.

However, this enormous gain through mortality control has been lost through a social change—a drastic increase in divorce. In the 1860s about 3.3 percent of existing marriages in the United States were broken each year, almost entirely by death. By 1970 virtually the same percentage (3.4) were broken, but nearly half of these were dissolved by legal divorce or annulment, and the proportion was rising rapidly. The divorce rate, which in 1890 was only 0.3 percent of existing marriages, rose persistently until it reached 2.7 percent in the twelve months ending with January 1977. Today, the wife's likelihood of being divorced before her marriage has lasted twenty years is more than eight times the likelihood of her being widowed. Accordingly, divorce far eclipses death as a cause of orphanhood. In the United States, the percentage of children under 18 who were in families but not living with two parents was 8.1 percent in 1960, 17.5 percent in 1975. Of those living with only one parent, six times as many were doing so because the mother was divorced or separated as were doing so because the mother was widowed.[4] With respect to the durability of family relationships, then, the United States has thrown away in social disorganization the potentiality that demography gave it.

Mortality Decline and Population Growth   The explosive population growth growing out of mortality control has gone through two phases—one within the industrial nations themselves, the other in the rest of the world as a result of what happened in these nations.

In the nineteenth century it was realized that the human increase in the industrializing countries was unprecedented. Europe not only became the world's most densely settled continent but also sent out millions of emigrants to new lands. As a result, the enormous energy made available from fossil fuels by industrial technology did not bring the utopia that the philosophers of progress had visualized. True, it did permit a long-run rise in the level of living, but the rise would have been faster if the population had grown less rapidly—that is, if the birth rate had descended parallel with the death rate. At the time, however, few observers grasped the genius of the Industrial Revolution. Still thinking of production as mainly determined by human bodies when in fact it was being increasingly determined by human skills and machinery, they generally welcomed the rapid population growth.

Ironically, by the time the birth rate was finally adjusting to the lowered death rate (in the early part of the present century), the second and more ominous phase of population growth was setting in, this time outside the industrial countries. It came because the medical technology gradually and laboriously invented in the industrial countries was beginning to prove readily exportable to the underdeveloped two-thirds of the world. After World War II death rates in these areas were reduced at a speed some four times greater than the rate of reduction that the industrial countries had themselves exhibited from similar levels. Since, however, the improvement came largely from the transfer of medical rather than productive technology, it involved little disturbance of those parts of the institutional structure governing reproduction. Birth rates consequently remained high. This meant that the ratio of the birth rate to the death rate became quite different from what it had been in the earlier history of the industrial nations.[5] As a result, the industrial nations were, and are now, confronted with the greatest problem they have ever faced—the explosive growth of population throughout the Third World. The United Nations medium forecasts indicate that by the year 2000 the less developed regions will add more than two billion people to their present population. This is half the world's population today. If the projection holds true, 90 percent of the world's population increase during the rest of this century will be in underdeveloped countries.[6] In these countries the average population density is already twice that of the industrial nations, and a majority of the people lack technical skills and education. Also, the enormous increase in population is coming at a time when the fossil energy that sparked the Industrial Revolution is giving out. Already millions of immigrants from these lands are streaming into the industrial countries, regardless of law or public opinion, and hundreds of millions are waiting to do the same. Already the international struggle for scarce resources is becoming intense—a struggle, it seems, in which the industrial nations must inevitably lose because so many people live in underdeveloped countries. Already, the demand for equality under conditions of scarcity is spawning Communist regimes in which equality is achieved by creating universal poverty, any surplus above basic needs being used for national rather than personal goals. In these regimes the old connection between industrialization and a rising level of living is being destroyed; its place is being taken by a new linkage between high technology and public poverty.[7] Thus the massive population growth in underdeveloped areas is having economic and political consequences not foreseen or desired. The miraculous achievement in death control, begun and managed by the industrial nations, has turned into a Frankenstein monster of world population growth.

CHANGING FERTILITY IN INDUSTRIAL SOCIETIES

Inside the advanced nations, a second consequence of the great gain in longevity has been the fall in the birth rate, which began in earnest about a century after the start of rapid mortality decline. Had the birth rate not fallen, the population growth would eventually have become impossible to sustain, as it is now becoming in the less developed countries. The level of living would have started down and finally the death rate would have risen again. By curbing their fertility, the people of industrial countries were able not only to continue their rise in consumption but also to continue their decline in mortality.

By what paths was fertility reduced? In the early stages, as the middle classes limited their births but the lower classes did not, pronounced class differences in fertility developed, which reached their peak in the first two decades of the present century. After that, as the lower strata took to birth control, a process of "standardization of reproductive performance" took over. For example, women tended to have more nearly the same number of children, the proportion at each end of the parity distribution being reduced (see Table 5). In the United States, 22.0 percent of the white women born in 1880 and surviving to age 49 never had any children, but only 8.8 percent of those born in 1925 ended up childless. At the other end of the distribution, 30.3 percent of those born in 1880 had five or more children by age 49, whereas only 11.7 percent of those born in 1910 had that many. (The distribution was affected in later cohorts by the greater immigration of Latin American women.) Women cut their fertility by stopping earlier rather than by lengthening the intervals between births. They thus reduced the median age of childbearing and shortened the length of a generation. They bore a greater proportion of their offspring in the modal ages—20 to 29. There was thus no tendency to reduce the birth rate by developing two mutually exclusive paths for women—one a career without family ties, the other a domestic role with numerous children. Instead, virtually *all* women sought to become mothers, but to have a modest number of offspring.

TABLE 5

Cohorts of U.S. White Women, By Parity at Age 49

Date of Birth	Percent with Each Parity at Age 49			
	Zero	1	2–4	5+
1880	22.0	12.6	35.1	30.3
1910	20.6	21.2	46.4	11.7
1915	15.6	19.5	52.9	12.0
1925	8.8	13.7	60.9	16.6

Source: National Center for Health Statistics, *Fertility Tables for Birth Cohorts by Color, United States, 1917–73* (Rockville, Md., April 1976), p. 317.

This standardization took a temporal form as well. In their reproductive behavior, all women tended to respond to changes in conditions in the same way at the same time, thus creating gyrations in fertility so great and sudden that the term "fashion" inevitably comes to mind. By the 1930s age-specific birthrates in industrial countries had fallen to the point where, in stable population terms, they were sufficient only for 70 to 95 percent replacement. Mistaking this for a permanent trend, many industrial nations adopted vigorous pronatalist policies. After World War II, however, the birthrate in all these nations went up remarkably, some achieving a net reproduction rate of 1.75 or above. A peak was reached in the late 1950s (see Table 6 and Figure 1), after which fertility universally declined until it is now, in most industrial countries, lower than it was during the Great Depression. The following tabulation shows the general fertility rate for white women in the United States:

CONSEQUENCES OF THE FERTILITY CHANGES

The social consequences of these changes in fertility can be seen both in the family and in the population at large. The effect of reduced fertility on the nuclear family, for instance, has been to make a fragile group even more fragile, thus again helping to cancel the benefit of lowered mortality in terms of the potential durability of family relationships it provides. Although children nearly all survive now, there are fewer of them to survive; and although marriage is potentially more durable, it is not actually so, because of the rise in the divorce rate. A parent's chance of being separated from his children is now still very great—the risk simply taking the form of divorce rather than death—and yet the number of children available to protect parents against that risk is very small. In the United States in 1850 white women had more children than the 3.40 they needed to replace themselves; they had

	Annual Births per 1,000 Women Aged 15–44
1928–45	80.5
1946–64	109.3
1965–75	77.1

about 5.42.[8] Now, even with greatly reduced mortality, they are having fewer births than needed to replace themselves—1.71 instead of 2.12. There is now no surplus against even the low risk of death, much less against the high risk of divorce. Inevitably a doubt is raised as to whether—or at least how—the nuclear family can be a viable unit under conditions of very low mortality and fertility (conditions the opposite of those under which it evolved). The very fluctuations in the birth rate suggest the uneasiness of this institution. Other features of modern society—the rise of divorce, of illegitimate births, of welfare-supported children, and of hostility between the sexes—also suggest that the nuclear family is in trouble.

THE CHANGING AGE STRUCTURE

With reference to the population as an entity, the most prominent consequence of fertility trends is their effect on the age structure. Changing fertility alters the age structure more powerfully than does changing mortality for a simple reason: people can die at all ages but can be born only at zero age. Accordingly, if the birth rate changes, the

TABLE 6

AVERAGE GROSS AND NET REPRODUCTION RATES
FOR 17 INDUSTRIAL NATIONS, 1940 TO 1973

	Average Rate for Each Year						
	1940	1950	1955	1960	1965	1970	1973
Gross Reproduction Rate							
Australia-New Zealand-United States-Canada	1.213	1.580	1.755	1.830	1.513	1.317	1.106
Japan	2.0	1.77	1.15	0.98	1.042	1.030	1.010
Europe (12 countries)	1.071	1.308	1.302	1.261	1.247	1.059	0.977
All 17 countries	1.159	1.399	1.399	1.378	1.298	1.118	1.009
Net Reproduction Rate							
Australia-New Zealand-United States-Canada	1.115	1.505	1.683	1.765	1.461	1.276	1.074
Japan	1.6	1.52	1.05	0.92	1.009	1.010	1.040
Europe	0.923	1.195	1.226	1.207	1.205	1.027	0.950
All 17 countries	1.008	1.287	1.323	1.322	1.254	1.084	0.984

SOURCE: United Nations, *Demographic Yearbook*, various years.

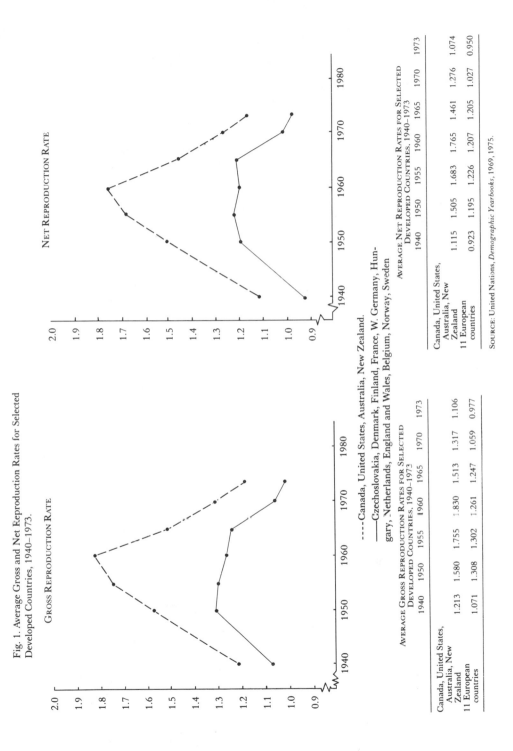

Fig. 1. Average Gross and Net Reproduction Rates for Selected Developed Countries, 1940–1973.

NET REPRODUCTION RATE

GROSS REPRODUCTION RATE

- - - - Canada, United States, Australia, New Zealand.
———— Czechoslovakia, Denmark, Finland, France, W. Germany, Hungary, Netherlands, England and Wales, Belgium, Norway, Sweden

AVERAGE NET REPRODUCTION RATES FOR SELECTED DEVELOPED COUNTRIES, 1940–1973

	1940	1950	1955	1960	1965	1970	1973
Canada, United States, Australia, New Zealand	1.115	1.505	1.683	1.765	1.461	1.276	1.074
11 European countries	0.923	1.195	1.226	1.207	1.205	1.027	0.950

SOURCE: United Nations, *Demographic Yearbooks*, 1969, 1975.

AVERAGE GROSS REPRODUCTION RATES FOR SELECTED DEVELOPED COUNTRIES, 1940–1973

	1940	1950	1955	1960	1965	1970	1973
Canada, United States, Australia, New Zealand	1.213	1.580	1.755	1.830	1.513	1.317	1.106
11 European countries	1.071	1.308	1.302	1.261	1.247	1.059	0.977

youngest age group differs in size from the others, and this difference lasts until the people then living have all died.

In contemporary industrial societies, changes in the age distribution are of two sorts—those produced by short-run fluctuations in fertility, and those brought by the long-run decline. With short-run fluctuations in fertility during any particular period, different parts of the age structure will grow at quite different rates. In Table 7, for example, it can be seen that between 1960 and 1975 the number of children in the United States under ten years of age *declined* by 15 percent while the next two older groups *increased* by 38 and 67 percent, respectively. Such changes create radical shifts in the demand for goods and services geared to specific age groups and alter the relationships between adults and youth. In 1933, for example, there were in the United States 21.6 million white children of elementary school age; ten years later there were only 18.9 million. By 1960 the figure had shot up to 30.7 million.

TABLE 7

CHANGES IN THE AGE-STRUCTURE OF THE UNITED STATES, 1960–1985

	Absolute Change (Thousands)			Relative Change (Percent)		
Age	1960–75	1975–80	1980–85	1960–75	1975–80	1980–85
0–90	–5,751	168	3,888	–14.8	0.5	11.6
10–19	11,343	–3,053	–3,788	37.7	–7.4	–9.9
20–29	14,509	3,658	1,227	66.9	10.1	3.1
30–39	1,164	5,627	5,272	4.8	22.0	16.9
40–49	489	–296	2,891	2.2	–1.3	12.7
50–64	6,357	912	–327	25.0	2.9	–1.0
65–79	4,050	1,828	1,715	29.3	10.2	8.7
80+	2,144	295	420	90.0	6.5	8.7

SOURCE: Future estimates based on *Projections of the Population of the United States, 1975–2020* (Washington, D.C.: U.S. Bureau of the Census, Series P-25, No. 601, October 1975).

Youth Conflict and Generation Size

Each cohort bears throughout life the onus of its relative size. In many ways, for example, the cohort stemming from the postwar baby boom is disadvantaged. Each member has more competitors his own age. The cohort reached adolescence to find there were not enough facilities for so many youths and, above all, not enough adults. The peak years of the baby boom were from 1947 to 1961. The persons born then were 9 to 23 years old in 1970. The adults who had to cope with this wave of youths were themselves born mainly in the late 1920s and the 1930s, and they were very few. For each one of them—that is, for each adult aged 30 to 44 in the white population—there was less than one youth aged 10 to 24 in 1950, but by 1970 there were 1.62, a rise of 64 percent in the ratio. This flood of young people into the population was, I believe, one of the conditions helping to give rise to the youth rebellion and college riots of the late 1960s and early 1970s. The baby boom generation will bear the scars of this conflict the rest of its life. It will never fully recover from the withdrawal philosophy and the deliberate underachievement it assumed during the formative years of its youth. A further result of the conflict is that, as parents, these disciples of freedom are likely to have low fertility, because marriage is a demanding relationship and children are an extremely confining responsibility. The ratio of youths to adults will therefore probably fall drastically. By 1990, according to the "E" projection of the Census Bureau, the ratio will be down to 0.93, some 6 percent lower than in 1950.

The Aging Population

In contrast to the short-run influence of gyrations in the birth rate, the effect of *prolonged low fertility* is to age the population and thus permanently give industrial societies one of their greatest problems. This effect, however, is delayed. At first, as the birth rate falls, the age structure becomes more economically favorable than any ever known, because the generation born earlier (at higher birth rates) moves into the productive ages but has not yet had time to reach old age. This can be seen in Table 8. In 1940, 70.2 percent of Sweden's population was aged 15 to 64, whereas before that the highest percentage was 62.3. By 1973, however, the percentage had dropped to 64.7, almost entirely because of the rise of the proportion aged 65 and over. In the United States in 1975, the proportion of the population aged 65 + was 10.5 percent; according to the "E" projection, this is scheduled to rise only slightly, to 10.9 percent, by the year 2000, but the small size of the increase is a temporary phenomenon resulting from the fact that persons 65 + in the year 2000 will mostly have been born in the late 1920s and early 1930s. If we had a birthrate that forever matched the death rate of 1975, the proportion aged 65 + would be 16.4 percent. After life-expectancy reaches 70 years or more, further gains in longevity tend to age the population. Thus, if our life-expectancy rose to 80 years, as it well may, over a fifth of the population would be 65 +.

Since capacities at older ages decline at an exponential rate, it should not be overlooked that the population 65 or over is itself aging rapidly, as Table 9 shows. Soon nearly half of these elderly people will be 75 or over.

The problem of an aging population is made worse, not better, by the way it is currently being handled. In the first place, there is no good evidence that the increased survival of the aged is a function of improved health. Indeed, many oldsters are now being kept alive only to suffer illnesses and disabilities that, in a former day, would have killed them. In the second place, since there is great individual variation at older ages, a productive policy would be to keep those senior citizens in the labor force who wish to work and are capable of it. However, the opposite policy is being followed—compulsory retirement at some arbitrary age like 65. As a result, as Table 10 shows, the decline in labor-force participation among those aged 65 + has been precipitous; it has occurred among women as well as men despite the general trend toward female employment. Detailed data show that, for men, retirement is increasing at ages under as well as over 65. As late as 1955 the proportion of men 55 to 65 years of age who were working was 87.9 percent, but by 1975 it was only 75.8 percent.[9] The trend for women aged 55 to 64, for reasons that will become plain later, is in the opposite direction.

The disemployment policy for the elderly seems to stem from the job-fund fallacy (the notion that there are a fixed number of jobs) and the confusion of jobs with productive work. At any one time the number of jobs may not equal the people seeking them, but this does not mean that the number is fixed, for it varies greatly with the business cycle and with the field of enterprise. In any case, a job is a claim on a salary or wage, not a guarantee of productive work. A person may hold a job without doing productive work or any work at all; and, conversely, he may not have a job but still be doing productive work and getting a return for it. It follows that an economy in which everybody has a job is not necessarily very productive. Production is not determined by rights to salaries but by work—that is, by the number of workers, their skills, and the kind of work they do. Given the same skills and the same productive type of work, the greater the proportion of people who are working the greater will be the production. This being the case, to retire elderly people from work is not to help the economy but to hurt it. An alternative would be to test those over age 60 for their skills and put them into the activity for which their skills best suit them. This alternative, however, is not likely to be followed because, having confused jobs with work, people unconsciously assume that if the old continue to work they must continue to hold a job—that is, continue to draw a

TABLE 8

CHANGING AGE STRUCTURE OF THE SWEDISH POPULATION, 1750–1973

Age	Percent of Total Population in Specified Age Group								
	1750	1800	1850	1900	1920	1940	1965	1973	1974
0–14	33.2	32.3	33.0	32.4	29.3	20.4	20.7	20.7	20.7
15–39	38.9	38.3	41.1	36.6	39.0	41.5	33.8	34.5	34.6
40–64	21.7	23.7	21.1	22.6	23.3	28.7	32.6	30.2	29.9
65 +	6.2	5.7	4.8	8.4	8.4	9.4	12.9	14.5	14.8

SOURCE: Historisk Statistik för Sverige, vol. 1 (Stockholm: Statistiska Centralbyrån, 1974), p. 68; United Nations, *Demographic Yearbook*, 1974, pp. 182–83, 1975, pp. 216–17.

TABLE 9

AGE COMPOSITION OF U.S. POPULATION AGED 65 + (PERCENT)

Age	1940	1976	2000	ZPG $e_0 = 80$
65–74	70.5	61.9	55.8	51.5
75–84	25.4	29.5	33.7	35.3
85 +	4.1	8.6	10.5	13.2
Total	100.0	100.0	100.0	100.0

SOURCE: U.S. Bureau of the Census, *Current Population Reports*, Series P-25, No. 98 (August 13, 1954), p. 15; No. 643 (January 1977), p. 13; Special Studies, Series P-23, No. 59 (May 1976), p. 3. The last column is from a life-table computed by the author.

TABLE 10

PROPORTION OF PERSONS AGED 65 OR MORE IN LABOR FORCE, UNITED STATES

Year	*Percent in Labor Force*	
	Males	Females
1890	68.3	7.6
1900	63.1	8.3
1920	55.6	7.3
1940	41.8	6.1
1960	32.2	10.5
1970	25.8	9.2
1975	20.8	7.8
1990 (projected)	16.2	7.2

SOURCE: *Historical Statistics of the United States, Colonial Times to 1970*, Part I (Washington, D.C.: U.S. Bureau of the Census, 1975), p. 132, and *Statistical Abstract of the United States 1976*, p. 355.

salary. This view is strengthened by another feature in our system, the seniority principle. This principle means in effect that the older a person is on the job the higher is his pay. The only way to beat that principle is arbitrary retirement from the job, but this implies to most people retirement from work as well. The old are given pensions and social security, which are salaries for not working, and which are less than the salaries in the jobs they left. If those among the elderly who wanted to work had their skills tested and were given the kind of productive work for which they are best suited, whether in a job or in self-employment, this would create goods and services that would help raise the demand for work by younger people.

Not only is the policy of compulsory retirement rendering useless a sizable portion of the adult population, but it is placing an oppressive burden on that portion of the population that does work. Social security payments in the United States (excluding disability insurance) rose from $26.3 billion in 1970 to $54.8 billion in 1975 (a doubling in five years). The cost per person in the labor force rose from $306 to $578. Of course, social security payments only scratch the surface. Much of the governmental expenditure for medical services—a category growing faster than any other form of government subsidy—goes for the aged, whose need for medical attention is virtually inexhaustible.

If the elderly are increasing as a proportion of the population and yet are being increasingly excluded from the labor force, one way of enabling those who work to meet the burden is by expanding the number of workers in other age groups. This is not being done by recruiting a larger number of youths but rather by drawing a greater number of women into the labor market. Indeed, in the United States, for every person aged 65 or over who withdrew from the labor market in 1970 as compared to 1950, there were six women under age 65 added to take his place. This is what might have been expected. As the tax burden on the worker increases, couples find that to maintain their level of living both must work. There were 8.1 million more women in the labor force in 1970 than would have been expected at the 1950 participation rate.

In an agrarian economy, the old were proportionately few, and they were cared for by family and kin. The close relatives knew the old people, knew their capacities, and had a vital interest in keeping them at work as long as possible. In turn, the old were highly motivated to be as useful as possible. Now we have handed the care of the aged over to impersonal agencies—pension schemes, government handouts, savings and financial institutions. These do not know the aged individual personally, and they give him little motivation to reduce costs. The reason for this profound switch is largely demographic. As Table 11 shows, there are now far more aged parents per adult than there used to be. The children have readily turned the care of aged parents over to whatever impersonal agencies will assume it, thus shifting the costs to all workers rather than just themselves (the children). The only trouble is that, due to the impersonality of the system, there is no rein on the escalation of the costs.

TABLE 11

RATIO OF AGED PARENTS TO CHILDREN IN THREE MODEL POPULATIONS

	I	II	III
Fertility	High	High	Low
Mortality	High	Low	Low
Parents 60 + per surviving child	0.289	0.301	0.601
Average years a parent lives beyond age 60 per year lived by child between ages 30 and 60	0.14	0.18	0.36

SOURCE: United Nations, *The Aging of Populations and Its Economic and Social Implications* (New York, United Nations, 1956), p. 76.

THE MALE VERSUS THE FEMALE AGE STRUCTURE

It is not only the age structure *per se* that becomes distorted to an unprecedented extent in industrial societies, but it is the sex ratio as well. This can be seen if we combine the sex distribution with the age distribution to get the sex ratio by age (the sex ratio is computed as follows: [males ÷ females] × 100). The age-sex composition of the American white population in 1975 is shown in the first column of Table 12. The sex ratio is masculine up to about age 30, but feminine (and increasingly feminine) after that.

A factor that can greatly influence the sex ratio, especially in the young adult ages, is differential migration as between men and women. Thus at one time the Chinese population in the United States was overwhelmingly masculine, because it was males who immigrated. If migration is omitted, then the sex ratio by age is ultimately determined by three other factors: the sex ratio at birth, the relative mortality of males and females, and the rate of natural increase of both sexes combined. The relative influence of these three factors varies according to the age group considered.

At exact age 0, for example, the sex ratio at birth is of course the only influence. If no other factors appeared later to alter this influence, the sex ratio throughout the age structure would be identical to the ratio at birth (which ordinarily is around 105 males per 100 females). In fact, however, from the moment of birth the difference in mortality between males and females exercises its influence; at older ages this influence accumulates and becomes predominant over the influence of the sex ratio at birth. The effect of the mortality differential can be seen in Table 12 where, in the second column, the sex ratio due to mortality alone is shown. Since (in the absence of infanticide or selective neglect) boys start dying more frequently than girls from the moment of birth, the sex ratio from mortality alone cannot be masculine at any age. How important the sex ratio at birth is in keeping the population masculine

TABLE 12

ACTUAL, STATIONARY, AND MODIFIED STATIONARY SEX RATIO
BY AGE, U.S. WHITE POPULATION, 1975

	Sex Ratio		
Age	Actual	Life Table Population*	Sex Adjusted Life Table Population†
0–19	104.4	99.5	105.3
20–29	101.9	98.3	104.1
30–39	98.6	97.4	103.1
40–49	96.5	96.0	101.6
50–64	91.2	90.5	95.8
65–79	73.4	70.6	75.7
80 +	52.4	43.3	43.4
Total	95.8	90.0	95.3

SOURCES: U.S. Bureau of the Census, "Estimates of the Population of the U.S. by Age, Sex, and Race," *Current Population Reports,* Series P-25, No. 643 (January 1977), p. 8. *National Center for Health Statistics, Monthly Vital Statistics Report,* vol. 25, No. 11, Supplement (Rockville, Md.: February 11, 1977), p. 8.

*These are the ratios that would result from the influence of mortality alone. They are obtained by dividing the L_x in the male life table by the corresponding L_x in the female table. Since both have a radix of 100,000, the sex ratio at birth exercises no influence.

†These are the ratios arising from both the force of differential mortality and the sex ratio at birth. They are obtained by calculating a sex adjusted life table, in which the ratio between the male and female radixes equals the sex ratio at birth.

through the reproductive ages is shown by the contrast between the second and third columns of Table 12. In the third column, the ratios shown are those that would be produced if both mortality and the sex ratio at birth (without any other factors) were determining the sex ratio by age. The distribution is fairly close to the actual one shown in the first column, except that the latter is influenced by migration, the underenumeration of males, and the past age-sex structure.

Another way of describing the numerical relation of the sexes is in terms of "surplus" males or females—the number or proportion above a 50–50 ratio. Table 13 (in the next section) repeats Table 12 from this point of view, using the female population as the base for percentages. Again it is the sex ratio at birth that saves the situation up to age 50, but after that the surplus of women grows rapidly because of the cumulative force of the male-female mortality differential. Thus, it is once more clear that the miraculous extension of life in advanced countries has given rise to a major development that no one anticipated. Not only has it forced a reduction in fertility and therefore an aging of the population, but by favoring females more than males, it has produced an imbalance of the sexes at older ages, which probably never occurred in the past.

An estimate of what will happen in the future to differential mortality between the sexes depends on the theory of the causes of the differential. In the absence of any theory, the female and male mortality can be extrapolated. In the U.S. white population, by the year 2000 the difference in life-expectancy would be 10.0 years (based on the 1900 to 1975 trend) or 10.6 years (based on the 1940 to 1975 trend). If, however, one believes that the chief cause of the differential is the protected life of females—that is, that they escape stress and hardship by not having to earn a living for a family—one can foresee a decline in the differential as an increasing proportion of women enter the labor force and become heads of families. On the other hand, the advantage of females in mortality appears at all ages, both before and after the working ages; it is not wholly explicable in terms of temporary differences in habits such as smoking, diet, and exercise.[10] Perhaps women are biologically more capable of resisting the environmental poisons and stresses of industrial society, especially since women are now freed from a high rate of childbearing. If so, the mortality gap may continue to increase, giving rise to sex ratios still more distorted than those observed today.

MARRIAGE AND THE SEX RATIO BY AGE

Having considered the imbalances of the age-sex distribution, we can now add another dimension—marital status. Since the primary division of labor between the sexes occurs within the family, the family would seem to be a good place to examine the impact of imbalances between the sexes. However, in modern societies the family has an automatic mechanism—monogamy—which keeps the imbalance from intruding into the family itself. In other words, the sex ratio of the married population is 100. This being true, any imbalances, or "surpluses," are concentrated in the *un*married population—i.e., those who are single, widowed, or divorced.

The sex ratio of the unmarried population by age is governed in part by the same factors mentioned above as determining the sex ratio of the total population by age. The surpluses shown in Table 13, for instance, must be found exclusively in the unmarried population. But for specific ages there is an additional factor exacerbating the imbalances. This is the differential marriage behavior of men and women. A larger proportion of men remarry after divorce or widowhood, because they are outnumbered and in other ways have more opportunity to remarry. Furthermore, as is well known, when they do remarry they tend to marry women considerably younger than themselves. With this source of distortion added to that caused by differential mortality, the imbalance in the sex ratio of the unmarried population becomes spectacular. Table 14 shows the sex ratio by age of the unmarried population in the United States and the unweighted average for nine other industrial nations and nine developing nations around 1970. In the younger ages, there are far more unmarried males than females (hence the masculine sex ratios) but in the older ages, the reverse is true. In the population aged 20 to 24 in nine industrial countries, for example, each unmarried woman has, on average, 1.68 unmarried males her own age. After that age one is surprised by the swiftness of the change (around age 37) from male surplus to female surplus. At age 50 to 59, there are more than two unmarried women for every unmarried man; at age 60 and over, the ratio is three to one.

A look across Table 14 shows some similarity of pattern between industrial and non-industrial countries. In the younger ages the surplus of males is greater in the non-industrial countries, but in the older ages the surplus of females is less, doubtless reflecting a younger and more rapidly growing population and a smaller sex difference in mortality.

TABLE 13

"Surplus" Female Population by Age in Actual and
Theoretical Populations, for U.S. Whites, 1975

	Percent of Female Population "Surplus"*		
Age	Actual Population	Life Table Population	Modified Life Table Population
0–19	−4.43	0.53	−5.30
20–29	−1.93	1.65	−4.11
30–39	1.23	2.62	−3.08
40–49	3.32	3.98	−1.65
50–64	8.73	9.54	4.24
65–79	26.65	28.50	24.30
80 +	48.49	56.74	54.21

Sources: U.S. Bureau of the Census, "Estimates of the Population of the U.S. by Age, Sex, and Race," *Current Population Reports*, Series P-25, no. 643 (January 1977), p. 8. *National Center for Health Statistics, Monthly Vital Statistics Report*, vol. 25, no. 11, Supplement (Rockville, Md., February 11, 1977), p. 8.

*"Surplus" means the amount by which females exceed males. This amount is divided by the female population in the age group to get the percentage "surplus." A minus sign means that males are in surplus.

Among industrial countries, the United States stands out in having a young age at marriage, especially for men. Accordingly, at young ages an unusually high proportion of men in this country are married and thus do not swell the ranks of the unmarried.

The rough similarity in sex imbalance between industrial and non-industrial countries does not mean similarity with respect to the proportion of all women affected. If we take the "surplus" women at, say, ages over 50 as a proportion of all women aged 15 and over, as shown in Table 15 (in the next section), we discover why the number of older unmarried women seems particularly large in industrial societies. It is not so much that the old in these societies are less married but that there are simply far more old people.

Of course, our calculations are based on the assumption that individuals within the same age group are the most likely potential marriage partners. Since this is not true, the tables only roughly approximate the reality. When we make calculations in terms of men five years older than women, the results are not very different from those shown in the tables above, but in general the excess of females at older ages is still greater. One can argue, of course, that in view of higher male mortality, the marriage of women to men older than themselves is ill advised (assuming the union is going to last). From the standpoint of the couple's joint survival, marrying a man of the same age would be an improvement, but marrying a man five years younger would be a still greater improvement.

TABLE 14

SEX RATIO OF THE UNMARRIED POPULATION, BY AGE, FOR THE UNITED STATES
IN 1970 AND THE AVERAGE FOR NINE OTHER SELECTED INDUSTRIAL
AND NONINDUSTRIAL NATIONS AROUND 1970*

Age	U.S. White Population	9 Industrial Countries†	9 Developing Countries††
15–19	111.4	114.4	118.2
20–24	134.4	168.1	184.0
25–29	127.0	117.6	199.7
30–34	99.0	133.2	118.5
35–39	85.8	103.2	83.2
40–49	71.5	55.7	53.7
50–59	49.5	39.5	40.8
60–74	33.0	32.4	36.4
75 +	31.6	30.2	41.2
Total	78.7	82.0	102.1

SOURCE: United Nations, *Demographic Yearbook, 1973*, Table 26, pp. 414–59, and U.S. Population Census 1970, Subject Report PC(2)4C *Marital Status*, pp. 14–17.

*In the United States the "unmarried" population includes the single, divorced, widowed, and separated. In only three of the other industrial countries are the separated included (these are Australia, Finland, and Norway), but they are included in six of the developing countries—Brazil, Malaysia, Mexico, Panama, Puerto Rico, and Thailand. It should be noted that for the United States the data omit armed forces overseas. Hence the sex ratio is more female in the military ages than it would otherwise be.

†The countries are Australia, Austria, Belgium, Czechoslovakia, Finland, Hungary, Japan, Norway, Yugoslavia.

††The countries are Brazil, Malaysia, Mexico, Morocco, Panama, Puerto Rico, South Korea, Thailand, and Turkey.

TABLE 15

EXCESS MALES OR FEMALES IN EACH AGE GROUP AS A PROPORTION OF
"SURPLUS," UNMARRIED U.S. WHITE POPULATION, 1970

Age	Excess in Age-Sex Distribution		"Surplus" Unmarried Persons		Excess as Percent of "Surplus"
	Male	Female	Male	Female	
15–19	548,324		826,010		66.4
20–24		441,509	1,006,965		– 43.8*
25–29		115,710	290,265		– 39.9*
30–34		134,711		7,129	1789.6
35–39		157,587		99,009	159.2
40–44		188,691		178,183	105.9
45–49		360,996		337,476	107.0
50–54		339,061		512,765	66.1
55–59		375,174		726,256	51.7
60–64		488,090		970,108	50.3
65–69		710,056		1,146,487	61.9
70–74		753,111		1,214,772	62.0
75–79		672,059		1,084,026	62.0
80–84		497,397		740,900	67.1
85 +		398,165		513,371	77.6

*A negative percent here means the proportional amount by which the "excess" fails to account for *any* of the "surplus." In other words, marital behavior accounts for more than 100 percent of the "surplus."

Demographic versus
Nondemographic Explanation

In explaining the causation of the sex imbalance among the elderly unmarried, we can separate the effect of the purely demographic factors previously discussed from the influence of marital behavior. This can be done by comparing the two-way age-sex distribution with the three-way age-sex-*marital status* distribution. Since the difference between the two is purely a function of marital behavior, the effect of the latter can be measured by the extra proportion of "surplus" females it contributes. It turns out, surprisingly, that in general marital behavior is not the main contributor, as Table 15 shows. At ages 15–19, two-thirds of the male surplus is a function of demographic factors alone, and at ages 30–49 the female surplus is overwhelmingly explained by these factors. After those ages, the proportion explained by demographic factors goes down, but it is always above 50 percent. Only at ages 20–29 does marital behavior dominate, explaining all of the male surplus.

Having decomposed the data on surplus females into two components—the age-sex distribution and marital behavior—we can now go further and decompose each of these components as well. As seen already, the female surplus in the age-sex distribution is almost 100 percent accounted for by sex inequality in mortality. The slow rate of population growth also contributes by minimizing the effect of the masculine sex ratio at birth, but its influence is negligible compared to differential mortality. The sex ratio at birth, the only other possible influence, would create a male rather than a female surplus at all ages.

Within the marital behavior component, things are more complex. One can see from Table 16 that in the United States the unmarried surplus is masculine up to age 29; this surplus is entirely explained by the fact that at young ages there are more *single* males than females. At those young ages there is no other marital status in which males exceed females. The predominance of males in the "single" category at young ages can be explained by the fact that males up and down the age structure compete for young females, who can therefore get married in greater abundance than their male age mates. At age 30 and above, the surplus unmarried population is always feminine, and at first this surplus is explained in young ages primarily by divorce and separation and, at older ages, by widowhood. Since at age 40 and above, widowhood accounts for more than 50 percent of the surplus unmarried women, we again see that the rising sex difference in mortality is playing a strong role.

TABLE 16

Proportion of "Surplus" Unmarried Attributable to Specific Marital Status, U.S. White Population, 1970

Age	Sex of Unmarried Surplus	Percent Attributable to			
		Single	Widowed	Divorced	Separated
15–19	M	100.0	F	F	F
20–24	M	100.0	F	F	F
25–29	M	100.0	F	F	F
30–34	F	M	29.8	47.7	22.5
35–39	F	M	35.6	45.7	18.7
40–49	F	M	58.4	30.6	11.0
50–59	F	3.1	79.7	13.7	3.5
60–74	F	6.3	88.7	4.5	0.5
75 +	F	7.6	91.2	1.2	M

Source: U.S. Population Census 1970, Subject Report PC(2)4C *Marital Status*, pp. 14–17.

CONCLUSION

This brief excursion into contemporary demography demonstrates, I think, that industrial societies are traveling an unknown road at high speed—expanding their complex technology with little knowledge or appreciation of the long-run consequences. They ingeniously find short-run solutions, then discover that the solutions have given rise to new problems for which again short-run solutions must be found. Longer term consequences are either not foreseen or else ignored in the hope that somehow they will not materialize or will succumb to new technological miracles.

Given the character of human societies as collections of individuals, the unplanned and unforeseen character of social change seems inevitable. There is no group mind or authority, but only the mind and authority of particular individuals; these are necessarily limited in knowledge and power, and they have short lives and individual interests. As long as the technology was rudimentary and the society stabilized by tradition, the future was fairly predictable except for external catastrophe. Now, however, industrial societies tend to generate their own catastrophes.

The blind character of contemporary social change becomes particularly clear in the light of demography, because demographic changes are interlinked. A change in one demographic component eventually must affect others, with quantifiable results. The first great demographic achievement of the Industrial Revolution, the prolongation of human life, was a boon that hardly anything else could equal. Aside from the sheer value of staying alive, it made possible more durable social relationships, freed women from the necessity of constant pregnancy in order to replace themselves, and contributed greatly to economic efficiency. But like a spendthrift who has inherited a million dollars, the industrial societies never reckoned, or could reckon, with the ricocheting imbalances and distortions that this fundamental change would give rise to. Lacking control over their destiny, they dissipated or canceled most of the potential advantages that a lower mortality could bring. The possibility of more durable family relationships was eventually negated by rising divorce rates and by deterioration of the parent-child relationship. The potentiality for an economic wonderland was eroded by the rapid growth of population, first in the industrial countries themselves and then in the world at large. Eventually, about a century late and without it being planned that way, fertility in industrial countries did fall, and it is now almost in balance with the death rate, but this in turn has given rise to another major problem of industrial societies—an aging population. Instead of working out an adjustment to this easily predictable development beforehand, industrial nations have failed to make an adjustment to it even after it has happened. In fact, the new circumstance has been made worse by patchwork responses that seem guided by misconceptions rather than truths. As the elderly become an increasing proportion of the population, they are, of all things, being eliminated from the labor force, regardless of their desires. Similarly, a less foreseeable problem—the widening gap between men and women in life-expectancy—has received little attention even after it has happened. Certainly no deliberate institutional restructuring has been undertaken to avoid or make more palatable the "surpluses" we have documented among the older unmarried population. Such restructuring may gradually evolve, but only as a result of cumulative individual adjustments rather than collective planning.

In the absence of societal foresight, individuals flail as best they can, seeking some solution to their personal situation under the circumstances of the day. Taken *en masse*, these individual flailings foot up to social change, but it is blind social change. It can be seen, for instance, how the alteration of demographic circumstances is helping to turn women toward increased labor force participation, abandonment of traditional sex roles, and entry into quasi-marital arrangements; it can be less clearly seen, but nevertheless deduced, that these changes themselves will have demographic consequences with still other social repercussions, few of which will be anticipated by collective effort. In perspective, it looks as though the industrial societies are simply advanced manifestations of man's basic dilemma—great capacity to make and use instrumentalities, little capacity to think through what he really wants.

Religion and the American Future

Peter L. Berger

M'GUINNESS

3 In an age of arrogant ideologies it is curious how many Americans have lost confidence in the political symbols upon which their society has been built. And, while virulent nationalism is rampant in the world, large numbers of Americans seem to apologize for the basic character if not the very existence of their own country. The national mood, despite some recent upswings, still appears to be one of pervasive anxiety, self-doubt, and pessimism. To be sure, this need varies in degree among different segments of the population and regions of the country. It is most intense in the college-educated upper middle class, which has been going through a whole series of orgiastic self-denigrations. To the extent, however, that this particular segment dominates the media of mass communication, the educational system, and the general "knowledge industry," its attitudes carry over into other groups. This situation constitutes a crisis for the polity. There has been a hollowing out of the beliefs and values on which the polity depends for its continuing credibility, a failure of nerve paralyzing both action and imagination.

In a different way, and for a longer time, there has been a comparable crisis of credibility in the American religious community. Here too there has been a loss of self-assurance, an apologizing stance in the face of what is perceived as the spirit of the age, a hollowing out of the traditional symbols. Again, this mood has not been uniform throughout the society. Not surprisingly, it has been strongest in those Christian churches that are closest to the upper middle class and that take their cues from the cultural oracles of the latter, that is, in the denominations of mainline Protestantism and, since Vatican II with a vengeance, in the Roman Catholic community. American Judaism, despite its distinctive problems, has passed through its own credibility crisis.

The purpose of this paper is to explore the character and linkage between these two varieties of what may well be called decadence. In seeking to understand these phenomena, as a sociologist, I try to be objective. I have no intention of trying to be dispassionate. I have a very big stake both in the vitality of religious faith in our time and in the continuing viability of the American experiment. In what follows, then, I will not restrict myself to detached analysis, but will take the liberty of making statements with policy implications.

The failure of nerve in the churches is not a new phenomenon. It is an attitude of obeisance to the "cultured despisers of religion" that goes all the way back to the Enlightenment. It is rooted in the confrontation of Christianity with both the institutional and cultural dynamics of modernity. I may add that there is nothing mysterious about all this; the relationship between modernity and secularization is fully analyzable in sociological and social-psychological terms (and since I, for one, have done so interminably over an embarrassingly long number of publications, I will refrain from expounding on the matter here). What has happened in America during the last two decades is an acceleration in the secularizing forces, most of it to be accounted for, on one level at least, by an increase in the cultural influence and power of the afore-mentioned upper-middle-class stratum—a group that widely controls the knowledge industry and that I like to call a cognitive elite in the society. As the aggressive secularism of this group has come to be more strongly felt, those in the churches taking their cues from this elite or wanting to belong to it have intensified their accommodating moves.

Secularism as a world view means, above all, a denial of transcendence. On the cognitive level, therefore, there is a rather simple formula for the accommodation to it by Christian thinkers: all references to transcendence in the tradition are translated into terms of immanence. This general formula can then be filled with just about any secular contents, just so long as they are secular. Thus the true meaning of Christian faith can be understood in terms of philosophical, psychological, or social doctrines: to be a Christian then means to become authentic, or to attain mental health, or to live in a true community. This translation of transcendence into immanence can also, of course, take place in political terms. The concepts and the imagery of biblical eschatology are particularly handy for this: the symbols of the Kingdom of God are then identified with whatever political program happens to be plausible to the translators. It is very important to understand that this political version of the translation procedure can be ideologically "right" as well as "left." The identification of the Kingdom with the

American nation, its alleged historic mission or its allegedly superior way of life, has precisely the same cognitive structure as the application of the eschatological symbols to the revolutionary struggle, the building of socialism, or to this or that liberation movement. The "right" version of political eschatology has, of course, a long history in America, in the idolatry of the nation and its institutions. It so happens that the "left" version is more in vogue at the moment.

America is a very big country, and a sociologically complex one. As a result, a lot of very different things are going on simultaneously. Thus there are still many people who, in fact, worship the American way of life, while others are engaged in worshipping Che Guevara; what is more, in the first group there are people who have never heard of Che Guevara. Commentators on the religious scene who reside in the Middle West keep chiding others not to confuse the two coasts with the country as a whole: what is the last cry in small-town Iowa may be taken for granted in New York City—and, let it be emphasized, the reverse may be true too. (Since I live in Brooklyn, let me add that it is equally dangerous to think that all New Yorkers are moved by, or even aware of, the allegedly burning issues negotiated at cocktail parties on the Upper West Side of Manhattan.) The crisis in the churches does not mean that most religious people in America have lost their faith. It does mean that those who still find the traditional symbols credible find themselves typed as backward or reactionary by the most prestigious, *avant-garde* spokesmen in the field of religion. In consequence, there has opened up a serious gap between large numbers of the laity and that segment of the religious leadership that has set the agenda of the churches in terms of radical accommodation to the shifting fashions of the cognitive elite. Jeffrey Hadden, in his book *The Gathering Storm in the Churches,* warned that this would happen (the book was published in 1969); it did not happen as dramatically as he thought, but, on the whole he has been right.

Let me now turn to the other crisis, to the failure of nerve in the polity. By contrast with the former one, this is a very new phenomenon in America, perhaps some ten years old. It is a deepening and spreading conviction that the symbols of the American political creed are, precisely, hollow. The old sense of self-assurance (let alone messianic zeal) is weakening and becoming increasingly hard to find. Instead, there is a vision of America as a fundamentally predatory and oppressive society, or at best a sick one. In its more developed forms, this new attitude is a vitriolic anti-Americanism: whatever is American (culturally, socially, politically) is bad; conversely, the good must be sought elsewhere. The psychological masochism of this cannot arrest us here. The political implications are far reaching. While, of course, the extreme versions of the new anti-Americanism are limited to a relatively small group (the relevant variables are class, race, and age), its more moderate expressions are, I think, spreading: there may not, or not as yet, be too many people in the country who think of it as a late manifestation of the Third Reich; there are more and more who perceive America as fundamentally sick, in decline, or even coming apart at the seams.

In the liberal conventional wisdom, three major events of the last decade are commonly cited as causes for this disillusionment: the racial conflict, the war in Indochina, and the Watergate affair. I have no doubt that these events were important factors. Let me also state that I, for one, find good reasons for moral anguish in each one of the three: America's treatment of its racial minorities, expecially of blacks, is the one most shameful aspect of its history; the war in Indochina was, I continue to believe, an unjust war; the Watergate affair was a serious assault on liberty. (I shall also take the liberty of saying that I was personally involved in fights for racial justice when I lived in the South in the 1950s, long before this became fashionable, and that I was vocally opposed to the Vietnam War.) What these events signify, however, is not the cause but rather the consequence of a certain vision of America. In my own view, the significance of these events is pretty much the opposite of what the new anti-Americanism makes it out to be: the astounding fact is the degree of progress in racial justice that we have seen in America in the very few years since the beginning of the civil rights movement. Minorities of every sort are brutally oppressed all over the world—there are few countries that can match America in the will to render justice to its minorities. It is not remarkable that an imperial power conducts a cruel colonial war in a faraway country, but it is remarkable that, in the case of the American war in Indochina, a public opinion that was at least partially motivated by moral considerations forced a reversal of policy. As to Watergate, the significant fact is not that the Nixon administration tried its "dirty tricks," but rather that the attempt failed—with major political institutions (a free press, an independent judiciary, and a responsible legislature) finally functioning in almost incredible fidelity to the prescriptions of the American creed.

This world being what it is, every ideal fails to be fully realized. To the individual who believes in the ideal, such failures are occasions for shame or guilt, but more importantly for renewed efforts. To the one who has lost faith in the ideal, every failure, and indeed every adversity, confirms that loss of faith. I think that the recent convulsions of American society are not causes but rather contributing factors, and to a degree even symptoms, of the political failure of nerve. The latter, in my view, is rooted in intrinsic tensions and discontents of modern society, which are always present but which erupt under certain conditions; I cannot elaborate on this here. Let me only make the additional observation that other societies—without racial problems, colonial adventures, or dramatic public scandals—manifest very similar symptoms of political and ideological malaise.

To repeat: not all sectors of the American population are affected equally by the crisis of the political creed. There is an educational divide which is to a considerable extent coterminous with a class divide. With the important exception of the black community, the disenchantment grows as one goes up in the class system (a fact, by the way, which remains inexplicable in liberal or "left" terms). Most importantly, the failure of nerve is strongest among intellectuals—broadly speaking, those who produce and distribute the metaphors by which the society can understand itself. What we are witnessing is another instance of the *trahison des clercs*. The ideological mood of these circles right now is "left." It is all the more important to understand that the collapse of belief in the viability of the American polity could just as easily take a "right" turn. Indeed, I suspect that this will be the greater danger if the credibility crisis of the system continues. We may then expect some movement that will combine a militantly resurgent nationalism with various populist noises (which, I suppose, is as good a definition of fascism as any). We may also expect that many of those who now admire and legitimate miscellaneous despotisms abroad will find ways of adjusting their ideology so as to celebrate a new tyranny closer to home.

The two crises, that in the religious and that in the political community, are related. They are not related, needless to say, in the simplistic sense that one cannot believe in America without believing in God—or, for that matter, that being a good Christian or Jew necessarily implies being an American patriot. The relation is more complex and subtle. There is a general relation, by no means limited to the case of America, in that the same underlying processes of modernity that have produced secularization also weaken the plausibility of all belief systems—not just the religious ones, but also those in the realms of morality and politics. There is, however, a special relation between the two crises in America. As Richard Neuhaus points out in his book *Time Toward Home* (1975), there has been throughout American history a complicated interplay between the sacred covenant of the churches and the social contract of the polity. More than in most other modern societies, the political institutions of the American republic rest upon beliefs and values of religious provenance. Even if, then, the two crises have distinct characters and, to a degree, separate causes, it would be surprising if they were not also connected in significant ways.

In the present situation, I think, the nexus between the two crises can be seen more clearly if one asks the following question: what is to be done about the crisis of the American creed? The question, of course, assumes that something ought to be done about it—an assumption I make without the least hesitation: if nothing is done, the ensuing scenarios are, in my opinion, dismal not only for America but for the world. But if something is to be done, there are really only two options.

The first option is the reimposition of the old political faith by force—if you will, this option is that of an "Augustan age" of the American republic. If it is followed, democracy as we know it would not survive—and this means that the option is self-defeating in the most elementary sense, since the democratic experiment is at the very heart of the American creed. The other option is a revitalization of the American creed from within, not by imposition but by renewed conviction. But how is that to be accomplished? Well, once again, I think, one may envisage two possibilities. One possibility is that the American state (and that means the federal government) would transform itself into an aggressive ideological entity. The state, that is, would take on the job of "mobilizing the masses" under the banners of the American creed. One may amuse oneself trying to imagine such an eventuality: it would probably look like the script of Mao's Cultural Revolution rewritten by Woody Allen. (The scene that I enjoy imagining is one of President Carter sending off hordes of screaming Boy Scouts to beat up federal bureaucrats!) In other words, the American state, as we know it, is not made to undertake such a task—and let us be thankful that it is not. If, on the other hand, the federal government did successfully transform itself in such a way as to become an agent of ideological mobilization, it would only do this by giving up the principles of liberty and diversity that, once again, are essential to the American creed. In other words, that option too would be profoundly self-defeating.

The reasons why the American state (except perhaps in moments of acute national emergency) is unable to function effectively as a mobilizing entity are deeply rooted in American history. Unlike the democratic states that emerged from various European and Latin American revolutions, the American polity largely refrained from understanding itself in messianic terms (although, of course, there were strong messianic themes at various moments in the history of the republic). As was already seen by early observers, like de Tocqueville, the vitality of American democracy derived not from the state but from a plurality of communities and associations within the society. Put differently: the polity has depended for its vitality (and, indeed, credibility) upon a variety of value-generating institutions outside itself. It is these institutions that have served to mediate between the state and the mass of the citizenry. Precisely this reliance upon natural communities and voluntary associations has served as a powerful brake on the totalitarian tendencies that, I think, are intrinsic to the modern state.

With this we come to an important point: organized religion occupies a strategic, if not paramount, position among the value-generating institutions in American society. There are others, to be sure—the family, the small community or neighborhood, a variety of voluntary associations, the grass-roots components of political parties and labor unions, as well as ethnic subcultures and groupings based on miscellaneous "life-styles." With the possible exception of the family, however, it is difficult to conceive of these as having the same potential as the churches for creating and sustaining human values. If this is so, there is a simple but far-reaching implication: the vitality of organized religion is a public interest of the larger society. To the extent that there is a crisis in the churches, this too is a matter of public concern—not because the state itself has a religious quality, but because the state, at least in the form prescribed by the American creed, is dependent upon the moral values that the churches embody and mediate.

I recognize that what I have just suggested will sound in many ears like a reactionary call for a "Christian America," presumably coming out of some corner of the right-wing lunatic fringe. I have made enough public statements and published enough books to know that nothing one says guarantees that one will not be misunderstood. All the same, I want to say a few things to reduce the risk of this particular misunderstanding: neither the concept of the churches as mediating structures nor the policy implications of this concept run counter to the constitutional separation of church and state. They only run counter to a narrow, doctrinaire understanding of this separation in terms of a newly aggressive secularism. Of course I'm not recommending a federal establishment of religion. Of course I'm not advocating the infringement of the religious liberty of anyone, Christian or non-Christian, or indeed the liberty of people to be left alone in their irreligion. On the contrary, I'm strongly committed to the peculiarly American combination of freedom and pluralism, which indeed has been the special foundation of our constitutional provisions in this area of life.

Yet what I have suggested does run counter to the way in which both the courts and liberal opinion have tended to interpret the First Amendment in recent years. For what some of these interpretations have done actually amounts to a reversal of the traditional neutrality of the American polity in matters of religion—to wit, it amounts to a new establishment, an establishment of secularism as the quasi-religion of the republic. Needless to say, this establishment is by no means an accomplished fact, nor would any judge or opinion-maker put it in these words. Nevertheless, there has been a trend in this direction, and what I'm recommending is that this trend be reversed. Let me cite some facets of this trend. There is the belligerent attitude of some liberal groups, increasingly supported by the federal courts, to deny tax support in any shape or form to education that takes place under religious auspices—an attitude of extraordinary sociological blindness, spurred by an unappetizing amalgam of old-time anti-Catholic sentiment and abstract liberal doctrine. There is the trend of state-run or state-controlled agencies to take over, or even to liquidate, welfare and health institutions operated by the churches. Before the courts of New York there is at this time the important case of *Wilder* v. *Sugarman,* in which an alliance of civil liberties groups is trying to coerce church-affiliated social agencies to give up their practice of giving preference of treatment to members of their own religious groups. As in many of these cases, there is a curious mixture of motives involved—the best of intentions to see that all who need care in the society get it in a nondiscriminatory manner, coupled with abstract doctrine, and the imperialistic urges of government bureaucracies and professional monopolies.

Education and welfare are two major areas in which the new secularism should be challenged—not in a reactive or unthinking way, but carefully, in full cognizance of all the legitimate interests involved. There are other areas as well. There have been ominous threats to the tax-exempt status of religious organizations taking moral stands on political issues. These threats can cut against the "left" as much as against the "right": threats were made against groups protesting against the war in Indochina on grounds of religious morality, as they are now being made against groups opposing abortion on similarly religio-ethical grounds. It is instructive to reflect upon the question of how many moral issues will be left to the churches once there is a principle of exclusion of any that bear on law, politics, or public policy. What is on the horizon here is an abuse of the taxation powers of the state to inhibit the free expression of religious conscience. Another area of concern should be the secularist drive to eliminate all religious symbols from the public sphere. The climax of this drive thus far was the Supreme Court decision against prayer in the public schools—another exercise in doctrinaire abstraction and sociological futility. But the drive has by no means exhausted itself. Recently the courts of California have decided that the closing of judicial agencies on Good Friday, even if only for a few hours, is a violation of the constitution. Again, what is required here is opposition that is both carefully thought through and politically responsible. Over and beyond these particular issues, it is very important that there be a wider understanding, especially among intellectuals, of the importance of religion in American society—and, consequently, of the social as well as political consequences of any further erosion of that religious presence.

What I have said so far I have said *qua* sociologist and *qua* concerned citizen of the United States. I must now also say something *qua* Christian—and it is something to which I attach very great importance indeed: none of the above-mentioned social and political considerations should be a motive for the churches in seeking a revitalization of their faith. It is not the mission of the Christian church to legitimate the American or any other political system. The only acceptable motive for the revitalization of the faith is the conviction of its truth. Those of us who came together in January 1975 in Hartford and issued "An Appeal for Theological Affirmation" (an event that, much to our satisfaction, has created a certain amount of controversy) were very clear about this: whatever else we disagreed about, we very much agreed about this. And, indeed, one of the notions we repudiated strongly was precisely the notion that "the world must set the agenda for the Church" (theme 10 of the Hartford statement)—no matter whether this agenda is politically "right" or "left"—in other words, no matter whether the legitimation refers to the *status quo* or to some utopian vision of the future. I believe that, *mutatis mutandis,* a similar position emerges from Judaism.

This has another important corollary: in the biblical perspective, faith always drives a hard bargain with the polity. It not only refuses to simply legitimate the polity; it also reserves the right to judge it. This was so from the earliest days of the strange covenant between God and Israel, and it has been a persistent affirmation (sometimes submerged or denied, then breaking through again) in the entire history of the Christian community. In our situation this means the following: if one wanted to speak of a "Christian America" at all (I, for one, don't, as I tried to make clear), this would mean above all that one understands America to be under the judgment of God. I doubt if this is what the Congress had in mind when, some years back, it introduced the phrase "under God" into the Oath of Allegiance. Jews as well as Christians, I think, will have to take these words in their full and awe-inspiring biblical significance. And it is precisely in this aspect of judgment, as Neuhaus has very nicely shown in the previously mentioned book, that the covenant theme in American history must inevitably collide again and again with a purely secular understanding of the social contract. Thus the last thing in the world I'm suggesting is that organized religion should be some sort of "blessing machine" for the American polity. Indeed, I would personally go one step further and say that the normal political mission of the churches is to say no, and that silence is the closest they should ordinarily come to saying yes.

This does not mean that the political world is a night in which all cats are gray, a *massa perditionis,* from which one can only withdraw. In my last book, *Pyramids of Sacrifice,* in discussing models of national development in the Third World, I have argued that what is needed is a new ethical procedure of "cost/gains analysis"—that is, a careful weighing of putative goals and of the human sacrifices deemed necessary to achieve these goals. I cannot elaborate this argument here. I would only add that such a procedure is very much in accordance with my own conception of biblical ethics, an ethics that knows all the projects in this world to be less than ultimate. Applied to the case of America, such a procedure will most certainly not be conducive to self-righteousness or self-congratulatory smugness. But neither will it support the masochistic self-denigration that has of late been common in many Christian quarters. America is neither "God's own country" nor the major source of evil in the world today. I believe that American Jews and Christians, with great assurance, can repudiate both these distortive visions—and, with equal assurance, condemn the moral atrocities legitimated by either.

One further comment is, I think, necessary. The necessity flows from the fact that the major non-Christian presence on the American religious scene is that of the Jewish community, with which the Christian churches are inexorably linked by ties not only of a common biblical heritage but of an anguished history of evils perpetrated in the name of Christianity. For thoroughly understandable reasons, talking along the lines suggested in this paper is particularly disturbing to American Jews. For it is obvious that a closer relation between religion and the polity will mean, in this country, a greater public prominence of the Christian churches. Even if it will not mean a Christian America, it will tend toward a more Christian America. Jews have good historical reasons to be apprehensive about such constellations. Accordingly, many American Jews, both as individuals and in organizations, have felt a strong affinity for the secularist interpretation of the First Amendment. Secularism, it was thought, would be "good for the Jews." It appears that there have been some changes in this conception recently, as it has become painfully clear that secularism is no reliable defense against anti-Semitism.

All the same, in speaking as a Christian about these things in the American situation it is necessary, I think, to make two affirmations over and beyond a general commitment to pluralism and religious liberty. First, it is necessary to affirm that anti-Semitism, always and in all places, is a sin against both God and man—not just because all hatred is sinful, but because the hatred of the Jews is a particular offence against the God whom Christians worship. Second, it is necessary to affirm that, in our time, the existence and safety of the state of Israel is a vital concern of Christian conscience—not because Christians must recognize some transcendent right of the Jews to this particular stretch of land, but because Christians cannot view the emergence of the state of Israel apart from the horrible reality of the holocaust with which it is historically linked. In my own mind, there is no contradiction between this affirmation and a recognition of the human and political rights of the Palestinian people, nor does it imply an endorsement of any and all policies of the Israeli government or of a particular set of international boundaries in that part of the world. I believe that American Christians of very different persuasions can and should agree on these two affirmations. I, for one, would add the further statement that the conversion of the Jews is not an item on the agenda of the Christian churches, and for theological rather than sociopolitical reasons (a statement, needless to say, that does not infringe on the liberty of individuals to choose a change in their religious affiliation).

I must come to an end. This is not an inspirational discussion, and I am not under the obligation to end on an upbeat note. I'm far from sanguine about the future, and I cannot supply recipes for success in either the political or the religious arenas. But, in the perspective of religious faith, the hope of success (humanly inevitable though it is) is not the final motive for our efforts on the stage of history. Rather, it is obedience to the moral imperatives of our situation. I believe that the revitalization of the American political community is such an imperative, and an urgent one. An awesome number of human values ride today on the survival of the American experiment. The revitalization of the religious community is an even deeper imperative, for it points beyond America and indeed beyond history.

Constitutionalism, Federalism, and the Post-Industrial American Polity

Daniel J. Elazar

MGUINNESS

4 Federalism is the form of government of the United States. The now somewhat antique term *form,* used here in its eighteenth-century meaning, signifies principles, relationships, structure, institutions, processes, and techniques all wrapped into one. In order to properly understand federalism as form, we must first understand federalism as the political relationship that animates American civil society. Too often today federalism is treated as simply an administrative principle or, less frequently, as a legal one. However, a closer look at American politics leads to the recognition that federalism is a political principle that defines a particular set of relationships—something more than simply an administrative device or even a legal-constitutional one, although both are vital facets of federalism.

In its most immediate sense, federalism in the United States has to do with the constitutional diffusion of power so that the general and the various constituent governments share in the processes of policy-making and administration by right, while the activities of government are conducted in such a way as to respect their respective integrities. Implicit in the idea of federalism as it is understood in a democratic regime is that governments will be organized so as to reflect the popular will and will be directed toward serving public purposes or ends. They will be republican in the sense that each government will be a *res publica*— a public thing rather than the private preserve of a ruler or small group of powerholders.

In the last analysis, however, federalism is more than simply an arrangement for power-sharing among territorial units of government. Especially in America, it is also a fundamental principle of social organization that has to do with the relationships among people and their associations, as well as governments and polities. European theorists have recognized this explicitly in their writings because they have sought to foster federalism in societies where federal principles were not indigenous.[1] Americans have generally ignored federalism as a comprehensive set of relationships precisely because those relationships are so deeply imbedded in American culture and in the psyches of the American people. A secularized version of what the Puritan founders of so much of the United States termed "federal liberty," with its linked political and social facets, has long been part of the American experience as a subconscious set of behavior patterns, the matrix within which American political behavior is rooted.[2]

The essence of the federal relationship is partnership based upon a convenant binding the partners in free association. The term *federal* is derived from the Latin *foedus,* which means covenant. The idea of cooperation to link free people and institutions in common tasks without violating their respective integrities as partners, with all that it implies regarding the building of unity amidst diversity (note the thrust of the American motto, *E Pluribus Unum*) is endemic to the American scene. American institutions—the pioneer congregations, the early business partnerships and corporations, and the first governments in so many of the colonies—were organized as associations by covenant or compact on federal principles that linked the political and social aspects of the federal idea to build a new society. In fact, the more ideologically committed to building a new and better society a particular group of colonists were (viz: the Puritans), the more they relied upon federal principles in organizing their institutions. Alexis de Tocqueville understood this well, which is why he chose to concentrate on studying state and local institutions in New England in his effort to get to the heart of American democracy.[3]

This federal relationship is what has governed the progress of America, what made the American revolution unique in the modern era and kept it from the pitfalls of totalitarianism. The question before us is whether it will survive with sufficient force in the post-modern era.

THE FRUITS OF THE 1960s

The American people have recently emerged from one of the most trying decades in American history, marked by a near-deadly combination of foreign war, domestic upheaval, unsettling reforms, and disruptions in the cultural continuity of society. In one sense at least, the history of that decade paralleled that of similar periods in the American past. The middle of the 1960s saw a great acceleration of federal activity and expansion of federal programs of the kind that comes regularly once in each generation.[4] It was then followed (in some respects, almost immediately) by a thrust toward reemphasizing the role of state and local governments in the American partnership, again, a common response to the generational burst of federal activity. Superficial parallels can be misleading, however, and in this case they appear to be, for in the last half of the 1970s the United States is faced with a major paradox and some corollary ones.

The movement of the past decade or so ostensibly (and sincerely) designed to revitalize the federal system of government actually turned out to be, in certain respects, a movement away from federalism and toward something else entirely. Elsewhere I have written about the true character of federalism as one of the rightful diffusions of power among many centers by constitutional arrangement so that no single center of power can be said to exist.[5] The United States as a compound republic is the model of this kind of noncentralized government with power dispersed across a matrix of power centers, each of which is an arena for political action in and of itself as well as part of the overall arena, with the smaller arenas linked to and parts of larger ones.[6] The national government seen in this way is the government serving the largest arena, not the center of political action but rather the most broad-based of the complex of institutions linked to the overall framework of popular sovereignty and constitutional government within which political action takes place. The matrix itself necessarily must function in what Morton Grodzins described as "mildly chaotic" ways.[7] I have termed the foregoing arrangements "noncentralization."

In recent years, noncentralization—the true principle of federalism—has been confused with decentralization. Decentralization is another phenomenon altogether, indicating as it does the devolution of power from a single center by decision of those who control that center. Decentralization is essentially an administrative device, and he who can decentralize can recentralize as well. A look at the history of the United Kingdom shows how this is so.[8]

Prior to the rise of the Tudors (1485), England itself was probably an example of a noncentralized polity with power diffused by right among a number of centers, which saw territorially based aristocrats sharing decision-making powers under the loose overall rule of the monarch. The Tudor rulers were able to replace this noncentralization with a more unitary system, not by overtly centralizing power but by subtly shifting the distribution of powers from a noncentralized to a decentralized basis. As the kings acquired authority to exercise new powers, they delegated the actual exercise of those powers to local officials who were formally linked to them, usually by royal appointment, but who actually preserved a great deal of discretion within the overall framework of "the king's peace." Thus, the practical changes in the distribution of power were at first less apparent than the constitutional changes. Over time, the royal government in London became the single center of governmental power, which, by its own will, allowed a practical diffusion of responsibility among the local governments.

Then, with the constitutional barriers removed, there began a natural trend toward reconcentration of power, this time in the hands of Parliament, which has superseded the monarchy as the locus of power in the now United Kingdom. Beginning in the mid-nineteenth century, the central government began to assert the authority that it had acquired, first to reorganize local government and then to shift powers from it to the center. In the past century we have witnessed a very substantial centralization of power in England, even where the forms of decentralization have at times been preserved, diminishing the scope, powers, and respect of local government.

In the United Kingdom as a whole, Wales also lost its constitutional right to local self-government and came to be ruled from London like the English "provinces." By contrast, when Scotland united with England in 1707, the bargain linking the two countries provided for the constitutional preservation of Scottish autonomy in the areas of religion and law and at least partially in education and administrative matters. The bargain was not a federal one, since Scotland was included in the unitary structure of the United Kingdom for matters of legislation and many aspects of administration, but it embodied federal principles by constitutionally guaranteeing the Scots a measure of noncentralization. Since the consummation of that union, the Scots have been very much at the mercy of Parliament in the last area, while in the first three, where constitutionally they are guaranteed a measure of autonomy, they have managed to preserve Scotland as a power center in its own right. More recently, they have even been able to build upon them to win back more administrative autonomy as well.

The recent suspension of the Parliament of Northern Ireland by Parliament in London is another case in point. Self-government in

Ulster (introduced by Act of Parliament in 1921) was a matter of decentralization, a privilege granted by Parliament, but not a (noncentralized) constitutional right. Hence it could be suspended unilaterally, over the objections of the majority in Northern Ireland. It is little wonder, then, that in an era of decolonization, Great Britain itself is now faced with a secessionist movement of real proportions in Scotland, a growing nationalist movement in Wales, and continued troubles in Ulster, while "devolution," the proposed solution of the ruling Labour Party that promises something of a return to Tudor patterns on a modern scale, has satisfied few.[9]

In the United States, the theoretical confusion of decentralization and noncentralization is now leading to some practical consequences that may well mark a radical shift in the federal distribution of power that characterizes the American compound republic and, carried to the extreme, the end of federalism as Americans know it. Much of the thrust in the last decade has been to replace noncentralization with decentralization, often in the name of federalism.

Nearly two decades ago, Morton Grodzins, in discussing President Eisenhower's efforts to turn functions back to the states—the last attempt to put into practice the old theories of dual federalism—pointed out that the president was doomed to fail because in order to achieve this reversal it would first be necessary for the national government to acquire sufficient control over the determination of how functions were to be shared by the several governmental arenas. Despite casual appearances that would suggest that national government activity necessarily meant control, the functions in question were being provided on a truly "federal" (meaning shared by the federal government, the states, and the localities) basis rather than on a "Federal" (meaning controlled by Washington) one. Neither the presidency nor Congress had such powers. In other words, what Grodzins was suggesting was that in order to decentralize it was first necessary to centralize power, but that, in a noncentralized political system, it is impossible to centralize power in the sense referred to here without changing the essential constitution of the system. The programs that President Eisenhower wished to devolve were themselves products of federal-state-local bargains in which all parties to the bargain retained a say over the fate of each program. Thus, the federal government could not unilaterally transfer those programs to any of the other partners, even under what it considered favorable terms. It was not a central government, and it could not make a central governmentlike decision on the matter. Grodzins continued, "a majority party powerful enough to bring about ordered decentralization is far more likely to choose in favor of ordered central-ization."[10] Today, we can see how correct Grodzins was. Powers transferred in one way or another to Washington have not brought more than token decentralization; rather there is a greater exercise of those powers by a newly enhanced national government.

When Grodzins wrote, there were still substantial constitutional and other barriers (including party, which he emphasized) to centralization of power in Washington, which were recognized by the public. Under the impact of the U.S. Supreme Court decisions and intellectual covenants of the 1960s, those barriers had by and large disappeared by the time that Richard Nixon became president. The result was that the Nixon administration, headed by President Eisenhower's former vice-president, was able to do just what Eisenhower could not, with consequences much like those Grodzins predicted. Although sincerely presented as an effort to reverse the tide of centralization, which he claimed had been running for the previous 190 years, Nixon's "New Federalism" actually became a loosely connected series of efforts to concentrate control over programs old and new in Washington so that they could be reformed to meet federal standards or goals and then be decentralized in their administration along lines more acceptable to the federal government. To the extent that the effort was systematic, the federal government seemed to be seeking to become the primary repository of policy-making and standard-setting powers across the gamut of American governmental concerns, ostensibly with the promise that once Washington had full power to make policy in any program area, the responsibility for executing the policies and managing the programs that resulted from them would be transferred to the states and localities. Thus, the Nixon years saw an increase in legislation—in the fields of education, health, welfare, environmental protection, industrial safety—which transferred policy-making authority to Washington from the states, sometimes accompanied by provisions for the devolution of responsibility for implementing the new policies and sometimes not.

No doubt President Nixon sincerely desired to strengthen the federal system. Nevertheless, if the concrete steps initiated in his administration are carried through to a successful conclusion, they will indeed change the thrust of the last 190 years—not toward greater power for states and localities as he advertised, but toward replacing a noncentralized governmental system with a centralized one, whether the centralized government chooses to act through its local instrumentalities or not.[11]

To a very real extent, Gerald Ford reversed that trend, in part by relaxing federal domestic efforts generally and in part by specifically directing his administration toward a reduction of the emphasis on federal standards. Moreover, there were few new federal initiatives during his years in office. At the same time, the U.S. Supreme Court, which bore much of the responsibility for initiating the trend toward centralization beginning in the Eisenhower years, also began to reverse itself to the extent of reemphasizing the residual powers of the states under the federal constitution. Here the influence of Nixon's appointments was discernible, as if he had somehow provided the remedy for his own disease.

President Nixon was successful in achieving a greater measure of centralization than his Republican predecessor because of changes in constitutional understanding on the part of the public and its political leaders that took place in the intervening years. What happened is that the courts, the Congress, the president and, apparently, the articulate public as well simply dropped the idea that there are any real constitutional barriers limiting the scope of federal action vis-à-vis the other partners in the federal system. This new freedom from erstwhile constitutional restraints was reflected in court decisions, legislation, administrative actions, and the general support given all of the former by those of the public who may be deemed the opinion-makers in American society. It soon built up a momentum of its own, one that may or may not be in the process of being arrested and redirected. It is the future of that momentum that will determine the role of constitutionalism and federalism in the third century of American independence.

INTELLECTUAL FORCES
UNDERMINING FEDERALISM

It is possible to trace the convergence of intellectual forces that have led to the situation described in the foregoing section. On one hand, there is the theoretical confusion of decentralization and noncentralization, discussed above, on the part of people who should know better.

This leads, at the very least, to the kind of confused action that we saw in the Nixon administration, whose leaders honestly wanted to strengthen the states and localities but often ended up doing the opposite.

The Impact of the "New View" of Federalism

On the other hand, the very promulgation of the theory of cooperative federalism has apparently had unanticipated consequences. The theory itself was developed between 1932 and 1962 as a new view of the federal system.[12] Its functional value as a framework that could accommodate the specific changes in intergovernmental relations that grew out of the New Deal led to its widespread adoption as the conventional wisdom in the 1960s.

Those who argued two decades ago (and this author was among them) that the federal system has always been basically cooperative rather than dualistic were attempting to describe historical fact and empirical reality; though their efforts were triggered by the development of the 1930s, their work was not necessarily designed to justify those developments *per se*. What happened, of course, was that once the theory entered the public domain it was possible to confuse all kinds of federal-state-local interaction with "cooperation" whether the interaction involved federal coercion or not.

Moreover, intergovernmental cooperation had existed prior to the 1960s in an atmosphere in which dual federalism was the expected norm, so that new federal government initiatives always had to be justified somewhat apologetically as not in violation of constitutional principles. They always were justified if there was a demand for them, but, in the process, the initiatives themselves were so designed as to utilize federal involvement to reinforce the position of the states and localities more than to undercut it.[13] However, once the idea that the federal government could act in any area as it willed became accepted as the norm under the theory of cooperative federalism, no further justification was needed, and the programs could be designed to place the thrust of the action on federal shoulders, thereby reducing the state and local roles in the programs that emerged.[14]

Apparently, the old theory of dual federalism was functional in its own way, not as a description of empirical reality, but as a constitutional restraint of a kind. With its abandonment came an abandonment of all restraint. While it is patently impossible to return to a disproved theory, a more sophisticated understanding of the way in which dual structures cooperate to advance common goals is needed to foster a less simplistic understanding of the differences between cooperation and coercion.

Federal versus Jacobin Democracy

Finally, it seems that the very idea of federal democracy, the theory upon which the United States was founded, has been lost by the American people in the twentieth century. Contemporary American discussions of what is democratic or not are derived from the far inferior Jacobin theory of democracy. Both theories are products of the eighteenth-century democratic revolutions—Jacobin democracy emerging from the French Revolution just as federal democracy emerged from the American.[15]

Jacobin democracy stands in direct opposition to federal democracy. According to the Jacobin theory, democratic government must be an expression of the "general will" of the citizenry. The general will, in the Jacobin sense, is not simply a synthesis of separate wills or even a simple matter of consensus. Rather, as a "whole" it must be greater than the sum of its parts. Consequently, it must, in any specific case, be expressed in a uniform manner through a strong central government. Only in this way can government give expression to it; otherwise government becomes a umpire choosing from among competing views. Both in theory and practice, this search for the general will is the enemy of pluralism, diversity, minority expression, and the diffusion of power. In the real world, it tends either to unrestrained majoritarianism (50 percent plus one on any issue is sufficient to determine the results) or to rule by an elite that claims special capability to ascertain the general will.

The Jacobins were (or tried to be) the first such elite. While they failed to retain power, their theory of democracy prevailed in France and many other parts of the world. In our times, the Communists make similar claims. Indeed, the very serious claim made by the Communist movement that the countries it dominates are democratic is based precisely on the theory that polities organized on Marxist-Leninist (or Maoist) principles properly embody the general will and, even more properly, entrust the practical interpretation of the general will on a daily basis to a Communist party elite.

This, in turn, leads to the use of the plebiscite as a means of seeming to give the public a voice in decisions, whereby a one-time vote on one of two policy options becomes a surrogate for continuing public deliberation and the right to exercise continuing public oversight in governmental matters. Whatever its precise form, Jacobinism requires the concentration of power in a unitary pyramidal way, ostensibly as the basis for democratic political organization, but actually to safeguard the interests of the state.

Federal democracy is the creation of the American founders. It emphasizes recognition of human and social diversity as the underlying basis of popular government, with its corollary of respect for minorities and rule through changing coalitions of interests. It fosters constitutional respresentative institutions as the means for popular decision-making, reflecting the view that the polity is called into existence by a compact which both empowers its institutions to act and limits their scope in order to maintain the freedom of the parties to the compact. And it is built upon the constitutional diffusion of power as the basis for democratic political organization to safeguard the rights of individuals and groups.[16]

In their impatience with the misuse of the principles of federal democracy as they were distorted by a big business-oriented "establishment" at the turn of the century and in their fascination with what seemed to be the utopian possibilities of the administrative state, many American opinion-molders effectively abandoned these federal principles for what seemed to be a more attractive set.[17] Two generations later, the views of those people and their allies have become dominant in the press, the schools, the academies, and increasingly in the halls of government. The change, when it came, was sudden, as a new generation educated in the principles of Jacobin democracy, often without even being aware of it, came to occupy center stage in American politics. Such people now fill the courts and legislatures, not to speak of the bureaucracies. Moreover, in many respects, there was no systematic effort to propagate a new doctrine as such. Consequently, even now the change has not been recognized for what it is.

Thus, over the course of a relatively brief period of time, federal court decisions, congressional legislation, and executive action removed what used to be seen as rather clearly definable limitations on federal (and, in some cases, state) action in order to accommodate demands for activist government. In doing so, they changed the ground rules by which the various planes or arenas of government—federal, state, and local—must play. Where they have been changed, the new ground rules are more akin to those of a unitary system in which Washington has the last word than to those traditionally and properly associated with federalism.

Extreme Activism in Government

Aside from the theoretical and doctrinal factors encouraging the breaching of constitutional barriers, it would be remiss to ignore the importance of the new thrust toward activist government. The demands for ever higher levels of governmental activity and ever-increasing government responsibility for the welfare and happiness of the citizenry are necessarily tied very closely with the character and locus of governmental action. Under the original theory of the American republic, however, interpreted in practice, it was generally accepted that, while government could be and even should be energetic in the pursuit of those tasks allocated to it, the tasks of government were not coterminous with the tasks of society as a whole. Rather, government was to be limited to the assistance of the citizenry in their private definition and pursuit of happiness, primarily by protecting life and liberty.

Over the years this position was interpreted in various ways. There were those who held that simple exercise of the police powers of government was sufficient as a governmental role, since the exercise of those police powers would serve to guarantee life and liberty, thereby enabling individuals to pursue happiness as they saw fit. Others recognized that the very preservation of life and liberty required more active governmental intervention into the affairs of society in order to ensure such things as equality before the law and more or less equal opportunity to engage in the pursuit of happiness.

Whatever the position adopted by the opinion leaders and policy-makers of a given time, they all generally agreed that government was to be more a facilitator than an initiator on the domestic scene. Government was to respond to public initiatives in some appropriate way rather than generate its own initiatives. This approach held through the New Deal and into the 1960s. Even the massive expansion of governmental activity in the 1930s was a reflection of the idea that government had to respond to enable the American people to achieve what still remained essentially private goals.

More recently, there has been a subtle (and sometimes not so subtle) change. More and more American opinion-leaders have been suggesting that government establish the goals that people should pursue and then develop policies and programs that will effectively force people to pursue them. Here we must be quite frank. While changes in the thinking of Americans as a whole were clearly necessary for this process to begin, the proximate cause of the change was and is the racial issue. The fact that white Americans pursued private goals that at best neglected the interests of black Americans and at worst prevented blacks from pursuing the same goals provided an opening for government intervention in the name of the Constitution to limit the rights of the former to pursue goals of their own choosing. It can be properly argued that the limitations on personal freedom that have resulted from this intervention, while painful and perhaps even unconstitutional in the abstract, were necessary as the price that white America had to pay for its treatment of its colored minorities since the very founding of European settlements on this continent. Nevertheless, the principle was then extended into unrelated areas in an expansion of the welfare state idea encouraged by partisans of extreme governmental activism on behalf of a planned economic and social order.

THE ENVIRONMENTAL BASIS OF THE NEW CENTRALIZATION

The problem of maintaining a political system that encourages private responsibility and the diffusion of political power among many centers is rendered additionally complex by the increasing centralization or standardization of other major pillars of civil society, particularly the economic and communications systems and recent efforts to that end in the religious and educational systems.

The Economic System— The Consequences of a Common Market

American federalism has always had to confront an integrated economic system; indeed, the federal constitution was written to promote that integration as a means of achieving peace and prosperity.[18] It is a mistake to think of the American economic system of 200 years ago as local and fragmented compared to the contemporary economic system that is clearly nationwide and integrated. The economic interdependence of the various parts of the Union goes back to its origins.[19]

What has changed is the way in which the economic system is organized and the manner in which it is integrated. These changes have been of two kinds. One involves the interstate unification of economic enterprises, and the other, the development of complex organizations to undertake economic as well as other tasks in society. To some extent, the second flows from the first and to no little extent the first was and is encouraged by the Constitution as interpreted and generally understood.

Five principal consequences have flowed from the changes in the economic system. In the first place, the sheer size of economic organizations and their nationwide, if not transnational, character brings them to focus on the national political arena and requires national action to deal with them and the problems they engender. This point need not be made other than in passing at this stage in our history, nor does such action represent a departure from fundamental constitutional principles. John C. Calhoun stated the principle in its simplest form in 1819 when he suggested that no government can allow a private source of economic power to become more powerful than it or out of its potential reach.[20]

The second impact also has to do with the size of economic organizations. In part, this is simply the bureaucracy problem in one of its many guises. The sheer size of many corporate organizations today changes their internal character and the character of their impact on the environment. The problems of alienation and inadequate lines of communication, which are endemic to large organizations of all kinds, have become increasingly endemic in the great corporations that employ such a high proportion of the American labor force in one capacity or another. These problems, coupled with the increasing detachment of large economic enterprises from the local community, transform what begins as a social problem into a political one.

Third, the overriding American commitment to the free flow of commerce and all that derives from it in the way of limiting state and local efforts to shape their own economies through governmental intervention has eased the rise of these corporate giants that shape the market. The small businesses that survive are dependent upon the giants, which support them through subcontracts, set the prices they pay for goods and materials, and often even call them into existence through franchise arrangements. By preventing the imposition of state and local barriers to this kind of economic consolidation, the American people have succeeded in creating the most successful common market yet seen on the face of the earth but, as in every human endeavor, a price has been paid for it. This common market could only exist because of decisions made in the political arena, decisions taken consonant with a reasonable and even proper understanding of the intentions of the constitutional framers. In the process, however, Americans have created a situation that now virtually foredooms the development of serious local responsibility, because the kinds of ties to local community that promote responsibility and concern have been consistently diminishing since at least the late nineteenth century.[21] It is this nationalization of interest rather than the simple nationalization of economic organization that is of such great consequence to the American federal system, as it is designed to encourage and foster local resourcefulness and commitment.

Fourth, the reduction in the proportion of locally owned firms of economic significance, particularly since the end of World War II, has had a major impact on the relationship between the economic leadership and the local community.[22] Many communities that were once minor centers of commerce and industry in their own right, are now no more than branch office or plant sites staffed by managers who look forward to moving up the corporate ladder and out of the community to do so. Today, even people who plan to live their whole lives in a particular community no longer expect their children to remain in the same community. Hence, any interest on their part in planning for the future is far more likely to be focused on the larger national arena.

This in turn cannot help but lead to a certain general alienation from government. I think that it is not unfair to say that most people develop national loyalties by projecting the satisfactions gained from their personal connections to the most immediate surroundings onto the larger whole. To Americans of generations past, "America" was family, church, and local community writ large. When they were called upon to make sacrifices for the country, they did so because of their ties on this immediate personal level. They simply projected their particular local version of the American way of life onto the national scene. This meant, among other things, that a broad range of variations in that way of life, each rooted in a particular locality, could exist without damaging (and even enhancing) the overall American consensus.[23] When the nature of those local and personal attachments is changed, corresponding changes occur, as has been seen in recent years.

There may well be a connection between the elimination of constitutional barriers and the changes brought by recent trends in economic organization. For nearly twenty years, beginning in the mid-1950s, the Supreme Court of the United States intervened to limit the autonomy of local communities to determine social and moral policies that shape the local social climate, particularly in the areas of censorship, social behavior, and the relationship between government and religion. The Court did so on the premise that the nation as a whole must be the basis for determining "contemporary community standards," i.e., must be considered the primary community of the citizenry.[24]

In many cases, the Court's decisions were consonant with the constitutional standards imposed on the federal government but involved the breaking of accepted (and correctly accepted, in the opinion of many constitutional interpreters) constitutional barriers, which had enabled state constitutional standards to vary and had thereby allowed local communities to assert their individual policies without imposing them on the country as a whole. Since the range of impact of each of these local decisions was confined locally, the country could tolerate a great deal of diversity based on the principles of territorial democracy without necessarily committing American society and government as a whole to one particular course of action or policy over or against another. Nationalization of standards in these areas drastically changed the possibilities of maintaining diversity of this kind, not by imposing a real national standard in place of local ones but by forcing the standards of a few large local centers, where the taste-makers gather, upon the rest of the country. The ultimate unworkability of this approach even came to be recognized by the Court itself, which began to withdraw from the extreme formulation of its new doctrine by the early 1970s.[25]

Finally, the impact of the economic system has had a major effect on shaping Americans' conceptions of what government should be doing in the United States, how it should be doing it, and how governments should be organized to do it. In a certain sense, Calvin Coolidge was perhaps more right than we would credit him when he said that "the business of America is business." He was simply providing us with an overly simplistic paraphrase of the idea of the union as a great commercial republic. As we have already stated, commerce, understood in its broadest sense as the production and exchange of goods, services, and ideas (the sense in which it was understood in the eighteenth century), is a matter of fundamental concern to the Constitution.

More than that, American conceptions of efficiency are based on the extent to which commerce thus understood can be freely promoted. In fact, the way in which commerce is promoted in any period becomes the touchstone for determining proper organizational methods in spheres other than the economic. Americans seem to have developed a belief that whatever is good for business in the way of organization should also be good for government.

In the eighteenth century, commerce was organized in a non-centralized fashion similar to the kind of political organization implicit in the federal and state constitutions of the period. Many small competing units functioned within a marketplace that was rather sharply defined and delimited by governmental action. Even within these small units, relations between employer and employee were more those of partners-in-work than anything else.

After the industrial revolution, this form of organization of commerce was replaced with a highly centralized and hierarchical one in which great corporate entities were built, pyramidlike, by great entrepreneurs who concentrated policy-making in their own hands, delegating it sparingly within the hierarchy as they saw fit. This new corporate model became the pervasive one in the economic realm and was then transformed into the model proposed by reformers for the political realm as well. Edward Bellamy worked it out in great and seemingly perfect detail in his Utopian tract, *Looking Backward,* and many of the best-known Progressives and liberals of the early twentieth century espoused it as part of their programs as well. Only the existence of constitutional barriers plus the entrenched patterns of politics that have made the American federal system so durable prevented the hierarchical model from being transferred lock, stock, and barrel from the economic to the political realm. As it was, serious steps were taken in that direction in the largest states and cities where reforms in general and in school government invariably meant the concentration of power in new bureaucratic hierarchies; and, with the coming of the New Deal, similar centralization was introduced in the federal arena as well.

While that was happening, however, the model of efficiency was changing in the economic realm. The great entrepreneurs passed on and were replaced by management teams that, in effect, became oligarchies sitting on top of each corporate pyramid. This in itself brought a certain diffusion of power at the top. It led, in turn, to new theories of corporate decentralization embodied in such great corporations as General Motors and AT&T whereby centralized decision-making authority was partially devolved to units lower down in the hierarchy so long as they conformed to the overall policies set unilaterally at the top.

This new kind of decentralization was reflected in President Nixon's "New Federalism." Because it is the dominant economic model today, Americans, whether radicals or conservatives, socialists or oriented toward free enterprise in the Goldwater tradition, all seem to share a common desire to transfer that model to the contemporary political realm, without even realizing it. In the end, this penchant for adopting notions of efficiency more suitable for the economic realm as the norm for the political realm as well, may be the most lasting and least beneficial political impacts of the American economic system.

The Communications System— Nationalization Run Wild

The impact of the mass media cannot be minimized, nor is it in general discussion these days. Here we need only focus on certain immediate political impacts. Nationalization and standardization have been most extensive and pervasive in the communications system, in part because the indigenous thrust of the system itself is toward both but mostly because the currently dominant means and modes of communication are all products of the twentieth century when the process of national integration in the economic realm has already reached its zenith. At no time in the history of mankind has the technology of communications functioned to ease communication as it does today.[26] Yet, it is still true that more than halting use of the new technology is available to only a select few. Only recently has the number of Americans who have flown at least once reached 50 percent, a figure that drops precipitously for those having flown twice or more. Use of television and radio to broadcast communications is in the hands of even a more select few. Only the telephone and the automobile among the new communications devices offer something like equal access. Certainly, political communication is not rendered more equal for all by the new technology, simply more convenient for some.

The fact is that it is easier for the mass media to report news from the national government and as a result give national officials a platform from which to make their names better known than it is for them to ferret out equally important stories and equally able people in 50 different states or tens of thousands of different local governments. The president of the United States has a decided advantage over all others in this respect, a factor that contributed in no small measure to the growth of the "imperial presidency." Even Jimmy Carter, seeking to reverse that trend, takes to the air waves and offers the public a taste of direct communication with him (it cannot be more than that), thereby upstaging congressmen, not to mention governors and mayors, who may make themselves more available over the long run but in far less visible and dramatic ways.

Even when the mass media seek to report on local events, their newsmen usually take the easy way out of reporting on New York and Washington where they are based, even though New York and Washington are perhaps the least typical cities or metropolitan regions in the United States. Not only is it easier to do that but it is also because the decision-makers in the mass media are conditioned by living in New York and Washington to identify the problems and conditions of those two areas with the problems and conditions of the United States as a whole. What all this adds up to is a kind of communications-based imperialism of ideas and culture whereby the entire United States is treated as part of a New York-Washington-Los Angeles metropolitan area.

Education and Religion—Contradictory Trends

The pervasiveness of commercial principles has been the major contributory factor encouraging centralization or standardization in other spheres as well, including education and religion, but in both, other factors have been at work to blunt the impact of commerce. Unlike the economic system, both the educational and religious institutions of Americans were built on the principles of localism and noncentralization and maintained in a noncentralized manner. Recent changes, again based on principles of economic efficiency, have introduced a measure of centralization in both areas. Nevertheless, radical change has been avoided because the counterpressures are great, whether with regard to state and local powers in the educational sphere or voluntarism in the religious ones.

The educational system was based on the local school and the local college, with the former tenuously linked into statewide systems and the latter given state support and serving statewide or regional constituencies. Religious organization was based upon the local congregation, so much so that even the hierarchically organized Roman Catholic Church had to transfer more and more power to the parishes in the process of adapting to American life. Larger church *bodies* remain, for the most part, federations or even confederations of congregations whose actual power diminishes the further removed they are from the congregations themselves.

In the nineteenth century, education and religion remained organized in this fashion while the economy moved in an opposite direction because both were considered functions that had to be kept as close as possible to those benefiting from or engaged in them. Only in the twentieth century has there been any serious movement toward change, in education because of economically based arguments reenforced by the new conventional wisdom of the educational professionals, and in religion in part because of the subtle influence of arguments that associate efficiency with bigness and central control. In education, the movement toward centralization took the form of school district consolidation and greater state control and was coupled with an equally strong movement toward standardization through the professionalization of school personnel and the development of common standards nationwide. In religion, the movement was manifested in a strengthening of the role and powers of national denominational headquarters.

Since the organization of education remains intimately tied to the political system (despite its ostensibly apolitical management), the degree of centralization or standardization achieved has depended upon political decisions first and foremost. The thrust of political decision-making in the educational realm today seems to be toward setting informal national standards in some areas, primarily through the professional associations and court decisions coupled with greater state oversight and fiscal involvement in local school affairs. Even more important is the trend of generally removing responsibility for the character and content of their children's schooling from parents.

Americans are only beginning to recognize that the latter represents a revolutionary trend in American society, part of the transfer of the right of Americans to define the pursuit of happiness for themselves and their families from the private to the public domain. One apparent practical consequence of this trend is the proliferation of private schools—religiously oriented or otherwise—as the public schools become less and less open to parental influence.[27]

Although the process of standardization and nationalization in the organization of religion also took a leap forward in the twentieth century, it seems to have now come to a halt, primarily because of the voluntary character of religious affiliation in American society. People may be limited in their ability to rebel against dictation from central offices in realms under governmental or business control but they are not so limited in the religious realm. To the extent that they are dissatisfied with centralized direction, be it within the local congregation or from the national office, they can either leave the church or leave their particular congregation. The growing threat of many members to do just that, which has surfaced in the last several years, has apparently arrested the trend towards nationalization and standardization in the churches, if only in self-defense. The liberal Protestant bodies, the champions of centralization, have been losing members consistently and have had to cut back on the staffs in the national offices. On the other hand, the growth of evangelical Protestantism, characterized as it is by strong organizational localism, is testimony to the desires of so many Americans in that direction.[28]

Thus in both these spheres, Americans are voting with their feet against further centralization. Insofar as the public schools are ceasing to reflect local values, they are ceasing to be the dominant factor in American elementary and secondary education. Insofar as certain churches allow national spokesmen to set their tone and national bureaucracies to develop, they are giving way to a more militant localistic brand of religion. Both cases have real implications for the third century of American independence.

A NATION OF COMPLEXES

The Public-Private Mix

Another bulwark of the American federal system has been the mixture of public and private activities. The mixture in itself has been federal in character. That is to say, inherent in the federal idea is the recognition that separate public and private spheres can coexist and even interact without overwhelming one another. Indeed, each is dependent upon the other for its very health. In the American experience, the interaction of public and private parties for communal or social purposes is central to the preservation of individual liberty precisely because it encourages the wide diffusion of power within civil society and obviates the necessity for reliance upon government for all social benefits. This principle is so fundamental to democracy as we know it that it must be embodied in the constitutional arrangements of the regime. It is radically different from the often totalitarian thrust of Jacobin democracy, which recognizes no inherent right of a private sphere to exist and function independently of the public sphere.

What has emerged over time from this mixture of activities has recently been labeled—correctly if pejoratively—the "complex." Abstracted from its use in connection with the "military-industrial complex," we can identify a complex as the bundle of public and private entities that interact in pursuit of common interests linked to a particular public activity. From the perspective of those in the complex, the activity can be seen as a "game." Mixing metaphors, what we have is something like an atomic model with the game serving as a nucleus that attracts various interests that fall within that field, causing them to revolve around it.[29]

While the term has been used most frequently in connection with the military-industrial complex, in fact complexes are all pervasive in the United States. Most public business is accomplished through such complexes, whether in the federal, state, or local arenas or, as is usually the case, across them. The United States can be seen as an "ecology" of games and complexes overlaying the basic matrix of territorial political units.

The virtue of this ecology has been to allow for a public-private mixture of activities without having the public overwhelm the private sphere as is the case in totalitarian democracies, or the private overwhelm the public sphere as is the case in civil societies lacking republican government at all. Moreover, the mix enables the government of the United States to overcome the limitations that structural separation imposes upon them. As a consequence of their common interests, the participants in each game relate to each other in ways that transcend the formal political jurisdictions and thereby serve as bridges to link the jurisdictions through an alternative communications network.

Today the system of games and complexes is under heavy assault, in part because certain of the complexes got out of control in the 1950s and

1960s. The problem is really how to control the complexes and keep them within the bounds of public morality rather than follow what seems to be the thrust of some recent reformer-inspired efforts to eliminate them. Here several problems present themselves. In the first place, complexes do have certain inherent problems. While they provide for an effective mobilization of energy that has encouraged beneficial public activity without relying entirely upon government as the source of that energy, if unrestricted, complexes can lead to favoritism for those private players in the game who are from the private sector. In fact, it is testimony to the universality and durability of complexes that the framers of the constitution essentially anticipated this problem and suggested that the constitutional system that they were erecting would provide the kind of structural checks on their activity that could lead to procedural checks as well.[30]

In part this was a correct argument, but in part it was not. There may be a point in its expansion where big government, like any other big organization, becomes more of a liability than an asset simply because it is big and doubly so because it is big and possesses coercive powers.

When a big governmental department such as the Department of Defense can be linked with private interests in a military-industrial complex the way it is, it may well be that government has become a problem in and of itself. Nor is DOD the only problematic agency of big government. When the various components of the Department of Health, Education, and Welfare are so far removed from the main body of the citizenry that they can truly pursue organizational policies and goals encouraged and supported only by their immediate clients (or worse, by their internal staffs alone), then we must reluctantly conclude that there is a deficiency in the structure in and of itself; that the complex is too detached from the totality of the body politic to do other than create an imbalance within the civil society.

It is this ability of complexes to grow so large as to be removed from the larger societal whole that makes it necessary to control even those whose purposes are humanitarian. Otherwise the complexes unite the various pillars of society with their governmental counterparts in what become tightly knit oligarchies, subordinating pluralism to a new kind of structured control over policies and programs.

One thing that can be done to bring these complexes under control is to sharpen the structural barriers that cut into them as they seek their own internal coherence. A federal structure is ideally suited for that task, as long as the constitutional barriers that keep it vital are maintained. By constitutionally and actually requiring the subordination at some point of every game and its complex to structures governed by different constellations of groups and interests, federalism creates a means of lateral entry into them and thereby offers multiple opportunities to subordinate them to the common weal. Even when this structural interference works imperfectly (and it cannot help but be imperfect in an imperfect world), it serves as an antidote to the iron law of oligarchy, which, all other things being equal, applies to organizations and complexes alike.

Just as the federal structure serves to control complexes, in all arenas procedures have developed for the conduct of public business that are not designed to prevent the existence of complexes but to facilitate their proper operation. (This is quite different from many of the procedures being recommended and even adopted today.) Complexes can be understood as analogous to political parties, extralegal but essential devices for the conduct of government in a democracy, which need to be given just enough legal recognition to be kept reasonably honest without either being absorbed into the public sphere or having all the abuses that are likely to flow from them eliminated.

The Public Sector:
Governmental and Nongovernmental

The Status of Public Nongovernmental Bodies   In this connection, it should be recognized that the public elements in a complex are further divided into governmental and nongovernmental components, the latter (conventionally, but mistakenly, referred to as "private") including a wide range of educational, health, welfare, cultural, and even public safety organizations and institutions. The mix of governmental and public nongovernmental activities is not only fully consonant with the federal principle but has been very much a part of American federalism from the first. Indeed, the existence of the mix is testimony to the way in which federal principles and relationships permeate American civil society and are not merely structural arrangements for American government. Because of the availability of such bodies, Americans traditionally preferred first to rely upon public nongovernmental bodies when public action was considered necessary, and to utilize government—even local government—only when necessary. Moreover, when and where government had to be involved, it was to be utilized in conjunction with the appropriate nongovernmental bodies.

The great growth of government in recent decades has to some extent dampened America's traditional reliance upon public nongovernmental bodies to undertake public activities, which was part of our traditional "limited government" outlook. The inclinations of many of those who have been the foremost champions of government expansion have been to reduce the importance of the public nongovernmental sector and even to prefer governmental assumption of public tasks where, all things being equal, nongovernmental bodies could handle them just as well. This trend is fraught with grave consequences, since it weakens public participation and self-reliance, on one hand, while extending bureaucratization, on the other.

In fact, public nongovernmental bodies are so well rooted in the American scene that most have been able to adapt to the new mix of governmental and nongovernmental activity and thus maintain a role in the overall bundle of public activities. Nevertheless, for many years now there has been no real effort to stimulate public nongovernmental activity as an alternative to further governmental expansion. The possible exception to this was the poverty program in some of its aspects where the desire to encourage participation by the poor was translated into encouragement of nongovernmental bodies in poverty neighborhoods. Unfortunately, what was there considered "sauce for the goose" was not also accepted as "sauce for the gander" as federally sponsored governmental programs were expanded to further encroach upon the public nongovernmental sphere outside of the poverty areas. Most constitutionalists have glossed over this denial of equal protection of the laws because of their concern for their goals but it is neither reasonable nor constitutional to continue to do so.

Who Defines the Pursuit of Happiness?

If there is anything that seems to be clear regarding the Revolutionary Era, it is that the Americans of the late eighteenth century wished to confine the definition of the pursuit of happiness to the private and the local spheres of civil society and to prevent the federal government from engaging in any active role in making that determination.[31] If there is any difference of opinion regarding who shall define the pursuit of

happiness stemming from that period, it is whether the matter is entirely private or whether it can (and even should) acquire a public
character in the local community (and perhaps in the statewide community as well, as many New Englanders would have argued). In general,
government was to be a tool for supporting and advancing nongovernmental initiatives regarding the pursuit of happiness.

One thrust in the two centuries following the Revolution has been
to restrict even the local community's role in defining what constitutes
the pursuit of happiness to make it even more a private matter. This
long-term trend intensified after World War I as a result of the application of the First Amendment to the states by the U.S. Supreme Court
via the Fourteenth, and has been carried to its logical conclusion in
recent years with the elimination of even those laws regulating individuals' moral behavior (e.g., abortion, homosexuality, pornography)
that were previously considered to be the minimum right of any government in recognition of the fact that even in the most open society certain
political decisions must be taken about private behavior to set the tone
for the society as a whole.

At the same time, there has been an increasing willingness on the
part of the public to tolerate new forms of federal and state government
intervention into what had heretofore been considered clearly private
arenas. Government intervention of this kind began in the nineteenth
century in the fields of health and education. Laws requiring people to
be vaccinated, even against their will, were sustained by the courts on
the grounds of an overriding public interest. Similarly, parents were
required by law to send their children to school for at least a minimum
period of time.

In recent years, this power of government to intervene has been
drastically increased. Parents today are not only required to send their
children to school for a specific number of years but are no longer able
to exercise very much control over what their children learn in school.
School consolidation coupled with the professionalization of educational personnel opened the door for this to occur. The expansion of
school curricula to include matters that touch upon values and life-
styles (such as the emphasis on scientific as opposed to religious measures of truth and the introduction of sex education which is not simply
technical by its very nature) as well as simple reading, writing, and
arithmetic is both a result of these institutional changes and still another extension of their impact. Bussing to achieve racial balance is an
extension of these phenomena in another direction.

These changes in the field of education are typical of the new thrust of government that is no longer acting simply to provide certain social basics necessary for people to build their own lives but is actively shaping the character of the society in which the people are to function. One result of this has been a creeping tendency toward entrusting the institutions of government with the task of defining what constitutes the pursuit of happiness. It is true that every government is empowered to rule out—or at least make very difficult—certain forms of this pursuit and to make others more acceptable or easier, but in the United States there has been a change in degree that may involve a change in kind as well. Of course, the "institutions of government" ultimately mean the people who man those institutions. Nor is it clear that the coercive power of government is brought into play, willy-nilly, to enforce them. Here, too, federalism can serve as a remedy as it once did, namely by offering the public choices as to which governmental institutions and arenas should be enpowered to act in different matters regarding the pursuit of happiness. But even that requires coming to grips with the bureaucracy problem.

The Bureaucracy Problem

So much has been written about the bureaucracy problem in recent years that little need be added here. The issues of organizational complexity, red tape, bureaucratic modes of behavior, and the like have been the subjects of everything from theoretical foundations to detailed case studies to irate letters to the editor.[32] One facet of the problem has been somewhat neglected, however, and is only now coming to the fore. That is the way bureaucracies have come to be able to generate their own agendas and then sell them to the political leadership and the public. In essence, by controlling the flow of information, large bureaucracies can bring issues of their own choosing to public attention and build them up to "problem" proportions. A very high percentage of the "problems" brought to public attention today are raised by government agencies themselves to further or enhance their own roles (and budgets). This is not neccesarily a result of Machiavellian maneuvers either. "Good men and true" having entered public service to be of service find themselves confined to routines. Wishing to fulfill their own aspirations of service, they are ever ready to discover new problems that will demand their energy and active attention. The fact that their zeal is also reinforced by self-interest only makes it more difficult to control them. But, such a situation is a sure guarantee of a continually expanding government, expanding governmental budgets, and greater governmental intervention in nongovernmental spheres. Moreover, since a problem, once manufactured, demands a solution, it creates strong pressures for centralization as well.

WHAT OF THE FUTURE?

By 1973, the ideational and operational trends of the postwar generation had more or less spent themselves. While in many ways both were carried along by their own momentum, new approaches were beginning to emerge and to influence action. In some cases—exemplified by the Ford administration—their emergence came about by default; in some—exemplified by the new localism of the churches—by popular action. In others—exemplified by state and local antigrowth measures—they emerged as a result of popular pressure, and in still others—exemplified by the shift in U.S. Supreme Court attitudes—as a consequence of rethinking. Behind all of these is a renewed popular concern for decentralization, local control, debureaucratization, and a general effort by Americans to regain some measure of control over their own lives.

Hence we have entered a period of transition and ambiguity, one in which the courts are allowing greater state and local interference with the national economy in the name of environmental and quality-of-life interests, even as national regulation of the economy grows. It is a period in which state and local powers to regulate morality have been restored in some spheres but in which little in the way of local consensus regarding moral standards can be found anywhere in the country, in effect neutralizing their restored powers. To the extent that the principles of noncentralization are being rediscovered, the U.S. Supreme Court continues to lead the way with recent opinions referring explicitly to the federal character of the American polity. The Court has even shown some tendency toward reviving the principle of constitutional limits on federal power to interfere with the states' prerogatives. The recent decisions regarding public employment in state and local government not only recognized the constitutional principle of reserved powers (or "so far and no farther") but began to rebuild a constitutional theory to that effect, suggesting that the states are entitled to maintain a basic minimum of structural and institutional integrity if the federal system is to be maintained.[33]

In sum, despite all the trends toward centralization, federalism remains vigorously alive in the United States, and continues to inform the American political system in all its parts. As a dynamic relationship, it has changed in the past 200 years and will no doubt continue to change whether in regard to federal-state-local, public-private, governmental-nongovernmental relations, or any other of its dimensions. As of now, American state and local governments retain primary responsibility for domestic programs, including responsibility for the major share of governmental expenditures and government purchases of goods and services. Federal-state-local relations have reemerged as a topic of public (in addition to specialist) concern after a hiatus of a generation or more. Indeed, public sentiment today is strongly behind strengthening state and local government and, for the moment at least, reflects greater public confidence in state and local institutions than in federal ones. Moreover, the states, which continued to be vigorous even when the wave of centralization was strong, are now becoming bold as well, more willing to take the initiative than at any time since the beginning of the century.

The business community has even begun to create a new model to encourage the revival of federalism. Conglomerates, with their pluralistic character, represent a move from decentralization to federation in the economic realm. Their organizational framework, coupled with cybernetic theories of communication and control, make many of the previous generation's assumptions about efficient management obsolete while at the same time reinforcing many aspects of the theory underlying federalism.[34]

Whatever the present wave of decentralizing tendencies may bring, however, it is reasonably clear that American federalism in the third century of the republic will be different in certain respects from what it has been in the first two centuries. For one thing, the greater interdependence of all parts of civil society will insure a greater integration of all governmental activities as well, a phenomenon that can lead to centralization and is often mistaken for it even when it does not. To date, Americans have managed to accommodate that integration without committing themselves to centralization; it seems reasonable to assume that as long as they have the will to do so, federalism will continue to inform the republic in years to come.

Judicial Activism

Martin Shapiro

M'GUINNESS

5 The legislator shall make the law. The judge shall apply it to the disputes brought before him. There is singular agreement on this model, not only in the course of Western history but in cultures as disparate as those of Islam and Imperial China. Even in the English legal tradition, where we openly speak of the common law as judge made, there has never been a successful challenge to the status of "king in Parliament" as the sovereign law-maker.

The model, however, is just as universally wrong as it is universally held. Americans often view our notable deviations from the model as the peculiar outcomes of the boldness of common law judges and/or the existence of a written constitution and judicial review. Thus it pays to look for a moment to the Continent, which did not, at least until very recent times, enjoy either of these blessings. To an outsider nothing could seem neater than the differentiation of legislative and judicial functions proclaimed in code law countries. The code is a systematic, complete statement of the law and is enacted by the legislature. The duty of the judge is to apply the code to the cases before him. Even where an automatic application of the code is not possible, because either the language of the code is ambiguous or does not seem to contemplate the exact situation that has arisen, the judge confines himself to the application of the intent of the legislature.

Again the model is neat, but it is not true. French judges have created thousands of lines of legal rules and exceptions often starting from a single sentence or phrase of the code.[1] The German Civil Code was designed to be more complete than the French. But its completeness is that of a highly elegant textbook. Only in portions is it a detailed set of rules.[2] Neither German nor French law students can learn the law from the code alone. Both must resort to bulky and carefully annotated volumes of judicial decisions to find the actual law of the forum on many subjects.

Indeed, Continental legal scholarship has had the same debates as our own over the scope of judicial creativity. Those debates have ranged from the position that the judge must faithfully carry out the intention of the legislature, to the position that the judge should freely resolve the conflicts of interests that come before him in any way that appears to him appropriate and is not literally debarred by the code.[3]

Why do we find so much judicial law-making even in places where the ideology of the sovereign and complete statutory law is so firmly imbedded? Because of a paradox or dialectic as old as human understanding. Each in his own way—Plato, Confucius, and Mohammed—tells us that the law must consist of general rules so that men may know the norm of action before they act. Each also tells us that the general rule will not yield perfect justice in each individual case. For no general rule can comprehend all the moral nuances of every potential human relationship that arises under that rule.

The universal solution, or at least palliative, to this paradox is judicial discretion. In the process of applying the general rule to the particular case, let the judge make those adjustments necessary to preserve the basic thrust of the rule while still doing substantial justice to the parties before him. Every one of the world's major legal systems recognizes the necessity of this kind of judicial tempering of the law. Moreover every one of these systems recognizes that the real world must throw up such a myriad of situation types that no legislator, no matter how wise and energetic, could possibly have anticipated them all. Thus to meet new particulars as they arise, the judge must not only temper his rule to the individual case but constantly invent new rules to more justly handle recurrent fact situations that the statutory rules have not fully anticipated. Even in Islam, where God himself is the sole legislator, we encounter approval of such judicial techniques of rule-making as reasoning by analogy, consultation of custom, and consideration of social utility.[4]

Less universal perhaps, but widely encountered in Western societies, is yet a third compulsion to judicial law-making. As the administrative organs of government have grown, both civil and common law systems have sought to ensure that administrators act according to law. Indeed a similar flowering of administrative law associated with a highly bureaucratized state is to be found in Imperial China.[5] The principal method of ensuring bureaucratic legality is a system of recruitment, socialization, promotion, and other devices of internal discipline that encourage the rational-legal bureaucratic thought-ways described by Weber. Judicial review of administrative action is, however, often added as a further device for ensuring bureaucratic legality. In the tripartite systems favored in the West, legislators have repeatedly set judges to watch administrators so that they will not exceed the authority granted to them by the legislature. Both the English and the French maintain ongoing traditions of judicial review of administrative action even in systems of government that have become far more bureaucracy centered than our own.[6] Yet ultimately, to what extent can courts enforce legality on administrators without substituting judicial for administrative and legislative policy-making? Whenever judges are set to watch administrators, inevitably there will be judicial law-making. Judges can only brand administrative conduct illegal by substituting their own version of the law for that proclaimed by the administrator.[7]

I have stressed the universal, or at the least broadly Western, characteristics of judicial law-making for two reasons. First, if we observe judicial law-making persisting in many places over long periods of time, even in the face of the accelerating trend toward bureaucratic government, we can reasonably expect it to persist into America's third century. Second, Americans have tended to peculiarly associate judicial law-making with the constitutional law jurisdiction of the U.S. Supreme Court. Yet, if we find judicial law-making spread across an enormous range of polities, with and without such constitutional traditions, then we can reasonably expect the persistence of judicial law-making in third-century America, whatever Professor Elazar sees for the future of American constitutionalism and federalism.

JUDICIAL REVIEW, THE NEW DEAL, AND ITS AFTERMATH

If judicial law-making is more or less a constant of man's political experience, then the long-standing American debate over judicial activism cannot be characterized as simply a debate over judicial law-making unless we are willing to attribute a totally quixotic character to one of the two sides. Judiciaries are always active. The questions are how active, and in whose behalf? Americans often confuse these two questions. That confusion is particularly evident in relation to the New Deal experience, which colors much of our thinking about the most peculiarly American form of judicial activism—judicial review of the constitutionality of statutes and executive acts.

The standard version is that the nine old men blocked the emergency efforts of FDR and the New Deal until our great president directed his righteous wrath against the Court, causing the switch in time that saved nine and ushering in the era of judicial self-restraint. After 1937 the Court announced it would never again substitute its economic policy views for those of the elected representatives of the people. Instead it would presume the constitutionality of statutes, thus showing its deference to Congress.

This political myth has long ruled as the orthodoxy of our constitutional law for the simple reason that almost every one of the lawyers and political scientists who have been prominent commentators on the Court and Constitution over the last 40 years were themselves New Dealers whose whole view of the Court was shaped by the partisan struggles of the 1930s.

That myth has two interesting and interacting features. The first has to do with the structure of political science and political commentary. The group of New Deal lawyers, historians, and political scientists who wrote about the Court, and the New Deal justices on the Court, expressed the doctrine of judicial self-restraint as judicial deference to the legislator—that is, to Congress. At the same time, but quite independently, another group of commentators was creating the New Deal doctrine of the "strong presidency" in which the president became, among other things, the Chief Legislator, whose legislative program was to be enacted by a dutiful and disciplined Congress.

Because the structure of American scholarship separated Supreme Court from congressional-presidential studies, the final product of this New Deal equation has long remained neatly camouflaged. But the equation runs clearly enough. If the Court must defer to Congress, and Congress must defer to the president, then it follows that the true New Deal doctrine is judicial deference to the presidency. That is the real moral of the New Deal myth about the Court.

A second doctrine of the late 1930s is even more significant than that of judicial deference to the presidency. It is the "preferred position" doctrine enunciated in 1937[8] by Justice Stone, a Republican appointee soon to become Roosevelt's chief justice. Because many of the nine old men truly were old, it was clear by the end of 1937 that the Supreme Court would soon be completely dominated by New Deal appointees. Why disarm a major political institution at the very moment of taking it over? What was needed was an explanation of why the old Court's activism had been wrong that would simultaneously justify a new judicial activism on behalf of the New Deal's clients. The old Court's clients had been the business interests that supported the Republican party. The Democratic party sought to build a coalition of union members, the poor, ethnic and racial minorities, intellectuals, and civil servants.

The Roosevelt Court proclaimed its judicial self-restraint in the economic realm by killing the evil dragons of economic, substantive due process and dual federalism.[9] In short, it stopped protecting business interests. Given that a new special court, the National Labor Relations Board (NLRB), had been established and staffed to favor the unions over management, a proclamation of judicial self-restraint by the Supreme Court in the economic sphere automatically transferred government patronage from business to labor. The proclamation of judicial self-restraint in the economic realm at a time when the remainder of government was dominated by those seeking to better serve the interests of the poor was a negative but sufficient judicial patronage of those interests. But what of the other deserving members of the Democratic coalition?

Here enters preferred position. Justice Stone argued that, while the Supreme Court should normally defer to the democratic processes of the legislature (read president), it might justifiably become active in defense of the rights specifically guaranteed by the first ten amendments and on behalf of minority interests not adequately protected in the legislative process. This latter was a particularly neat touch. For in practice the one area where legislature could not automatically be read as president was race relations, where Southern Democrats firmly resisted Rooseveltian "leadership." And in that very area, like magic, it was suddenly discovered that the Court need not defer to the legislature.

The most prominent initial use of the preferred position doctrine was, of course, the justification for judicial activism on behalf of freedom of speech. A distinction was drawn between fundamental political rights and economic rights. The libertarian wing of the Court concluded that while judicial deference was the rule, activism was the watchword where freedom of speech was involved.[10] Of course, it turned out that freedom of speech had a striking correspondence with the interests of the left intellectuals who formed a numerically small, but politically important, link in the New Deal coalition.

Having moved toward the passive protection of unions and the poor and the active protection of minorities and intellectuals, the one remaining element of the coalition to be protected was the government worker. Clearly the interest in a government job is an economic interest. How could a Court that had proclaimed the virtue of judicial deference in the economic realm now intervene to protect government workers?

Here the Court benefited from the fortuitous circumstance that attacks on the interests of government workers first came from McCarthyites, not budget cutters. The Court gradually moved from the old position that government employment was a privilege that could be conditioned or withdrawn at the pleasure of the government to the position that government employment enjoyed some constitutional protection. It did so in the context of the federal loyalty-security program.[11] The cases involved attempts to purge alleged Communists and fellow travelers from government either on the basis of their previous political activity or their refusal to reveal that activity. The cases were technically either freedom of speech, self-incrimination, or procedural due process cases, and so they remain neatly classified in constitutional law books to this day.[12] As a result the Court could actively intervene to create a new property right—the right to a government job—while still proclaiming the preferred position doctrine that the Court must be self-restrained in economic matters while active in defense of civil liberties.

There remained one major segment of the New Deal coalition in need of help: ethnic and racial minorities. Ethnic minorities turned out to need little help from the courts. Unlike Negroes, ethnics typically controlled local governments and local Democratic party organizations where they lived and thus could receive direct benefits down the New Deal transmission belt.[13]

We have already noted that the preferred position doctrine's emphasis on minorities deprived of electoral power provided a new rationalization for judicial activism in favor of minorities as a special exception to New Deal self-restraint. The plight of the Negro created a special difficulty, however. The constitutional clauses under which it could be alleviated, equal protection and due process, were the very ones that served as the basis for the bad pre-New Deal activism of the Court on behalf of business. The antislavery origins of the clauses could, however, be urged as more than sufficient reason for distinguishing Fourteenth Amendment activism on behalf of blacks from Fourteenth Amendment activism on behalf of the business community, which had earlier masqueraded as the "persons" the amendment was intended to protect. Civil rights joined civil liberties as the special province of judicial activism. The official position of the Court became that statutory racial classifications would trigger the highest possible level of judicial activism while economic classifications *directed against private business* would trigger absolute judicial indifference.[14]

Two further steps were necessary to complete judicial servicing of the Democratic coalition. First, after the McCarthy period, threats to the economic interests of government workers no longer came in First Amendment packages. And a whole new category of recipients of government largesse, the beneficiaries of various governmental welfare programs, had come into existence. In short, serving the interests of organized labor was no longer sufficient or synonymous with serving the poor. The solution was simple enough. The Court held that government employees and beneficiaries were protected by the due process clause from arbitrary deprivation of their government checks. In order to do this, of course, the Court had to create a new property right in government largesse.[15] It had to return to precisely the economic due process that the New Deal commentators had condemned. And it immediately began to transpose procedural due process into substantive due process as the old Court had done.

For a long time everyone simply pretended not to notice. Most commentators continue to pretend, even today, that the economic rights of the poor, unlike those of the rich, are somehow not economic rights at all but some kind of civil rights or liberties so that activism in this area can still be distinguished somehow from the old Court's economic activism.

The Court itself has all but abandoned the pretense. In recent cases it has openly characterized both the old and the new property as property. Then it has gone on to say that it simply doesn't care if the government deprives a private individual of his business, but that it will look very closely at any attempt by government to deprive a civil servant of his job or a beneficiary of his check.[16]

The final step in the New Deal program has to do with money and votes. After 1928 and 1932, the Democratic party had the votes, and the Republican party had the money and the entrenched status. It followed that a judicial activism, properly conceived, would insure that election outcomes were determined by votes, not money or position. New Deal canons of self-restraint called for deference to the legislative body, and legislatures had always made election laws. Nevertheless, the Supreme Court gradually built up a body of decisions on equality in the electoral process that has reached its most recent culmination in *Buckley* v. *Valeo,* the Campaign Financing Case.[17] In that case, we even begin to hear suggestions that the freedom of speech of the rich ought to be trimmed back to equalize it with the freedom of speech of the poor.

Viewing matters in the shorter run, most commentators on the Court have presented a picture of judicial self-restraint in the 1940s and 1950s followed by a new wave of judicial activism initiated by the Warren Court. From a longer perspective, however, we can see that the apparent self-restraint of the immediate post-1937 period was merely the negative phase of the transfer of judicial patronage from Republican to Democratic clients. After the early Roosevelt Court completed stripping business of its constitutional benefits, and did the spade work for a new set of beneficiaries, the Warren and Burger courts went on with the construction of a new system of benefits for workers, the poor, minorities, and intellectuals.

WARREN COURT ACTIVISM AND EGALITARIAN IDEOLOGY

The Warren Court was essentially engaged in testing the limits of New Deal consensus. In the McCarthy movement it met and compromised with those forces that terminated the New Deal's opening to the left. And with *Brown* v. *Board*[18] the Court confronted the most basic cleavages in the Roosevelt coalition, those between North and South and between the now more prosperous, unionized, blue collar workers and the last underdogs. Both these great crises of the Warren Court were often fought in the rhetoric of activism and self-restraint, but both were at bottom simply part of the general tensions that were developing in post-New Deal politics.

While the race cases may have been the most controversial, they were only one segment of the most important activism of the Warren Court, which was a systematic probing of the egalitarian, welfare state implications of the New Deal experience. The American approach to social services has been piecemeal and pragmatic. As we have been told repeatedly, the peculiar art of the New Deal was to help the needy without raising ideological boogies. Yet implicit in the rise of the positive or welfare state was an idea of equality.

That same idea was implicit in the whole body of Warren Court jurisprudence, from its rights of accused to its birth control decisions. The Warren Court went further, however, than implicit support of equality. It began to translate what the New Deal had treated as interests into constitutional rights.

So long as social claims are seen as interests, the legislature may distribute resources to each such claim as it thinks best. No theory need be announced except perhaps a kind of democratic pluralism. Legislatures may proclaim some of these interests to be rights as Congress proclaimed a right to a job in the Full Employment Act of 1946. But no one takes such proclamations very seriously, as the subsequent history of that act shows. Here the Supreme Court enjoys a comparative institutional advantage over president and Congress. When it calls a social interest a right, it is taken seriously. And once elevated to the status of judicially acknowledged constitutional right, the interest is raised above the hurly-burly of political bargaining.

By freely employing the equal protection clause and moving steadily toward declaring constitutional rights to subsistence, housing, education, and employment on a par with the constitutional right to vote, the Warren Court was moving the nation toward an open, official, consistent, and principled acceptance of the egalitarian ideology of the welfare state. If the Warren Court's doctrinal tendencies had been carried to their logical extreme, the end result would have been a judicially enforced constitutional obligation on government to bring all Americans above the poverty line and to provide substantively equal government services *to* all in any area where it chose to provide government services *at* all.

BURGER COURT ACTIVISM, THE IDEOLOGY OF PLURALISM AND JUDICIAL DISCRETION

In spite of the apparent radicalism of the 1960s and early 1970s, Americans did not seem prepared to elevate the social democratic tendencies of the New Deal into a consistent and official political ideology for the nation. The Warren Court gave way to the Burger Court at the very moment it seemed ready to take the crucial steps toward social equality. The key case was *San Antonio School District* v. *Rodriguez*,[19] which rejected the claim that there was a fundamental constitutional right to equal public education. The Burger Court has steadfastly refused to extend the list of fundamental rights to include subsistence, housing, and employment.

Thus the Burger Court has stopped short of demanding that government openly acknowledge and consistently pursue the egalitarian values of the welfare state. This rejection of the Warren Court tendencies does not, however, involve a return to judicial restraint as opposed to the activism of the Warren Court. Burger Court decisions on abortion, campaign financing, state aid to parochial schools, obscenity, rights of accused, due process, and school desegregation indicate that the Burger Court remains an activist Court but one with a different style from that of the Warren Court.

The Warren Court's activism tended to be expressed in firm, new constitutional rules. One man, one vote, and the exclusionary rule were the most famous of these, but there were others. The Burger Court continues to make policy decisions just as the Warren Court did, but it tends to announce them as the product of prudent judicial balancing of competing interests rather than absolute constitutional rules. This balancing approach takes on a myriad of forms in Burger Court jurisprudence. For instance, in obscenity cases, where the Warren Court had come to say that a work was protected by the First Amendment unless it was *"utterly"* without redeeming social importance, the Burger Court now requires the presence of *"serious"* social importance before First Amendment protections come into play.[20] In religion, the Burger Court changed the old rule of no entanglement between church and state to the rule of "no *excessive* entanglement."[21] In the abortion area it establishes a trimester approach that surely cannot be derived from anything in the Constitution and is quite clearly an attempt to compromise among conflicting public sentiments.[22] In free speech, the Court openly says that it will balance the government's interests in suppressing speech against the interests in freedom of speech.[23]

This balancing of interests approach of the Burger Court has two important consequences. First, it enormously increases the scope of judicial discretion. The rules of the Warren Court imposed new, sharply defined, judicially created public policies, but they bound everyone including the Court itself. The Burger Court's balancing doctrines impose new, vaguely defined, judicially created public policies. Because they are vaguely defined they leave legislators and administrators more elbow room. On the other hand, since the Court always nominates itself as the final determiner of just how "serious" is serious enough, or just what state interest is compelling enough to meet its constitutional tests, the Court assigns itself ultimate and unbounded discretion over nearly every policy area it chooses to enter. The Burger Court's style somewhat softens the impact of the Court's policy pronouncements on the nation at large, but increases the ability of the Court to continually alter its policies as circumstances and the justices' preferences change.

The second major consequence of the Burger balancing approach is a return to the incremental, piecemeal, pragmatic style of interest group politics that has traditionally characterized Washington policy-making. It is no coincidence that balancing of interests was the orthodoxy of the courts and the law schools during the era labeled "the end of ideology," or that the Warren Court began to speak the language of equality and fundamental rights during the ideological upsweep of the 1960s and early 1970s. Nor is it a coincidence that now that we have returned to the more traditional politics of the Ford-Carter era, the Court has returned to a balancing of interest approach. The fundamental ideology proclaimed by the Burger Court is that of liberal pluralism rather than that of the egalitarian welfare state.

Thus it would be a mistake to see the history of the Supreme Court over the last half century as a fluctuation between judicial activism and judicial self-restraint. Instead what we observe is a rather continuous judicial activism that has from time to time shifted its clients and ideologies. Given the universal character of judicial law-making and this continuous American tradition of judicial activism in constitutional law, it is not difficult to predict that Supreme Court activism will continue. Nor is it difficult to predict that the style of activism and its beneficiaries will continue to change in accord with changes in the general political context in which the Court operates.

JUDICIAL ACTIVISM, TECHNOCRACY, AND POST-INDUSTRIALISM

Judicial activism can be measured at quite another level from that of grand constitutional doctrine—in the amount of day-to-day judicial intervention we observe in the routine affairs of government and society. At this level there have been sharper discontinuities in judicial activism. These discontinuities are closely related to the shift from industrial to post-industrial society.

In the industrializing phase, we would naturally expect to encounter growing respect for technology and consequently growing prestige for the technical specialist. Of course anti-technology, anti-expert themes are always to be found in American life. Nevertheless, the success of technology is quite clear in twentieth-century America. The engineer, then the nuclear scientist, and finally the space man, became our culture heroes. By the 1930s, in which so many of our attitudes toward courts were generated, a quasi-religious cult of technology flourished. Twentieth-century American law has been dominated by sociological jurisprudence that characterizes law as "social engineering."[24]

Particularly in its Wisconsin and California varieties, the progressive movement defined good government as government by specialized, technical experts rather than "politicians." The city manager, the county agent, the budgeter, the sanitary engineer, in short, special experts in public administration and technologist civil servants were to replace the ward heeler and the spoilsman. The civil service movement in general, and particularly the early absorption of scientists and technologists directly into government that has been traced by Don K. Price,[25] meant that the government administrator became the recipient of the status ascribed to the technical expert in American society. The legitimacy and authority of many government agencies rested largely on their technical expertise. The regulatory commission was a peculiar manifestation of this technological legitimacy. It was to be preferred to a legislative or judicial solution to the problems posed by the technologically advanced segments of the economy such as railroads and broadcasting because it could build an organizational store of technical knowledge that legislatures and courts could not. Its decisions were expected to be better, more fair, more impartial, precisely because they added technical expertise to the political purposes embodied in the congressional statutes. This worship of technology became a central theme of the philosophy of judicial self-restraint built up during the New Deal.

As we have already noted, in a number of sectors of the economy the preexisting law and/or the courts favored business over the various clients of the New Deal. The solution was to change the law and/or transfer application of the law from courts to new or newly expanded administrative agencies packed with New Deal stalwarts who could be trusted to reach the right decisions. The transfer of decisional authority from courts to administrators was not complete, however, because of the deep-seated American sentiment in favor of judicial review of governmental decisions. Even those statutes providing the most sweeping delegations to administrative experts typically contained provisions for judicial review of the legality of administrative acts. What was necessary, therefore, was a theory of judicial deference that would provide the substance of administrative sovereignty while preserving the form of judicial review.

Justice Holmes once said that the life of law was not logic but experience. Common lawyers had always defended their peculiar vehicle from critical onslaughts by insisting that no matter how complex, impenetrable, and illogical the common law might appear to the unlearned, it was the repository of the practical wisdom of the English people. In short, in the commercial age and well into the early stages of industrialism, the common lawyers and judges could claim a superior technological expertise since they were the repository of a body of transactional techniques honed to perfection over the centuries, essential to the operation of an agricultural and commercial economy, and too complex to be understood except by the legal technocrats themselves.

The intellectual self-confidence of those learned in the artificial reason of the law, as Coke had called it, was shaken by the new scientific and technological ethos that accompanied an industrializing society. That ethos was reflected in the Benthamite attack on common law.

The lawyers were, however, gallant fighters, albeit often under the banner "If you can't lick 'em, join 'em." They invented the case method of teaching, and purported to believe that by using it the law schools could discover the scientific principles of law.[26] Faced by the challenges of science and technology in the fully industrializing society of late nineteenth-century America, lawyers responded by asserting that law itself was a science, an organized body of knowledge that rested on legal principles derived by induction from a body of social experience gained from centuries of experimentation.[27] The judge was as good a technocrat as any of the others he encountered.

Stealing the name of science was not likely to work indefinitely, however. By the 1930s no one, least of all the lawyers themselves, believed that they were scientists or technologists, in the sense that engineers or even accountants were. The claim to scientific or technical authority rested on the acquisition and organization of empirical data. At the turn of the century lawyers had made their claim to such authority on the basis that law represented the accumulated factual experience of the race. But in the twentieth century it was new facts, new theories, new inventions that gave the technologists their authority. Clearly litigation and case method teaching were not routes to the rapid generation and digestion of new facts and the rapid creation of new technology.

It was the administrator and his agency, which continuously did research, rapidly accumulated and evaluated new facts, and either employed or directly consulted technical experts, who necessarily out-scienced the judge, who did no research, accumulated no data, and heard from experts only sporadically and at the behest of litigants. In a world of science and technology, the judges lost confidence in themselves. Judges knew that the administrators they were called upon to review, not they with their ancient and creaking legal lore, were the real technocrats.

Thus the shift in government patronage dictated by the New Deal could be readily accomplished in the sphere where judges and administrators met by a doctrine fully compatible with the values of the times. The authority to decide ought to be vested in those who knew the facts. Administrators knew the facts. Judges did not. It followed, therefore, that judges ought to defer to the technically expert decisions of administrators.

This deference became a central tenet of orthodox administrative law in the late 1930s and 1940s and a centrally held belief of the generations of New Deal appointees who filled the federal bench during the forties and fifties. The result was a litany of incompetence constantly preached by the federal judiciary and the dozen leading law schools.[28] Federal judges, and at a somewhat slower rate their state colleagues, lost faith in their own abilities to make sound public policy. They had read themselves out of the technocracy that rules the industrialized state.

The use of the expression "post-industrial" is itself a symptom of a certain malaise or loss of confidence both in the goals and techniques of technocratic government. One of the first signs of this malaise was the rather widespread feeling of the 1950s that the federal bureaucracy had lost its New Deal snap, had become middle-aged, pessimistic, and lacking in self-confidence about its ability to solve real-world problems. On a much broader intellectual front, old conservative mumblings about government red tape and inefficiency had been supplemented by an elegant sociology of organizations that confirmed the careerism, sluggishness, and parochialism of large organizations and particularly stressed the capacities of organizational subunits to distort, suppress, or ignore the facts in the pursuit of organizational self-interest.[29] Instead of being the cure-all, organizational division of labor according to technological specialization began to be seen as a threat to the rationality of public administration.

So long as the New Deal was both new and dominant, the shared values and esprit de corps of New Deal politicians and New Deal bureaucrats masked the latent contradictions for a democratic political system posed by the shift of political power to a technocratic bureaucracy. As New Deal esprit began to break down, and particularly after a Republican president inherited an aging New Deal bureaucracy, those contradictions began to come to the fore. The unease with the bureaucracy began to show itself in diverse ways. The Hoover Commission, Schedule C, the growth of the White House staff, PPB (Program, Planning, Budgeting)—there were these and many other signs that America was losing faith in the bureaucracy.

In administrative law there was a slight dampening of enthusiasm for judicial deference to administrative decisions.[30] It began to be admitted, albeit with a certain tinge of guilt, that judges sometimes did intervene against the agencies. While using the cover of procedural language, they were sometimes actually intervening because they found the policies of the agencies parochial, self-serving, or otherwise not in the public interest. It was even suggested that these interventions might be justified on precisely the grounds that had previously been offered in favor of judicial deference, namely that the administrators were technical specialists and the judges were not. Once it was recognized that the virtues of technical specialization brought with them the vices of narrowed and distorted perspective and clientelism, the judge, precisely because he lacked technical perspectives, suggested himself as a generalist watchdog against the pathologies of bureaucratic specialists.[31]

That the judge was entitled to political power precisely because he knew nothing was still a startling notion even in the 1960s. In the 1970s, of course, a number of presidential and gubernatorial candidates have ridden to success on the claim that their peculiar virtue lay in their noncontamination by the technocrats in the capital. It is this general ebbing of faith in technocracy in a "post-industrial" age that has led to the tremendous resurgence of judicial self-confidence that we have witnessed in recent years.

THE JUDGE AS POST-INDUSTRIAL HERO

Today no action of government seems complete without litigation. Our newspapers tell us of judges who forbid the transfer of air-force squadrons from one base to another, delay multimillion dollar construction projects, intervene in complex negotiations between public employers and their employees, oversee the operation of railroads, and decide the location of schools. In the course of these litigations we have seen judges blithely intervening in precisely the kinds of massive and complex technical matters about which they would have automatically disclaimed competence twenty years ago. Judges now joyously try their hands at everything from the engineering of atomic reactors to the validation of IQ tests. They run school districts, do regional land use planning, redesign welfare programs, and calculate energy needs. They make policy decisions with massive financial and political consequences for every level of government. They destroy and direct the rebuilding of educational, electoral, tax, and public utilities systems that are the products of thousands of hours of legislative negotiation and hundreds of complex statutes. Today there seems to be no public policy issue, no matter how massive, complex, or technical, that some judge somewhere has not felt fully capable of deciding, aided only by the standard processes of litigation.

This resurgence of judicial presumption is, of course, part and parcel of the very currents of opinion that have led to constant talk of "the greening of America," "appropriate technology," "ecology," "the limits of growth," "the new property," "small is beautiful," "humanistic values," and the "post-industrial" society. We are in the midst of a revolt of the intellectuals against the establishment technocracy and the methods and goals it has traditionally espoused. At the heart of this revolt are a number of key premises. One is that the lay consumer of technology, not the technician, must be the ultimate decision maker about how and where technology will be applied. Another is that division of labor among technologists has gone so far, and the self-interest of the technologists has been so enlisted in the technical programs they operate, that they cannot be trusted to present or evaluate their own technologies impartially and with an eye toward the general good.

Now that the technologists have allegedly failed us, it follows that we need new champions of the public good and the higher human values. Such champions must be uncorrupted by technology, unattached to the bureaucracy, and independent of the "special interests" with whom the technocrats have become allied. Enter the judge: by constitution separated from the technological bureaucracy and the special-interest-dominated legislature; by education and experience devoid of technical expertise; by popular mythology armed with impartiality; and by his service to "the law," "the constitution," and "justice" pledged to the highest and most universal human values. In a society in revolt against expertise, the judge emerges as the prophet armed— armed in his ignorance of every one of the technologies that make the society run. The judge is transformed, in his own eyes as well as those of others, from the industrial idiot to the post-industrial hero and wise man.

Our faith in judicial policy-making is certainly not entirely misplaced. Precisely because he is a generalist hearing a wide range of cases as they arise, the judge can interject a useful element of lay perspective and general public concern into the governmental decision-making process, particularly in those instances where the process is dominated by a single group of technicians and clientele. Moreover the presence or potential presence of the judge provides a certain incentive to explain and justify its decisions, which is healthy for any bureaucracy. And litigation or the threat of litigation insures a more complete hearing for interests that might otherwise be disregarded. The presence in the political process of at least one decision maker who formally treats the opposing parties as equals rather than in terms of their unequal economic and political power, is useful, particularly where one of the opposing powers is that of the government and the other that of an individual or minor group.

THE COSTS OF GOVERNMENT
BY JUDICIARY

Nevertheless, the costs of government by judiciary can be enormously high. Much of the current judicial intervention is done under courts' equity powers. The instinct of equity courts is to freeze the situation or return it to the status quo ante until such time as the court wends its leisurely way to a final resolution of the competing equities. Other public policy makers have long since learned to treat time as a resource and delay as an important cost, often one that can be fairly precisely calculated in terms of interest rates or other discounting methods. The equitable injunction originated in an agricultural setting in which the greatest damage was likely to be done by alteration and little harm would result from leaving the land as it was for a few more years. The injunction may insure that ultimately the best justice will be done, but in the meantime, particularly in periods of rapid inflation, it may lead to unacceptable disruptions in fiscal management and cost escalations that outrun the eventual benefits of correct legal outcomes. Yet the enjoining courts cannot be forced to directly face these costs since they are costs that must be borne by other agencies than the courts themselves.

More generally the current tendency of courts to extend their hospitality to everyone claiming even speculative injury means that litigation costs become a substantial cost of nearly every project, both public and private.[32] These transaction costs do not necessarily constitute a rational or desirable charge on the society's resources.[33]

Case-by-case litigation is often a very awkward way of making social policy. For instance, courts have recently been examining so-called snob zoning ordinances of suburban communities. Considered individually, each of these ordinances may have the laudable purpose of maintaining low population densities and the character and amenities of the communities. Collectively they may create a wall sealing less-than-affluent minorities in central cities. Thus in many instances a suit centered in one small community lures the judge into the most complex problems of regional land use. A series of judges in a series of uncoordinated decisions about a dozen scattered communities may be attempting a task of regional, ecological reconstruction that would challenge planning institutions with a thousand times the resources.

One defense of social decision by litigation is that the judge is confronted with the rival technical experts of the two parties and is thus freed of the domination that technicians exercise over laymen who are entirely dependent on one source of technical advice. In theory the layman judge will discern the real technological truth by comparing the conflicting technical testimony. In reality the judge often cannot understand the technical testimony on either side, has no mode of independently evaluating the accuracy of either, and is reduced to an act of faith in one side's technicians or the other's. The judicial weighing of technical testimony often comes down to a law clerk, fresh out of law school and with no technical background, juggling footnotes to support whatever guess the judge is making.

While the prerequisite for the outburst of judicial activity of the sixties and seventies was the return of judicial self-confidence, its immediate cause lay elsewhere. *Brown* v. *Board* became a new judicial parable and instructed interest groups that the judicial shop had fully reopened for interest representation business. Such groups quickly learned to translate their political goals into the language of legal and constitutional rights. New judicial lobbying organizations, the so-called public interest law firms, arose to meet the new needs.

Among the many results of this new phase of American interest group politics was one particularly significant for judicial review of administrative action. Congress had long since fallen into the quite conscious habit of adopting statutory language that delegated a great deal of discretion to the federal bureaucracy. It has been less conscious of another habit. Congress had been passing a great deal of legislation that either created major new claims for public services or imposed extremely severe sanctions on private conduct, fondly trusting that incremental budgeting and differential or delayed enforcement would avoid sudden raids on the treasury or excessive disruption to the private sector. The implementation and enforcement of statutes was, after all, the business of the bureaucracy which would be trusted to round off the sharp edges of the legislation and make the necessary adjustments to bring the law into accord with social, economic, and technological reality.

Much of the untoward judicial activity of the last twenty years is part of a period of adjustment. When statutes are an essentially private channel of communication between congressional committee and executive branch bureau, a great deal of statutory language may be nicely declaratory but essentially harmless. Such language may take on an entirely new and different significance when a militant interest group waits in the wings anxious to get the language into court where an activist judge stands waiting to fully enforce the litigants' legal rights. The incredibly costly and congressionally unanticipated saga of the "environmental impact statement" provision is the most dramatic illustration of this point. Today we face almost daily emergencies that could have been resolved twenty years ago by bureaucratic discretion but which are now insoluble because an exercise of such discretion will be followed by litigation insisting that the letter of the statute be enforced immediately.

Congress will have to learn to write its statutes with an eye to the new litigational scene. Paradoxically the result is likely to be a further increase in bureaucratic discretion. For if the statute maker now wishes to provide for practical adjustment of the rigidity of his statute through bureaucratic discretion, he is going to have to provide for such discretion openly in the language of the statute in order to insulate it from litigation. As we become more and more aware of the costs of judicial policy-making, such statutory vesting of discretion is likely to become more and more popular.

For the ultimate cost of judicial policy-making is that judges are essentially irresponsible. The older New Deal exponents of judicial self-restraint denounced judicial policy-making as antidemocratic on the grounds that the federal judiciary was non-elective. This argument is hardly persuasive in light of the proclivities of New Deal congresses and presidents to turn vast spheres of discretionary policy-making over to non-elected federal bureaucrats. The true irresponsibility of courts lies along two other interrelated dimensions.

First, courts can and frequently do impose enormous financial and political demands on other portions of the political system without themselves taking any responsibility for finding the resources to meet those demands. The Court that orders bussing does not have to find the money to pay for the bussing or the police to protect the buses. The Court that enjoins the construction of a new power-generating facility does not have to find the electricity to meet the future shortfall. Policy-making through the vehicle of litigation means that the judge enters highly complex ongoing situations just far enough and just long enough to pull out a crucial brick and then scampers away, leaving it to the rest of the political system to somehow make sure that the wall does not fall down. Alternatively, as local judges handling school desegregation have discovered, the judge stays and finds himself becoming responsible for the whole wall, a responsibility for which his training, knowledge, and staff resources are insufficient.

This antinomy of too little or too much responsibility largely arises because of a second dimension of judicial irresponsibility. Judges clothe their policy intervention in the language of legal rights. When particular social, economic, and political interests are translated into legal or constitutional rights, they cease to be political agenda items to which varying priorities can be assigned and become absolute claims on available resources. This is particularly true when the judicial language of equal rights is employed. So long as the handicapped have an interest in obtaining public transportation, the decision makers can consider whether it is worth investing millions in bus lifts and subway elevators or whether the total benefits to the few persons involved are outweighed by the benefits that would accrue from alternative investments of the money. Once a court declares that the handicapped have a right to equal access to public transportation, then the money must be spent even if the cost benefit ratio is insane.

Because courts too often speak in the language of rights rather than interests, they find it difficult to engage in reasonable and responsible collaboration with other portions of the policy-making machinery. For they are always demanding that the particular interest that they choose to prefer at the moment be given absolute priority over all of the other interests at play.

If there has been any point central to "post-industrial" commentary, it is that the seamless web of modern life requires careful adjustments between interests and goals with special attention to the unanticipated consequences of unidimensional development. The paradox of judicial policy-making in a post-industrial age is, then, that the very teachings that have given the judges confidence to intervene against the technocrats are constantly contradicted by the kinds of interventions that the judges do. For judicial intervention tends to be unidimensional and to be made without regard to the radiating chains of consequences that follow from such interventions. In short, because of its preoccupation with "rights," judicial decision-making is frequently itself a kind of technocratic decision-making, suffering from a narrowing of perspective similar to that afflicting other technologists.

JUDICIAL ACTIVISM IN A POST-INDUSTRIAL AGE

The prediction and prescription for judicial activism in a post-industrial age is, therefore, a relatively simple one. American courts are likely to remain active policy makers. Statute makers, however, are likely to react to the current embarrassment of judicial activity by being more cautious in the creation of statutory rights and more open in their delegation to administrators of discretion to waive or vary statutory rules. We examined the constitutional style of the Burger Court at some length in part to indicate that the judges themselves are already beginning to learn not to invariably translate interests into equal rights. Instead they are beginning to treat such claims as matters of degree that must be coordinated with other claims in the society. Unlike the use of similar balancing language by the New Deal proponents of judicial self-restraint, however, the new balancing language is not a cloak for judicial withdrawal. Instead it seems to be an announcement that judges will actively exercise policy discretion but do so in the context of reasonable collaboration with the rest of the policy-making machinery.

The renewed emphasis on individual rights protected by law, which inspired and was inspired by the outburst of judicial activity in the sixties and seventies, was a natural part of the revolt against technocracy that marked the transition from the industrial to the post-industrial society. That revolt was, however, only partial and more one of style than substance. The Warren Court and its judicial subordinates participated in the extreme style of the greening of America generation. The Burger Court has already moved to the lower-keyed style of the Jimmy Carter electorate.

As the costs and institutional incapacities of judicial intervention become clearer, we can expect courts to voluntarily relinquish or be barred from the more quixotic adventurism inspired by their brief emergence as post-industrial hero. Judicial activism will not disappear. Instead it will become part of an armory of political institutions designed to insure lay or generalist participation in government decision-making, the need for which, I think most of us would agree, has been demonstrated by our rocky passage into post-industrialism.

The Prophylactic Presidency

Sanford Weiner
Aaron Wildavsky

*Calls for national planning—the coordinated effort to antici-
pate and forestall national problems—are once again abroad
in the land.*
                                   New York Times (December 12, 1975)

*The problem of politics is less to solve conflicts than to prevent
them; less to serve as a safety valve for social protest than to
apply social energy to the abolition of recurrent sources of
strain in society.*
                        Harold D. Lasswell (*Psychopathology and Politics,*
                        University of Chicago Press, 1930, p. 197)

*A president who does not raise hopes is criticized as letting
events shape his presidency, rather than making things happen. A president who eschewed inspiration of any kind would
be-rejected as un-American. For as a poet once wrote, "America is promises." For people everywhere cherishing the dream
of individual liberty and self-fulfillment, America has been
the land of promises, of dreams. No president can stand in the
way of this truth, no matter how much the current dissatisfaction about the size of big government in Washington, and its
incapacity to deliver the services it promises.*
                        Thomas E. Cronin ("The Presidency and Its
                        Paradoxes," p.11, unpublished)

6 Most decisions most of the time are reactions to what has
already happened. Evils occur and we attempt to mitigate
them. Our security depends on our collective capacity to
cope within changing circumstances. Suppose, however, that collective
confidence declines either because of a decrease of trust in internal
social relations or an increase of external menace. The institutions
through which people relate may be in disrepute or their environment
may be perceived as precarious, the slightest error ramifying throughout the system to cause catastrophe. Instead of reacting to difficulties
that can be overcome, we would want to anticipate those from which we
could not recover. Now the evils that do occur are limited, if by nothing
else, by our capacity to recognize them. But the evils that might occur
are potentially limitless. Shall we err by omission, then, taking the
chance that avoidable evils might overwhelm us? Or shall we err by
exhaustion, using up our resources to prevent evils that might never
have occurred in order to anticipate those that might do us in? The
prophylactic presidency, with its rationale in preventive planning based

on reducing risk through market socialism, answers this question in favor of an anticipatory democracy.

Planning is again being offered as the solution for government's inability to prevent the crises of recent years—energy, environment, economics. And the proposals inevitably center on the presidency—the only person who is also an institution—as the locus of the effort to plan. Demands that the president be more of a planner have emanated from many quarters. A national committee of prominent businessmen, labor leaders, politicians, and academics, chaired by Nobel Prize winner Wassily Leontief, issued a manifesto. Senators Javits and Humphrey introduced a bill embodying the committee's ideas, and the Senate then held well-publicized hearings. A planning scheme was also incorporated into the Humphrey-Hawkins "full employment bill," which became a prominent part of the Democratic platform in 1976. Conservatives, including economist Herbert Stein, have responded to these initiatives with their own speeches and articles denouncing the whole idea.

However, this paper is not about the desirability or feasibility of planning. For if we take the most common definition of planning— present actions undertaken in order to achieve better future results— then everyone plans and is in favor of it. In this sense, planning is not only ubiquitous but also varied and problematic. There are many different ways of planning in addition to a formal written plan, and their outcomes are uncertain. Planning per se, therefore, cannot be a solution to a problem, only a restatement. Rather than an answer to the question of what to do, planning provides only a question disguised as an answer. To say "Let's plan" does not tell us who should plan, how to plan, what it will contain, whose interests it is supposed to serve, or what the consequences will be. Planning conceals unresolved conflicts about power, knowledge, and purpose.

The litany of demands that presidents become planners leads us to unsettled questions about the power and purpose of the presidency itself. We intend to use the concept of planning, then, as a diagnostic probe, to illuminate unresolved conflicts about the appropriate functions of the presidency in American life.

THE PLANNERS' VISION

What makes planning attractive to its advocates? What characterizes a good plan, and what benefits is it meant to bring?

First, good planning reflects anticipation. Through planning, future problems can more readily be foreseen in the present. Henry Ford II, for example, told the *New York Times* that recent shortages in the supply of metals and other industrial materials "could have been anticipated if there had been planning." However, this point of view is not limited to business leaders or to such specific forecasts. George Meany is one of many advocates of planning who expect it to anticipate society-wide crises, even a decade in advance:

> We need long range economic planning and priorities to minimize unforeseen major developments and reduce the degree to which American society has stumbled and fumbled along in the past few years . . . . the United States was not prepared for the Urban Crisis of the 1960s which could have been foreseen by sensible long run economic planning in the 1950s.

But anticipation is only half the effort. Planning is also meant to be the ability to control the future by current acts. "Planning," says the advocates' manifesto, "can spare all of us the sense of helplessness we feel as the economy drifts from crisis to crisis and replace frustration with a sense of hope, with the conviction that we can, in fact, exert some control over our affairs." This control escalates quickly from a point of satisfaction to a matter of duty. Not only is planning "an economic and social necessity" but, for Leonard Woodcock of the United Auto Workers, "It is a crime to allow millions of workers to lose their jobs because we refuse to plan."

Wassily Leontief, the committee's chairman, has drawn the themes of anticipation and control together. For him, planning is the "preventive medicine" the United States needs to "inoculate itself against forever repeating the same miserable mistakes." Thus, its advocates view planning as essentially prophylactic—it is a technique to foresee future evils *before they have manifested themselves* and to act in the present to prevent them.

Special mechanisms, moreover, need to be established to achieve these aims. Planning advocates believe that a technocratic process, embodying comprehensive rationality, is urgently needed to override the messy, decentralized political institutions that now make decisions: as the committee says, "We leave so much to chance. . . . Instead of systematically trying to foresee the needs of the nation in years ahead we have dozens of separate uncoordinated agencies making policy. . . ." The hallmarks of this approach are that planning is conceived as a direct antidote to politics ("Planning could help us look beyond the next election"); and that it ultimately embraces all governmental decisions. When one pursues comprehensive choices, everything becomes relevant. The planning manifesto cites energy, housing, and transportation as "obvious examples" of policy areas in need of planning. But—the logic is inescapable— "a planning office cannot look at energy alone, transportation alone, housing alone, or at any other sector of the economy in isolation, all these sectors interact. . . ."

Robert Dahl has recently described how initiatives for activist reform in America tend toward the presidency as the natural focus for their efforts: "The presidency became the institutional center from which a majority coalition . . . would be mobilized, organized, and given voice." The advocates for planning also display this state of mind—their Office of National Economic Planning "must be set up at the center of our economic and political life . . . within the White House."

Nor will this be just one more high-level advisory body. The planners envision an office that will dominate all existing institutions. Its director is to be the president's chief economic advisor, and the six-year plan is to be the guiding document for the Executive Branch. The president, through the planning office, will oversee the implementation of the plan, in all major policy areas, throughout the bureaucracy. This new and potent arm of the presidency is the centerpiece of the planners' vision.

Thus a felt need for more control over the future leads to a call for greater central control in the present, and—inevitably in our system— to demands that the president do something about it. Hence, we now turn to the full implications of this vision of a prophylactic presidency.

THE PROPHYLACTIC PRESIDENCY
IN ACTION

How might a presidency remade in the planners' vision function, and would we like a prophylactic president if we had one?

To fulfill these new demands, the president would have to become our great anticipator—first foreseeing evils hidden in the future, then forestalling them in the present. But carrying out this dual role would require shifts throughout the political system that are only implicit in the planners' design. If we demand that presidents undertake the task of avoiding future evils, we cannot then deny them the power to act on their foresight, even when our own vision is less clear.

This logic carries a faint but still familiar ring. In the era before Vietnam a similar deference to superior presidential foresight was known as bipartisan foreign policy. Then the future evil was envisioned as Soviet expansion toward world domination, which required American containment around the world. In such a complex and perilous situation, it was argued, only the executive could properly anticipate the measures needed to forestall future Soviet gains. So domestic differences must be submerged in favor of presidential judgment on the Marshall Plan, the Truman Doctrine, NATO, SEATO, etc. (These may have been warnings well taken, but, despite Vietnam, no one without infinite knowledge can yet really know whether Soviet behavior was accurately foretold.)

The similarity arises because the full flowering of the planners' vision would approach a domestic equivalent of this Cold War urgency. Indeed, as Harvey Sapolsky has pointed out, the key to the oft-mentioned "success stories" of systematic planning, Polaris submarines and the Apollo landing, was actually the Cold War consensus, which gave each unchallenged priority status.* This agreement on urgent goals was far more important for both programs than any special analytic techniques.

The centerpiece of the new call to swift, centralized action is again the domino theory—now generalized to all the evils of domestic policy. Once we feared that an unfriendly regime in Laos would inevitably bring the "fall" of Vietnam and Cambodia, and that in turn would undermine Thailand, then the Philippines, then even Japan or West Berlin. Our alliances appeared as a tightly linked, explosive system, where every action carried a cumulative impact, so that if the initial evil were not countered, the international system would explode.

Nowadays, after Vietnam, one may ask, who believes this sort of thing? Why do (among others) environmentalists, who see nature's tightly linked systems violated with catastrophic consequences as the earth freezes or boils over, ozone is depleted, oceans die, on and on?

Just as in our perception of the balance of power, each action in the

---

* Harvey M. Sapolsky, *The Polaris System Development: Bureaucratic and Programmatic Success in Government* (Cambridge, Mass.: Harvard University Press, 1972).

planners' proposed system is linked to the next, where one misstep today leads to greater danger tomorrow, on into the future. When all systems are interrelated, a single mistake opens the door to cumulative evils ahead. The variety of areas where this approach might be applied can be seen from the numerous calls for impact statements. Inflation impact statements may have lapsed with Gerald Ford, but energy, health, research, and safety statements are all on the agenda. Environmental impact statements have now permeated the smallest segments of governmental activity. As we write this, the city of New York is processing a 50-page environmental report, pursuant to federal regulations, for converting a vacant lot in Flatbush into a playground. (There has even been a proposal that planning itself should be subject to *planning* impact statements.)

Discerning the impacts in any one of these areas could be productive and effective. But the process, in essence, is a claim for special priority for certain types of impact. Applied to all impacts it creates a world of all constants and no variables. Where each possible impact must get precedence there is no room for tradeoffs, bargaining, or judgment. One consistent voice must be dominant.

When all policy areas are subjected to interrelated impact statements we would achieve an anticipatory democracy. In that world we would expect each of these areas to take on the same characteristics prominent at the height of the Cold War: secrecy, "cooperation" or deference to executive leadership, and an insistence on the moral authority of the president to make these (unending) crucial choices. A prophylactic presidency, in fact, could only succeed if it were invested with enormous faith (action in the absence of things seen), for that is what is required to trust leadership when it acts to control dangers that cannot yet be observed.

Which activists believe that their policy concerns would be better served by a prophylactic presidency in an anticipatory democracy? Only environmentalists, public health doctors, energy analysts, cancer researchers, White House aides—the list grows quickly.

The planning and orientation of President Carter's energy program, for example, might be a blueprint for anticipatory democracy. As reconstructed by the *New York Times,* "the plan was conceived in secrecy by technicians," and "reflected a detached, almost apolitical attitude." The Secretary of Transportation was not privy to the plans for automobile taxes, and even the senior economic officials were in the dark until the last minute. The atmosphere "was one of wartime urgency." Schlesinger and his aides "functioned as if they were a self-contained unit and their task as hush-hush as the Manhattan Project."

The program that came out of this process was then presented to the public in exactly the same spirit. The key to the plan, noted Richard Rovere, "was to convince the public that a crisis existed or, at least, was imminent, and that a failure to meet it with a 'comprehensive' policy would invite 'national catastrophe.' " It was only consistent, then, with the overall approach for Carter to summarize the proposal as "the moral equivalent of war."

These hallmarks of the prophylactic presidency—secret and centralized policy-making, then demands for urgency and faith—appear (in less virulent form) in several other recent experiences. The swine flu vaccine decisions also were made swiftly and privately. Only when President Ford had committed himself to the new vaccine were Congress and the country informed. Then, in another atmosphere of emergency, Congress was bidden to ratify the president's choice before the impending evil arrived. No independent evaluation was desired or achieved.

In another area, norms consistent with anticipatory democracy have already been routinized through legislation. The saccharin decisions highlighted the fact that the Food and Drug Administration (FDA), by statute, must ban any food substance that shows any trace of carcinogenic properties in animals. This freezes into law a two-step scientific extrapolation. First, it assumes that any cancer found in animals will be similarly produced in humans; and second, that cancer produced in a few animals by very high doses (the normal testing procedure) is equivalent to the cancer that might be found if large numbers of animals were actually given normal doses. This type of data can only be appropriate within a larger scientific context, where overall risks can be weighed against benefits lost. Where, as in the saccharin case, benefits vary with individuals, only they can judge the tradeoffs.

The FDA, however, is given no discretion to consider ambiguous or even contrary scientific evidence, economic costs in relation to probable benefits, or public opinion. Under the law (only special legislation can provide exemption) a showing of potential carcinogenic danger, no matter how uncertain, leads to immediate action.

This pattern might be called the collectivization of risk. Citizens are not allowed to decide for themselves what risks they will face. Individual judgment and choice are replaced by governmental action that automatically wards off evils before they manifest themselves. Yet if presidents act to avoid every imagined evil, where will their control end . . . or begin?

FOUR TYPES OF PRESIDENCIES

The prophylactic or preventive presidency is an ideal type. Its features have purposely been exaggerated so they will stand out in bold relief. In order to make the contrast even sharper, we should compare it with several other presidential models. The evident opposite of a preventive presidency is a reactive presidency, which would attempt to deal with problems after rather than before they manifested themselves. Its information costs would be lower, because it would be reacting to problems instead of trying to anticipate them. Its political costs would be mixed: on one hand, because the problems would be apparent, it would be less difficult to mobilize consent; on the other hand, because the evils were already being experienced, discontent might reduce its political support.

Both prevention and reaction, however, deal only with the scope of decision, that is, of which problems are accepted or rejected as worthy of solution. To get at the means to these ends, at the mobilization of consent, we also need an explicitly political dimension, focusing on power. The political problem is whether the presidency is to remain the institution par excellence that steps in when all others fail to function, as it has often done in recent times, or whether it will be content to play its part by performing its essential functions. The dualism inherent in the office has never been between an active and inactive presidency, as if the question were one of individual vigor, but of the relative domain of the institution.

A pluralist presidency operates in a constitutional context (as Neustadt put it so well) of separated institutions sharing powers. Its purpose is to perform the tasks especially entrusted to it, but it is not responsible for the functioning of other institutions, nor, when there is disagreement, is it required to coerce them. The pluralist presidency takes a systematic view; it is but one part of a larger whole whose interaction (hence its stress on compromise and bargaining) is more important than its individuality. All elements of the system, not only the presidency, have legitimate mandates from the people.

Governor Brown's style in California illustrates this view in un-usually pure form. Coming from a tradition of egalitarianism and sus-picion of the moral meaning of mass consumption, Brown was the first to apply both these norms—more equality, less consumption—to gov-ernment; hence balanced budgets, and salary increases for state em-ployees in absolutely equal (instead of proportional) amounts so as to help the worst off economically. The cartoon showing a motorist ap-proaching the California border gazing at a sign saying Depress Expec-tations captures the prevailing impression that the governor is telling people what they have long known—to wit, that government cannot make them happy.

The governor also expressed an idea about proportioning responsi-bility. Just as government was not properly responsible (i.e., should not be held accountable in public) for the state of society, which had its own inner dynamics, so too the governor, as chief executive, should keep himself in order (hence his refusal to live in the opulent new mansion) but is not responsible for the legislature. If, after reasonable activity on his part, the legislature refused to share his views on farm labor, he would wait until a more propitious moment for it to agree. For a time, then, he accepted stalemate as proper.

The theory expressed in the Federalist Papers (though no wholly authoritative interpretation can be given) suggests that stalemate was both possible and proper until majorities in House and Senate, and the president, were well agreed.* Justice might be divine but transient majorities were not. The framers hoped that time would cool passion, size would dilute it, and institutional invention confound it, so that no interest opposed to most men's ideas of justice would last long enough to prevail. About defense, to be sure, they were more concerned and gave presidents larger powers, but they did say that Congress alone could declare war or supply the armed forces. To prevent war or to prepare for it, presidents were made commanders in chief, but the thing itself—the power to declare and wage war—was not given to presidents alone.

Several recent presidents, in contrast, operated on the assumptions of a different model, where superiority instead of stalemate is the proper relationship. This predominant presidency tries to overcome

---

* This sentence is based on a lecture given by James Sterling Young at the Graduate School of Public Policy, University of California, Berkeley.

obstructions created by other institutions. It assumes the right to step in when, in its opinion, they fail to function. Its electoral mandate, being the only one that comes from all the people, has the largest legitimacy. When the predominant presidency is thwarted, therefore, it feels, as we say, free to go over the heads of other institutions to renew its mandate so as to coerce them into compliance.

Putting the two dimensions of scope (prevention versus reaction) and power (pluralist versus predominant) together, we get a fourfold table. Categories A and B are symmetrical: a preventive presidency should work well if it is also predominant (category A); a reactive presidency appears comfortably imbedded in a pluralistic system (category B) where its limited scope facilitates accommodation. Category C (where a predominant presidency is also reactive) is easiest because its capacity to mobilize resources is far greater than the tasks it assigns itself. The Eisenhower presidency with regard to foreign policy fits this model well. It is category D that deserves our attention because a presidency whose aspirations are preventive must work within a political system that remains essentially pluralist.

Of course, the prophylactic presidency is only a model and an extreme one at that. No one expects an entire presidency to become prophylactic in all areas all at once. The question is one of proportion and degree.

The struggle of a preventive presidency with its pluralist heritage, its efforts to escape the bounds of pluralism into the peace of predominance by making its power compatible with its desires, is in the making. The would-be prophylactic presidency, combining prevention with predominance, makes huge demands for knowledge and power.

FOUR TYPES OF PRESIDENCIES

Scope

	Preventive	Reactive
Pluralist	D	B
Predominant	A	C

Power

Knowledge is required for anticipation, and power for support of its broad-gauged policies. The demand for knowledge means that those who can produce it will be favored. The demand for power means that other institutions will be threatened.

What will they fight over? Money, naturally. The politics of prevention is expensive. The cost of anticipating evils, those that might have come about as well as those that might not, is enormous. (Biologists tell of organisms that die not so much because they are invaded by lethal foreign bodies as because the attack immobilized all their defense mechanisms at once, thereby leading to annihilation by exhaustion.) Ways must be found, therefore, either to raise huge sums by taxation or to get citizens to bear the costs themselves. By asking who benefits from (as well as who pays for) the prophylactic presidency, we should be better able to discern its future patterns of action.

THE POLITICS OF PREVENTION

Who benefits from the prophylactic presidency? Its purpose is to ward off evils that have not yet manifested themselves, by spreading the risk around. Who gains from the collectivization of risk?

To find out we must examine how costs are assessed when risks are collectivized. We might call the process "market socialism." Instead of costs appearing directly in the government budget, to be supported by taxes or borrowing, they are passed on to consumers indirectly through higher costs for producers. Indeed costs may even appear as government revenues—taxes on business—that are also ultimately passed through to consumers. When new safety standards are imposed, for example, relatively small governmental expenditures appear for inspectors, but much larger ones are incurred by industry for more equipment, additional safety supervisors, and new tests, which become part of production costs. Naturally, the consumer identifies the company, not the government, with the higher price. Think of restrictions on housing density, more insulation, safety features, and the like: they raise the cost of housing, diffusing it among the population, with only a few inspectors to show on the side of governmental expenditure. And, finally, consider effluent charges: by placing a tax on pollution, government hopes to make it in the interest of producers to reduce levels of noxious substances, without direct regulation. Rather than spend money to clear up streams, government gets money from producers who become, in effect, tax collectors from private citizens. Market socialism is the name for this reverse tax process—government controls private behavior not by taxing citizens and spending the proceeds, but by getting private companies to do the taxing while still supervising the spending.

The chief concomitants of market socialism are its low visibility, its capital intensity, and its social selectivity. Consider first the obscurity of market socialism. By combining collective control with private collection, market socialism obfuscates cause and effect between the public and private sectors. Which one, for instance, is responsible for the increase in housing costs? Which one is responsible for the higher cost of safety features in manufacturing? Suppose, to make the contrast vivid, the government closes down a plant because it is unsafe for workers or neighbors. Everyone can see what is happening. Should workers and neighbors prefer to accept existing hazards to losing employment, they might make their will felt. Suppose, however, that environmental and safety regulations prevent a plant from locating in this low-income area and shift it to a suburb. Who would know about the mental calculations of a manufacturer passing over a location? It is more difficult to mobilize over things no one ever had in distinction to those about to be taken away.

Allied with low visibility, adding an element of intellectual mystery, is market socialism's widespread displacement of expensive effects on to unsuspecting (and unconsenting) adults. Take the well-known potential for drug lag: by requiring innumerable trials and procedures, as well as levels of safety difficult to prove, drugs that might be forthcoming may not be produced, are produced later, or at a higher cost. But this is not all; drug companies, desirous of following up promising leads, try out new drugs in foreign countries where standards are lower. Our safety is, therefore, bought by their risk.

Though problem displacement in place of problem solution has come to prominence in law enforcement (where plentiful police patrol in some precincts leads criminals to move their operations to adjacent ones), the phenomenon has distinct analogues in the field of auto safety. As various safety measures have been mandated—seat belts, collapsible steering columns, shatter-resistant windshields, etc.—accidents have declined in severity. But, as drivers have gained in security, the number of accidents per mile driven has increased. Not only have accidents been displaced from severity to frequency, however, but also from drivers to pedestrians, larger to smaller cars, faster to slower cars, newer to older cars, etc.

So much attention has been devoted to policies concerning safety because this area is openly concerned with the socialization of risk. The signs of the times if one cares to look are also evident in less likely places. Consider the phenomenon of "redlining," which refers to the practice of mortgage lending institutions refusing to loan (or loaning less) in neighborhoods where they believe the risk is too great. Initial discussions focused on whether these neighborhoods had actually declined so that the risk really was excessive, or whether banks were actually contributing to the decline through discriminatory practices not based on economic considerations. Of late, however, there is less interest in empirical investigation of the charge (several studies suggest it is unfounded in certain places) and more in defining redlining. Why? By emphasizing this charge, pressure is put on lenders to expand resources available for mortgages in poor and minority neighborhoods. In effect, if discrimination is not practiced, this is a housing subsidy. Now the government could provide direct subsidies, but a more sophisticated generation of officials has come to believe that government does a bad job of containing risk in housing whereas banks are better. Who, then, pays for provision of funds to high-risk neighborhoods? Bank stockholders or other mortgage holders who respectively receive less or pay more. Instead of government paying a subsidy, which shows up in its budget, the subsidy is diffused among numerous stock and mortgage holders, and administration is left to the lending institution. By bearing the costs of a social welfare policy, the housing market is being socialized though not nationalized. Considerations of this sort suggest that a prophylactic presidency, collectivizing risk through market socialism, has a differential impact on people of different social and economic status. The lower classes—with no car or a smaller one and lesser income to absorb price increases—will not do so well. The very people, presumably, who are supposed to benefit from the collectivization of risk turn out to be the losers. Why this should be so, how the underlying mechanism works, should be clarified by investigating the other sides of market socialism, its capital intensity and social selectivity.

What happens when government seeks to anticipate a wide variety of risks or to mitigate those that do exist? There is a decrease in the amount available for investment to create future jobs or for current expenditure to support jobs. To some extent, however, there is a substitution effect as jobs devoted to production give way to jobs supporting safety. (Whatever happens, however, the price goes up because consumers buy safety whether they want to or not.) What kinds of jobs are these? They are filled by middle-class technicians and upper-middle-class professionals—inspectors, clerks, lawyers, etc. What jobs did they displace? Working-class production jobs. Wherever possible, in addition, companies make intensive use of labor-saving machinery, because that is where they can make economies, thereby displacing manual workers. But they have no choice, according to government regulations, other than to hire middle-class people who can perform the necessary regulatory functions. In this there is a certain symmetry: the prophylactic presidency is a style of government suitable for people who already have more than enough and want to safeguard it; why shouldn't they be the ones to make jobs out of preserving their way of life?

Having shown who gains economically from the prophylactic presidency, it remains to be seen who is in the best position to profit politically. The answer is twofold: those who run it and those who run on its platform. Who is most capable of anticipating evil in order to eliminate it before it can get started? Imaginative intellectuals, otherwise known as theorists or model builders. The day of large-scale systems analysts, with their computer simulation models of all important sectors of the economy, will have arrived. What happens inside their models, where it is difficult even for experts to see because of the interaction of myriads of variables, will be of much greater importance than whatever is observable outside—witness swine flu, saccharin, et al.—because the object of public policy is not corrective but preventive. Who loses? People who trade in common sense because the purpose of public policy is precisely to avoid experience.

What kind of party could make most use of the politics of prevention? Its class composition would be upper-middle and upper because maintaining old amenities would be more important than creating new ones. It would be opposed to compromises to maintain production and employment, because this is the very mentality—wait until evils manifest themselves before correcting them—against which they have organized their struggle. Only a party of purists—no risks, no compromises—would promote a prophylactic presidency. It would, therefore, need principles that would unite its members who otherwise might split into differing professional or ethnic or partisan groupings. Decision-making would approach the unanimity principle. Policies would necessarily be procedural—one man-one vote, open hearings, periodic review of all programs, publication of assets by office holders, legal due process—because it is easier to get agreement on how to act as opposed to what to do. Prophylaxis and purity, after all, have much in common. Substances must be pure, procedures must be pure, politicians must be pure.

The closest we have yet come to a party of purists are the public interest lobbies, Ralph Nader's various entities, and Common Cause. But they are not political parties. They oppose parties because parties cannot be pure. These public interest lobbies have made it their mission to weaken all other intermediary organizations—parties, corporations, labor unions, interest groups—that stand between government and citizen. These intermediaries cannot be pure because they must go beyond procedures to bargain over the substance of legislation designed to benefit certain groups at the expense of others. A no-growth ethic fits well with prophylactic politics. Only if there is a larger domestic product, with more for everyone, or more for some but not less for others, would severe social conflict be mitigated. But this would mean putting resources into production, not prevention. The struggle over who should pay for a politics of prevention, therefore, is likely to aggravate conflicts among institutions over who should rule, i.e., over whether a pluralist presidency should become more predominant.

THE PROPHYLACTIC PRESIDENCY
VERSUS THE FEDERAL SYSTEM

If planning is to be more than an eternal exercise, it must actually guide the making of governmental decisions. Governmental actions (and the private activities they seek to influence) must in large measure conform to the plan if it is to have practical effect. Yet as soon as the prevalence of disagreement over social goals or policies is admitted into the discussion, it becomes clear that there can be no planning without the ability to cause others to act differently than they otherwise would. Hence effective planning assumes necessary power.

Demands that the president become planner in chief, viewed in this light, become demands for a radical redistribution of power within the federal system. If planning assumes power, then lurking behind the facade of planning without politics is a president whose power allows no opposition. These new prophylactic presidents must discern future evils and then carry out their plan for preventing them.

That assertion of coercive power goes to the heart of the unresolved relationship between the presidency and the other actors in a federal system. For power is a reciprocal relationship that must be viewed in its social context. It depends not only on what one actor can do but on how the other relevant actors respond in turn. The wielders of power are restricted not only by the limits on their own resources but also by the capacities of the respondents. Thus prophylactic presidents need not only increased authority of their own, but also to directly diminish the resources that could be employed contrary to their will. Other federal actors must be subordinated to the plan.

A prophylactic presidency can emerge, then, only through a determined struggle to undermine other independent political actors. There is no consensual way for the new demands to mesh with our traditional system. So far we have only seen the first moves in this conflict.

Consider, for example, the full implementation of the swine flu decisions described earlier. While the presidentially proclaimed emergency carried the day with Congress and much of the press, other actors were not so easily swayed. The actual inoculations were the responsibility of state and local health departments, who need not be responsive to the president, since they have their own resources and constituencies. As a result, there was extreme variation in local activity and thus in the proportion of the population ultimately reached. They ranged from over 70 percent in Wyoming to less than 20 percent in New York City. Massachusetts declined to conduct any mass campaign at all.

The drug companies, the major interest group involved, also played a key role. They declined for several months to schedule full-scale distribution of the vaccine, until Congress accepted the precedent that the government rather than the companies would be liable for damage suits arising from its use. Even the armed forces defined emergency in their own fashion, choosing a different type of vaccine, with higher immunity but more side effects, than that recommended by civilian scientists.

A fully established prophylactic presidency could have tolerated none of these deviations once the emergency was invoked. Presidents engaged in forestalling evil could not allow states to make independent choices; rather they need French-style prefects who are in place to carry out orders, not to question their value. Nor could interest groups be allowed to trade issues of value to them in return for cooperation. Negotiations take time and compromises weaken the consistency of the plan. Most of all, prophylactic presidents would have to make the federal bureaucracy responsive to their will, for others would not follow the path that their own troops openly abandon.

But all these independent actors are more than inconvenient obstacles to presidential rationality and control—they are the heart of the federal system. The essence of federalism, as Martin Landau has written, is overlap and redundancy:

> . . . what appears is a truly messy system—one that is anathema to our prevailing conceptions of a viable organization. There is no unity of command, and there are no unequivocal lines of authority. Domains overlap, jurisdictions are confused, and accountability is dispersed. And for each citizen there is at the least, two of everything. . . . Virtually every aspect, every feature, every agency, and every structure of government was duplicated and still redundancy was not exhausted.*

The crucial point unseen by advocates of planning is that this system is *intended,* in fact planned. But it is planning with a different aim: fostering choice through careful structuring of social interaction.

Traditional planning is defended not for what it accomplishes but for what it symbolizes—rationality. Planning is conceived to be the way in which intelligence is applied to social problems. Its virtue is that it embodies universal criteria of rational choice: the efforts of planners presumably result in policy proposals that are systematic, efficient, coordinated, and consistent.

Planning by intellectual cogitation is meant to avoid surprise by conscious control instead of allowing social interaction to proceed willy-nilly. Life is organized as if it occurred in a single mind with all actors assigned roles and given a script in which the hero triumphs over the villain. Federalism seeks to structure choice in a different way. Choice is the result of many preferences that interact as the participants bid and bargain with each other. Interactive modes of choice depend on learning from error as it occurs, in a series of adjustments in which

---

* Martin Landau, "Federalism, Redundancy, and System Reliability," *Publius* 3 (1973): 188.

participants compare what they want with what they can get. A preventative politics substitutes a single mind for many as all must play their preassigned parts to avoid drastic disorder. Federalism seeks to structure choice in a different way. Social interactions occur and those deemed good are rationalized after the fact as appropriate. When results are regretted, social interaction in political arenas and economic markets is not replaced by central control but given structural adjustment to perfect the pattern of outcomes. Interactive modes of choices depend on learning from error after it occurs, in a series of adjustments, not all at once through a preventative politics because that substitutes a single mind alone for many.

This complex, messy system is a permanent challenge for those who find their rationality in hierarchies. The model of social interaction implicit in the planners' vision has no place for the varied intermediary groups that characterize our political system: political parties, congressional committees, interest groups, states, semi-autonomous agencies. None of these are needed if cognitive calculation can provide one best choice; and all stand in the way of the "direct" relationship between a prophylactic president and the people.

The potential political consequences at stake in these alternate models can be seen if we consider the extreme case—if our political institutions were indeed reshaped to eliminate duplication and to promote coherence. First the executive and the legislature would not need staggered terms, nor different constituencies, nor for that matter distinct representation. One set of members could serve all the roles, like the British M.P.s they would then resemble.

The British parliamentary system, however, has evolved a set of informal norms that diffuse the enormous pressures that a unitary system would otherwise channel to the prime minister at its center. British government is a federation of departments. Individual ministers themselves take responsibility for departmental choices, and the Cabinet, not the P.M., is collectively responsible for major decisions. Responsible parties also serve as an independent focus for policy-making.

Yet a prophylactic presidency, unprotected by British conventions, would face increased pressures toward the center with less buffers than before. For no president can ever assemble the knowledge and power needed to control all the future dangers he would then be held responsible for. (What if we run short of oil after a master energy plan has been implemented?) At the same time these unruly intermediary groups, which now serve to buffer the expectations directed toward presidents, would be undercut. They would be too strong to take over and too weak to share responsibilities that could overwhelm presidents. Hence the planners' model, seeking to impose central cognitive choice in place of social interaction, would probably just disrupt the interaction instead. A prophylactic presidency, enmeshed in the remains of a federalist system, could well combine the worst aspects of both.

Yet demands for increased presidential power, Watergate notwithstanding, are bound to grow. Left opinion is momentarily immobilized around fear of excessive power crushing liberty, and concern that the executive may become too weak to implement social programs. The right is divided over whether to stop at the present level of government expenditures, thus accepting a higher proportion than doctrine deems desirable, or to attempt to drive it down, thus courting disaster at the polls. Conservatives might be willing to give up a strong domestic presidency, where the more done the better, but not at the expense of a strong defense and foreign policy presidency, which must be operated by one and the same individual and institution.

The prophylactic presidency is, of course, a developmental construct designed to push certain trends, as yet dimly perceived, to an extreme conclusion. Insofar as it is not wholly a product of our disordered imaginations, it reflects a lack of confidence in existing social relations. When people trust each other, and they have confidence in the institutions through which they relate to one another, they have sufficient belief in themselves to deal with most difficulties as these arise, and sufficient faith in their leaders to follow them in trying to head off a few evils before these occur. When trust declines, the need for leadership increases. Clues to the future of the presidency will be found more in how we-the-people feel about ourselves than in what presidents do to (or for) us.

The American Party System Today

Everett Carll Ladd, Jr.

M'GUINNESS

7 In the 1830s, Alexis de Tocqueville examined the U.S. party system. He reviewed the considerable contributions of the Federalist party to the republic, arguing that "the period of Federalist power was, in my view, one of the luckiest circumstances attending the birth of the great American Union."[1] But for all their virtues, Tocqueville noted, the Federalists "had the disadvantage of being inapplicable in their entirety to the society they wished to control . . . ," and they came to ruin. For the first time in U.S. history, but not the last, one part or feature of the party system became "out of phase" with the demands of the society.

Over the last decade, there has been a renewed sense of something "out of phase" in American party politics. Each of the last four presidential elections, for example, has manifested much negativism, frequent suggestion of voter dissatisfaction with the alternatives before them, the sense of electoral outcomes both unsatisfactory and in some sense unexpected.

Even if one is quite persuaded that something substantial has been wrong, of course, one can still hesitate before laying blame at the doors of party. Political parties must process the conflicts of the society they inhabit. And a period which began with the assassination of a popular young president, which was racked throughout by bitter divisions precipitated by the Vietnam War, and which culminated with the first forced resignation of a president in U.S. history, produced enough rancor to unsettle any party system.

Entirely aware that many of the dissatisfactions associated with party performance are not attributable to the party system, I nonetheless argue that the latter is malfunctioning. My concern in this essay is not with all the ills that beset the polity but with one set of related problems that appears to have its origins in the way parties are organized to go about their job. I find the malperformance basic and in the structure of the contemporary party system, and I find the consequences serious.

Having chosen to view party performance critically, I would caution against overstating the magnitude of the problem. Tocqueville comes back to mind. He was not at all happy about the state of affairs in U.S. politics in the 1830s, especially as it involved the party system. But with characteristic wisdom he recognized that there were at least two ways of interpreting the condition he deplored. "To a foreigner almost all the Americans' domestic quarrels seem at first glance either incomprehensible or puerile and one does not know *whether to pity a people that takes such wretched trifles seriously or to envy the luck enabling it to do so.*"[2] I feel much the same today. It is indeed a lucky republic where critics can permit themselves to become preoccupied with the order of the problem I emphasize here.

THE PROBLEM

Political parties in the sense we know them—as instruments designed to organize mass publics politically and to serve as linkage between the public and the government—first took form in the United States in the 1790s. While parties are now found in most countries, the chronological record of party systems is coterminous with that of the American republic.

The intimacy of the connection between the United States and political parties does not rest solely, of course, on the fact that the two share a common birth. The character of the party system has been closely linked—as effect but also as cause—to the character of American social-political experience and performance. Clinton Rossiter had this in mind when he offered this "string of assumptions". "No America without democracy, no democracy without politics, no politics without parties, no parties without compromise and moderation."[3] American society had delivered accommodationist parties, Rossiter argued, and such parties in turn had left a distinctive stamp on the political life of the country.

The United States, like any polity with a high level of popular participation, has asked much of its party system. Such changes as the development of a pervasive electronic communications system, a significant further elaboration of interest groups, and an increasingly leisured, educated, and hence independent-minded citizenry distinguish the contemporary context for party activity from that of earlier periods in the country's first two centuries. But the party system retains exclusive custody of one core democratic function—aggregating the preferences of a mass electorate for political leadership and thereby converting what was general and diffuse into specific electoral decisions.

Performance of this aggregation-conversion function is the *raison d'être* of a democratic party system. Because this function is so critical to a democracy like the United States, it matters much how well or how poorly the parties perform it. And though other institutions have come forward to claim certain of the functions associated historically with the American parties—such as the transmission of political information and assessment, which has been assumed increasingly by the national communications media—there is no rival claimant in sight for the aggregating-converting role. The parties must play it, or it does not get performed. Today in the United States, that performance leaves much to be desired.

To do an effective job of aggregating and converting popular wishes, the American party system must manifest three distinct capabilities.[4] First, the parties must be able to plan for nominee selection. Whatever the song may claim, it's a big world after all, specifically a big country. The potential electorate in the United States (persons of voting age) numbered in 1976 about 150 million. This public comprises a considerable range of interests, hopes and fears, values, preferences as to candidate style, and the like. It will never be possible for two national parties (or three, or four) to offer presidential nominees who will seem "an ideal choice" to everyone, and in some electoral circumstances it may be hard to avoid frustrating many voters. The chances that any given pair of presidential contenders will produce various unforeseeable dissatisfactions among the electorate are also high—whatever the selection system. But for there to be a reasonable prospect that the candidates will be seen regularly by most people as a good distillation of their interests and expectations, the parties must have a mechanism that is at once able *to assess popular wishes and to convert those wishes into candidates.* This is what, in my usage here, planning requires. The capacity of the Democratic and Republican parties to plan for presidential nominee selection, in particular, has diminished notably over the last fifteen years.

Second, and following on from the capability just mentioned, the parties' selection mechanisms must insure representativeness. Any party must be expected to include groups more inclined to the selection of nominees whose public philosophies are compatible with the group's, than to the choice of nominees with views that best fit the expectations of the rank-and-file party supporters. But effective aggregation and conversion of popular wishes require that each major party begin general election campaigns with candidates broadly representative of the wishes (style, policy perspectives, and the like) of those voters making up its "regular expected majority." To the extent selection processes and mechanisms advantage sectors of the party with particularistic (as opposed to catholic) preferences for candidates, the ability to be representative is diminished. Such a diminution has occurred in the United States, again especially at the presidential level.

Third, the party system must be able to deliver sustained and reasonably even competition if the aggregating-converting function is to be performed effectively. Assume that one party is in control of a set of offices—for example, Congress—and that citizenry dissatisfaction with legislative output is substantial. If a second party closely challenges the majority alignment, the conversion of the dissatisfaction into electoral decisions is readily accomplished. The "outs" become the "ins." But if the majority party goes underchallenged, voter discontent finds restricted expression. Third parties and protest movements may materialize, but these are likely to be consequential only in selected races, not as a vehicle for sustained electoral expression.

Especially in selecting nominees for national leadership, the American party system now has a notably reduced capacity to plan. And its representation capability is diminished. Throughout, the party system is insufficiently competitive. As a result, while it continues to aggregate and convert popular wishes, it does so less well than it might—less well than we might reasonably expect—and the polity suffers as a result.

THE INABILITY TO PLAN

In the fall of 1976, together with Martin Lipset, I directed a national telephone survey of the electoral preferences of America's professors.[5] We found that faculty did not intend to sit out the election—96 percent of them said they would vote. And those going to the polls planned to vote in the now-customary academic fashion, heavily Democratic. Jimmy Carter led Gerald Ford by a margin of roughly two to one in academe. But the most notable feature of the faculty's candidate perceptions involved not their ultimate choice but rather their dissatisfaction with both principal contenders. An extraordinary 54 percent of the professoriate argued that "We really do not have any adequate major party nominee this year. Neither the Republicans nor the Democrats have nominated a man well suited to be president." A full 50 percent of those professors who intended to vote for Jimmy Carter maintained that their choice was not well suited to be president; 44 percent of Ford backers made the same judgment of their candidate.

This negativism characterized the population generally. All polls revealed an exceptionally high proportion of the population undecided right up to election day as to how they would vote and unenthusiastic about both Ford and Carter. Why was there this dissatisfaction?

The easiest answer, and at one level obviously the right answer, is that neither contender performed especially well—that we happened to have in 1976 two candidates who did not particularly impress the American people. It could have been only a chance occurrence.

But negativism has been with us for four presidential elections now—since 1964—although the form has varied considerably. We know, for example, that while Nixon won by a large margin in 1972, many people were dissatisfied with the alternatives offered them that election year. Eight years earlier, Lyndon Johnson had trounced Barry Goldwater in a contest more notable for its rejection than its affirmation.

In earlier writing, I described the 1964 and 1972 elections as "unnatural landslides":

> Twice now in eight years, presidential candidates who might have normally expected to win at best modest majorities, have become the recipients of massive victories, winning by margins at the upper limits in American presidential history. Perhaps more impressive than the issues of 1964 and 1972, and personal attributes of the victorious and vanquished candidates, is the fact of landslides which by conventional rules of American presidential politics should not have been— "unnatural" landslides.[6]

Richard Nixon was never an exceptionally popular political figure. With the country still mired in the Vietnam War, with the economy in considerable trouble, it would be hard to argue that the events of the day were so massively favorable as to ensure an easy triumph for the incumbent party. And Nixon was, as well, leader of the minority party. Yet even though the usual conditions for a landslide did not apply, he won such a victory. His 60.8 percent of the popular vote and his 23.2 percentage point margin over his principal challenger rank among the largest electoral margins in U.S. history. Other than Johnson's position as the majority party candidate, much the same thing had occurred in 1964. In an election that might have been expected to yield a modest Democratic victory, Johnson won by 16 million votes over Goldwater and received the highest proportion of the total popular vote ever recorded by an American presidential candidate.

There is every indication that the consequences of these "unnatural" landslides were severe. The only way an electorate can leave its mark upon the policy process is by saying yes or no to the alternatives presented to it. An era of negative landslides carries serious consequences, then, for democratic decision-making. Large numbers of voters feel deprived of a satisfactory choice. Big majorities are produced, but these are in no sense mandates. A lack of competitiveness and a general atmosphere of negativism reduce the incentive to participate and render campaigns a far less meaningful medium for policy debate. Ultimately demoralized oppositions are unable to test the victors effectively.

The 1976 presidential election did not, of course, produce a landslide victory for either of the major party contenders. The Democratic nominee enjoyed a slight edge, but the election remained in doubt until the early hours of November 3. Still, the 1976 election appears to be part of the series begun in 1964. With this twist. Rather than an "unnatural landslide," 1976 produced "unnatural deadlock."

The Democrats by all rights should have won easily in the 1976 presidential balloting. They came out of their presidential nominating convention in New York a relatively united party. After the searing defeat of 1972, there was an inclination to sheath ideological knives, to rally around the nominee in the interest of regaining control of the White House. At the same time, the Republicans were laboring under exceptional burdens. Both the president and the vice president elected under the Republican banner in 1972 had been forced to resign in disgrace amid major scandal. The economy suffered through high unemployment and high inflation under the Republican administration. The body of core supporters of the Republican party had reached its lowest point since 1856.

Were this not enough, the Republicans were led in the 1976 election by a relatively weak candidate. While widely admired on personal grounds, Gerald Ford never showed any signs of capturing his party, much less the presidency, until a beleaguered Richard Nixon nominated him for the vice presidency in the wake of Agnew's resignation. Ford's initial weakness in presidential leadership followed because he had never, in a quarter century of public life, become really a national leader—the head of a faction seriously contesting for control of the presidential party. After assuming the presidency, Ford continued to suffer from a widespread perception, held by both elites and by the mass public, that he was insufficiently "presidential," lacking in those leadership qualities demanded by the office.

This public perception was dramatically reinforced by the events of spring and early summer 1976. While Carter was locking up the Democratic nomination, Ford was in deep trouble within his own party. He lost the North Carolina primary of late March, was clobbered in Texas and Georgia, lost Indiana and Nebraska, was trounced in Nevada, dropped in South Dakota, and was solidly defeated in Montana and California. In between these setbacks, there were triumphs, of course, but an overall image was reinforced: Ford was seen to be "weak," not a leader. He could not master his own party—how could he expect to lead the free world?

This list of Republican debits and initial Democratic advantages in 1976 can be extended, but the point is evident enough. When a united majority party confronts a divided, incumbent minority party, beset by one of the most celebrated political scandals in U.S. history, by a deteriorating economy, and by a citizenry clearly inclined to changes in leadership, it should have been no contest—1976 presented a situation where the "ins" should have been trounced.

There are many reasons to describe such a trouncing as desirable, apart from one's personal partisan preferences. When things go sour, kicking the incumbents out can contribute to a restoration of confidence. The other side should be "given a chance." The retirement of the "ins" in times of trouble appears part of the natural rhythm of democratic politics.

But the "ins" were not trounced in 1976, they were barely beaten. The electorate was dissatisfied with the incumbent, but it appeared no more attracted to the Democratic challenger.

Unnatural landslides and unnatural deadlocks: what is happening? Like a number of observers, I find the answer in the weakness of political parties in the contemporary United States. Specifically, the disappearance of party organization as the decisive intermediary in the selection of presidential nominees has made planning virtually impossible.

I should attempt, before proceeding further, to clarify what I mean by *party* in the context of this discussion. For there are two quite different uses of the term in common circulation. On the one hand, party is *symbol* and *identification*. Partisan conflict has been fought out for the most part only beneath the Republican and Democratic banners, for a span that exceeds the lifetime of any living person. Buttressed by habit as well as current application, Republican and Democrat still command the allegiance of large numbers of people. But *party* is also *organization*—by which I mean leadership and the structure and processes through which leaders operate. Here, when I refer to the weakness of parties, I intend this latter usage.

The historic weakness of political parties as organizational entities in the United States is an old story. I will not review it except to assert that it follows in large measure from the much-vaunted American individualism. Such extreme individualism seems to have been incompatible with strong party organization. Too many people have made claim on their individual rights to determine electoral outcomes—specifically, their rights, rather than those of party leaders, to control the nomination process.

Over the last decade, a new era of party "reform" activity has opened. This new surge has originated largely within the Democratic party, but in a less rapid and dramatic fashion it is evident within the Republican party as well. It comes in response to new participation claims by a substantial segment of the American public. A rather prosperous, relatively leisured, highly schooled, self-appreciative populace, able to command at a flick of a TV dial political information from an elaborate national communication structure, is simply not inclined to grant party regulars the measure of control over the presidential nominating processes they long enjoyed. Americans generally, but especially the expanding professional middle classes, want highly porous parties. *This means the dominance of primaries, and mechanisms in which the discretion of party elites or regulars is severely limited.*

In this climate of extended egalitarianism, the claim of established party leadership, working through such formal mechanisms as state committees and conventions, to a privileged place in the determination of party affairs—and in determining who secures the party nominations—became increasingly hard to defend. Over the last decade, we have added our own variations to the distinctive American conception of what democracy requires vis-à-vis internal party operations. There now seems to be remarkably wide acceptance of the idea that any substantial ability of regular party leaders to dominate the delegate-selection process and thereby to control the party's presidential nomination represents an unacceptable violation of democratic requirements.

This argument is tricky because Americans have long manifested an individualism and a lack of deference incompatible with strong party organization. But there has been a significant change over the 1960s and the 1970s. In 1952, Estes Kefauver, the Tennessee Democrat, had considerable success in the primaries. Party leaders, and Kefauver's principal rivals, Stevenson and Russell, could watch this with little concern—because they knew that control of the nomination lay within the state party organizations. The latter were not inclined toward Kefauver, and the Tennessean's edge in the primaries could be disregarded.

Why was this so? The conventional answer is that primaries were still few and that most delegates were selected by party-dominated processes. This is, of course, true, but it begs the real question. Why did the public accord legitimacy to a nominating process in which it was reduced to bystanders? Because there was still the general inclination in the United States—as there is even now and more strongly in other Western democracies—to defer to "party regulars" in the process of choosing presidential nominees.

The organization of the nomination process is obviously a key factor determining performance of the core aggregation-conversion function. And in American presidential politics up to the 1960s, state party organizations, operating through the national conventions, controlled nominations. This is no longer so—the arrangement having succumbed to the party "reform" of the late 1960s and early 1970s.

The tumultuous 1968 Democratic Convention created two commissions, one headed by George McGovern to study and make recommendations bearing on delegate selection (a commission subsequently chaired by Representative Donald Fraser of Minnesota), the other led by Representative James O'Hara of Michigan to examine convention rules and operations. Recommendations of the McGovern-Fraser Commission, implemented for the 1972 Convention, proved particularly important and generated rancorous intraparty debate.[7]

The commission insisted that internal party democracy was the primary value to be promoted. And in this context, it attacked such prevailing practices as the absence of clear rules governing delegate selection (in twenty states), a condition that left "the entire process to the discretion of a handful of party leaders"; the ability of majorities to use "their numerical superiority to deny delegate representation to the supporters of minority presidential candidates"; frequent recourse to "secret caucuses" and other vehicles of "closed slate-making"; underrepresentation of blacks, women, and youth at the national conventions; and frequent use of the "unit rule," a practice whereby a majority at a party meeting could bind a dissenting minority to vote in accordance with majority wishes. The achieved changes required that state Democratic parties "overcome the effects of past discrimination by affirmative steps" to ensure the representation of blacks, women, and young people at the national conventions and other party functions "in reasonable relationship to [the group's] presence in the population of the State." They stipulated that state parties must adopt rules that facilitate "maximum participation among interested Democrats in the processes by which National Convention delegates are selected"—through such devices as broad publicization of the time and place of all selection meetings. Use of the unit rule was banned. Minority views were to be represented in slate-making sessions, including those in states where final selection of delegates was left to statewide primary elections. The practice whereby "certain public or Party officeholders are delegates to county, State and National Conventions by virtue of their official position" was proscribed. If a state Democratic party insisted on permitting its central committee to choose delegates to the national convention, it was required to limit the number of delegates thus selected to not more than 10 percent of the total.

Two commissions set up by the 1972 Convention continued the changes in party organization and procedures: the Democratic Charter Commission, chaired by Terry Sanford; and the Commission on Delegate Selection and Party Structure, headed by Barbara Mikulski. After nearly two years of argument befitting in its complexity the internal heterogeneity of the Democratic party, the work of these commissions culminated in decisions of the Democratic National Committee and of the 1974 Conference on Democratic Policy and Organization, the so-called Kansas City miniconvention.[8]

The 1972 requirements that delegates be selected through open processes (primaries or caucuses) in which any party adherent wishing to participate could do so—at the expense of the influence of party regulars—was continued. Winner-take-all schemes of delegate selection were banned, with proportional representation required:

> At all stages of the delegate selection process, delegations shall be allocated in a fashion that fairly reflects the expressed presidential preference, uncommitted, or no preference status of the primary voters, or if there be no binding primary, the convention and caucus participants, except that preferences securing less than 15 percent (15%) of the votes cast for the delegation need not be awarded any delegates.[9]

The historic 1974 Democratic meeting, which formally adopted a charter for the national party, sustained virtually all the 1972 reforms, and in fact served to extend them.

As the Democrats were making these rather dramatic changes, the Republicans were plodding in much the same direction of openness and democratization. The low-profile Delegates and Organizations (DO) Committee served as the McGovern-Fraser Commission counterpart, and the Rule 29 Committee paralleled the Mikulski Commission.

The "reform" struggle was in large part a power struggle, as ascendant middle-class strata confronted party organizations substantially unresponsive to their claims for influence and their policy perspectives. Reform was also spurred, though, by the more disinterested intent of some to perform aggregation-conversion better—by letting all the Republican people choose their party's nominee and all the Democratic people choose theirs. But it has not worked out this way.

It is no longer possible for the parties to plan for presidential nominee selection. Party leaders can still contemplate the question of who is best suited to be the nominee, of course, but they are not able now to ensure the implementation of their judgment. At the same time, we have not achieved—probably because it is not possible to achieve—a mechanism through which "the people," meaning popular majorities, pick the candidate who is their considered choice. All sorts of bizarre outcomes are thus possible in party candidate selection and subsequently in the elections themselves. The 1976 contest is a case in point.

Were political parties still intact, were the Democratic party an organizational entity still controlling nominations for the presidency, Jimmy Carter would not have been chosen. This would have been partly for the wrong reasons—he lacked an established network of "old-boy" ties—but it would have been in part for the right reason. In the context of national presidential politics, Carter was unproved. We Americans have now created a party system that is extraordinarily contemptuous of the notion that leaders are to be "brought along," tried and seasoned gradually, rather than suddenly tossed upon the national leadership stage.

In reviewing the weakness Carter displayed and his inability to enthuse the Democrat-inclined electorate of the nation in 1976, there has been much commentary on his personal weaknesses or errors. He made mistakes, of course, but it seems more productive to emphasize problems of the mechanism rather than those of the man. Is there any reason to expect a candidate chosen through the currently employed procedures to be a strong contender in the general election? There is no place at present to introduce coherently the standard of the candidate's ability to bring together the various groups and interests in the national party and convince the electorate he is well fit to govern. One may get a strong candidate, but since there are presumably many indifferent candidates for every strong one, a mechanism that eschews planning is risky indeed.

Jimmy Carter was not perceived by the American public during the 1976 campaign as either a fool or a knave. The public mood—with regard to both contenders in fact—was one of doubt and skepticism, not hostility. Carter was seen as an inexperienced person in the context of presidential politics. The voters were not sure how he would handle the presidency. They were somewhat dissatisfied with things as they were, but they remained quite unsure that things would be better if Carter were elected. Since only 3 or 4 percent of the electorate knew who Carter was nine months before the November voting, since the vast majority of voters lacked any behavioral base on which to assess him, since most electors had seen him only on the campaign trail, is it surprising that they considered him something of an unknown, something of a question mark?

Jimmy Carter's 1976 march on Washington can properly be described as an electoral tour de force—or as an indifferent showing. To come from so far back and capture the nomination of a major party (and then the presidency) is an extraordinary achievement, one that surely should not be dismissed lightly. But Carter also manifested striking weaknesses.

He led the field by only 4,300 votes in New Hampshire, or by 5.5 percent. If Jackson, Wallace, Brown, or Humphrey had entered the New Hampshire primary, it is almost certain that Carter would not have attained the plurality that gave him a badly needed bit of early momentum. Carter had "right field" all to himself in New Hampshire, while the liberal vote was divided. After getting only 14 percent of the Massachusetts vote and running fourth, Carter won Florida with one-third of the popular vote and a lead of only 4 percent over George Wallace. Humphrey was not entered. Neither was Brown. Jackson got going late. Carter then won the Illinois popular vote handily (with 48 percent of the total vote, and a 20 percentage point lead), but only Wallace, Shriver, and Harris were on the ballot with him. The *New York Times*-CBS News Poll indicated that Hubert Humphrey would have swept the Illinois primary had he been entered.

With all the momentum thus generated, Carter won Wisconsin by only one percentage point, Michigan by two-tenths of a point. He lost in Nebraska, was trounced in Idaho, Nevada, and Maryland, was solidly beaten in Oregon, was defeated in the New Jersey delegate voting, was swamped in California. He had much earlier done poorly in the New York delegate race. Out of these raw materials one could easily build a hypothetical progression of early defeat, loss of momentum, drift back into the pack, and disintegration.

There is also the largely forgotten fact that after Carter had acquired a lead during the primary season, he was typically unable to hold it. Thus, in state after state, from Florida through Michigan and Wisconsin, he saw his lead over contending Democrats weaken in the last days before the primary voting—a datum indicated by the surveys of the candidate's own pollster, Patrick Caddell. Just as once his nomination appeared well-nigh irresistible, he began to get beaten badly by a young California governor.

One may argue, still, that winning primaries is the best test of electability, and that Carter won more of those in 1976 than any other

Democrat. The weakness of the claim that presidential primary victories indicate a popular mandate is revealed most clearly by the following: only 20 percent of the voting-age public in the states that held presidential preference contests actually cast ballots in the Democratic primaries of 1976; Carter received the votes of about 6 percent—and this in the context of crowded fields and a changing mix of possible alternatives from one state to another. This 6 percent was more than any other Democrat received, and as translated through the party's current delegate selection procedures it gave Carter the victory. But it hardly indicates he was the choice of "the people."

We have been reduced presidentially to an overweening individualism. Each individual entrepreneur (candidate) sets up shop and markets his wares—himself. The buyers—the voters—don't find the same choice of merchandise in all the states, and one seller, who may attract only a small segment of all the buyers, is finally granted a monopoly. Candidates are able to win, then, because of crowded fields, low turnouts, strategic miscalculations by their opponents—but above all because there is no one to mind the store.

Shortly before the 1976 election, James Reston scolded his *New York Times'* readers for their lack of enthusiasm and commitment. Even though you don't know Carter very well and you feel uncertain about him, Reston argued, you know the Democratic party very well, and Carter is the Democratic nominee. Vote for the party, not for the man.[10] The advice is entirely reasonable—in some other electoral system. We have built a presidency shaped by individual attributes of the person who holds the office at a given point in time. We have systematically dismantled national party mechanisms. In this situation, voters can do only one thing—they can look at the individual nominees and decide which one is better fit to be president. It is little short of nonsense to substantially remove party from both the selection of nominees and from the functioning of the presidency and then to insist that the voters should choose the party rather than the man. Party leaders, were they again to have the power to control presidential nomination, would sometimes plan badly. But at present, no party-wide planning is possible.

In another piece published just before the 1976 election, in an interview that he gave to *U.S. News and World Report,* Richard Scammon described the contest as a return to normality after a prolonged string of abnormal presidential struggles.

> This year we have the first really normal election in a generation. We had Eisenhower—a big charismatic figure—in 1952 and 1956. We had Roman Catholicism as a disturbing issue in 1960, when John Kennedy ran. In the last three elections, we've had a perceived extremist on the ballot—Goldwater, Wallace, and McGovern. What we've got this time is a moderate conservative running against a moderate liberal, neither of them greatly charismatic figures. It amounts, frankly, to a feeling of pedestrianism. Now, pedestrianism may not be a good thing to stimulate voters, but it's not necessarily a bad thing for the future of the Republic.[11]

While sharing Scammon's belief that pedestrianism is far from being a bad thing for the country, I disagree that 1976 represents a return to electoral normalcy. Neither Carter nor Ford was ideologically distinct—as, for example, Goldwater and McGovern were in the past—but the 1976 presidential race did not proceed as one would have predicted. The impact of the loss of the capacity to plan on a party-wide basis in selecting presidential nominees was very much evident.

A LACK OF REPRESENTATIVENESS

Even in the absence of system-wide planning mechanisms in the political parties, of course, decisions get made. Chance does become especially important under the present arrangements of party leader weakness, low primary turnouts, crowded candidate fields, and the like. It is by no means true, however, that outcomes in the absence of party-wide nomination planning are totally random and unpredictable. Control over presidential nominations in both parties has been wrested from the "regular leadership" and turned over to a larger body of people—to the highly participant or activist cohorts in the mass party. There is extreme pressure to select nominees deemed acceptable by ideological groupings in the two main parties, as a result, and a serious problem in terms of how representative the resultant nominees are of party-wide sentiment.

We have seen over the past four presidential elections a series of successful (in the sense of being able to secure the party's nomination) and near-successful candidacies of a very distinctive ideological character: Goldwater in 1964, McCarthy in 1968, McGovern in 1972, and

Reagan in 1976. In each case the contender enjoyed the support of only a tiny fraction of the regular party leadership and was the first choice of only a distinct minority of all party identifiers. But two of these candidates managed to capture their party's nominations, and the other two came very close indeed. In each instance, the candidate enjoyed disproportionate support among the middle-class and upper-class cohorts, which are the prime beneficiaries of the weakening of party. These strata tend to emphasize issues and eschew party organization.

As the national parties have been made more open to the activists of the day, an interesting polarization of the activist cohorts has occurred. We can see this by examining the opinions of all college-educated Americans, the principal stratum from which activists are drawn. In the 1930s, 1940s, and 1950s, there was no polarization of college-educated Republicans on the one side and college-educated Democrats on the other. But over the last fifteen years, such a polarization has occurred. Today, college Democrats are noticeably more liberal than their party's rank and file on all issues, while college Republicans are consistently more conservative than their party's rank and file. Since the college educated are more highly participant in the new "open" processes of candidate selection, we have a situation in which the chance of unrepresentative nominees is increased.

There is now an abundance of data on the emergent activist cohorts within the parties showing a lack of fit of their views with those of the rank and file. For example, in 1972 Jeane Kirkpatrick conducted a study, in conjunction with the Center for Political Studies of the University of Michigan, in which the policy perspectives of all Democratic identifiers were compared to those of delegates to the 1972 Democratic Convention. Kirkpatrick found the convention activists far to the left of the party's rank and file.[12] The tone and style of the 1976 Democratic Convention was very different, but a *Washington Post* study found over half the delegates describing themselves as liberals, a proportion twice that among all Democrats.[13]

Another recent survey by the *Washington Post* demonstrates even more convincingly the pronounced polarization of the activist cohorts of the respective parties, in the absence of any polarization of the rank and file:

> Republican party workers by majorities of more than 4 to 1 believe that poor people are almost always to blame for their poverty. Their

Democratic counterparts, by margins of more than 5 to 1, believe just the opposite: that the American system is to blame, in that it does not give all people an even chance. Republican party workers, by margins of more than 3 to 1, say that justice is administered equally to all in the United States; their Democratic counterparts, by margins of more than 4 to 1, say that justice favors the rich. By margins of almost 4 to 1, Republican party workers oppose public financing of elections, while by more than 5 to 1 their Democratic counterparts favor it. . . . If the two parties are poles apart [the activist cohorts, that is] the electorate stands almost midway between the poles. . . . The result, almost invariably, was a positioning of this kind: at the far left were the Democratic party workers. In the middle were the citizens who identified themselves as Democrats; to the right of them were those who identified themselves as Republicans. At the far right were the Republican party workers.[14]

The polarization of activist cohorts becomes most consequential, of course, in the context of low turnouts in primaries and caucuses. Turnout in the 1976 presidential primaries was 29 percent, about half that in the same set of states (not all states held presidential primaries) in the 1976 presidential election (Table 1). And the most highly participant Americans manifest an extraordinary over-representation of the college educated and the above average in income.[15]

So the slice actually voting in the new open processes is small *and* unrepresentative of the population generally. Not surprisingly, in view of this, extraordinary warpings of public wishes can occur. The most striking of these in 1976 involved Ford and Reagan. The Republican president was found consistently to outdistance his California rival in popular support among all Republicans and independents from March through June, by margins up to two to one. Yankelovich, for example, showed Ford leading Reagan by 71 to 29 percent among all Republicans and independents who declared a preference in April 1976; in June, the Ford margin was 62 to 38.[16] According to Harris, Ford was ahead of Reagan—again, among Republicans and independents—60 to 40 percent in late February, 66 to 34 in late March, 67 to 33 in May, and 61 to 39 in July.[17] Ford and Reagan split the primary vote almost evenly, however. Democratic crossovers accounted for only a small part of the discrepancy between survey descriptions of rank-and-file Republican preferences and the actual primary distributions. The main factor was that the primary voters were not a microcosm of the rank and file. Much of the recent commentary on choosing presidential candi-

TABLE 1

PERCENTAGE OF THE VOTING-AGE POPULATION CASTING BALLOTS FOR U.S. HOUSE
OF REPRESENTATIVES CANDIDATES IN 1974, FOR PRESIDENT IN 1976, AND FOR
PRESIDENTIAL NOMINATION CONTENDERS IN THE 1976 PRIMARIES, BY STATE

State	Percentage turnout, 1974 House elections	Percentage turnout, 1976 presidential election	Percentage turnout, 1976 presidential primaries
Arkansas	29.9	54.2	37.7
California	40.2	54.2	39.5
Florida	18.3	54.3	32.9
Georgia	25.5	45.3	21.4
Idaho	48.2	66.3	31.8
Illinois	37.2	61.7	27.3
Indiana	48.0	61.7	34.6
Kentucky	29.6	50.8	19.2
Maryland	31.4	51.8	27.3
Massachusetts	41.6	62.4	23.1
Michigan	41.7	60.5	29.3
Montana	52.5	68.0	40.7
Nebraska	41.9	56.8	36.9
Nevada	44.0	52.9	32.2
New Hampshire	40.0	61.8	34.0
New Jersey	40.9	59.1	11.8
North Carolina	27.2	46.2	21.9
Ohio	40.4	56.5	27.3
Oregon	47.4	64.9	46.0
Pennsylvania	40.5	55.4	26.2
Rhode Island	44.0	59.5	10.8
South Dakota	58.6	64.9	30.8
Tennessee	31.3	51.2	19.9
Vermont	44.6	58.2	22.9
West Virginia	33.6	60.7	42.6
Wisconsin	38.4	67.4	42.7
All of the Above States	34.4	56.7	29.4

dates displays an unfortunate insensitivity to the distinction between *participation* and *representativeness*. The scope of the former has been extended by the new nominee-selection mechanisms—more primaries, open caucuses, and the like—but the latter may have been diminished. In 1976, we saw ample evidence of a persisting representativeness problem.

Gerald Ford was the choice of a large majority of GOP elected officials around the country. If they, together with party organization leaders, were still in charge of the candidate-designation process, Ford would have easily won the nomination in 1976. The Republican leaders wanted Ford, not because they were strongly attached to him personally, but because they concluded partisan *raison d'état* required his nomination. He was the incumbent, had not done badly, was well positioned between the main ideological camps, was accepted by a broad spectrum of the electorate, had at least an outside chance of winning, and almost certainly would not lose badly. And the rank and file wanted Ford. It seems that the established leadership was more representative of the general public than was the primary participant stratum whose elevation had been achieved over the past decade and a half. To understand fully the problem thus posed and the special democratic dilemma presented, two things must be appreciated. One applies to party regulars; the other to the activist stratum.

Party regulars—the leaders of the "organization," such as it is— have been inclined in the American two-party system to use what control they have over the nomination process to advance rank-and-file preferences for candidates. People who spend their lives within party organizations necessarily want to ensure the survival and promote the growth of these organizations. In some fashion, their individual aspirations have been attached to the fate of the party—the reason why they have been willing to labor on the party's behalf.[18]

In a multiparty system, of course, interest in party maintenance may lead to an espousal of particularistic appeals. With many contenders, the party survives by distinguishing itself and thereby maintaining the loyalties of its own special slice of the electorate. The distinctive base must be defended at all costs. But party organization leaders in a two-party system have been conditioned to think very differently. Success requires regularly attaining the votes of at least 50 percent plus 1 of the general public. Particularistic appeals might bring the intense approval of, say, 30 percent of the public; but if the rest were thereby lost, there would be a massive debacle for the party one is committed to maintain. Success requires a promiscuous search for supporters. Thus the psychological attachment to party is translated into an intense majoritarianism, which eschews ideological distinctiveness and enthrones accommodation.

There are times when hard choices must be made. The party organization leaders of the U.S. system have long been socialized to be suspicious of principled appeals that cannot be generalized. They have been "taught" that the pursuit of party success requires that they be mushy majoritarians. Presumably those not psychologically inclined to such a stance—those for whom a principle must be pursued whatever the national majority may desire—frequently have "selected themselves out" of party leadership positions thus defined, or have tried to stay in but have failed in struggles with more flexible (less principled?) rivals.

Thus a special type of party leader has been produced by the U.S. party system historically. He has had his attractive and not-so-attractive features. Here, one characteristic stands out: he has been willing—nay, eager—to subordinate personal ideological predilections in the interest of articulating majority wishes.[19]

This is why "boss-dominated" national conventions so often have produced nominees with high support and low resistance standing among the rank and file. The "bosses" have not been candidates for democratic sainthood. But they have pursued party maintenance, which in a two-party system has required pursuit of the majority.

When one moves outside that small slice of the population tied into party maintenance into the rest of the activist or participant stratum, one finds a mix of participation motivations that do not on the whole mesh so easily or consistently with complete majoritarianism. Some of the activists may be strongly wedded to advancing a program. Others articulate the claims of an interest group. Still others may be moved by personal attributes of a leader. And so on. None of these are incompatible with majoritarianism, and one can entertain any of these motivations and still devoutly seek electoral victory; but there is no necessary structural link between the motivation for participation and majoritarianism.

So it is not surprising that the Richard Daleys of the United States tried to articulate majority wishes in the choice of candidate. And it is not surprising that the present ascendancy of a participant stratum frequently produces a disjunction between popular wishes and party nomination decisions.

The new nominating processes, in which the elite "filter" has been largely removed, are not more democratic, in the sense of more representative of popular wishes. But they reflect the current conception of democracy and the participation demands of an expanding professional middle class.

THE DECLINE OF COMPETITIVENESS

Competition is important to the successful conversion of citizenry wishes through the party system, I have argued, because voter discontent can be best expressed in support for a challenger to the "in" party. A number of related points can be made on behalf of partisan competitiveness.

A party in power, knowing that it may be expelled if it does not perform, is more likely to attend to popular interests than one that has grown fat and complacent from a lack of challenge. The same general claims apply to party competition as to competition in the economy. The level of productivity is apt to be higher when the contending parties or producers feel their success or failure is dependent upon, in some significant measure, the job they do.

A competitive party situation is desirable from a standpoint of the trust and confidence of the electorate. It is nice to think one's vote matters. Sustained party competition increases the sense of electoral efficacy. When there is such competition, voters have reason to believe that they have a remedy in the event of shoddy performance by the incumbents.

It should be noted that competition requires something other than the presence of a reasonably even balance between or among contending parties. It requires that the public be satisfied that the choice before them is a meaningful one—that the differences between the parties are those which most matter to the people. A party system becomes truly competitive, then, when it provides easy opportunity for alternating ins and outs and when its internal divisions are seen to mirror the conflicts that occupy the society.

The United States lacks a competitive two-party system at the present time—primarily because of the exceptional weakness of the Republican Party.[20] The now-common observation that the two-party system in the United States has been replaced by a "one-and-a-half party system" does not contain much exaggeration.

Looking only at presidential voting, one is still inclined to take issue with this description of the GOP as "half a party." The Republicans have won four of the eight post-World War II presidential elections. A Democratic presidential nominee has received an absolute majority of the popular vote only twice in the last eight contests, and only once has there been a decisive Democratic victory. Adding up all post-World War II presidential votes, we find Republicans actually leading the Democrats, 270 million to 256 million.

In fact, of course, the presidential contests have long since ceased to be party affairs. A contender described as Republican or Democrat wins, but it is not primarily a party victory. Voters pass judgment on the character of the candidates, on the issue positions the candidates take, and on the "nature of the times."

In those contests where one gets media-utilizing and media-assessed candidacies of such visibility that voters attend to candidates' personal attributes rather than to party—and this includes in many instances elections to state governorships and to the national Senate—Republicans can win without particular difficulty when they nominate attractive candidates (and sometimes when they don't). But everywhere outside such contests, everywhere party is a prominent element in voting, the Grand Old Party is weaker today than it has been at any time since 1856.

The point is often made that the GOP experienced a big decline in support during the Depression decade. Its support did drop off substantially in that period, of course, as the party fell from majority to minority status. But the Republicans were a very healthy minority party—in their ability to provide sustained competition—throughout the period from 1932 to the 1960s. Even in 1936, with the Democrats riding high and the Republicans perceived as the party of economic failure, the Democrats had a lead of only 15 percent in party identifiers. And this lead shrank to only 4 or 5 percent in the early 1940s. It took the GOP only a decade after their 1932 rout to return to a really competitive position in Congress. Of the 436 representatives elected in 1942, for example, 208 bore the GOP label. The Republicans captured both houses of Congress in 1946, again in 1952, and they stayed close to the Democrats throughout the 1950s until the 1958 recession-year election.

Looking at state legislative races, we find a Republican party that was similarly competitive up to the early 1960s. By 1938 the GOP had recovered from its Depression debacle to the extent that it claimed 43 percent of state legislators in the country. In 1948, the Republicans actually gained a state legislative majority by a 53 to 47 percent margin over the Democrats. In 1956, 44 percent of state legislators carried the Republican label.

Over the last decade and a half, however, the GOP has slipped into its "half-party" status. Little more than one-fifth of all Americans now identify as Republicans. In 1977, only 32 percent of state legislators in the country were Republicans and this low has been reached through a steady secular erosion. The GOP state legislative contingent has actually declined slightly from its 1974 Watergate low point. The Republicans have become—and this is only the second time in American political history that we have had such a development—a permanent minority party in Congress, one unable to secure a majority in either house no matter what the prevailing conditions are in the country. One must go back to 1953 to find Republican congressional majorities.

For a full quarter century, then, the Democrats have had at least a nominal majority in both houses of the national legislature, and for the last decade and a half that majority has been essentially unchallenged. The only other period in which one party controlled Congress over a comparably prolonged period was that between 1801 and 1825 when the Jeffersonians reigned. Need we remind ourselves that that period saw the death of the Federalist party and the inauguration of a temporary "era-of-good-feelings" one partyism. The present-day Democratic control of Congress has already exceeded in number of years the domination of the Democratic-Republicans.

In 1972 when Nixon was winning by 17.5 million votes, the Democrats were winning a majority of the popular vote in U.S. House of Representatives' contests, a 47-seat edge in the House, and 60 percent of all state legislative seats. In 1976, when Ford contested evenly for the presidency, the Republican position declined even further. Fewer than 42 percent of all congressional ballots cast in 1976 went to Republican nominees.

Why are the Republicans so weak? At one level, we have a laundry list. That is, there are all kinds of contributing factors. At the risk of erring grievously, however, I will suggest an explanation that seeks parsimony and tries to provide some theoretic coherence. Let me begin with a few basic observations.

The Republican party is not in especially bad shape today among those groups associated with the old New Deal coalition—Catholics, city dwellers, blue-collar workers, southerners, all the principal New Deal Democratic groups except blacks. The GOP position among them is minoritarian still but rather healthy. In many ways, the Republicans are now stronger among such groups than they were three or four decades ago. In the case of southerners, the GOP position is now vastly improved.

The Republican problem appears most notably among their "own people." We have grown up with a picture of the Republicans as the party of the relatively well-off in contrast to a lower class Democratic coalition. But the Republicans manifest striking weaknesses today among the higher status cohorts. The society has grown much wealthier over the past quarter century, and in many ways it is accurate to talk about a burgeoning of the middle classes, but the GOP keeps getting weaker in those middle-class sectors that were considered for so long to be its natural territory.

Let me offer a little data, and before that a few definitions. Consider *high socioeconomic status* to include people who are college educated and hold professional and managerial positions. Consider *middle socioeconomic status* to include high-school graduates in skilled-worker occupations. Finally, consider *low socioeconomic status* to include persons who at once are of less than high-school education and hold semiskilled and unskilled jobs. In the 1948 presidential balloting, 70 percent of the high-socioeconomic status people were Republicans, compared to a 40-percent Republican vote in the low-status cohorts. In congressional balloting that year it was much the same thing: a 67-percent Republican figure among the high-status groups as against a 36-percent Republican support figure among people of low socioeconomic status.[21]

Over the last decade and a half, there has been a pronounced erosion of Republican strength in the middle-to-upper strata. The 1974 congressional landslide was the first in the history of the Republican party in which it was demolished in the upper strata. The contrast between the 1974 vote distributions and those of 1964—the great congressional landslide a decade earlier—is sharp. The Democrats did no better among the middle-to-lower status voters in 1974 than in 1964, apparently not quite as well, but they bettered their performance markedly within the high-status cohorts. While conditions in both elections evoked memories of the New Deal—some said Goldwater wanted to repeal it, and some felt we were entering anew in 1974 a situation that precipitated it—there was no reappearance of class voting in the more recent of the two contests. The distance between high- and low-status voters, immense in 1964, was modest a decade later. Indeed, where noncollege whites under 30 years of age were 18 percentage points more Democratic than their college-educated age mates in the former election, there was no difference at all between the vote of these two groups in 1974. Nearly three-fifths of all high-socioeconomic status Americans voted for Democratic congressional candidates in 1974, and a full two-thirds of all high-status people under 30 years of age voted Democratic in the 1974 congressional balloting.[22]

In the 1976 congressional elections, the Democrats did somewhat better among low-status whites than among the high-status, but major-

ities of virtually every high-status group voted Democratic. In congressional balloting, the Democrats look like the "everyone party." Even
though the 1976 presidential voting evidenced a return to class voting
patterns similar to what prevailed in the early 1960s, Republican
weakness among high status electors was still striking. Robert Reinhold
of the *New York Times* was correct in observing that "Mr. Carter
succeeded in eating into the groups that normally tend to vote Republican. For example, he did better among professional and managerial people than any Democrat in the last quarter century [it could be
extended to the last half century, at the very least] except Lyndon
Johnson."[23]

The growth of Democratic strength in higher status circles sounds a
little bit like the old "transplantation" phenomenon—people moving
up the socioeconomic ladder in growing national prosperity—and taking their older party loyalties with them. Haven't I simply been reviewing the fact that the composition of the high-status cohorts has changed
since World War II as a lot of new people have moved into them? There
is some of this, but something quite different is happening as well. We
get a sense of the new if we look at the behavior of young people of high
socioeconomic status. These cohorts were solidly Republican throughout the 1930s, 1940s, and the 1950s. Then a Democratic surge began,
and as I have noted, in the 1974 congressional voting this stratum was
two-thirds Democratic. It remained Democratic in 1976.

Student studies show the same thing. Harvard undergraduates,
for example—an establishment group if ever there was one—were
Republican throughout the Depression and post-Depression elections. A majority of them favored Landon, Wilkie, Dewey, Dewey,
Eisenhower, and Eisenhower from 1936 to 1956. John Kennedy in
1960 was the first Democrat to run for president and be favored by a
majority of Harvard students, and Kennedy's margin over Richard
Nixon in Harvard yard was modest. By 1972, however, Harvard students, like their counterparts at other Ivy League schools, were voting
for McGovern by overwhelming margins.[24] (In 1976, even though
Jimmy Carter was not especially popular on our college campuses, he
held a lead of about 2 to 1 over Ford within the Harvard student body.)
There have been changes in the social background of Harvard students,
of course, but nothing sufficient to account for such major shifts in
electoral behavior.

While the absolute distributions are different from campus to campus, the student populations of the 1930s and 1940s were generally

Republican, following the normal class distributions of the time. During the 1950s, as well, students were solidly Republican in presidential politics, supporting Eisenhower by margins far in excess of the general public.[25] By the late 1960s, however, the national college student population was decisively Democratic—or more precisely, heavily anti-Republican, since large numbers of students were self-described independents consistently voting against Republican presidential nominees. Gallup found a marked drop-off in Republican allegiance among students during the late sixties and early seventies. In 1966, 26 percent of college students described themselves as Republicans, 35 percent as Democrats, and 39 percent as independents; by 1970, Republican identifiers in the student population had declined to 18 percent, compared to 30 percent self-described Democrats and a massive 52 percent independents; and in 1974, the Republican proportion stood at its all-time low of 14 percent, as against 37 percent Democratic and 49 percent in the independent category.[26] Among graduate students, an almost unbelievably meager proportion of 9 percent identified with the GOP, while 43 percent thought of themselves as Democrats, and 48 percent as independents.[27] A 1973 CBS election-day survey found 54 percent of students in the 18 to 24 age category voting for McGovern, 16 points higher than the proportion among the public at large.[28] Gallup reported in October 1972 that 68 percent of graduate students planned to vote for McGovern, compared to just 31 percent for the Republican incumbent Richard Nixon.[29]

These recent distributions are really quite extraordinary. Not only are college students an important component of the intelligentsia, but from their ranks will come the bulk of the leadership of all of the principal institutions in the United States. When only 14 percent of all students and just 9 percent of graduate students profess an affinity for the Republican party, the extent of the latter's decline, and even more the scope of its potential decline, among the political classes become evident.

And the position of the GOP is even bleaker than these data suggest. Among students at major colleges and universities, Republican electoral support falls below that within the general student population. For both faculty and students, the most prestigious and influential sectors are the most solidly Democratic.[30]

One basic fact comes through with absolute clarity from the data on recent electoral preferences of high-status Americans. While these cohorts were solidly Republican throughout the New Deal era, sometime around the early 1960s they displayed a pronounced move toward the Democrats. In 1964, for the first time, Democrats outnumbered Republicans (in terms of self-identification) throughout many high socioeconomic status groupings, and majorities of these strata backed Democratic congressional candidates as well as the party's presidential nominee. While there was some temporary falling off in Democratic support among these groups immediately after 1964, the overall secular progression has not been interrupted. Substantial portions of the high socioeconomic strata in the United States are consistently displaying absolute Democratic majorities in self-identification, and in congressional and presidential balloting.

Let's return to the original question. Why is the Republican party so weak? In part it is because this old bourgeois party has become a decidedly minoritarian coalition among today's middle and even upper-middle classes. And with each succeeding generation, this Republican weakness becomes more evident. The professional, college-educated cohorts have grown, and it is in their ranks that the GOP decline has been most notable.

To locate the social group base of declining Republican fortunes, of course, isn't really to explain the dynamic of declining support. Why is the Republican party increasingly less attractive to the professional middle classes of the contemporary United States? I would suggest that the answer involves the diminished ability of the party to adapt its appeal to the intelligentsia, to the idea-generating and idea-consuming communities in the United States. There is a growing lack of fit between the Republican world view and that of the intellectual community specifically and of the college-educated professional classes generally.

The most obvious observation that comes to mind is that the intelligentsia, variously construed, is more liberal than the national Republican party. This is true, but the significance of it is probably overstated. Of deeper importance, I would argue, is that the Republican position is seen by intellectuals and by a large proportion of college-educated Americans generally as reactive, as having no positive vision. The Republicans claim to be little more than the party one turns to when one is uneasy with what the majority Democrats propose to do programmatically. It has not always been thus.

Samuel Beer has noted that the Federalists, the Whigs, then the Republicans long served as the party of the *national idea*.[31] They had a positive vision—promoting the building of an industrial society. One can find fault with this vision, but it was in many ways progressive—in keeping with the directions of social development which for large numbers of people constituted progress. Like the Federalists and Whigs before them, the Republicans enjoyed apparently widespread backing within the intelligentsia up until the last quarter century.

But the Republican position is now seen by the intelligentsia as antiquarian, as poorly suited to advanced industrialism, as lacking in new ideas. It isn't simply that the Republicans are conservative, but that they have given up any claim to a distinctive national vision. The public philosophy that guided and vitalized the party in the last decades of the nineteenth century, and indeed through the 1950s, has ceased to be appropriate—at least in its current manifestations—to the perceived needs of an advanced industrial society, and the party has been forced back upon a nakedly reactive position.

The Republicans are unable even to fully exploit this reactive stance. As Kevin Phillips and other proponents of the neopopulist, "new conservative" Republican party have noted, the GOP's leaders and activists represent far too narrow a slice of the socioeconomic and the ethnic-religious spectrums.[32] At the activist level, the Republicans remain remarkably the party of white Protestants. So the party is poorly equipped in style and tone to pick up the frustrations of other segments of the newer, emergent American petite bourgeoisie—southern white Protestant, Catholic, black, and the like.

At times, notably between 1966 and 1972, when social issue resentment has been greatest, Republican candidates have been beneficiaries of it. But the party's leadership, national and local, appears very uncomfortable with the constituents of George Wallace and the "cop candidates." Some conservatives now speculate that the symbol *Republican* puts off many natural supporters of a conservative party and hence that the symbol should be scrapped. In fact, it isn't the symbol but the social composition of the party, especially the composition of the party's leadership cohorts, which puts off these putative supporters.

CONCLUDING OBSERVATIONS

Planning, representativeness, and competition continue to be required of American political parties. To the extent they are absent, the party system must find diminished its ability to aggregate the public's preferences for political leadership and to convert such preferences into satisfactory electoral decisions.

These capabilities have been allowed to deteriorate over the 1960s and 1970s. The reasons for this are complex and, to a large extent, beyond the scope of this essay. But it may be noted that the extreme individualism that has distinguished American liberal democracy historically figures prominently in the current partisan condition. Nomination processes that deny any substantial measure of control to established party leadership and that are instead responsive to the participation claims of the more activist strata of the public represent a natural extension of individualism. The current "reform" of party procedures may have quite undesirable consequences, but its stated objectives are more individual rights, more democracy, and these are hard to argue against.

Americans have not proved to be very sensitive to systemic requirements. Many of the newer partisan arrangements I have criticized are reasonable enough as responses to individual demands. But the party system as a whole has a diminished capacity to perform the core aggregation-conversion function that the society requires.

This tension is not new. It surely will not disappear, for it has roots deep in the American ideology. We may hope, nonetheless, that there will be somewhat greater appreciation of the fact that American democracy does not demand internally "democratic" parties. It may even suffer from attempts to achieve such an intraparty standard. It requires a party system able to translate preferences for leadership that are enormously varied and diffuse into sets of electoral choices at once narrow, popular, and responsive to national needs.

The Future
of the American
Labor Movement

John T. Dunlop

8 There are two known ways of avoiding the hazards of a prophet called upon to predict the future. One is to predict so frequently that one can change the vision of the future as necessary; this method is used profitably by economists and other soothsayers forecasting the economic outlook. The other is to predict for fifty or a hundred years ahead by which time no one will remember or care; this gambit appears to be the approach of the title of this series of lectures. The concern of this lecture is rather a moderate period of a decade or two, to the threshold of the next century.

THE PERSPECTIVE OF PAST PREDICTIONS

A sober way to begin a discussion of future tendencies is with predictions made in the past. We may be better prepared to think about the future of the American industrial relations system, and modesty will be enhanced, if we review briefly some of the predictions of earlier generations of students of American labor.

In the first decade of this century, Werner Sombart, the economic historian, wrote: "I believe that a close examination of the American movement will lead to the conclusion that its tendency is more and more toward Socialism and the class war. . . . Already the Social Movement is beginning to show the same tendencies as in Europe . . . and the result is as obvious as it is unavoidable."[1]

Shortly before the Great Depression, William Z. Foster urged that the Marxian predictions for capitalism would soon come true in America. "The present situation is only the calm that precedes the storm. Inevitably, through the very contradictions inherent in the capitalist system, intensified by the extension of American imperialism itself, the employers and workers, with violently clashing interests, will be thrown against each other in greater and deeper going struggles than ever before."[2]

George E. Barnett, that pioneer student of trade union government and collective bargaining, devoted his presidential address before the American Economic Association in December 1932 to the future of the labor movement. He predicted ". . . the lessening importance of trade unionism in American economic organization." This careful scholar went on, ". . . I see no reason to believe that American trade unionism will so revolutionize itself within a short period of time as to become in the next decade a more potent social influence than it has been in the past decade."[3] The Great Depression that intensified this pessimism also created a political and economic reaction that was to destroy the prediction.

"Old Before Its Time: Collective Bargaining at Twenty-Eight" (1963) was Paul Jacobs' attempt to bury the mainstream of the American labor movement and collective bargaining. His title identified the origins of collective bargaining with the Wagner Act, and he predicted that "the place of unions in the structure of industrial justice will continue to grow smaller unless unions return to the political function that once was primary with them."[4] Bad history on both counts.

Once in a rare while one comes upon a set of predictions that stands well the test of time. E. Levasseur's *The American Workman*, written in the 1890s by a perceptive French visitor, is such a volume. In the following twenty or thirty years he foresaw that "labor unions will have increased in numbers and improved in organization . . . and they will constitute a power which will have to be treated seriously, and which, thanks to the improvement of custom and law, will probably work with greater regularity. . . ."[5]

A thorough search of previous predictions of the future of the American labor movement would no doubt reveal the same pitfalls that have trapped this brief sampling of seers: the excessive influence of contemporaneous events, wishful thinking and the desire to remake the labor movement and collective bargaining in the image of the prophet, or an ideology that portrays an inevitability and necessary logic to the course of society and the place of labor organizations.[6] In the intellectual community, views on the labor movement and collective bargaining and likely future developments have often been dictated largely by ideology. It is essential, in this audience, accordingly to consider at the outset the relations between intellectuals and American labor organizations.

INTELLECTUALS AND LABOR
ORGANIZATIONS

The mutual perceptions of intellectuals, left or right, and labor leaders in this country have been hostile and discordant in the main for a century, although some periods have been more contentious than others, as in the past decade with the turbulence over Vietnam and foreign and defense policies. (I exclude from the term *intellectuals* for the present purposes those who are also professional practitioners in industrial relations, in labor, management, government, or as private neutrals, since their orientation is largely shaped by operating experience which tends to banish ideological illusion whatever other biases such involvement introduces.)

Fifty years ago, as a culmination of the Wisconsin school of labor history, Selig Perlman wrote that "there is a natural divergence in labor ideology between the mentality of the trade unions and the mentality of the intellectuals."[7] A vital struggle arises both over leadership positions and over the framing of programs and policies toward the reform of society. In Perlman's view trade unionists struggle no less against the "intelligentsia" who would frame their program and policies than they do against employers for income, security, and liberty in the shop and industry.[8]

The mainstream of American labor has resisted intellectuals, save for a few selected technicians used as staff,[9] on grounds that have varied with efforts of intellectuals to impose an ideology that is anticapitalist, to use labor unions for a separate political party or a major faction, to use them as a base of support for the latest reform idea, to infiltrate leadership posts, or to advocate a view of society that in the end alienates and loses the support of American workers.

A second-order qualification should be noted in the garment, clothing, and related unions, led in their formative years largely by Jewish immigrants who combined in rare proportions ideology and bread-and-butter activities, where there prevailed a more comfortable and longer relationship between socialist ideology and trade unionism. These interactions, particularly in the New York area, have helped to maintain viable relations among some leaders in both groups through such organizations as the League for Industrial Democracy and Social Democrats, U.S.A.[10] These are minor variations on the main theme of the American labor movement.

The pragmatism of the emerging national unions and Samuel Gompers's design of a federation survived the half century after the 1880s rather than the ill-fated efforts of intellectuals seeking to organize workers under many other banners. Even Louis Adamic candidly recognized the indigenous and survival qualities of business unionism. "Left-wing radicals and liberal intellectuals are forever finding fault with the A.F.L. policy and tactics, for its obvious short-comings from the viewpoint of the working class and society as a whole. But the A.F.L. is, I believe, the only kind of labor-unionism that could have been effective and survived in the extremely chaotic, narrowly pragmatic, blindly violent and dynamic period of the last forty years in the United States."[11]

The intellectual left has typically been highly critical and even ashamed of the American labor movement. "The backwardness, ideologically and organizationally, of the American working class has long been notorious. . . . The organized workers of this country constitute the only important labor movement in the world which still frankly supports and defends the capitalist system."[12] That support for private enterprise today, fifty years later, is more unabashed and even stronger. The principal complaints of intellectuals with the American labor movement, which have varied in their emphasis from one period to another, have been over "bureaucratic union leadership, class collaboration with employers, reactionary nonpartisan politics, high salaries and expenses of union officers, graft and corruption in some industries, a craft rather than industrial structure, a lack of interest in the unskilled, racial discrimination, and autocratic and undemocratic control of unions."[13] Harold J. Laski reflected these views, although the principal focus of his criticism was the absence of a political party. "The trade unions in the United States obviously exercise great influence; they do not exercise responsible political power, and they do not train their members to know how to use it."[14] These themes, apart from their merits, have been reiterated on numerous occasions by various shades of the left.

In the CIO challenge to the AFL the intellectuals climbed aboard the destiny of the CIO, proclaiming the demise of the AFL, only to discover that at merger in 1955, the AFL had far outdistanced its rival in membership (10.6 to 4.6 million).[15] They applauded the expulsion of the Teamsters for corruption from the merged federation only to be chagrined that membership in this outcast grew from 1.4 in 1957 to over 2 million members recently, far outdistancing any other union. Walter Reuther, deeply admired as a champion of the non-Commmunist left, had been a cofounder of the merged federation in 1955; in 1968 he led the autoworkers out of the AFL-CIO without attracting a single former CIO union to take the same step.[16] These developments suggest how poorly intellectuals have understood the character of American workers and their organizations.

A survey of articles on labor in major periodicals catering to those of a liberal or left persuasion in 1970 revealed the same old themes.[17] The root problem of American labor in these views lies in the inadequacy of its leadership and the failure to construct a more powerful political arm to promote the interests of working people. These diagnoses and implied prescriptions derive fundamentally from an idealized and romantic view of the American worker, which bears little relation to reality, and a "deep rooted faith that labor is somehow the chosen vessel of whatever may be the power that shapes the destiny of society."[18]

Labor leaders have been quick to return these compliments of intellectuals over the years in bitter terms. The following excerpt is illustrative from the discussion before the Commission on Industrial Relations between Gompers and Morris Hillquit, Chairman of the National Committee of the Socialist party, May 1914:

MR. GOMPERS: ... when a fair and reasonable opportunity presents itself for continued improvement in the condition of the workers, that movement must necessarily go on, and will go on.

MR. HILLQUIT: And that movement, Mr. Gompers, must be a movement of the workers as workers, is that correct?

MR. GOMPERS: Yes, Sir, undominated by the so-called intellectuals or butters-in.[19]

An address of Lane Kirkland is in the same spirit: "Among government policy makers, the occupants of think tanks, and what Arthur Koestler has termed the call girls who have learned papers and will travel to Aspen, Bellagio, Salzburg, Persepolis and other notorious sweat-shops to ply their trade, the notion is epidemic that labor's voice in world economic affairs is simply an interference, producing regrettable distortions in the proper order of things."[20]

The hostility was exacerbated by the February 1977 election within the Steelworkers Union, where many intellectuals indicated their financial and public support for Sadlowski over McBride, the choice of Abel and the established union administration.[21] J. K. Galbraith and Lewis D. Sargentich urged such financial support in a letter of invitation to a dinner including these words: "Sadlowski is in the forefront of a movement that is sweeping the steelworkers and many other unions— a movement to turn the American labor movement around and make it into the democratic, progressive political and economic force its founders intended it to be."

There has been a widespread tendency to date the labor movement from the New Deal period when it is thought there was full collaboration between unions and intellectuals and to see only subsequent deterioration. There is no doubt that the social legislation and the new unions, particularly some affiliated with the CIO, attracted intellectual involvement. The common war effort, particularly after the entry of the Soviet Union, further influenced these alliances. But by the end of the 1940s the CIO had expelled ten national unions on charges of communist domination. In most older unions, AFL or CIO, including John L. Lewis's coal miners, there never was much flirtation with the intellectual left.[22] The longer term view clearly shows that the 1930s and 1940s were not an aberration in the mainstream of the labor movement in its view of intellectuals. For many intellectuals, however, the romance of the New Deal and World War II with labor unions created an illusion and a trajectory that ever since has proven to be a bitter disappointment.

Then there is a cannonade from the right. The arguments run that labor organizations and collective bargaining are monopolistic and artificially raise the price of labor and make for an uneconomical allocation of resources; they create work rules and inefficiencies reducing the national product; they are a major independent cause of inflation; and they foster unwise public policies. Unionism is disruptive "because it will cause an amount of lasting unemployment or a degree of continuing inflation which will become so serious that the competitive price system will be abandoned in the search for remedies."[23] Then strikes and lockouts are held to be antisocial conduct. Although unions are required under law to represent "without hostile discrimination" all employees in a bargaining unit, the negotiation of a requirement for the payment of union dues for all employees in a unit is held by many conservative forces to be an invasion of individual freedoms and liberties. And Senator Helms distributes for Americans Against Union Control of Government a fund-raising letter that reflects the feelings of the right. "I am gravely disturbed, and I think you are too, about the very real possibility of a relative handful of union bosses seizing control of America's government.... Let me say at the outset that this letter should not be construed as an attack on labor unions. What I oppose— and I hope that you oppose it also—is the abuse of power by labor union bosses."

It may not be surprising that intellectuals from the left and right come to opposing views as to the role and impact of labor organizations on American society, but they both focus on leadership and politics. The left holds that union leadership is inadequate, too bureaucratic and businesslike, and not sufficiently concerned with political action. The right holds it is too autocratic and too powerful in the political arena. The left holds unions have little vision of the future of society, are not democratic enough, and are too weak to make significant changes in society; the right complains labor bosses have too much power and distort the working of the market-system economy, contributing seriously to inflation, unemployment, and inefficiencies.

The role of labor leadership, its relations to members, the quality of democratic processes, the impacts of unions and industrial relations on the economy, and their role in our domestic and international future are complex questions on which informed people may reasonably differ. But these issues should not be predetermined by a somewhat hidden ideology that is ingrained in much of the intellectual community and its heritage.[24] But neither should it be presumed that past roles are unchangeable regardless of circumstances.

THE CENTRAL THEME

The central theme of this chapter may be briefly stated. American labor organizations reflect long-term continuity with gradual change and adaptations to evolving challenges and opportunities. The dominant method is collective bargaining, which has grown enormously in content, diversity, and complexity in new circumstances. Legal enactment, including the use of administrative proceedings, and participation in political elections are supportive and collaborative secondary methods, which have also expanded in organization and scope in recent years. This view rejects as out of character the aspirations of those who would like to remake the AFL-CIO into a "genuine social movement" modeled after European labor movements rather than have it be the "political arm for market-unionism."[25]

Sumner Slichter's judgment as to the past was correct:

> I think the United States should consider itself lucky. It possesses a system of industrial relations that, in its basic characteristics, fits conditions here reasonably well. The system has been developed without being planned. Perhaps that is why it represents a pretty good adaptation to conditions. . . . We seem justified in being grateful that we have been favored by fortune and perhaps also in taking modest pride that we have pursued opportunistic policies with considerable flexibility and good sense.[26]

These central directions of the past are likely to continue since they reflect well the character of American workers and the economy and society. Fundamental changes in the methods of the American labor movement and in its basic directions might arise, however, should certain unlikely developments take place; in particular, should national labor leaders lose touch with local union officials and the rank and file of active members; should major employers operating under collective bargaining agreements launch a concerted attack on the legitimacy of unions; should the political leaders of both parties refuse to make accommodations to the aspirations of labor organizations; or should a period of prolonged economic stagnation and inflation preclude advances in wages, benefits, and other rules of the workplace. Such drastic changes in the American industrial relations environment appear remote, but should they occur they could well produce a marked shift to the ideological left and to a social movement closer to those constituting the labor movements of Western Europe.

STRATEGIC ISSUES FOR THE FUTURE

The present discussion selects six strategic issues that confront the labor movement in the next several decades, the outcome of which will determine whether the American labor movement continues on its trajectory or develops significantly new directions and methods. The list of six is not exhaustive, but it provides one compressed view of decisive strategic issues. These issues are portrayed as confronting the labor movement, labor leaders and their organizations, but they no less confront American management and the industrial relations system.[27]

Workers' Attitudes

Widespread attention is attracted from time to time to the view that the American work ethic has eroded, that dissatisfaction is increasing rapidly at the workplace, and that union rebels are "mining a deep vein of worker discontent." After a long strike the phrasing is likely to continue, "relations between management and labor have degenerated into bitter parochial conflicts incapable of resolving the mutual discontents."[28] But the evidence is clear that these conclusions are in the eye of the beholder and in phrasemakers of "blue-collar blues" and "lunch-pail lassitude" rather than in the workplace or workforce. It would seem that if any events call for explanation in our times it is not so much the occasional wildcats at the auto assembly lines at Lordstown, Ohio, as the fact that the great inflation of 1973–74, with declines in real income, and the large-scale unemployment of 1975–77 have produced so little industrial unrest or protest.

Periodic polls have asked employees, "On the whole, would you say you are satisfied or dissatisfied with the work you do?" An overall response for 1973—77 percent satisfied, 11 percent dissatisfied, and 13 percent no opinion—is rather characteristic of responses from those with paid employment over the past quarter century.[29] The study of more substantial behavioral measures such as productivity, quit rates, absenteeism, accidents, and strikes reflects that their changes over time are explained by conventional economic determinants, and there is no basis to ascribe any role to changes in worker attitudes and motivation.[30] The Survey Research Center (University of Michigan) made careful surveys for 1969 and 1973 that conclude there were no major changes in overall job satisfaction for the labor force as a whole or for any major demographic subcategories in the traumatic period 1969–73.[31]

There are, of course, differences among employees in various types of jobs as to their job satisfaction, whatever the term *satisfaction* may mean. Younger workers appear to reflect more dissatisfaction than older workers, but the jobs they hold as newcomers pay less well and are probably less challenging than jobs they subsequently achieve. Moreover, the proportion of the labor force below age 25 has begun to decline, and absolute numbers in this age group may well decline in a few years. The evidence indicates that women are less satisfied than men with the financial rewards and challenges of their jobs, but their overall satisfaction scores do not differ significantly from those of men. Racial differences in job satisfaction appear pronounced, although differences within occupational and age groups are much less. Job dissatisfaction among racial groups and among women in part reflects resentment at discrimination.

Changes in the workplace seem, if anything, gradually over time to have been favorable to workers. Unskilled work has declined relatively, and professional and technical and clerical positions have increased substantially.[32] Higher wages, fringe benefits, and legislation provide increased protection against risks of the workplace and modern life. An increased emphasis on education, retirement, changes in the schedules for working hours, and increased opportunities for part-time work have tended to mitigate job dissatisfaction. Company policies in larger enterprises have become more concerned with people at the workplace, reflecting in part the consequences of professional personnel functions and the effects of labor organizations on management. These changes are not frozen; they continue to be made in response to aspirations, pressures, and the opportunities of economic growth. Indeed, it is likely that as wages, leisure, and educational attainment rise, with progressive income taxes, employees may well seek in the future to take a higher fraction of their rewards in improved conditions of work. These are opportunities for collective bargaining and some legislation, not the seedbed of worker rebellion or a revival of the class struggle.

Union Growth

The most vital issue confronting labor organizations continues to be their capacity to grow, to convert workers to vote for and join unions, and to persuade managements to enter into collective bargaining agreements. The unions have often seemed to confront a perverse fate. In the 1920s employment fell off in the highly organized sectors of that period in railroads, coal mining, and construction while jobs expanded in the non-union sectors of automobiles, rubber, glass, and electrical manufacturing. In the 1960s and 1970s a similar development has been taking place, apart from government employment. The unions' capacity to extract high settlements from union firms in construction, food retailing, apparel manufacturing, and other competitive industries greatly exceeds their capacity to organize non-union enterprises in these sectors or to prevent imports in these industries. Meanwhile employment has expanded in less well-organized white collar jobs, the professions, finance, and services.

In a number of industries, unions need to organize and assimilate each year a number of employees equivalent to their full membership to maintain their dues-paying totals, on account of high turnover rates in, for instance, retail trade and some construction unions. But it should be recognized that union growth into new sectors, occupations, or regions is a long-term social change, akin to the waves eating at the base of a cliff. The belated rapid organization of federal, state, and local government employees in the 1960s and 1970s and the penetration into commercial agriculture and the medical sector are illustrative. It may not be too much to suggest that some day, as growing industry changes the character of much of the sun-belt, labor organizations may eventually penetrate this area more fully. The concern of the federation with labor law reform in 1977–78 is with means to increase its capacity to win elections and agreements; it seeks to remove from hostile managements the delays and opposition conduct which the National Labor Relations Board (NLRB) and the courts have allowed.

One of the major changes in labor organizations, proceeding gradually, is the tendency for merger of small local unions within the same national union and for some mergers as well among international unions. Union growth rates are greater among larger and better staffed locals and internationals that are equipped to render better service to members. These mergers are largely voluntary and take considerable time and persuasion to achieve. It is often the pressures of reduced membership in a sector and higher financial costs of operations relative to dues that have been the underlying considerations encouraging merger. There are 109 out of 175 national unions with a membership of 50,000 members or less; 26 of the 109 have only 5,000 members or less. These figures indicate the possibilities of consolidation, but they also suggest the heavy influence of tradition and parochialism.

Participation in Management.

Workers' participation in industry has received widespread public attention in recent years, and European developments appear to extend significantly worker participation in management. Participation is urged as a solution to such widespread problems of industrial society as worker alienation, industrial conflict, and political unrest. It is also said to contribute to effective management and productive efficiency.[33]

German codetermination was adapted in 1976 from the iron and steel industry to provide nominally equal worker and management representation on the supervisory boards of companies employing more than 2,000. At least one of the worker members is to represent plant-level supervision; in the event of a stalemate in the board, the management chairman is to cast the deciding vote. German law also provides, as does the law of many other European countries, for an elected workers' council in plants, and for company-wide councils, comprised of all segments of the workforce, to meet with management and supervise plant-level issues. German authorities are keen on the results of codetermination and hold that it has contributed significantly to German labor peace, stability, and productivity.

The Bullock Report in Great Britain, presented to Parliament in January 1977, proposed to place worker directors in boardrooms of enterprises with 2,000 or more people, estimated to comprise the 738 largest firms, when unions demand it and when endorsed by a vote of all the workforce.[34] It is argued that this form of union participation is essential to improve the deep-seated industrial relations malaise of Great Britain.

> It is our belief that the way to release those energies, to provide greater satisfaction in the workplace and to assist in raising the level of productivity and efficiency in British industry—and with it the living standards of the nation—is not by recrimination or exhortation but by putting the relationship between capital and labor on a new basis which will involve not just management but the whole workforce in sharing responsibility for the success and profitability of the enterprise.[35]

The Sudreau report of February 7, 1975, represents President Giscard's concern with *réforme de l'entreprise.* The report rejected German codetermination in order to preserve management's responsibility to direct the daily affairs of the enterprise and on the grounds that it is not suited to present-day France. But, the report says, there exists a need for conscious participation by all in the organization of their work. A radically different approach to participation by employees on the boards of companies is necessary. The report proposes that consideration be given to a one-third worker participation in supervisory boards or boards of directors with supervisory functions, a new form of participation designated cosupervision. In view of general misgivings in France, cosupervision should be introduced gradually. The report contains a number of other areas of company reform, including means of strengthening work councils.

In the United States, labor organizations have not only failed to show interest in codetermination, but also they are hostile to such ideas. They also look unkindly toward stock ownership as a means to interest workers in management. Our unions regard collective bargaining as an adequate means of influencing management. The words that follow are those of Thomas R. Donahue, George Meany's executive assistant, but the views are widespread: "We do not seek to be a partner in management—to be, most likely, the junior partner in success and the senior partner in failure. We do not want to blur in any way the distinctions between the respective roles of management and labor in the plant. . . . And we probably bargain on as many, if not more, issues than the number we might have any impact on as members of a Board of Directors."[36]

Economic Consequences

The economic consequences of labor organization can be briefly considered under three headings: conflict, productivity, and inflation. In the period immediately after World War II, as after World War I, the concern over disruptive economic strikes reached a peak. The national emergency provisions of the Taft-Hartley Act (Title II) were enacted in 1947. The statute was seriously defective from the perspective of labor-management relations (e.g., the role of the board of inquiry and the last-offer vote), but emergency disputes have ceased to be perceived as a significant problem, if they ever were one.[37] On rare occasions, however, one may continue to expect a sticky situation as in a chaotic coal organization or in public employment. Protection of the public interest in private employment is likely to be better served by bargaining between the parties, informal influence of senior labor and management leaders, imaginative mediation, and forebearance of Congress with ad hoc legislation designed for the particular dispute as a final resort, as against the patent solutions of compulsory arbitration or the application of antitrust laws. In local and state government employment, state legislatures and courts are in the process of experimenting with a variety of procedures, and in due course the complex issues of the competing interests of taxpayers and public employees will be brought under more clearly delineated procedures.

Alfred Marshall well understood, as few contemporary economists do, that labor organizations have materially increased productivity by their impact on training, morale, methods, forms of compensation, safety, support of orderly procedures, and discipline at the workplace and in the work community.[38] The favorable influence through the "prodding of management" (Meany's phrase) or "the making of exacting demands on management" (Slichter's phrase) is recognized to be very considerable by those familiar with the processes of business organizations. These influences are a continuous process and may be expected in general to continue. Moreover, in a growing number of enterprises formal labor-management production committees outside the bargaining mechanism are operating to reduce waste, improve quality and performance, and to tap the ideas of workers regarding the production process.[39] These joint efforts are likely to be significant in only a minority of situations with special problems, opportunities, or leadership.

The net impact of labor organizations and collective bargaining on productivity is obscured in public discussion by a few outdated work rules, such as the fireman on the diesel engine. The elimination of obsolete practices is a continuing function of periodic bargaining, and the view has been widely accepted in American collective bargaining that such practices are a form of property-right of workers to be purchased or traded for wage increases or other benefits in negotiations if they are realistically to be eliminated. In the interests of efficiency, American managers with some exceptions have done well in this process.

The inflationary potentials of collective bargaining have been obscured in recent years by the worldwide inflation in 1973–74 derived largely from food and energy. But with major collective bargaining settlements averaging 9 to 10 percent (at 6 percent increase in the cost of living) to 1979 or 1980, the persistent concern with wage-cost inflation has already revived. As Arthur Okun of the Brookings Institution sees it, "a happy ending to the stagflation story *must* involve some incomes-policy or social-compact arrangement."[40] It is well that economists of both political party persuasions now recognize that wage and price guideposts cannot be effective without full consultation with labor and management, but they have little experience, and one might add capacity, in the art of consensus building in this area.

In the United States an income policy or a social compact, as those terms are understood in Europe, is not a viable policy save in a dire national emergency. The decentralized labor federation has no capacity to commit its constituents, and they in turn have little authority or disposition to control their members on vital collective bargaining matters. The ultimate test of any wage restraint policy is what happens when a union strikes against the policy, as the Heath government discovered in the coal industry in England. Moreover, the use of a single yardstick (be it the 3.2 percent of Kennedy-Johnson guideposts or the 5.5 percent of Pay Board) is a crude and inappropriate measure to distinguish inflationary from non-inflationary settlements. Noncompliance with these so-called voluntary standards creates strong pressures for controls. Inflationary periods distort the wage structure, and the primary task of effective stabilization as wage agreements come open is to achieve a result in which different amounts are negotiated for variously situated parties in order to restore wage relationships and eliminate continuing efforts to catch up or to move ahead of closely related groups. A single guidepost number is incapable of producing wage stability.[41]

The alternative policy for the United States is to identify sectors with severe wage and price problems, to diagnose the underlying difficulties, and to work with the labor organizations, managements, and government agencies involved to moderate the structural inflationary pressures, be they labor supply and training, plant capacity, collective bargaining structure, productivity, etc.

A significant problem of public policy prescription in the area of inflation is that formal analysis at the level of the whole economy is no longer adequate to the issues, if it ever was very helpful. The hard problems of public policy ahead on unemployment are less aggregate numbers than they are the special problems of youth, minority, and particular regions or localities. Similarly, the problems of public policy ahead on inflation are not reducible to issues of money supply and the federal budget, important as these factors certainly must be regarded, but they deeply involve particular labor and product markets and government policies. A different type of specialist and analytical body of economic ideas is required in the years ahead for this work.

Collective Bargaining
versus Government Regulation

One of the critical issues shaping the future of labor organizations and collective bargaining, and the extent to which they are likely to deviate from past methods, concerns the relative roles of private collective bargaining and government regulation in setting the rules of the workplace. In recent years the role of the federal government, through legislation, administrative agencies, and the courts, has expanded substantially as illustrated by measures on health and safety, pension reform, civil rights, and affirmative action. One measure of these developments is the fact that the Labor Department administered 16 major statutes in 1940 and 134 in 1975. The labor movement has been a vital factor in pushing for this expansion in government's role.

The greater the role of government regulation the greater the imagined capacity to deal with serious problems of workers in workplaces that are unorganized. The government is able, it is thought, to marshal the technical knowledge without direct costs to the union, to require information to set standards, and to compel compliance. But labor organizations are also finding, in many circumstances, that workers and elected union officials lose a voice in determining conditions of work to union staff experts, government bureaucrats, and the courts. The resulting rules of the workplace are often complex and impractical, and long delays occur in comparison to a grievance procedure and arbitration in the resolution of problems. Moreover, government regulations not only impact the specific problem area, they also have significant side-effects on other rules developed through collective bargaining. Thus, the pension law reform may considerably increase the costs of pensions and compel many employers to leave multiple bargaining associations, thereby increasing non-union competition. The extent of these conflicts is only now beginning to appear in the legislation of the early 1970s.

The NLRB in its administration of the Wagner and Taft-Hartley acts confronts numerous problems of conflict between private solutions to problems, including the grievance procedure and arbitration, and public law. The labor movement has tolerably adapted its historic jurisdictional concepts and internal disputes procedures to the necessities of "established bargaining relationships" mandated by legislation. The law has never, however, accommodated the necessities of collective bargaining in construction where the agencies do not know how to conduct representation elections. Disciplinary actions by management, supported by arbitration, from time to time are overruled by governmental determinations that the conduct of employees was determined to be concerted activity permitted under the statutes rather than a violation of company rules and the collective bargaining agreement.

While an uneasy accommodation between the NLRB and arbitration is likely to continue, a more serious problem arises should the courts expand the area of constitutional rights to include private employment generally. "The role of government and the courts would be enhanced; individual employee rights will receive much broader protection; the authority of unions as collective bargaining representatives of employees will be substantially diminished; and our system of collective bargaining based largely on private, consensual arrangements will be supplanted by one more nearly resembling the pattern in Western Europe. . . ."[42]

The continuing interaction between government regulation and collective bargaining and between decisions of courts and the private interpretation and application of collective agreements is a decisive arena shaping the operation of collective bargaining and the role of the labor movement. The capacity of collective bargaining and labor organizations to accommodate, encompass and, indeed to confine, the governmental regulatory processes will be a measure of their vitality and survival in their historical mode.

The International Arena

American labor unions have a long tradition of interest and involvement in international labor affairs. Gompers was a leading figure in the founding of the International Labour Office. American unions continue to participate actively in the various international trade secretariats that deal with international standards in various industries such as transport and metal trades. The federation vigorously opposed the spread of Communist influence in the labor organizations of Western Europe after World War II; it has sought to encourage and support the growth of democratic trade unions in the developing countries. Although the federation has withdrawn from the International Confederation of Free Trade Unions in a dispute over policies, it has expanded its activities to assist leadership development, education, technical assistance, housing, medical and other social programs in developing countries through the American Institute of Free Labor Development (Latin America and Caribbean), the African-American Labor Center, and the Asian-American Free Labor Institute.

The labor unions of the United States could be an extremely important resource in the policy aims of the country in international relations. In Western Europe and some other countries many government officials are former labor union leaders, and the complex interactions of labor unions, labor and allied democratic parties, and their governments are intertwined in ways more readily understood by those sensitive to the labor scene. Personal relations in labor forums often go back many years. In a number of developing countries, the influence of our labor organizations directly and through associates in third countries, can make a contribution to the emergence of institutions more compatible with our long-term interests and values. It may not be remiss to note that among Western countries there is none that enjoys more loyalty and security from its labor movement.

There is no more contentious issue for the future in this field than trade policy and taxes on corporate earnings abroad. The deep unemployment has exacerbated the concern in labor groups over imports and created in many communities deep hostility to the trade negotiations envisaged by the 1974 act. These are developments despite the fact that the devaluation of the dollar against the currencies of trading partners and greater inflation abroad increased the relative competitiveness of American enterprise. The magnitude and spread of adjustments required by expanded imports in the projected economic climate in such industries as clothing, shoes, electronics, and specialty steel are certain to create strong economic and political reactions favoring bilateral restraints on imports.

It is naive to assume that workers are fungible and that one can simply add up the employment gains and losses or the gross national product effects from trade and be persuasive in trade policy. Trade adjustment assistance in the 1974 act in the form of a measure of higher unemployment compensation, retraining grants, and moving allowances is an improvement over earlier policies. Workers affected, however, do not see why they should bear the material and psychic costs and risks of adjustment. Their labor and community leaders, particularly in the present and projected economic climate, are persuaded that the United States is simply accommodating to subtle forms of autarchy abroad, which encourage American firms to locate abroad and to keep out American exports, with resulting damage to American employment, while at the same time the foreign autarchy subsidizes in various ways the costs and exports of its own enterprises. The state trading companies of Communist countries and government operated enterprises elsewhere have compounded the problem. Until labor leaders are much more involved in the formulation and execution of policy in this area, beyond the formalism of advisory committees, and until responsible officials are prepared to carry on a much more vigorous campaign against autarchical forms abroad, there will be little change in the present hostile policies and attitudes among labor leaders. These developments will require a long time with new approaches and much new and detailed data.

A concomitant major issue concerns the growth in this country of people without documents, to use the language of diplomacy, or simply illegal aliens. Various informed estimates now place the figure in the 8 to 10 million range, with significant impacts on competition for jobs, wages and benefits, and welfare among the least skilled. A country of immigrants and relatives has difficulty facing the issues. Police action is ineffectual. The economic interests of some employers combine with civil rights interests against identification cards that are likely to be used in a discriminatory manner to preclude strong legislation. Population pressures in other countries combined with large wage differentials is an invitation to movement across borders, temporarily or more permanently. It has been suggested that citizens may not be willing to perform menial jobs, and illegal aliens are essential for many activities.[43] Serious attention to this area, including further negotiations with our neighbors, is a major item on the agenda for the future likely to affect as well labor attitudes toward trade.

Tbe American labor movement and collective bargaining are well-established institutions, deeply rooted in the character of the American worker, the economy and its structure of markets, and our political system. They have the virtue of pragmatism rather than ideology, and they respond gradually to new challenges and opportunities at the workplace and in the polity.[44]

Any appraisal of the past performance or future prospects of labor organizations in this country decisively depends on the expectations that are applied. Intellectuals have often expected our labor unions to perform activity for which they were ill designed and were never intended to accomplish and which they abjured. Some have looked to unions for the working-class revolution; often they have preached mutually inconsistent objectives of radical reform and economic responsibility; others have hoped for a new political party. Consider the following aspirations:

> Labor has no more urgent job in the '60s than the focusing of its political energies on the conquest of want, illiteracy, intolerance; the building up of both health and decent housing; the realization of limitless promise of the scientific golden age. And apart from their general social necessity, these undertakings would be vastly more inspiriting, to union membership and leadership alike, than the present ever more routine function of the policing of day-to-day plant grievances and the writing of mechanized contracts.[45]

Labor unions will undoubtedly gradually continue to make some contributions toward some of these objectives primarily at the workplace and secondarily through social and legislative activities. But in the depreciation of collective bargaining and grievance handling, and the enhancement of political methods, the statement again seriously misreads the nature of American workers, their organizations, and the practicalities of the American economy and society.

American Catholics
The Post-Immigrant Century

Andrew M. Greeley

9 That one-quarter of the American population that identifies itself as Roman Catholic finds itself in the interesting situation of being caught in the intersection of two monumental social changes: a largely peasant immigrant population is well on its way to becoming predominantly upper-middle-class professional; a church held in the grip of Renaissance pietism for several centuries is in the process of returning to its more ancient open, pluralistic, and democratic styles. That intersection creates both problems and possibilities for American Roman Catholics—a short-run expectation of more problems than possibilities and a long-run expectation of more possibilities than problems. I propose to divide this paper, therefore, into three sections: Religious Change; Social, Economic, and Political Change; and Problems and Possibilities.

RELIGIOUS CHANGE

The penultimate draft of this paper was being prepared during the "year of the three popes," indeed, in the preconclave period, after the death of Pope John Paul and before the selection of his successor. Computer simulation of the conclave, done on James Coleman's decision-making model, was performed at the National Opinion Research Center (NORC) two days before I began this draft (computerized conclave simulation in itself will be a symbol of change in Catholicism). A cluster analysis of the coalitions within the college of cardinals revealed sharp divisions in that body, divisions that reflect the monumental struggle that has been going on within Catholicism since the French Revolution, and in particular, since Pope John convened the Second Vatican Council. The majority coalition within the sacred college is mostly non-Italian, accounts for about two-thirds of the members of the college, and rallies around Cardinal Aloisio Lorscheider of Fortaleza, Brazil, who, as its leader, is a man with an almost ideal "papal profile," according to the Coleman model (Lorscheider, a German ethnic born in Brazil, is sufficient proof that European immigration went not only to the United States). Lorscheider himself is not a candidate for the papacy because of cardiac problems, despite the fact that his relatively youthful 53 years makes him one of the youngest members of the college. A number of other candidates, such as Italians Salvatore Pappalardo and Ugo Poletti, as well as non-Italians, such as Bernardin Gantin of Africa and Eduardo Pironio of Argentina (both of whom work in Rome), Basil Hume of Westminster, and Johannes Willebrands of Utrecht, also come close to the ideal profile. The majority coalition probably represents more or less adequately the more than two thousand Roman Catholic bishops throughout the world since Lorscheider was also elected the permanent counsel of the Synod of Bishops (which meets every three years) after the Synod of 1977. The only other man to be so elected was the American archbishop of Cincinnati, Joseph Bernardin, of whom one of his strong admirers said, "If Joe were in the conclave his profile would be even closer to the ideal than even Lorscheider's." Interestingly enough, it was Lorscheider for whom Albino Luciani came to Rome in August to vote, and for whom he voted up until his own election.

The minority coalition, on the other hand, is mostly Italian (though by no means all Italians belong to it) with some foreign allies, like Munich's young (fifty-year old) Cardinal Ratzinger, once a theologian but now a militant anti-Communist. This minority coalition is organized around the seventy-two year old Archbishop of Genoa, Cardinal Giuseppe Siri, who once said it would take a half-century to undo the harm that Pope John had done to the Church. The curial minority, so-called because most of its members serve in the Church's sensitive administrative body (though by no means are all curial cardinals in this minority), will fight to one step short of the bitter end for Siri but will finally settle for any, or almost any, Italian cardinal in order to keep the papacy in Italian hands and to continue to be able to manipulate the next pope, and to decelerate if not stop completely the forces of change in the Roman Catholic Church.

The important points about October 1978 are two: first, whoever is pope will not be elected without the support of the majority coalition, and will have to accept the sweeping revolution in papal style and the commitment to collegiality (power sharing) made in the September pontificate of John Paul. For the first time, perhaps, the majority of cardinals will so understand the enormous symbolic power of the papacy as a world beacon for hope (the curialists, however, do not perceive this; they can only think about the stacks of unsigned papers on John Paul's desk). The second point is even more important for the social science study of American Catholicism: in the October 1978 conclave the forces for change were an overwhelming majority and even if the conclave does not elect a non-Italian or a Third World pope to represent the shifting power balance in the Roman Catholic ecclesiastic institution, the counter-Reformation is over; the Ecumenical Age has begun.

At the last minute in preparation of this manuscript it is possible to include a paragraph written after the extraordinary election of the Polish pope, John Paul II, a professional academic philosopher who climbs mountains, canoes rivers, plays a guitar, writes poetry, and sings folk songs—and can address the world in eleven different languages. Interestingly enough, in the computer simulation of the two conclaves described previously, the profile of Cardinal Wojtyla was virtually the same as the profile of Cardinal Luciani, only two points on a scale of 200 points separating the two. By accident at the first conclave the cardinals elected a pope with worldwide media appeal. At the second conclave they realized that they had been through one revolution and had to find a replacement who could speak with equal effectiveness to a world in which the pope was immediately available through mass communications. Not finding an Italian cardinal who fit the new job description, they sought another, who happened to be Polish, one of the most gifted men who ever sat on the papal chair. The Ecumenical Age has indeed begun and with a vengeance.

Since the time of Napoleon the official Church has hesitated about the modern world, at times listening to those men of genius within it— LaCordaire, de Lammenais, Rosmini, John Henry Newman, Maurice Blondel, Pierre Teilhard de Chardin, John Courtney Murray—who claim that the world that emerged at the beginning of the nineteenth century was one with which Catholicism could engage in a constructive dialogue; at other times listening to those who saw in the modern world an enemy even more furious than the Reformation—the Enlightenment, the industrial, political, and social revolutions, democracy, liberalism, pluralism, modern science and modern scholarship, all were an attack, perhaps diabolic, on the mission of the Church and must be resisted with the same garrison mentality with which the Church responded to the Reformation.

Liberal or quasi-liberal popes were followed by intransigent popes and the contest swayed back and forth. In the process, the careers and even the lives of many great men were destroyed and the working class and intelligentsia of Europe were decisively, if not irrevocably, lost to Catholic Christianity. In the reign of terror initiated by St. Pius X in 1903, any discussion about modern methods of scholarship was banned.

There were three central issues in this historical debate: democracy, modern science and scholarship, and the office of the pope. Intransigents saw liberal democracy as an assault on the Church, scholarship as an attack on Christian truth, and the pope as an absolute spiritual and, ideally also, absolute temporal ruler to defend Christian truth and ecclesiastical rights against these assaults. The other side of the debate argued in reply that the Church had once elected all its leaders by democratic votes, that Western democracy grew out of the ecclesiastical democracy of the Middle Ages, that the Church had once been the patron of science, art, and culture and ought to be so again, and that the pope had far more power when he presided as a symbol of hope and principal religious leader of humankind than he did when issuing solemn definitions and proclamations.

In the middle of the twentieth century, after World War II, the first two issues were well on their way toward solution. The Church had made its peace with liberal democracy. It had become through the Christian Democratic parties in Western Europe an ardent defender of democracy against totalitarianism. In a letter on the study of sacred scriptures (authored apparently by Augustine Bea, a dazzlingly brilliant and politically adroit Jesuit scripture scholar) Pius XII formally endorsed the use of modern scholarly techniques in the study of the scriptures. The Church had not yet caught up to modern art and culture but the war was over and the stage was set for John XXIII to convene the Second Vatican Council in which the modern world would be formally embraced (ironically enough, just at the time when many of the defenders of the modern world were losing faith in it), and religious liberty definitively endorsed (in a document largely authored by the American John Courtney Murray).

It is not to minimize the contribution of Pope John XXIII to assert that the time was ripe for the Second Vatican Council. Something of the sort would have had to happen in any event to validate the intellectual and social revival in Catholicism after the Second World War. It was John's merit to see which was the way of history and to climb aboard.

He was replaced after the first session of the Vatican Council by the far more enigmatic figure of Paul VI, who tried for his fifteen years to balance the majority conservative force supporting change with the curial minority resisting it—often struggling in his own conscience as he did so (the curia early learned how to manipulate Paul VI's conscience: issuance of the famous encyclical renewing the Church's ban on birth control, *Humanae Vitae,* against the virtually unanimous recommendation of the commission he had appointed to investigate the matter, as well as the abandonment of plans to reform and broaden the base of papal elections are both attributed by vaticanologists to curial manipulation of papal conscience). But for all the hesitancies, the mistakes, the wasted opportunities, and the false starts, one can now see in retrospect that the fifteen years of Paul VI were of enormous importance. For the first time in the two centuries of struggle a liberal pope had not been replaced by an intransigent one. The changes of the Vatican Council had time to take root and become irreversible. Ecumenical dialogue with non-Catholics, as well as power sharing with the bishops of the world (in theory, since in fact this world Synod of Bishops was manipulated and stage managed by curial bureaucrats) became a part of the Church's posture. Finally, while papal election procedures had not been reformed, and while Paul VI kept most of the trappings of the Renaissance monarchical papacy, the composition of the college of cardinals at the time of his death was such that the intransigents no longer dominated. It was a major achievement of Paul VI, noted one Roman observer at the time, that his successor, at the very worst, could scarcely take a position to the right of him.

Then, in a dazzling September, John Paul swept away the trappings of the Renaissance papacy, and proved beyond any doubt, even to the cardinals returning to choose his successor, that the symbolism of hope was far more powerful than the infallible definition (John Paul substituted the personal "I" for the majestic "we," but during the first week and a half of his short administration, curial censors still changed the texts of his documents before they were published in *Osservatore Romano* or broadcast on the Vatican radio. Paul VI's last spoken words on earth involved the use of the majestic "we," "We thank. . ."; it is almost inconceivable that any pope would attempt to undo this important symbolic change).

The battle between the progressive (but scarcely radical) majority and the right-wing curial minority (and a scattering of Catholic traditionalists under the leadership of the retired French missionary, LeFebre) will go on no matter who is elected pope, but the year of the three popes left little doubt as to what the outcome would be. Pluralism and modernity have won.

The euphoria of the Vatican Council and the subsequent disillusionment produced a traumatic impact on the clerical and lay elites within American Catholicism, totally unprepared for the change. Many priests, religious, and activist lay people found their intellectual and religious structures come apart, their personalities badly shaken. There were fashions and fads, alarums and excursions, enthusiasms and disillusionments in abundance. Approximately a sixth of the priests in the country resigned and as many as a quarter of the religious left their communities. "Vocations" declined precipitously (though they have since leveled off; a project sponsored by the Knights of Columbus, currently under way at the NORC, will attempt to analyze the "vocation" decline). American Catholic scholarship, which had a profound effect at the Vatican Council through the influence of Murray, turned to romantic radicalism, seeking everywhere else but in its own experience to find structures of meaning. The decline of morale among the clerical and lay elites, then, the crisis caused by the Second Vatican Council, was serious and is still unresolved. However, the majority of the laity was able to respond much more easily to the post-Reformation Church. Two-thirds of them approved of the Conciliar changes (60 percent of them even approving the frequently denounced "guitar" folk mass), 30 percent endorsed the English liturgy—thus putting aside a 1500 year tradition with scarcely a single backward glance. Exits from the Church increased (from 7 to 15 percent), but these defections were unrelated to post-Conciliar change.[1] The reception of holy communion doubled and support for Catholic schools remained unchanged (attendance at these schools declined because the church authorities expanded the school system to keep pace with the suburb-migrating Catholic population). Church attendance declined, as did Sunday contributions (standardized for inflation), support for a vocation in one's family, and acceptance of ecclesiastical authority. However, all these changes could be accounted for in a complex, mathematical change model,[2] not by changes in the Vatican Council, but by a disillusionment that would set in after the birth control encyclical.*

---

*Some Catholic critics have argued that this explanation "can't" be true, and appeal to other various dynamics at work such as "secularization," or the "sexual revolution." They are rarely ready to submit such speculations to empirical testing. In fact there was an enormous sexual revolution in Catholicism during the sixties and early seventies—a change in attitudes toward sexual pleasure, family size, and toward family planning, though none of these changes can account

The Church's sexual effort is no longer taken seriously by an overwhelming majority of Roman Catholics. Only 15 percent oppose artificial birth control, only about a third accept the Church's stand on divorce, and almost half see no great harm in premarital intercourse among engaged people.* However, the overwhelming majority of Catholics seem to be able to harmonize disagreement with the Church on sex and their continued membership in the Church. Indeed, as Professor Westoff's research has demonstrated, there are a substantial number of Catholic married people to whom birth control and weekly reception of holy communion are not at all incompatible.[3]

The shift then from the counter-Reformation to the Ecumenical Age has created a crisis of confidence and of meaning structures for Catholic elites but seems to have been absorbed with remarkable equanimity by the Catholic masses. The nativist conviction that Catholicism would eventually fade away was given a new lease on life in certain advanced cultural and intellectual circles after the Vatican Council. Catholicism, it was thought, would eventually become indistinguishable from, let us say, Methodism. Such hopes were without foundation. Catholicism changes; it remains Catholicism. The sooner the nation's intellectual and cultural elites prepare to take the Catholic tradition seriously, and not wave it away with patronizing contempt, the better the nation's cultural life will be.†

Thriving upper-middle-class suburban parishes between the great metropolitan centers, with their pressure of organizations running full gamut, glossolalia-speaking Catholic charismatics, ardent supporters of liberation theology, crowded teen dance clubs, vivid Sunday liturgies, and often flourishing Catholic parochial schools are sufficient evidence that with sensitive, intelligent leadership American Catholics enjoy the pluralistic Church.

They should, because their great leaders at the end of the nine-

---

for the decline in religious practice and indeed none of the variables correlate with church attendance. It is precisely attitudes toward birth control and toward papal authority which correlate with church attendance and account for the change in church attendance.

*Leaving aside as too complex for the present paper discussion of the abortion issue, it suffices here to say that in terms of the *legalization* of abortion, there is little difference between Protestants and Catholics.

†For a discussion of the Catholic approach to reality, see David Tracy's forthcoming *Analogical Imagination* (New York: Seabury Press), and my own, *No Bigger Than Necessary* (New York: New American Library, 1977).

teenth century urged, in language that anticipated many of the documents of the Vatican Council, precisely the changes that have occurred.[4]

SOCIAL, ECONOMIC, AND POLITICAL CHANGE

In an article in the *Irish Times* on August 15, 1978, an expatriated, alienated Chicago Irishman named William Leahy contemptuously dismissed his fellow Chicago Catholics as being the descendants of uncultivated peasants, a dismissal that doubtless pleased some Dublin Irish intelligentsia who, economically inferior to the American Irish, have a powerful need to feel culturally superior. But Leahy's article, stripped of its contempt, is demographically accurate: the American Catholic population is, for the most part, the offspring of impoverished, illiterate peasants.

Who else would migrate?

Indeed, in 1964, the first NORC national study of American Catholics conducted of the adult population found they were either immigrants or the children of immigrants. The Catholic families in the country are descendants of those who came to our shores within the last hundred years and a very large proportion are those who came in the twentieth century. American Catholics still live very close to the immigration trauma.

Yet, in terms of educational achievement, occupational prestige and income, American Catholics are now above the average for white Protestants, even standardizing for region and city size. Without resurrecting the hoary and outmoded debate over Catholic intellectualism, Catholics are above the national average now in the proportion attending college, in the proportion seeking academic careers, and in the proportion with tenured appointments and publication records at the country's best universities (which normally means state universities since Catholics are still notably underrepresented on the faculties of the most prestigious private universities). In income, Irish Catholics are the highest of any Gentile ethnic group in the country, followed closely by the Italians. Even the bigotry of the sort that can appear in the prestigious magazine *Science*[5] to the contrary notwithstanding, intellectually, socially, and economically Catholics have arrived. They may still be excluded from the prestigious private foundations, the presidencies and the faculty clubs of the great private universities, the corporate boardrooms of the most powerful financial institutions, the means to influence through some of the most influential national journals (unless they have abandoned their Catholic heritage), but they have still "made it" in America, despite prejudice, despite skepticism about the evidence of success, and despite the inferiority feelings of their own intelligentsia who still find success hard to accept.[6]

One can even specify the time of the change for these ethnic groups. Irish Catholics crossed the national college attendance curve for whites in the first decade of this century; Polish and Italian college attendance rates climbed parallel to but below the national average during the era after World War II, then curved sharply upward and crossed the average in the 1960s. Not only the proportion engaged in white collar work but the proportion in managerial and professional occupations also crossed the national line in the years immediately after World War II. The blue collar ethnic, so loved by *Time* and *Newsweek*, is no longer appropriate, for the Catholic ethnics are less likely to be blue collar than are white American Protestants.

The Catholic Church as an institution has not even begun to cope, even to face intellectually, the fact that it is in the process of becoming upper middle class—in the archdiocese of Chicago, for example, more than 40 percent of Catholics have attended college. (Nor, for that matter, has it been able to cope with the enormous wave of new, mostly Spanish-speaking immigrants whose Catholic culture is dramatically different from that of the European immigrants, even from the other major Latin immigration from Italy; however the special issue of Hispanic Catholics is beyond the scope and the competency of the present article.)

Even, for that matter, those who explain and interpret and analyze American society, either for the mass media consumer or for the scholarly consumer, tend to be much less absorbed by the following critical facts about American Catholics:

1. Despite predictions to the contrary, ethnic immigrants did adjust very rapidly to the new society. Within the space of a new generation or two at the most, they caught up with and indeed passed the white Protestant average on social status measures.

2. Also, despite convictions to the contrary, these groups did achieve success in American society without giving up either Catholic commitment or in many cases much of their ethnic culture.*

For the non-Catholic scholar (as well as for the alienated and sometimes self-rejecting Catholic scholar), one of the major problems coming from the embourgeoisement of the immigrants and the emergence of the Ecumenical Age is that of understanding American Catholicism. These two enormous changes have had a profound influence on one-quarter of the American public. Neither of these changes is very well known or even understood by the nation's intelligentsia. I must confess that there does not seem to be any great deal of unrest about this lack of knowledge.

There is a younger generation of Catholic scholars, all of them under forty, most of them under thirty-five, who are deeply involved in examining the American Catholic experience, but there is little sympathy for them among tenured faculty, government funding agencies, or scholarly journals. Curiously enough, the official Church seems quite uninterested in their work. Neither the bureaucracy of the national hierarchy nor the American Catholic universities take seriously scholarly research on the American Catholic experience. Indeed, ethnic studies programs are conspicuous by their absence in the Catholic universities. One professor of Catholic history is about all even the most important Catholic universities seem able to afford.†

Absence of interest in self-conscious study of the American Catholic experience prompted the assertion of two Canadian scholars who, in a recent review of literature on Catholicism and the intellectual life, concluded that the empirical evidence overwhelmingly disproves any conflict between the two. There is no reason why an American Catholic cannot also be a good scholar. A Catholic intellectual class has emerged in the United States that is both intellectual and Catholic. However, the

---

* For a discussion of the survival of ethnicity, see Andrew M. Greeley, *Ethnicity in the United States* (New York: Wiley & Sons Interscience, 1974); also Andrew M. Greeley, William McCready, and Gary Thiesen, "Explaining Ethnic Subcultures," as yet unpublished.

†Two qualifications must be added to this sentence: the University of Notre Dame is acting vigorously to expand its program of research and teaching on American Catholicism and, as I prepare the draft of this paper, the U.S. Catholic Conference, under the leadership of Monsignor Francis Lally and Dr. Francis Butler, are preparing to convene a meeting of Catholic "ethnic" scholars. Better late than never.

authors add, there is no evidence that the emerging intellectual class has had any impact either on the institutional Church, its official bureaucracy, its diocesan administrative structure, or its higher educational institutions.*

PROBLEMS AND POSSIBILITIES

In the short run two problems face the American Catholic Church: leadership and scholarship. In the long run, a more serious problem faces it: once the twin changes of the achievement of middle-class status and the arrival of the Ecumenical Age have been absorbed, it will have to fight the last-ditch battle with anti-Catholic nativism.

The impact of the Americans at the Second Vatican Council was much stronger than anyone had expected. Scholars such as John Courtney Murray, Godfrey Diekmann, and Gustaf Wiegal impressed their European counterparts and some of the American bishops. Meyer of Chicago, Ritter of St. Louis, Wright of Pittsburgh, Primeau of Manchester (not Manchester in England, as he once told the assembled fathers of the council, but Manchester, New Hampshire; the other fellow is one of the Separated Brothers) were frequently heard as influential voices. Meyer, an unappreciated great of American Catholicism, made seven major addresses to the council, each one of them either a theological or a practical masterpiece.

Curial leadership was particularly angry at the American influence since they viewed American Catholicism as docile and subservient. It was made quite clear to reporters as the council ended that the American Church would be punished for its impertinence. In the last years of the council and the years immediately after the council until 1970, the curia filled virtually every major American see with one of its own

---

*A personal note: there were two meetings last year between younger social scientists and theologians and several leaders in the American hierarchy under the auspices of a committee of the National Conference of Catholic Bishops. The conferences were immensely successful and a very warm and friendly environment arose in which scholars and bishops were calling each other by first names and clearly enjoying themselves. The NCCB committee quickly phased out the program, apparently fearing the scholars would contaminate the bishops (presumably there would be no worry about the opposite occurrence). As one who believes in the presence of "Grace" in the cosmos, I must report that particularly the second meeting was one of the most "Graced" experiences I've had in my life, and the destruction of the program by bureaucratic ineptitude was a monumental absurdity.

appointees. Thus, Ritter was replaced by the ineffectual Carberry in St. Louis; Meyer, by the madcap Cody in Chicago; Cushing, by the ineffectual Medeiros in Boston; Hallinan by the silent Donnellan in Atlanta; and Primeau was left to retire after fifteen years in New Hampshire. Most Vatican appointees were "safe" men; that is to say, safe from the curia's viewpoint, but hopelessly ineffectual in respond- ing to the crisis among the Catholic elites in the United States. One natural leader remaining, Cardinal Dearden of Detroit, resolutely re- fused to exercise his ability of leadership. A younger generation of curial choices, men like Baum of Washington and Quinn of San Fran- cisco, surely intelligent and able men, are neither inspiring nor chal- lenging leaders. Only Joseph Bernardin, general secretary and then president of the U.S. Catholic Conference, now archbishop of Cincin- nati, seems to have combined the political adroitness, intellectual flex- ibility, and sensitivity to have emerged as an immensely important leader out of the dark days of the 1960s. Then undersecretary of state, Giovanni Benelli (as cardinal archbishop of Florence, a major pope- maker in the August conclave), paid a long visit to the United States, in part to learn more about America and in part, one suspects, because the Vatican was uneasy about what it was reading in *Time* and *Newsweek* concerning the American Church. Benelli was horrified at the low state of morale and the authoritarian and inept leadership he encountered throughout the country, and also shocked by the fact that the apostolic delegate who represented the Holy See in Washington had not accu- rately reported the conditions in the American Church, particularly among the clerical and lay elites. Immediately after his return, a new apostolic delegate, the Belgian, Jean Jadot, was sent to Washington. Jadot is a special kind of papal diplomat. With no formal training in the diplomatic service, and only a minimal knowledge of Italian, he had been a military chaplain commissionary and then papal representative in Asia and Africa. His staff members said that the energetic demo- cratic, smiling Jadot learned more about the United States in three months than his predecessors had in all their terms in Washington.

Jadot went out of his way to meet with American Catholic scholars, and to discuss at length with them the problems of the American Church. His choices for promotion in the hierarchy were of a very different sort from his predecessors' choices—for the most part, open, flexible, and pragmatic men. Like all of us, Jadot has made some mistakes in his appointments, and some of his open men became remarkably closed as soon as they donned the episcopal purple. Furthermore, the open pastoral leader needs ideas (unlike the closed chancery bureaucrat who has no need of ideas at all). Not a few of Jadot's appointees have been content with simplistic clichés as a substitute for nuanced thought. Nonetheless, the principal problem of Jadot's administration has been that none of the major archdioceses—New York, Chicago, Boston, St. Louis—have come open during his period of influence. Most of the American cardinals at the conclaves in 1978 were ineffectual, harmless men, wanting only to find out who the winner was so they could vote for him.*

The leadership crisis in the American Church is on its way to resolution but it has not yet been completely solved and will not be until some of the younger and more effective leaders, mostly notably Bernardin and Rembert Weakland of Milwaukee, become cardinals and exercise the dominant influence in the American Church. Of all the American hierarchy, Weakland, whose doctoral work in musicology at Columbia included editing the text for the *Play of Daniel,* has first-rate scholarly credentials. Jadot has acknowledged that he searches for other scholars to make bishops, but has been unable to find any, since American Catholicism currently finds itself in a situation where it is beginning to acquire leadership, but the leadership in its turn needs ideas and direction, and has yet to learn where to look for them. Thus the new generation of episcopal leaders are consumers in the marketplace of ideas with little access to the producers other than those who write articles for the Catholic journals such as the *Commonweal* and the *National Catholic Reporter.* The staff members of the National Conference of Catholic Bishops all too frequently have little in the way of either professional or scholarly training and turn to fashions and clichés for guidance (an exception, the thoroughly professional staff of the Committee on Technology, Science, and Values, was phased out in an economy move this year). Many of the staff members seem threatened by serious scholarship. A whole generation of ecclesiastically ori-

---

*Another personal note: Jadot invited me to Washington to learn of my work, and my colleagues and I have briefed him periodically on our efforts ever since. Indeed, I now lunch with the apostolic delegation a couple of times a year—even though I've been dropped from the mailing list in my own archdiocese. I kept this relationship with the apostolic delegate confidential because I was afraid of embarrassing him—until I found out that he was going around the country telling everyone that we were friends. Archbishop Jadot is not everyone's idea of a diplomat, much less a papal diplomat, but he is an extraordinary man and something of a saint. Since he says it, I must acknowledge it: a very good and loyal friend.

ented Catholic scholarship seems to have been wiped out in the religious and political crisis of the late sixties when enthusiastic confrontations precluded both planning and scholarship. Hence, many of those who received graduate school training in the 1960s have either abandoned or not developed their professional skills and are content to rely for theory on mishmash liberalist fashions—feminist and liberation theology imported from Latin America (though actually from Germany with a stopover in Latin America).

It is not so much that self-understanding of the American Catholic experience is deemed unnecessary as that the possibility of such a matter being an issue is not even considered. Furthermore, the shallowness of most clerical education, the intellectual naiveté of immigrants striving to find a place in their society, pietistic suspicion of intellectual pride, and the exaggerated pragmatic concern for immediate results contributed to the absence of serious scholarship within the institutional Church. There are now Catholic scholars and it is now possible to be a scholar and still be a Catholic, but the Church does not yet quite perceive any institutional use or relevance for scholars. It does not know what to do with them so long as they go to church, make the Sunday contribution, and perhaps send their children to Catholic schools.

Catholic scriptural scholarship in the United States is first-rate and respected all over the world, and younger Catholic theologians like David Tracy and John Shea are earning worldwide reputations. Scholarly resources are available and will be even more available in the years ahead. *Lumpen* intelligentsia of Catholic journalism and national bureaucratic staff still stand in the way of serious dialogue between the institutional Church and the scholars who are professionally competent and loyal to it.

Leadership, then, is improving but the leadership does not yet have a theory to replace the old theory of protecting the faith of the immigrants in a hostile society. Hence, it drifts, making ad hoc decisions, devising Band-Aid solutions, missing both the serious possibilities and the difficult problems, with unofficial institutions such as Catholic magazines, publishing companies, religious goods shops, and bookstores all suffering acute difficulties at the same time as the well-educated and affluent Catholic population grows in size. Problems of religious education, whether in the Catholic school or in the Sunday sermon, are given little attention (only 11 percent of the college graduates in the country rate their Sunday sermons as excellent).

Although Americanization and modernization have not destroyed or even notably weakened the commitment of most American Catholics to the institution, Catholics have reluctantly come to the conclusion that they can expect little from the institutional Church other than certain liturgical and ritual functions and the offering of some organized services. One must look elsewhere for meaning, motivations, and skills to cope with the complex problems of modern life. American Catholics are apparently relatively content with the situation. Whether the next generation will be equally content remains to be seen.

American Catholicism's leadership, scholarship, and creative imagination problems are likely to diminish as the century winds down. The result will be a Catholicism that is simultaneously American and Catholic, that is, even occasionally critical of American society and yet loyal to a universal Church, which presumably, by the end of the century, will be far more pluralistic and decentralized than it is now. Catholicism will still have to face the unresolved problems of nativist prejudice which lurk in American society and which, in recent years, seem to have increased in virulence—evidenced in television jokes, in cartoons in college newspapers, in discrimination against Catholic ethnics under the guise of racial quotas, in fomenting anti-Catholic animosity among the McGovernite bureaucracy which swarmed to Washington after the Carter election. A notable recent example of this resurgent nativism was the attack on Catholic schools during the tuition tax-credit bill controversy. Whatever one may think of the proposed educational reform, the charges in newspaper ads and on the floor of the Senate that Catholic schools were segregationist—"rich men segregated enclaves" (to quote verbatim from the National Parent-Teachers Association)—could only happen in a society where the opponents of Catholic schools were confident that no one, not even Catholics, would seriously challenge them. The charge could be made with impunity despite the fact that Catholicism subsidizes inner-city schools used now by hundreds of thousands of non-Catholic black parents and by the Spanish Catholics with no tradition of parochial schools in their culture and which provide the only major alternative to the deteriorating public school systems in the central cities of America. The money to maintain this system must certainly run into the tens of millions of dollars a year. Of the Catholic school students on Manhattan Island, for example, 60 percent are black or Hispanic. To describe such institutions as segregated rich men's enclaves is simply to lie. To ignore the enormous financial contribution Catholics are making to support such alternative schools for people who are not of their religion is to violate not only common justice but human decency.

Several liberal senators, many of them depending on Catholic votes for their election, sat on their hands during the Senate debate without rising to the defense of Catholic schools; and Senator Kennedy took it for granted that he could go to Pope Paul VI's funeral and return to vote against aid to Catholic schools without any threat either to his senatorial reelection or to his presidential ambitions.

Senator Kennedy may have misread the signs of the times because there is growing resentment in the Catholic community against nativism, not only among Catholic intellectuals who have encountered it in their daily existence, but also among the Catholic masses who now encounter it in television and the press. The American bishops are belatedly aware of the problem and seem to realize that unless they find an effective way of responding to neonativism (which Senator Moynihan has suggested will be the last of the three great prejudices to be eradicated—the other two being racism and anti-Semitism), then leadership may be taken out of their hands by a far more militant and pugnacious right-wing laity.

The Catholic Church in the United States and the American Catholic population have survived twin crises much better than anyone might have expected. Both have become, or are in the process of becoming, American and yet remain Catholic. Given the fears of the immigrant clergy, what is surprising is not that there have been losses but that the losses have been thus far relatively few. American Catholicism, then, faces the end of the twentieth century with far more possibilities than problems; indeed, the biggest problem of all is that it may not recognize its own possibilities.

American Jews:
Three Conflicts
of Loyalties

Nathan Glazer

10 Since the late 1960s, American Jews have been uneasy. This uneasiness is surprising; perhaps it is unwarranted. After all, probably no Jewish community in world history has been, at the same time, as numerous, as prosperous, as influential, as secure, as American Jews during the past twenty years. American Jews have surpassed in these respects the remarkable position achieved by the Jews of Germany in the Weimar Republic. Taking account of their much smaller numbers (1 percent of the German population, against 3 percent of the American), German Jews were, if anything, more distinguished than American Jews in scholarship, science, and culture, and probably more prosperous. But as events demonstrated, they were far from secure politically. Their place in German society, economy, and polity was always under attack by important elements in German society. Despite their great accomplishments in German and world culture, they were considered strangers, and thus their position was precarious. As we know, they were driven out or killed and only a few thousand Jews now live in Germany.

In contrast, American Jews live in a society in which, in truth, there are no strangers. The United States is unique among the great nations of the world in the degree to which it refuses to define itself in ethnic or religious or national terms, as our basic founding documents make clear. This is not an "English" nation, or a "Protestant" nation, or a "Christian" nation, or even a "white" nation. In practice, of course, it took almost two centuries before the promises of the founding documents were fully realized. In practice, blacks were slaves, free blacks were without political rights; Chinese and Japanese were allowed to enter the country freely during only brief periods, deprived of the opportunity to become citizens, subjected to fierce official discrimination and, in the case of the Japanese, deprived of their property and removed to relocation camps. And in the 1920s, we set up a hierarchy of favored and disfavored peoples and races by means of our immigration laws.

But since 1965 theory and practice have become one in the United

States. No group is restricted in its right to enter the country and seek citizenship on grounds of race, national origin, or religion. No group is restricted in its political rights (by the powerful sanctions of the Voting Rights Act of 1965, and its extension in 1976), its right to employment or education, or its right to housing (the Civil Rights acts of 1964, 1968, 1972). Admittedly there is controversy about how each of these rights is being fulfilled. One hears that they are paper rights, evaded, without effectiveness. But the fact is we can see a revolution in the participation of formerly deprived groups, principally blacks, in political life, in the economy, in education. Tens of thousands of people are engaged in, and hundreds of millions are spent on enforcing and securing these rights, often to the point indeed where many protest that the rights of others have been ignored.

All this established, we return to the question: Why the uneasiness? Does it simply reflect a paranoia created by the events of the past, the ingrained fear of persecution, the expectation of renewed massacres, because of a 2,000-year history in which persecution and disaster have been the norm? Perhaps. But I will argue that in the beginning of America's third century, there are more substantial reasons for uneasiness.

To give legitimate reasons—legitimate, in the sense of being understandable, rationally based on evidence—is not easy. In part, the reason for this is that, if one predicts difficulties, one's readers—Jews and observers of Jews—easily leap to the worst, since the holocaust after all is only thirty years away. Anything like that to my mind will not happen in America—cannot happen—is inconceivable. I do not even believe that there is any chance that the United States will revert to the racism and anti-Semitism of the past that made possible the rigid two-caste system in the South, the incarceration of the Japanese-American population, or the massive exclusion of Jews from broad reaches of the economy. The course this country set in the middle 1960s is secure and firmly fixed. I see no withdrawal.

But one cause of Jewish uneasiness is what has happened as we have moved on this course toward creating a more equal, multiracial society. What has happened, I have argued in my book *Affirmative Discrimination* (1976), is that a statistical standard to test for discrimination in employment and education has rapidly grown up, and has been accepted widely by federal, state, and local administrators, and by regulatory agencies and courts. Congress, I believe, opposes the statistical standards. As early as 1964, it asserted that racial balance in schools or in employment was not the objective of the Civil Rights Act, and could not be required by federal agencies. Nevertheless, federal agencies do require no less than that. Statistical representation of a number of groups determined by administrators as having been the special object of discrimination is now required, though nothing in the civil rights legislation or the Fourteenth Amendment refers to any specific group. Nevertheless, the Equal Employment Opportunity Commission, the Office of Civil Rights of the Department of Health, Education, and Welfare, the Office of Contract Compliance of the Department of Labor, and other government agencies require employers and institutions of education to report on the number of blacks, Hispanic-Americans, American Indians, and Asian-Americans they employ, promote, admit to educational programs, and the like, and government agencies take action on the basis of these reports.

The Supreme Court may in time limit the increasing tendency of federal agencies to require public and private employers and educational institutions to take into account the race and ethnicity of potential and actual employees and students in making decisions on employment, promotion, and admission, and by the time this essay appears in print we may see a somewhat different legal situation affecting the use of racial and ethnic categories. But it is hardly likely that the vast structure enforcing what we call affirmative action, and which does require taking the racial and ethnic status of individuals into account, will simply be dismantled, and that we will return to the situation naively called for in the Civil Rights Act of 1964, in which public and private institutions would become blind to color, race, religion, and national background.

One may see why this rapidly spreading development is a problem for all Americans, for our policy is built on individual rights, not group rights, and we all share a certain repugnance to being forced to report on, and being judged on the basis of, our race, ethnic origins, or religion. We had hoped that in a country built on individual rights these affiliations could remain private matters, of no concern to government except insofar as they were used to discriminate. Indeed, some states still forbid requiring such information from job applicants or applicants to educational programs. And aside from this repugnance—based on fears as to where all this will lead—there is the inevitable consequence that if one does take into account race or national origin in deciding on employment or access to education, individual rights will be limited by group characteristics. But why should this be specifically a problem for Jews? There are a number of reasons, and each is rooted in a distinctive part of American Jewish experience.

First, Jews have committed themselves unreservedly to a color-blind (or religion-blind or national origins-blind) approach to rooting out discrimination. When Jews developed political influence in New York and other states, they were the most vigorous fighters for the state legislation which banned employers and schools from seeking information on race, religion, or ethnicity, and from acting on such information. Admittedly Jews had no problem in presenting decent qualifications for education and employment, and thus, it may be argued, this principle served their own self-interest. No one would deny this. But the fact is that all groups subject to discrimination agreed on such measures, and were equally fervent in seeking them. And some of these measures—for example, forbidding the employer or institution of education to request pictures from applicants—did specifically aid Negro rather than Jewish applicants, for the names of blacks give little evidence as to their race. Of course it helped Jews, too. Many Jews change their names, and Jewish defense organizations could fear that employers and admissions officers would recognize a Greenberg or Rabinowitz behind a Green or Robbins.

But having become so fully committed to nondiscrimination as color-blind action, Jews felt the ground shifting under them as a completely new definition of nondiscrimination—as color-conscious action—began to take hold and be enforced. Certainly to see a deep value one holds undergo a transformation into its opposite—and the shift from color blindness to color consciousness could be seen as no less than that—was a deeply upsetting experience.

Second, as a result of this change, Jewish organizations discovered that long-term alliances they had taken for granted with other civil-rights groups were broken. It was and is truly agonizing for many Jewish liberals (and most Jews are liberals) to decide on their position on these issues, and many Jews, because they are lawyers, civil rights activists, judges, community leaders, must take positions. Whatever position they come to does not make them happy. Many found that principles they held deeply and considered liberal were now attacked as conservative, reactionary, or even racist.

Third, Jews found themselves more deeply split on these issues than any other group, another cause for discomfort. This split, which divides Jews it would seem almost evenly, first became evident in 1966, when New York City voted on a police civilian review board. This became identified as a race issue—if you were for it, you were for black rights; if you were against it, you supported police authority against blacks. A study demonstrated that Jews, of the major ethnic groups in New York, were unique in being evenly divided on this issue. The same phenomenon was evident in the 1969 mayoralty campaign, when John Lindsay ran a second time for mayor. Jews were once again evenly split, and it is fair to say the main issue over which they split was whether it was proper for Mayor Lindsay to favor blacks and Puerto Ricans, as he was perceived as doing, particularly in his handling of riots in black areas. Other groups in New York had no difficulty coming down solidly on one side or another of these issues. And one could see the same split at work in the hotly contested primary for Democratic senator in 1976, when Jews divided between Bella Abzug and Daniel P. Moynihan. What divided them, and liberal Democrats generally, was Moynihan's perceived position on black issues, and black attitudes toward him. The issue in none of these contests, one may note by the way, was that of whether one voted for a Jewish candidate or not. Jews have generally voted for the more liberal candidate, regardless of race or religion. The more liberal candidate *is*, to Jews, the "Jewish" candidate, regardless of race, religion, or national origin.

In this even division of Jewish votes in New York races in which race was an issue, it was on the whole the more prosperous Jews who voted for the issue or candidate that was seen as pro-black; the poorer and working class Jews voted for the opposing candidate or position. But while it is of some interest just how Jews divided, what I would emphasize is how strongly divided they were, how salient for them had become the issue of public policy toward blacks and minorities.

I concentrate on New York races because it is there that we have the greatest concentration of Jewish population, and it is therefore easiest to analyze Jewish voting behavior because of their numbers and concentration. But the salience of these issues is true for Jews everywhere. In the important ruling of the Supreme Court of California on the case of Allan Bakke who was denied admission to the Medical School of the University of California at Davis, and who argued that he would have been admitted were it not for unconstitutional discrimination against whites, it was one Jewish justice who wrote the majority opinion, another who wrote the dissent. And as the case reached the Supreme Court, the divisions between Jews intensified.

Of course, Jews are not different from other citizens in dividing on these difficult issues. But I would argue they divide more evenly, and with greater intensity. For in taking a position they make a judgment about their entire political past. They decide whether they were right or wrong in fighting so vigorously and consistently for the color-blind position; and whether in doing so they were simply promoting their individual and group interests. In taking their position they also decide on who are their allies and who are their enemies; they must question their basic political outlook; and they find, if they come out against quotas, that they are now allied with groups they have never been allied with before. This is uncomfortable as well as surprising.

Thus there are a number of reasons in these domestic developments for Jewish uneasiness. We may well describe it as a conflict of loyalties, whether to old principles of equality, or to new ones. But are there deeper reasons for this uneasiness—fear for the Jewish position, for example for the careers of young men (less so for young women) who find their hopes for becoming doctors, lawyers, professors, managers, and the like made more difficult by the new forceful affirmative action? There are such fears, but they do not explain behavior. I know of young Jewish graduate students who know their chances for jobs in a tight market under affirmative action are very poor, but who cannot bring themselves, owing to their political commitments, their own conception as to who they are and where they stand—to attack the new regulations that have reduced their opportunities to pursue a chosen career. Is it healthier for them to be angry at the regulations? I do not know. But it is clear it is deeply troubling—a touch of schizophrenia, if you will—to find one's interests adversely affected by public policy, but at the same time to find one cannot criticize those policies. Thus we have a conflict of loyalties: of loyalty to nondiscrimination and individual rights, in conflict with loyalty to goals of black and minority progress.

But the problem of the impact of these regulations on Jews is not one of individuals alone. There is also a group aspect. If to be "underrepresented" in employment or education is to be interpreted as evidence of discrimination, the same logic can apply to groups that are "overrepresented." Now if the group that is overrepresented is simply perceived as that of "white males," no Jewish interest is involved. But the matter is not so simple. As Michael Novak, Andrew Greeley, and others have pointed out recently—and as I argued in *Beyond the Melting Pot* many years ago—it is naive to think of American society as divided between a "white (and non-Hispanic) majority" that is over-privileged and a "colored and Hispanic minority" that is under-privileged. These categories, while they can be made—and are, for purposes of affirmative action—are to some extent fictitious. Each must be disaggregated into religious, ethnic, and socioeconomic subgroups. Whites are made up of Protestants, Catholics, and Jews, Poles, Italians, Greeks, and others, the rich and the poor. Now some of these groups have been subject to discrimination in the past, as have been colored groups; some today are still "underrepresented" by some measure in the economy, the polity, and the major institutions of society. Jews, even though they are a minority with a 2,000-year history of prejudice and discrimination, nevertheless happen to be highly overrepresented in many of the occupational and professional areas which are most often in the center of disputes: as doctors and lawyers, as professors, and as students in graduate schools.

Increasingly, it would appear, political advantage is based on being able to show group disadvantage. But Jews are at a disadvantage in the United States in not being able to show disadvantage. In this respect, they may be likened to a number of groups in different countries that have, despite minority status and political powerlessness, achieved high incomes and professional positions, and have as a result become targets of governmental policies trying to raise the position of other groups. This has been the fate of the Chinese and Indians in Southeast Asia, Indians in East Africa, and other groups. Now we in this country have a very different polity from some of those in the developing world. In law and sentiment no group is here considered strangers, and thus subject to despoliation. Nevertheless, we are still a multi-ethnic society, and while I am not sure what consequences will follow for a small overrepresented group as the politics of disadvantage take hold, one can be sure it will not be to Jewish benefit.

Conceivably Jews and others who hold high positions in terms of income and status will be seen increasingly as having unfairly gained those positions. I have already seen some rather harsh statements of judges imposing quotas in which they dismiss the claims of those who are going to be discriminated against by saying that they do not have the right to hold on to advantages gained through discrimination. Of course these judges are speaking of all whites or nonminorities, as they con-ceive them, and yet the language chills me, and suggests that, having overcome the disadvantages of discrimination, Jews will now be charged themselves with being the beneficiaries of discrimination.

Will it matter? I don't know. But one thing is clear: Jews would be better off if the color-blind principle still prevailed, if each person were indeed treated as an individual regardless of race, religion, or national origin. This development is properly not so worrisome for white Protestants, who are after all still the majority, and who have been the founding and shaping elements of American society and carry the prestige which comes from that status. It must be rather more worrisome to a small group, less than 3 percent of the population, with a long history of persecution by others.

Here then is one area where we see a clash of loyalties: between the interests of the Jewish group and of Jewish individuals, and of disadvantaged minorities; between color-blindness and commitment to individual rights, and the new governmentally dictated group-consciousness and commitment to measures of group progress.

But there is a second area, and here the clash of loyalties is potentially more serious. It is the clash between loyalty to Israel, and what are considered Israel's interests, and loyalty to the United States, and what are conceived of as American interests.

Israel has become the preeminent issue in American Jewish life, to a degree that could not have been envisaged in 1948, or 1957, or 1966. Newspapers, the mass media generally, political candidates, and preeminently presidential political candidates—as became clear in the Ford-Carter debates in the 1976 campaign—must be aware of how important Israel is to American Jews. What is not often realized is how relatively recent in time is the absolute predominance of Israel in American Jewish life and concerns. In the early postwar period, the Jewish community of Israel was only 6 percent of the reduced Jewish people. Within individual Jewish communities, including that of the United States, Zionism had been only recently a minority movement. Jewish organizations fought over how much of the funds raised for Jewish causes should go to Israel, and how much to other claimants. Jews in other countries who were in distress (particularly the Jews who emerged from the concentration camps of Europe or survived the war some other way, and the Jews of Arab lands) had a strong claim to Jewish charitable funds, and domestic needs—synagogues and temples, schools, hospitals, social service agencies—also rated high among Jewish priorities. Further, the Jewish community in Israel, after its first miraculous victory over the Arab armies, seemed secure. It had the support of the two great world powers (though the support of the USSR was very brief indeed), the support of most of the countries of Europe and the Americas, and there were, in that early postwar period, few independent nations in Asia and Africa to identify with the Arab cause.

A great deal has happened to change the position of Israel and to make it the central issue in Jewish hopes and fears. First, the great Jewish communities of Eastern Europe were not restored—most Jews there had been killed, the rest fled to Israel, or maintained pale shadows of their prewar community life under Communist control. The future of the one great Jewish community that remained outside of Israel and whose fate could still be a matter of fear and concern for Jewish organizations, the Russian Jewish community, became linked, particularly after 1967, ever more closely with Israel itself. The aid—political and financial—other Jewish communities provide to Russian Jews is for the most part aid that might enable them to emigrate to Israel. The Arab Jewish communities were reduced to tiny fragments, as the overwhelming majority of Arab Jews fled to Israel. Succor for Jews—an important element in Jewish communal affairs—increasingly meant succor for Israel. And finally, Israel became increasingly isolated in world affairs, and increasingly endangered, as a fierce hostility to Israel took hold in the Communist world, as the numbers of independent countries in Asia and Africa increased, and as Arab oil suddenly became central for the economically advanced countries.

Thus Israel became central in Jewish life in ways never expected, either by Zionist theoreticians and leaders or anyone else. In the early postwar years, there was still a substantial non-Zionist or anti-Zionist element within the Jewish communities of the Western world, and in particular in the largest of these communities, the United States. Here the American Council for Judaism insisted that the political loyalty of American Jews was owed to the United States, religious loyalty to Judaism, and since Jews were only American citizens of the Jewish religion, they owed nothing to Israel as such. Israel from this point of view was only another Jewish community. Most American Jews, I would guess, never thought much about the matter, and while the majority of those who did opposed the American Council for Judaism, it had its supporters. In 1957, when Israel occupied Sinai, and President Eisenhower insisted that Israel withdraw, there was no major outcry from American Jews.

The exclusive and overwhelming concern of American Jews with Israel dates from the crisis of 1967, when it appeared that Israel would be defeated and the Jewish inhabitants massacred. American Jews discovered then that Israel meant much more to them than they realized. Everything possible was done to save Israel—great political pressure was mobilized, huge funds were raised in a surprisingly short time, thousands of volunteers left to fight. If in the past it was possible for some Jews to separate their commitment to Judaism from their commitment to Israel, after 1967 this was no longer possible. Israel has become *the* Jewish religion for American Jews.

To those who think in terms of Christianity—and perhaps to some Jews, too—that may sound blasphemous or heretical. How can anything of this world—Israel, or the Jewish people—be absolutized to the point where it becomes the central theme of religion, and other-worldly things are put away? But that, I would argue, is a rather non-Jewish way of looking at religion. The Jewish religion has always been linked to a single people. Among the great religions, it is perhaps unique in this respect. Judaism is inconceivable without Jews, the actual and living people. Christianity is quite conceivable without the adherence of any particular ethnic group, as is Islam. After the holocaust, this apparently archaic feature of the Jewish religion becomes very modern again. The most creative Jewish theologian on the North American continent, Emil Fackenheim, emphasizes in his theology the centrality of the *physical* survival of the Jewish people, particularly when we live in the aftermath of a diabolical effort—which had considerable success—to physically destroy the Jewish people.

One can thus make an argument out of Jewish theology and history that the Jewish commitment to Israel has a religious character. (For many Jews, Orthodox Jews, it of course has a direct and immediate religious character.) The problem is that Israel is also a state, as well as the Zion whose restoration God promised to the Jews. And thereby hangs a potential difficulty that Jews have only recently become aware of, but a difficulty which must, it appears to me, become more serious with time. The difficulty is the potential conflict between loyalty to the United States and loyalty to Israel.

Put that bluntly, it may appear one is manufacturing problems out of thin air. After all, there is no danger that the United States and Israel will be on opposite sides in a war, which was the fate of German-Americans and Japanese-Americans. But in every other respect the problem of Israel raises the question of dual loyalty more sharply. Thus, Israel evokes a much deeper and more emotional commitment by American Jews than I think any homeland* ever has in an American ethnic group. For Israel is unique in that it is not threatened only with defeat or the loss of territories or the loss of respect—it has been threatened by annihilation up to, one assumes, the massacre of its inhabitants. At times, this threat has been very vivid and immediate indeed: in 1948, in 1967, in 1973. The startling change in the position of Egypt in late 1977 on the question of the acceptance of Israel and willingness to live in peace with Israel, followed up by the Camp David agreements, a change initiated by President Sadat but enthusiastically embraced by the Egyptian people, has suddenly pushed off, far off, this danger, which has been present so long. It has gone far to "normalize" the Israeli-Arab conflict, to make it somewhat parallel to other long-sustained hostilities, such as those between Greeks and Turks, or Pakistanis and Indians; conflicts in which the hostility has deep roots, the current issues seem enormously difficult to settle, but in which the *existence* of either side is not threatened.

Nevertheless, can one now simply put aside as no longer meaningful the fear of the possibility that Israel in defeat will face annihilation? Without any effort to give any rational estimate of the likelihood of such a tragedy, one can point to one trend and two historical facts which will certainly keep the possibility alive in the minds of Jews and Arabs. The trend is the growing strength of the Arab world. The historical facts are the fate of the Crusader states, and the very recent history of the holocaust. What has happened once—in the experience and memory of most Jews now living—can possibly happen again. But whether or not this fear is rational, there is no question that the *intensity* of American Jewish fear for Israel, the absoluteness of Jewish commitment to Israel's safety, raises a special problem for American Jews: it makes them different (just as, in connection with the affirmative action problem, their special concentration in law, medicine, and the academy makes them different). Perhaps only the issue of Ireland, when it was ruled by England, aroused the same intensity for an American ethnic group, and the Irish, as we know, were ready to go very far in support of Irish

---

*I use "homeland" for Israel even though of course few American Jews have come from Israel; but many—perhaps most—have relatives there; it serves the place of a homeland in sentiment, religion, and ideology, more strongly than "real" homelands do.

freedom. But there is no equivalent of Ireland for any ethnic group today, and thus Jews are alone in the intensity of their commitment, and the kinds of actions they will engage in to assure American support (we have to add the additional point that significant support is not really possible from any other quarter, owing to Arab power and Communist hostility). Jews would like to point to other ethnic groups that act as they do, and in a measure they can, but the difference in degree of involvement with homeland that marks Jews, owing to the special position of Israel, reaches to a difference in quality. Thus, we know that there was Greek pressure on Congress in connection with arms to Turkey, but all that was involved, serious as that was to Greeks, was the division of the island of Cyprus. Greece itself was hardly threatened.

The oddities of history further make the Israeli-Arab issue not one in a distant corner of the world. It now involves all the great powers intimately, and the world's most important source of energy, and it is seen as the one issue that may well lead to world war. Thus it is not only the intensity of Jewish feeling which attracts notice, it is also the centrality of the Middle East in world affairs.

If Jews were a small and uninfluential group, it would perhaps not matter much that they were deeply committed to the fate of Israel. Jews make up less than 3 percent of the population, and that proportion is declining. But despite their relatively small numbers as a proportion of the American population, there are enough of them—perhaps 6 million—and they are prominent enough, owing to how they are distributed through business, the professions, the academy, that they matter politically—and yet there are not enough of them to matter decisively. It is an odd position to be in, and if the needs of American foreign policy dictate, as they have for our leading allies, the withdrawal of support for Israel, what will American Jews do—and what will their fellow-citizens think of them?

Now there are various answers to the dual loyalty problem. Some argue that it does not exist—that every American has the right to support his homeland. We generally act as if that is so, and yet we know that dilemmas do arise. Ethnic groups, their leaders, their publications, and their organizations must often choose between what is seen as a homeland interest and what is seen as an American interest. I have already referred to the most drastic circumstance when they must choose—that is, when the United States goes to war against the homeland. I have suggested Jews do not face such a drastic possibility. But the possibilities they are faced with—owing to the reality that the extermination of Jews is possible, and severe public anti-Semitism is also possible—create drastic possibilities of another type: the possibility that they may have to stand by while American concern with Israel declines, and aid to its potential enemies rises, and it is argued that American national interests limit what American Jews should do to prevent it.

Here another recent historical memory becomes relevant to Jewish fears and concerns, the memory of the agonizing dilemma of World War II, when Jews were being destroyed, and opportunities existed—or so many believed—to save some by giving money to individual Nazi leaders. It was a tragic dilemma indeed—what pressure, after all, could one, should one, place on one's nation at war when our leaders insisted that not an iota of assistance could go to the Nazis to save Jewish lives?*

One may hope that the awful choices imposed on so many people by a demonic Nazism will never have to be faced again. But even if the issue of a strain on loyalties never emerges again in this most stark and drastic form, this does not eliminate the issue. Israel now increasingly has had only one major supplier of arms, the United States. These arms can only be acquired by means of large American loans and grants. There seems to be no likelihood that this situation will change radically soon. Any form of foreign aid is now unpopular among the American people. Israel's immunity to criticism—at least by respectable elements in American life—came to an end after the 1967 war, more so after the 1973 war, and even more so following the Sadat initiative in 1977. Widely syndicated columnists have felt quite free to take an actively hostile anti-Israel position and to draw attention to the fact that American Jews have lobbied strongly for aid bills for Israel and have tried to neutralize the influence of Congressmen who oppose aid to Israel. During the debate over sending planes to Saudi Arabia in 1978, the matter became uncomfortable for American Jews. They saw their secure position eroded as they invested their political resources in a lost battle. Investments of political influence in one area mean they cannot be used in another. A favor granted on one vote makes it harder to request a favor for the next vote, and the next. And the change in the political contribution laws reduces the influence of Jewish givers, because no single individual giver or group of individual givers can be that important any more.

---

*See Arthur D. Morse, *While Six Million Died* (New York: Random House, 1967); Henry L. Feingold, *The Politics of Rescue* (New Brunswick, N.J.: Rutgers University Press, 1970).

Thus if one looks ahead, and even in the absence of another war, one may see difficulties developing. Congressmen and their constituents will increasingly grumble at the heavy costs of aid to Israel. They will insist that the United States put pressure on Israel to come to some agreement with the Arabs about the return of the West Bank to Arab rule, even if the agreement in Israel's eyes is temporary and illusory and leads only to the weakening of Israel. In such a development, one can be sure that either some American Jews will join their fellow citizens in deciding Israel's danger is really not so great, or find themselves increasingly isolated as they insist it is. Most likely, both reactions will be seen, and the Jewish community will be split on this issue, as it was when Secretary Kissinger tried to negotiate some kind of agreement between Israel and Arab states. It is hard to see how American Jews can escape dilemmas which place a severe strain on their own conception of who they are and where they owe their loyalties.

One other factor that I have not referred to has made possible up to now the general American acceptance and even approval of the vigorous American Jewish support and pressure for Israel, and that is that the conflict is seen by Americans as not only a conflict of nations, but one of principles. Americans support democracies and imperilled small nations—and Israel is both. The loyalties of American Jews are under no strain when the foreign nation they support is seen by most Americans as worthy of support, without regard to the religion or ethnicity of its inhabitants. In this sense, American Jews have been fortunate. Israel is our ally and one of the small handful of democracies in the world to whose support we are committed—and the "our" and "we" there refers to the United States and most Americans. Jewish and American loyalties, which have flowed together so strongly for so long, in the long Jewish battle for rights for Russian Jews, which so many American presidents supported, and in the Jewish battle against Hitler, who was as fierce an enemy of democracy and the United States as of Jews, may continue to flow together for a long time to come in support of Israel. But this is the more optimistic possibility, and one must consider the alternatives too.

The alternatives, as I have suggested, are that American national interests as seen by our leaders, and by increasing numbers of Americans, and the interests of Israel as a state, will increasingly diverge as Arab strength grows. Even, ironically, the break in the solid front of Arab hostility to Israel may increase this divergence as Israel comes to be seen as a "normal" state, and Egypt and other Arab states escape from the stereotypes with which United States opinion has viewed Arab states. "Normalization" means Israel is no longer immune from criticism—even on the ground of human rights. Arab antagonists are no longer seen as irrationally hostile, and Israel's need for aid and assistance is therefore no longer seen as overwhelming. Israel's leaders of course will view the matter differently, and American Jewish leaders, whatever the differences among them individually, will feel it incumbent on them to provide a solid phalanx of support. And in the back of everyone's mind there will always be the memory of what has happened and may happen again to support the divergence of view between American national leaders and Israel and its American Jewish supporters.

There is yet a third conflict of loyalties, more internal to the Jewish community and the Jewish religion, that in some sense underlies these first two. Both in the first conflict, over group rights and individual rights, and the second conflict, over support for American national interests and Israeli interests, there is a fear among American Jews of standing out, of appearing exceptional. In both these conflicts, of course, we do not have a matter of only unique and idiosyncratic Jewish positions; we have basic disagreements, over which people divide on the basis of universalistic principles, as well as particularistic attachments. Thus, there are general reasons, aside from any Jewish interest, why one might support individual rights over group rights, Israel as a democratic state as against its antagonists. Nevertheless, it is also true that Jews on the whole do not think it to their advantage to have it pointed out how successful they have been in demanding and rewarding professions, or how special and distinctive is their support for Israel.

But then an underlying question emerges: How can Jews protect themselves from exceptionality and its dangers as long as they are, identifiably, Jews? This issue came up in Central Europe, as Jews escaped from the ghetto and became successful, and while one answer—at the time it appeared a somewhat eccentric answer—was Theodore Herzl's, who said the Jews could only escape the dangers of their position by leaving Europe to live in a state of their own, a rather more popular answer, in behavior if not in ideology, was assimilation. There were a great number of conversions to Christianity, a great amount of intermarriage, and in time, it could be argued, the issue of Jewish exceptionality would disappear as Jews disappeared. To return to the

United States: in the last decade or two one has seen the rise of an American equivalent, and this is a third cause of uneasiness among American Jews. Conversion has never been popular among American Jews, certainly not since East European Jews became numerically dominant in the late nineteenth century. But recently the extent of conversion has become at least a topic of conversation. There are three cabinet members of Jewish birth in President Carter's cabinet: *all* are converted. This is surprising, perhaps completely without significance, but it does suggest that loyalty to the maintenance of the Jewish religion and people is declining among successful Jews.

More significant—and certainly underlying much of whatever conversion does exist—is the very high rate of intermarriage among Jews. Until the 1950s intermarriage among Jews was low, as indicated in community surveys and special studies. In the 1960s and 1970s it became remarkably high, not surprising when one takes into account the very high proportion of young Jews going away to college, and the fact that fewer and fewer of the institutions they go to are dominantly Jewish. Finally, in recent years, demographers have been pointing to the very low Jewish birthrate, which is perhaps also not surprising, if one considers the high levels of education reached by Jews, and the high rate of intermarriage, factors generally negatively associated with fertility. Rabbis have, since the modern epoch, thundered against conversion and intermarriage. Jewish leaders are now beginning, more hesitantly, to discuss the birthrate and to project how many Jews there will be in the United States by the end of the century and beyond—undoubtedly considerably less than there are now.

The conflict of loyalties I see here is between individual choices—for marriage, for children—and a group demand, which has been a constant in Jewish history, but which it is increasingly hard to press on modern Jews raised in an individualistic and free society.

There are many reasons why this demand—for marriage within the group and for a higher birth rate—cannot be raised forcefully, or, if raised, has little impact. The main one, as I have suggested, is that marriage and children are seen as individual choices, which should not be affected by ideology or religion. The second is that it is very hard to present demands affecting marriage and having children as *religious* imperatives rather than as crudely national, or even worse, racist. The Jewish religion is a peculiar one. One can have Christianity without Italians, Islam without Arabs, Buddhism without Indians (one does), but one cannot have Judaism without Jews. Yet our common contemporary image of religion *is* universalistic, divorced from given groups, and the indissoluble and essential link between Jewish people and Jewish religion is not understood or accepted by Jews raised in an American environment; for here and now religion is seen as a purely personal choice, one which should be as little constrained as one's choice of marriage partner or number of children.

This basic underlying conflict of loyalties is between loyalty to individual choice, individual happiness, individual development, personal expression, wherever it leads, and to traditional group demands, rooted in an ancient religion, but which now, because of the general decline of faith, have been stripped of the dignity religion is capable of giving them. It is not easy to express or make credible the religious component in the demand that there should be more Jews, particularly since there are clearly explainable national and practical reasons for more Jews (the strength of Israel, the strength of the American Jewish community as an active support of Israel). Indeed, the strictly religious requirements that have evolved over many centuries to define what is a Jew, and which have the force of state support in Israel, are now attacked by many critics of Zionism and Israel—Jewish and non-Jewish—as racist, and it is a rare American Jew who knows enough, or is clear enough, about these issues to counter this devastating charge.

Loyalty to Jews and Judaism, I am convinced, cannot be made simply parallel to other American ethnic loyalties (perhaps none of them can be made parallel to each other, either; they all have elements of uniqueness). Jews may say they oppose affirmative action just as Italians and Poles do, or they support Israel just as Greeks support Greece and the Irish Ireland. But something more is at stake: an ancient history that has linked people and religion and made Jews exceptional everywhere. We do not see among Jews any large-scale, reasoned attack on the maintenance of this exceptionality, as occurred among German Jews in the nineteenth century. But we do see a silent departure, on a surprisingly large scale, from the actions that will sustain this exceptional people and religion. Nor do I suggest that we see this departure because "it is hard to be a Jew." It has never been easier than in the United States. But individual choice, modern culture, and the difficulty of justifying an ancient faith in an individualistic and modern society, all contribute to the reduction of the number of Jews. In the American Jewish community, which maintains this historic alliance of a religion and a people, it is hard to make the religious arguments against inter-marriage and a low birthrate understandable to Jews. But because Mussolini and Hitler wanted more Italians and Germans, because Jews, as an enlightened and educated group, are aware of the population crisis, it is not possible for American Jews to be happy with or responsive to the national argument for more Jews either. And only a minority are capable of making, or being moved by the religious argument.

These then, as I see them, are the issues facing American Jews at the beginning of the third century: the problems of the multi-ethnic democracy, committed to equality, and dividing Jews between those committed to individual rights and Jewish interests, and those committed to group rights and the progress of black and other minorities; the fate of Israel, which may—I believe must—introduce a strain between the loyalties of American Jews to their country and to the state that embodies today the special mixture of religion and people that is Judaism; and the most difficult issue of all, what Jews as individuals owe to the group—that difficult-to-comprehend but not-easily-dissolvable mix of religion and ethnicity.

These are lines of tension that seem to be inherent in the present situation of Jews in America, and they cannot be wished away. Nor do they suggest any immediate or even ultimate doom. American values—which Jews hold as closely as any other Americans—all suggest answers, none easy. Somewhere in the American commitment to individual rights and equality there are answers to the conflicts between them; somewhere in the long American commitment to democracy and the independence of small nations there are answers to reconciling distinctive Jewish political interests and larger American foreign policy interests; and one can even find in the tradition of American tolerance for diversity a place for the Jewish people and religion, however individual Jews manage to iron out the conflict between individualism and modernity on the one hand, and tradition and community on the other. The answers that emerge may not seem like answers to everybody, but only defeats. I emphasize my own values when I say that if, in each case, individual and group choices of distinctive values are respected, America's third century should turn out as good for American Jews as have been the first two.

The Black Community:
Is There a Future?

Orlando Patterson

11 In this essay I plan to discuss the black community in broad civilizational terms. There is a surfeit of narrow and wholly technical studies of the social and economic conditions of black Americans and little purpose can be served by simply repeating or summarizing these studies. What is now vitally needed is an interpretation of the development and role of the blacks within the context of wider developments in Western civilization, and in particular, American industrial civilization.

I propose to argue that the development of the black community since its catastrophic contact and enmeshment with European civilization can be seen as the unfolding of three great historical movements. Two of these have already occurred; the third is just beginning.

The first movement is concerned with the detribalization and rural proletarianization of the diaspora blacks in the New World. The second movement, which was no less traumatic in its impact, involves the massive urbanization of the black community, a process that has very nearly worked itself out in the United States and is now in full swing in other parts of the Americas.[1] The third movement only now shows signs of beginning: it concerns the critical catalytic role of black Americans in the coming post-industrial period of American civilization. The discussion of this last movement must, of necessity, be conjectural. It is more a scenario of one likely course of development, given certain clearly identified trends in the development of American society and the present condition of the black minority.

These three movements in the development of the diaspora black community were and are closely tied up with three major developments in Western industrial civilization: the first movement was part and parcel of the development of industrial society in the West; the second movement was intimately interwoven with the shift of the center of Western civilization from Europe to the United States starting at about the end of the First World War; and the third movement, as already indicated, will be involved with the coming of the post-industrial phase of American, and, as such, Western civilization.

THE FIRST MOVEMENT:
THE ENSLAVEMENT OF
THE BLACK COMMUNITY

The forced migration and enslavement of some nine million Africans in the Americas was, of course, occasioned by the demand for cheap and reliable sources of labor. A new world had been discovered. There was a fabulous abundance of resources—gold, silver, dyes, virgin soil. But there was little or no labor to exploit it. Indian labor, even were it sufficient, was culturally inappropriate. Wherever there is cheap capital and a severe labor shortage in a frontier situation one or both of two solutions present themselves. The yeomanric solution involves the use of free household labor in small-scale family-type operations. In the northern colonies of North America and in most areas of Spanish America this was the method employed.

The yeomanric system is not, however, a peasant economy. Cash crops are the main objects of production, whether for a local market, as in the Spanish haciendas,[2] or for a metropolitan, overseas market, as was the case with the North American colonies.[3] As such, there is some demand for labor beyond the limits of the family, and it was to meet this limited demand that slavery was introduced, beginning with the exploitation of Indian labor, then white indentured workers, and finally, African labor. The early small-scale settlers, then, were the pioneers of black enslavement, Protestants and Catholics alike. It was they who paved the way, set the tone, and formed the nucleus of the system upon which those who adopted the second major solution to the labor problem built.[4]

This second solution involved a radically new mode of production: large-scale capitalistic farming of specialized crops. This second choice was anticipated by the mining works of Spanish America. Extractive industries, however, by their very nature constituted a primitive form of capitalism. What is exploited is also what is sold directly to the consumer, with few intermediary processes. Thus little demand is made on the capitalist regarding the social relations of production. Not only are such relations brutal in their simplicity and harshness, they are essentially nongenerative.[5] The nongenerative nature of Spanish extractive capitalism partly explains the sterility and ultimate bankruptcy of the Spanish imperial system. Once the ores were mined out, the empire found itself to be an empty inflated shell.[6] The desperate attempt to imitate the generative capitalism of the North-West Europeans toward the end of the eighteenth century, especially in Cuba, came too late.[7]

It was the North-West Europeans, and to a lesser extent the Portuguese in Brazil, who were to develop true, generative capitalist structures in the New World. This development was closely related to similar developments in Europe itself.[8] Historically, the impetus came from changes in the metropolitan center, unlike the Spanish Empire where economic changes in the center were directed by developments on the periphery, in sharp contrast with the flow of political power. While the stimulus came from Europe, however, it would be a mistake to conclude that developments in the colony were secondary to developments in Europe. They were so only in a purely historical sense. Structurally, colonial developments were vital for developments in the mother countries. At any rate, mercantilist economists and imperial planners during the seventeenth and eighteenth centuries were in no doubt as to their significance. Colonies existed for the economic benefit of the mother country: as sources of raw materials and exotic products; as markets for the new industries, capital goods; and as an outlet for surplus population. To be sure, the last of these declared functions was in conflict with the first two. It soon became apparent that not only was European labor needed in Europe, but that this labor source could never meet the tremendous demand for labor in the colonies created by the shift toward large-scale production of primary goods for the industries of the home economy. Hence the constant paradox of mercantilist theory, which endlessly called for more and more emigrants to "people" the colonies, yet undermined such efforts both in the growth of the domestic economy of the metropolis, and in the creation of conditions unfavorable for the small settler in the plantation colonies.[9] If mercantilist economic theory was ambivalent on this issue, economic practice and policy were not. It soon became clear that pious calls for the "peopling of his majesty's colonies" was simply a code word for the forced emigration of troublemakers; and by the end of the seventeenth century the colonial offices of all the European imperial powers had fully committed themselves to the development of large-scale colonial economies based on African slave labor.

In shifting the focus of colonial economic development to large-scale monocrop production, the North-West Europeans, beginning with the Dutch, were to add two critically new features to the economic practice in the colonies which were to change the course of both the New World and the Old. One was a qualitative change: the mode of production that we call the plantation system. The second was a change in degree: the massive shift from a reliance on free white labor to a near total reliance on black slaves in the southern part of the United States, Brazil, and the Caribbean.

While the economic significance of this shift in focus has not gone unrecognized, its implications within the wider context of the history of Western civilization remain a matter of some controversy. What exactly did the forced migration of nine million Africans to the New World and their employment in large-scale slave economies mean for the West? How does this development relate to former historical epochs in Western culture? To answer these questions we must pause briefly to examine the origins and role of the plantation system in the ancient world, especially in Rome, where it reached its highest peak of development.

The plantation system may have been the invention of the Carthaginians.[10] The Romans, after their conquest of Carthage, rapidly adopted the institution and carried it to its most extreme development in the slave latifundia of southern Italy and Sicily, especially during the last two centuries of the republic.[11] There are many striking parallels between the ancient Roman slave latifundia and the modern slave plantation system. Both involved a radical change in the social relations of production, essentially the replacement of the small, independent farmer producing for the local market, by the large-scale monopolistic estate owner. Both involved a change in crops produced, from the production of grain and other locally consumed crops to the specialized production of crops for a metropolitan or foreign market (wine, olives, and meats in the Roman colonies and southern lands; sugar and cotton in the Americas). And both operated within the context of an expanding imperial system that made possible the conquest and displacement of vast numbers of peoples, in this way providing a ready supply of cheap labor. It is often claimed that the racial difference between masters and slaves in the New World is a vital point of contrast with the Roman slave systems. We think this issue has been grossly exaggerated. The ethnic and color differences between Roman masters and their Sicilian, Phrygian, Gallic, Scythian, Jewish, and North African slaves were as great, in subjective human terms, as those between Europeans and Africans.[12] The differences, admittedly, were more ethnic than racial; but the significance is minor when it is considered that ethnic differences had, in the ancient world, as much salience as racial differences to the modern. Furthermore, if pressed, a good case could be made for the view that the somatic differences between light-skinned Germanic and Celtic slaves and their relatively dark-skinned Roman masters were almost as great as those between Europeans and West Africans. It is an anachronism to assume that Romans would have given skin color as much weight among the wide range of somatic differences, as say, nose size and body height and weight. My point is not that the modern slave master might not have paid greater attention to skin color than his Roman counterpart. I am saying rather, that in the comparison this is to emphasize a trivial difference. More important are the total somatic as well as ethnic differences. With respect to the latter the differences were just as great.

This issue bears directly on a crucial debate in the development of the black community, namely, the origins of racism in the Americas.[13] It is often assumed that the ancient data have no bearing on this debate because of the racial similarity of slaves and masters. If my interpretation is correct (that the somatic and ethnic differences were just as subjectively significant) it strongly suggests that slavery does not necessarily generate racism or ethnic intolerance. Why then did racism become rampant in the Americas? It is tempting to argue that such racism must have preceded the establishment of slavery; that it was somehow endemic in European attitudes and culture. We reject this idealistic alternative explanation. American historians have couched the issue in rather narrow either/or terms: if racism was not the cause of slavery it must have preceded it and, as such, partly caused it. A more refined approach would pose the issue in another way. If racism is not necessarily the consequence of slavery, are there, nonetheless, special circumstances under which slavery generates racism? In other words is racism the consequence, not of slavery in general, but of certain kinds of slavery? This is where the comparison with ancient slavery becomes vital. Given the striking structural parallels outlined earlier, were there features of modern slavery that were unique, which gave it a special character? In isolating such differences we will have come closer to identifying genuinely structural factors accounting for racism. At the same time, we will have shown the unique role of the slave plantation in the development of modern industrial civilization.

Wherein then, does the modern slave plantation differ from its most advanced ancient counterpart? Marxist studies of ancient slavery offer us several major insights into the unique features of that system.[14] The slave mode of production in Roman antiquity went beyond all former modes of production in the new patterns of social relations of production it created. Its strength lay in its scale of operation and in its highly rationalized method of labor exploitation. Thus the ancient slave system was highly modern in its proletarianization of the worker. In this regard there was little difference between the experiences of the displaced African slaves in the New World and the displaced Syrians, Jews, Ethiopians, and Gauls in the latifundia of southern Italy and Sicily.

The fundamental weakness of the ancient slave mode of production was the fact that the revolution in the social relations of production that it wrought was not accompanied by any parallel revolution in the underlying technological base. As Marx, and later Weber, were to emphasize, the slave economy relied on a technology and an economic infrastructure that was just as primitive as those that served the peasant economies it partly displaced. The system, as Welskopf has argued, was unreproductive. This is not to say that there was not a process of accumulation. In terms of commodity production the system certainly generated vast surpluses. And while some of this wealth was reinvested such reinvestments were unable to generate any structural changes. The system merely repeated itself in a kind of stationary equilibrium for several centuries, one pitched at a higher level than the peasant economy it replaced, but which was unable to resolve its many internal contradictions (for example, the generation of a large urban *Lumpenproletariat,* which was artificially maintained by tribute from imperial conquests). Indeed, the pivotal contradiction of the system was that it retarded the very technological development that was essential for the resolution of its social contradictions.

Thus, Weber, who follows Marx closely in his writings on slavery, argued in a celebrated chapter on the subject, that Western man had to make a thousand-year detour via the traditional, feudal economy of the Middle Ages before returning to the task of generating the technological revolution that would transform the slave economy into a truly capitalistic system.[15] We now see that the historical timing of the modern slave plantation was no mere historical accident. The revival of the slave plantation was not a new beginning in Western man's history; it was a necessary resumption. In reviving it, Western man stretched across some fifteen hundred years of economic regression and literally took up where he had left off at the point of his most advanced development in the journey to modern capitalism. Now, however, the breakthroughs in navigation made possible a transportation system and an international commercial network that would have dazzled the ancient Mediterranean world. The era of the seaborne empire had come. Running parallel with this were the scientific breakthroughs that made possible the technological changes required to make the slave economy a truly generative system. The African slave, joined to the modern machine, especially in the Caribbean agro-industrial systems, became an infinitely more productive worker than his ancient counterpart.

But there was yet another difference which was even more vital. The imperial systems created by the modern Europeans introduced for the first time a highly integrated form of international specialization in which the exploitation of colonial lands complemented the exploitation of the metropolitan center. Unlike the ancient world where the slave latifundia existed both in the metropolis and in the colonies and ultimately undermined both systems, the modern imperial systems colonized their slave economies and in this way avoided on the one hand the inevitable deleterious consequences of large-scale slavery, and, on the other hand, tapped the resources of the colonized economies for the greater exploitation and accumulation by the metropolitan economic center.

Eric Williams, in his celebrated work *Capitalism and Slavery* (1944), argued that the slave trade and colonial slavery played a major direct role in the accumulation of capital necessary for the industrial revolution. The thesis has come under severe attack in recent years.[16] The criticisms are well taken, but they do not imply a rejection of the argument that the enslavement of Africans in the New World was a vital and necessary part of the development of European civilization. Williams's error was to posit a too direct relationship between the two developments; he was also wrong in over-emphasizing the role of capital inflow from the colonial areas. Seen as a single economic system, the modern European imperial economies depended on African slavery for their development in the effect that slavery had on the cost of labor, and the relation of labor to capital in the European metropolis. By incorporating millions of African slaves in a single international economic system the European capitalist class effectively reduced the price of the labor of the European working classes. Within this system, the European laborer was reduced to the economic status of the slave. He was literally a wage slave. Indeed, it is likely that he was materially worse off than his African counterpart in certain of the colonial areas of the imperial economy. We now see that the mercantilist emphasis on the "surplus" of population in the center was really not as anomalous as appeared at first sight. Seen within the context of the imperial economic unit, which was the way in which the mercantilist, rightly, saw it, there was indeed a vast surplus of labor. The only factor that accounts for the exploitation of one category of labor in one region rather than another was the cost of transportation. It was cheaper to buy African labor and transport it to the New World than to transport European labor to the Americas for this purpose. Racism had little to do with this. Had economic realities dictated it, there can be no doubt that European laborers would have been exploited in the New World in servile or semi-servile status. This, indeed, was exactly what happened in the early period of colonization before the international slave trading network was fully established.[17]

Cliometric critiques of the Williams thesis are deficient and, indeed, downright spurious in an even more important way. By interpreting the Williams thesis in the narrowest terms possible, critics such as Roger Anstey have persuaded themselves that they have demolished the argument because they have shown that the "contribution of slave trade profits to capital formation" was small (according to Anstey only 0.10 percent).[18] Such irrelevance is truly spectacular. These arguments fail completely to take account of macrosociological linkages in the development of Western society. Thus, if it can be shown that the development of Western industrial civilization depended on the resolution of certain critical contradictions, and that such resolutions depended, in turn, on the development of plantation slavery, the Williams thesis, admittedly elaborated, holds just as forcefully. A specified effect is no less important than one that is unspecified.

Just such an argument is presented by Eric J. Hobsbawm who shows persuasively that a major precondition for the emergence of Western industrial civilization was the resolution of the crisis that swept European society during the seventeenth century.[19] This crisis was due mainly to certain contradictions in the traditional East-West trade of Europe, culminating in the collapse of the Baltic trade in the 1620s, and to the contradictions in the sixteenth century colonial system of Spain, the bullion based, nongenerative character of which stimulated widespread inflation and severe economic dislocations, especially in the still backward agrarian sector of Western Europe. Economic failure, in turn, weakened the capacity of the European populations to resist disease and, as such, partly accounted for the demographic disasters of the seventeenth century.

Colonial slavery was not only critical in resolving these crises, but in so doing paved the way for the industrial revolution in England. The colonial investment, writes Hobsbawm:

> . . . turned out to be immensely stimulating to the economy in general, since they depended on a self-generated and constant expansion of markets all-round: more sugar sold at lower prices, more sales in Europe, more European goods sold in the colonies, more slaves needed for the plantations, more goods with which to buy slaves, and so on. Small wonder that the new colonial systems that emerged in the middle of the seventeenth century became one of the chief elements and it may be argued, *the decisive element,* in the preparation of industrial revolution. (emphasis added)[20]

Second, the plantation system made possible the emergence of an international economy, another essential prerequisite for the development of industrial capitalism: ". . . the capture of this entire world market—or most of it—by a single national economy or industry could produce the prospect of rapid and virtually unlimited expansion which the modest and confined capitalist manufacture of the period could not yet achieve itself and thus made it possible for this modest capitalist sector to break through its pre-capitalist limits."[21]

Finally, the slave colonies were partly responsible for the rise to power of the industrializing bourgeoisie. Plantation slavery in the West Indies and America "helped to enable the large—and increasingly concentrated 'capitalist sector' of the European economy to maintain its growth, and to move straight from the crisis period into an era of extremely rapid and dynamic expansion, notably in England between 1660 and 1700."[22]

All the above developments were attributable to colonial slavery, even if the direct contribution to capital formation in England were as small as those claimed by the cliometricians. The real issue is not the actual volume of profits generated by the slave trade and slavery, but first, the economic uses to which these profits were put, and more important, the social changes they made possible. There is, in human society, not only an economic multiplier effect but also a sociological one. Small concentrations of wealth in the right hands at the right time can have revolutionary consequences for a social order. The Industrial

Revolution was, above all, the socioeconomic multiplier effect of New World plantation slavery. This most important revolution in the history of Western man, and of mankind in general, would not have been possible without the enslavement and merciless exploitation of the labor of nine million Africans and their descendants, especially those who toiled in America.

Let us move now to a consideration of the consequences of these developments for the black community, especially in America. To understand what was unique about the American black experience it is necessary to compare it with other areas of the Americas. First, there was the sheer scale of the American colonization and its infinitely greater material resources when compared with the Caribbean or most of the Latin American areas. Variations in climate and geography combined with a vast frontier meant that the large monopolistic colonist could never displace the small farmer. The latter was protected in the Northern colonies by the fact that the environment was unfavorable to the growth of the kinds of crops that were ideally suited to slave labor. And in the Southern colonies the amount of land available in the South itself, plus the existence of the western frontier, meant that the medium-sized planter could never be placed at the mercy of the large-scale slaveholder. Neither of these conditions applied in the Caribbean, so we find that by the end of the seventeenth century, small-scale family farming by free whites was wiped out by the new breed of capitalistic farmers. Because slavery remained of minor significance in the North and was never totally dominant in the South (though certainly predominant), a large white majority remained intact in both areas. From very early it became clear that minority status would be the lot of blacks in America. By the opening of the eighteenth century blacks were demographically dominant in the non-Latin Caribbean, and blacks and mulattoes constituted the majority in many parts of Latin America.[23]

A second major difference between America and the rest of the Americas was, of course, the growing independence of the American colonies from the imperial system, and the emergence of industrial capitalism especially in the northern colonies, the whole process culminating in the political independence of 1776. The existence of a large industrial sector and of an equally large, viable sector of diversified free farming had major implications for the American slave system and, more particularly, for the black slave. First and foremost, it ensured the economic viability of large-scale slavery long after these systems had become economically bankrupt in the other areas of the Americas.[24] Unlike his Caribbean counterpart the American slaveholder had a ready and cheap supply of food and staples, as well as machinery for his farms. Closeness to the source of production of these vital inputs as well as the absence of heavy imperial taxes meant that the cost of these inputs was constantly decreasing rather than increasing as in other areas of the New World. The reliability and cheapness of food supplies also meant that the American slaveholder could make one crucial economic decision, which had never before been possible in the annals of large-scale slave systems: he could afford to breed his slaves rather than rely on an external supply of slave labor. Thus the collapse of the Atlantic slave trade and with it the drying up of external sources did not have the effect that it had in the Caribbean or in ancient Rome. In both Rome and the Caribbean the slaveholders found that the economics of slave breeding simply did not justify a continuation of the system. Cuba and Brazil, of course, continued to rely heavily on slave labor. But in the former, developments similar to those that existed in the United States took place, that is, there was a growing economic independence, a large group of free farmers, and a ready supply of inputs, which were available at prices that made slave breeding profitable.[25] And in the case of Brazil (as well as Cuba, though to a much lesser extent) the continuation of the slave trade, in spite of British opposition, ensured a continued supply of cheap labor.[26] The U.S. South then, and to a lesser extent, its structural counterpart, Cuba, became the first and only large-scale slave systems that could rely on natural population growth to supply their slave labor needs. The result, as we now know, was the massive increase in the U.S. black population (see Table 1). Black Americans, then, while remaining a minority in their society, for the reasons mentioned earlier, were for these very same reasons to become the largest single group of blacks in the Americas.

Apart from their permanent minority status, black Americans were to pay a heavy price for their greater material security and demographic expansion.[27] One of these was the simple fact that they remained slaves for a much longer period than their non-Latin Caribbean counterparts. The second is that they were forced to make greater compromises with the system than slave populations elsewhere. Thus in the Caribbean the sheer demographic weight of the slave population plus the high cost of maintaining the slave population forced the masters to develop a system in which the slaves largely maintained themselves. In doing so they had

TABLE 1

NATIONAL POPULATION AND ANNUAL GROWTH RATES 1790–1969

Dates	Population (000) White	Negro	Average Annual Growth Rates for Interdecennial Period White	Negro	Proportion of Total Population Negro
1790	3,172	757	–	–	19%
1800	4,306	1,002	3.06%	2.80%	19
1810	5,862	1,378	3.08	3.19	19
1820	7,867	1,772	2.94	2.51	18
1830	10,537	2,329	2.92	2.73	18
1840	14,196	2,874	2.98	2.10	17
1850	19,553	3,639	3.20	2.36	16
1860	26,923	4,442	3.20	2.00	14
1870	33,589	4,880	2.22	.94	13
1880	43,403	6,581	2.56	2.99	13
1890	55,101	7,389	2.39	1.25	12
1900	66,809	8,834	1.92	1.79	12
1910	81,732	9,828	2.01	1.07	11
1920	94,821	10,463	1.48	.63	10
1930	110,287	11,891	1.51	1.28	10
1940	118,215	12,866	.70	.79	10
1950	134,942	15,042	1.33	1.56	10
1960	159,467	18,916	1.67	2.29	11
1969	178,225	22,727	1.14	1.88	11

SOURCE: R. Farley, *Growth of the Black Population* (Chicago, 1970), p. 22.

to make major concessions to the slaves: free time and land had to be given them to produce their own food. Thus by the middle of the eighteenth century the Caribbean slaves, though more greatly exploited and used by the master class, ironically, had eked out a substantial area of freedom and independence for themselves. They had become what Sid Mintz aptly calls a "proto-peasantry."[28] Within the framework of this proto-peasant system they were able not only to resist white encroachment on their way of life, but to develop a syncretic subculture of their own, based partly on the fragments of African culture that remained, and partly on new developments in the New World.[29]

None of this was possible in America. The slaves remained wholly dependent on their masters for their survival, and the social patterns they evolved were couched within the framework of complete dependency.[30] Other factors reinforced this tendency. The master class in the United States was a resident ruling class highly committed to the system that it ruled. It also had the full support of a free white working class, which it could play off against the slaves and rely on for security. Absentee landlordism dominated the Caribbean slave economies; those whites who ran the system had no committent to it in social terms.

Hence another irony. The very same factors that account for the brutality of the Caribbean planters also explain why they not only had little interest in interfering with the lives of the slaves (as long as they got the labor they demanded) but also little interest in developing a highly articulated racist ideology. This is not to say, let me hasten to add, that they were not racists. Like their Southern counterparts they assumed the natural inferiority of the blacks. The important difference, however, concerns the degree to which they acted out such racist attitudes. There is a great difference between believing in something and acting in a manner consistent with this belief. The Southern planter not only believed in racism, but precisely because he lived with and among his slaves and was highly committed to the system, and because he had the luxury and motivation to worry about such weighty matters as culture and social morality, he fiercely developed, acted out, and institutionalized an etiquette of racial interaction, one in which blacks were seen as a viable and desirable part of the system, albeit a part that involved the perpetual status of the blacks as a dependent caste. Herein lies the origin of American racism.

The Sambo ideology of the master class was just that: a ruling class ideology that the ruling class took quite seriously. It is a gross libel of an entire people, and a distortion of historical realities, to argue, as Elkins did, that this ideology was a true picture of the way blacks actually were.[31] Naturally, the black American had to respond to this entrenched ideology, as all oppressed classes must respond to the ideological rationalizations of their oppressors. In this sense the Sambo ideology was a real and meaningful part of the lives of black Americans. It was, however, a part of the environmental burden of the group, another cross to bear; there is no evidence whatever to prove that they wholly internalized this image of themselves, any more than, say, Jews internalized the Christian conception of them during the long period of the Middle Ages, or the British working class internalized the equally nefarious ruling-class image of them in Britain.

In the Caribbean, on the other hand, the white managerial group, racists that they were, simply lacked the luxury and the motivation to actualize and develop to a finely articulated etiquette the incipient "quashie" stereotype that they held.[32] The blacks in the islands, then, did not have to put up with and adjust to an institutionalized racist ideology; and even if such an ideology existed they had the cultural resources and independence to resist it. What emerged in the Caribbean then, was a curious kind of psychocultural standoff: both groups mistrusted each other, but neither group was prepared to take each other quite seriously. It is a curious fact that, to this day, the typical response of a black West Indian peasant, confronted with whites, is to laugh at them. White people are somehow not quite real. They are rich, to be sure, and powerful when they want to be, but they are also funny, delicate souls lacking substance. This comes out clearly in their songs, in their folktales, and in their open mimicry of the whites on the slave plantations and in postemancipation peasant villages. The prowhite color bias for which West Indians are known[33] is actually true only of the brown-skinned and upwardly mobile bourgeoisie.[34]

We find, then, that the slaves in the Caribbean paid the whites back in ideological kind. If the slaves were, in the white image, an inferior group of "lazy bastards," the whites were, in the slaves' image, ghostly "red devils." Like all ghosts they were things to be lived with, part of the environment; they had great powers of evil, but they could be contained both by propitiation and retaliation. For if the white man had his whip and his guns, the black man had his obeah-men and "shadow-catchers" and there was always the welcoming tropical bush, ideal for escape and guerrilla warfare. In general, a creaky modus vivendi emerged wherein each group decided to live and let live, partly by providing the minimum requirements of the other group, partly by not taking each other too seriously, and partly by not attempting too strenuously to institutionalize their own views about the other group. The result, then, was the paradox that these, the most brutal systems of slavery ever devised, were also ones in which both groups mixed freely without any strong sense of racial purity or physical exclusion evolving. A white overseer could beat a slave to death during the day, then return to his great house, which was being run by his slave mistress and in which her word was law. He could mercilessly separate families by selling common law husbands from their wives or children from their mothers, and the very next day write a moving petition pleading with the assembly to allow him to leave more than the legal limit of 12,000 pounds for his illegitimate offspring. This, truly, was moral chaos, but it was the kind of chaos that a shrewd protopeasantry could exploit, and, more important, it was the kind of chaos that did not breed paternalism.

Quite the opposite was the case in America. While the black American did not become the distorted, twisted Sambo that Elkins simplemindedly claims was the consequence of his adjustment, the fact remains that the American slave was coopted by the system. It is impossible to see how be could have avoided it. The result, in cultural terms, was near total deracination; the loss of a sense of the past, of aboriginal traditions, and of independent values. This is not to say that he was not creative in his response. As Genovese has argued,[35] the black American slave made the best of a bad situation by evolving a symbiotic subculture within which there was some possibility of dignity. But it was the dignity of the oppressed and downtrodden. It was the dignity provided by a servile version of Christianity, which brought out all the latent slave soteria of primitive Christianity. It was the dignity of the protoserf, not of the protopeasant. Above all, the social patterns evolved by blacks in their adjustment to American slavery were too integrated with the social system that oppressed them to ever form the basis of a truly radical black proletarian culture. It is on this point that we completely depart from Genovese, in much the same way that he departs from his own data in coming to such an extraneously imposed conclusion.

To conclude then, slavery ensured the demographic survival of the black American to a degree unknown in any previous slave system in the annals of world history. Allied to this were unusually stable familial and community organizations. But it brought in its train the complete deracination of the group, the making of cultural compromises that involved a complete adjustment to the system and the development of a subculture which was merely a symbiotic variant of white society, one centered on a servile regression to primitive, conservative Christianity. It permitted a pseudostoic dignity. But it also entailed a complete loss of honor and independence. This is the price that black Americans were asked and were forced to pay for their survival.

THE SECOND MOVEMENT:
THE URBANIZATION OF
THE BLACK COMMUNITY

Between the Civil War and the end of the First World War the foundations of American economic and later political hegemony were laid. Arguments over the inevitability of the Civil War are usually confusing largely because there is often a lack of clarity concerning the exact forces that were in conflict. The simplistic "inevitability view" that the war was the inevitable result of the clash of two conflicting economic systems, one precapitalist and feudal, the other advanced industrial capitalism, is no longer tenable. The Civil War came about not because the economies of the North and the South were in conflict with each other but on the contrary, precisely because their economies had become so tightly interwoven.

The relationship, however, was not one of interdependence but rather of a highly asymmetric relation of dependence. The South bore the same relation to the industrializing North that a colonial society bears to its metropolitan center. As Dowd has noted: "The South. . .was not an extension or in an important sense even part of an industrializing America. The South was one of America's colonies."[36] As the West was settled and became the breadbasket of America and as Northern industry boomed to world prominence, the South sank deeper and deeper into dependency and stagnation. The institutional core of Southern economic backwardness, Dowd argues, had its origins in "three elements: cash crop monoculture, the plantation system and Negro slavery."[37] This is not to say that Southern slavery was not highly profitable, even efficient. Modern econometric studies suggest that it was, but the very profitability of the slave system on the micro-level of the plantation firm depended on a configuration of social, political, and economic institutions that ensured its overall economic backwardness and dependency.

Civil War and emancipation did little to change either this pattern of backwardness or the economic status of the blacks. As Rothstein has observed, the reconstruction South became a dual economy possessing a parasitic modern sector dominated by wealthy planters, many of Northern origin, and a large backward sector dominated by poor whites and blacks locked in a semifeudal sharecropping economic system.[38] Racism and caste were the social institutions used to divide the working classes and head off any populist threat from below. Internally the postemancipation Southern ruling class maintained its power by making race an ever-present issue.

> The profits of Southern industry were dependent upon cheap and abundant labor. The self-respect of the mass of Southern whites was dependent to a critical degree on the existence of the underprivileged and oppressed position of the Negro. The power of Southern business and political leaders rested on the creation and maintenance of

the one party system, a post-bellum development in the South. The maintenance of the South as an economic preserve of the North was dependent to an important degree on the continued political sterility of the South in national affairs. All these, of course, were interconnected.[39]

Externally the Southern ruling elite, especially its newly emerged middle segment, further reinforced its hegemony by collaborating with the Northern industrial elite in a compromise that involved the betrayal of black economic and political rights, the perpetuation of lower class white poverty, and the continued backwardness of the South.

It was this group [the new middle class] that gave as a quid pro quo easy access to the natural riches of the South to those on the outside, a process that greatly furthered the economic domination of the South by the North. And it was this group whose political power was ultimately dependent upon the continuation of the one party system—the North's role in this power play was to sacrifice what remained of abolitionist realism for the right to plunder the South and to look the other way in the decades after 1877 when the common principles of American Government were violated.[40]

For the blacks there was only one way out of this socioeconomic nightmare—massive flight from the rural areas. There were periodic spurts of migration in the nineteenth century but the sustained movement out of the rural South really began during the twentieth century and attained massive proportions during the depressed period on the eve of the First World War.[41]

The collapse of Southern agriculture under the impact of the boll weevil epidemic, natural calamities, and declining farm prices adversely affected blacks more than any other group. The growth of fascist assaults on blacks, especially by Ku Klux Klan groups, during the early twentieth century, was another important push factor, although it should be noted that these assaults were also closely related to the effects of the economic depression on the poor white community. Just as important, however, were the pull factors of a rapidly increasing demand for labor in the Northern industrial plants, especially during the war when immigration of cheap European labor was cut off. Tables 2 and 3 summarize the data on the urbanization of the black community between 1870 and 1960. Several points should be noted about the black experience of urbanization.[42] First, although the black rate of urbanization increased much faster than the white rate during the twentieth century, whites remained more urban than blacks up until 1960. In spite of the massive presence of blacks in Northern cities from the second decade of this century, it should not be forgotten that a sizable portion of blacks remained rural until quite recently. Second, the urbanization of blacks is as much a Southern phenomenon as a Northern one. Half of the black population still resides in the South. Third, blacks have a tendency to concentrate in large metropolitan areas rather than in smaller urban areas. Again, this is as true of the South as it is of the North. However, the Northern increase in black urbanization is closely correlated with the increase in the proportion of the urban population that is black in this region whereas no such correlation exists in the South, the absence of this correlation in the South being due to the equally rapid urbanization of the white working class community. It is this crucial difference that more than any other accounts for the popular perception of blacks as being overwhelmingly resident in large Northern cities. There is, however, a more substantial implication of this difference—the rise of the large inner-city urban ghetto, especially in the North—for while there are more black urban ghettos in the South than in the North, it is in the North that they first emerged and remain huge commercially and industrially eroded black communities.

Fourth, this ghettoization in the inner city was intensified first in the North and more recently in the South by the suburbanization of the white comunity beginning in the immediate post-World War II years. Finally, all the evidence suggests that black urbanization has now peaked and has been replaced by a new pattern, which has two effects. One is the increasing ghettoization of the black lower classes in the inner cities, both in the North and in the South. The other is the growth of black suburbanization, not however in integrated, middle-class suburbs but in equally segregated areas on the margin of the central cities, the so-called metropolitan ring. Harold M. Rose, in his study of this movement, observed that:

> A secondary urban environment is emerging which is increasingly becoming the place of residence of an ever larger number of black residents. The emerging environment is found beyond the margins of the central city but within what is sometimes identified as the metropolitan ring.[43]

TABLE 2

PERCENT OF URBAN POPULATION BY RACE AND REGION 1870–1960

Region and Race	1870	1880	1890	1900	1910	1920	1930	1940	1950	1960
United States										
White	27.5	30.3	38.4	43.0	48.7	53.4	57.6	57.4	64.3	65.5
Negro	13.4	14.3	19.8	22.7	27.4	34.0	43.7	48.6	62.4	73.2
Northeast										
White	44.2	50.6	62.5	69.0	74.0	75.7	76.9	76.1	78.7	79.1
Negro	54.0	62.7	71.5	78.3	82.6	86.7	89.0	90.1	94.0	95.6
North Central										
White	20.5	23.8	32.7	38.2	44.7	51.6	56.9	57.3	62.6	66.8
Negro	37.2	42.5	55.8	64.4	72.6	83.4	87.8	88.8	93.8	95.7
West										
White	25.3	30.7	37.9	41.2	49.2	53.0	59.6	58.8	69.7	77.6
Negro	44.6	50.8	54.0	67.4	78.6	74.0	82.5	83.1	90.3	92.7
South										
White	13.3	13.1	16.9	18.5	23.2	29.6	33.4	36.8	48.9	58.6
Negro	10.3	10.6	15.3	17.2	21.2	25.3	31.7	36.5	47.7	58.5
Secessionist South										
White	8.8	8.8	12.8	14.9	20.4	26.4	33.0	35.5	48.7	59.2
Negro	8.3	8.5	12.9	14.7	18.8	22.7	29.1	33.7	44.6	55.4
Nonsecessionist South										
White	23.8	24.3	27.6	27.4	29.9	35.8	39.2	40.2	49.7	56.5
Negro	26.2	29.4	38.4	42.1	44.3	49.4	54.7	60.8	71.6	79.3

SOURCE: D. O. Price, "Urbanization of the Blacks," in Clyde V. Kiser, ed., *Demographic Aspects of the Black Community,* Milbank Memorial Fund Quarterly, 48, no. 2, 1970, pt. 2. p. 48.

TABLE 3

PERCENT OF TOTAL NEGRO POPULATION IN RURAL AND
URBAN PARTS OF THE SOUTH, 1870–1960

Year	United States	South Total	South Urban	Rural
1870	100.0	90.6	9.3	81.3
1880	100.0	90.6	9.7	80.9
1890	100.0	90.3	13.8	76.5
1900	100.0	89.7	15.4	74.2
1910	100.0	89.0	18.8	70.2
1920	100.0	85.2	21.5	63.7
1930	100.0	78.7	24.8	53.8
1940	100.0	77.0	28.1	48.9
1950	100.0	68.0	32.5	35.5
1960	100.0	59.9	35.0	24.9

SOURCE: D. O. Price, "Urbanization of the Blacks," in Clyde V. Kiser, ed., *Demographic Aspects of the Black Community,* Milbank Memorial Fund Quarterly, 48, no. 2, 1970, pt. 2. p. 48.

Between 1960 and 1970 the metropolitan black ring suburbs grew by one million, from 2.5 million to 3.5 million, although the proportion of blacks in them remained stable at 5 percent. Significantly, the housing conditions of these new suburban areas are no better than those of the inner city ghettos. Indeed, they are often worse. White resistance is just as great here as it was to the movement of blacks to the inner cities. "The fight for turf . . . continues in a new arena among a new generation of urban residents."[44]

What were the major social consequences of the urbanization and ghettoization of the black community? We must distinguish two crucial periods in the impact of these developments. The first period began with the Great Migration and culminated in the Great Depression. We may call this the lumpenproletarianization of the black community. The second period began with the postwar years and is coming to an end and we may refer to it as the period of bourgeois development. There are many ironies in these two periods of development, especially with respect to the two main social groups within the black community, the bourgeoisie and the lumpenproletariat. The most significant feature of the first period is that blacks were never fully integrated into the industrial mainstream of the American economy. Overwhelmingly they were forced into the fringe sector of the economy, obliged to take what were essentially dead-end, low-paying jobs. They were systematically excluded from meaningful industrial jobs by a combination of protectionist pressures by the white working class, and racism on the part of employers.[45] It is impossible to explain their exclusion in this period in any but racist terms. Certainly market forces should have had the opposite effect. As Kenneth Arrow has written: "I do not see how the process of racial discrimination can begin in the economic sphere out of purely economic motives. It always pays any group with enough power to discriminate against some other—since color is seized on as a basis for discrimination, there must be an extra economic origin, although it is not precluded that its economic profitability reinforces the discrimination once started—the gains to the whites appear to accrue to white workers primarily."[46]

Incidentally, recent historical scholarship on black social and cultural life during slavery and the years after make nonsense of any cultural explanation of black exclusion from the mainstream of American economic life. The slave, we have been informed, was a highly efficient modern worker with a much higher productivity than his South European counterpart.[47] Thus the black migrants who applied for jobs in Northern industries were more culturally prepared and qualified than the Southern and East European peasants with whom they were competing. Racism alone explains their failure to secure meaningful jobs and not any such nonsense as the superior work ethic or the more stable family background of the European migrants since on both these grounds blacks were either their equals or their superiors.[48]

In spite of these obstacles a minority, and in some regions a substantial one, did succeed in gaining a toehold on jobs that provided some economic security and it is this group that, however precariously, formed the nucleus of a genuine working class in the black community. This working class, while socially significant for the black community, was always a minority of all blacks. From this group came the small black middle class that during this period was essentially a caste elite, that is, its economic base was the black group—in its roles as teachers, doctors, lawyers, bankers, insurance brokers, funeral parlor operators, ethnic publishers, and the like, all aimed exclusively at the black community. Like all caste elites it had a vested interest in the system of segregation, and the prevailing conservatism of its politics during this period must be interpreted in this light.[49] There was always, of course, a more progressive wing of this leadership, best represented by the NAACP, which struggled for greater freedom for the black community. However, the techniques and objectives of the NAACP were largely liberal and bourgeois. Their methods were primarily legal and their objectives were limited to the achievement of civil rights. Such rights, even were they won, would have been meaningless to the mass of lumpenproletarian blacks who were in no position to exercise them.

Collective action was also in evidence from lumpenproletariat leaders. In the face of white terror and economic oppression the character of this leadership was overwhelmingly retreatist. Escapist fundamentalist religion was the major form of communal social expression.[50] The major political expression of the period, the Marcus Garvey movement, was also retreatist, back to Africa millenarianism.[51] Both approaches, needless to say, failed to improve the condition of blacks, nor did the bourgeois legalism of the elite leadership.

The social and cultural impact of the urbanization and lumpenization of the black community is both complex and the subject of continuing controversy. It would seem obvious that these movements should have had a traumatic effect on social patterns. But what were these patterns and how exactly were they influenced? The traditional view that slavery resulted in the wholesale destruction of black family life is being strongly challenged by recent historical studies.[52] According to modern scholars the nuclear family emerged from the detribalization process and was reinforced by the economic self-interest of the planter class as well as the paternalistic ethos of the slave plantation. During the reconstruction period, as Gutman has argued, the already socially sanctioned nuclear family became legally sanctioned. Gutman, however, in his eagerness to disprove the traditional stereotype of the broken black slave family underestimates the impact of the migration on black life. The lower-class black family "did not disintegrate following emancipation" he tells us, "and it did not disintegrate as a consequence of the great migration to Northern cities prior to 1930."[53] Gutman is here attacking a straw man. Few observers now deny that the *typical* black family was a household with two parents. More important are the changes in the proportion of families with one head or with insecure socioeconomic foundations, and Gutman's own data clearly show a small but significant increase in the number of such families.

A more important critique of Gutman and the revisionists, however, is that they fail to note the important periodic lag in the effect of mass movements. As Jessie Bernard, in a far superior analysis of this period observes: "The succession of generations is a gradual one and it takes time for the traumata of any one generation to reveal themselves."[54] Thus if we really wish to assess the impact of the Great Migration and early urbanization on black family life, we should look not at the migrants themselves but at their children. Sure enough, when we observe the cohort of black women born since 1925 we find a high proportion of out-of-wedlock births among them and when we examine their children—the third generation, so to speak—those born after 1945, and who are now reproducing, we witness a massive disintegration in their familial patterns.[55]

This is in no way to deny the role of contemporary socioeconomic factors. Certainly these have been reinforcive. The point, however, is that the effects of the migration and urbanization have been delayed and are amplified with each new generation so that there is a real sense in which, current economic disasters aside, the effects of these developments are really only now being fully realized.

Urbanization, while the prime cause of the collapse of a significant minority of black lower-class families, was mediated through other more direct sociocultural forces. Poverty, welfare dependence, and unemployment have all been proposed as the critical intermediary variables but the most cursory examination of the relevant data suggests that the explanatory power of each, while not insignificant, is nonetheless quite limited.[56] Rather, as Bernard indicates, a deep division emerged during this period in the cultural strategies employed by blacks in their attempt to cope with the white capitalist world.[57] In summarizing a large number of studies that are uniform in making this distinction, Bernard calls one of these strategies the "acculturated," the other the "externally adaptive." The acculturation strategy highly values familial stability, sexual moderation, the work ethic, and in general those values we associate with white bourgeois society. There is an acute emphasis on respectability and restraint, perhaps even more so than among white middle-class Americans. The other response is self-consciously "unrespectable." It is hedonistic, sex-obsessed, nonfamilial, anti-intellectual, and pathetically macho. The externally adapted culture, during this period, was not a culture of poverty in the Oscar Lewis sense,[58] since one of its striking features was the fact that it cut across income groups within the black community. Rich and poor blacks alike adapted in this way.[59] At the same time the acculturated group could be found among both middle-class and working-class blacks. One weakness of Bernard's analysis is that she fails to explain the structural origins of this basic division in cultural strategies among blacks. I suggest that the two status groups or "stands" in the black comunity, to use Weberian jargon, are indeed economically related although not in the simplistic economic terms employed by advocates of the culture of poverty thesis. The cultural strategies were functions of the economic marginality of black Americans. We have stated that the majority of poor blacks were and are forced to accept marginal jobs in the urban industrial areas. However, it was and is possible to be rich and economically marginal in America. Considerable wealth can be and has been made by means of illegal activities. However, even certain legal activities, while highly rewarding financially, are equally marginal and precarious and not fully respectable in bourgeois society. Chief among these are the occupations of the sporting and entertainment industry. Many wealthy blacks derive their riches from these socially ambiguous and economically uncertain occupations. It is understandable then that wealthy blacks who so achieve wealth should remain committed to the externally adapted culture, whether in the "hip" variant of the legal occupations, or the more "funky" or "street" variant of those who rely on illegal means.

The acculturation strategy, on the other hand, is directly related to the secure and economically integrated jobs of those who share this style of living.

The second major period of black change, that between the forties and the end of the sixties, resulted in certain important modifications of the early patterns of development. The two major developments of this period were, of course, the passage of civil rights legislation resulting in the abolition of legalized segregation and civil disabilities and the rise of the black bourgeoisie, the main beneficiary of this liberal process. Great claims have been made for the changes that have taken place in the black community during this last period, some of them so exaggerated as to be laughable. More moderate is the recent assessment by the liberal sociologist Robin M. Williams. American society since the forties, Williams argues, has become more cosmopolitan. It is "more tolerant of dissent, diversity and nonconformity of beliefs, values and behavior."[60] This has been associated with major changes in the attitudes of whites toward blacks, reflected in the fact that 68 percent of whites express a willingness to live with blacks of a similar socioeconomic standing compared with 40 percent in the 1940s.[61] Relating to such changes in attitude have been changes in stereotypes about blacks, who are no longer considered an inferior race by a majority of whites. There have further been massive desegregation of schools, especially in the South, and total desegregation of the armed forces where "a massive, legally enforceable system of segregation and discrimination was dismantled in just under 5 years."[62] There has been increased political participation of blacks and a rapid rise in the number of black officeholders, especially in the South. The black middle class has increased from 5 percent to about 25 percent of the black population, and nonwhite income went from 51 percent to 63 percent of white income in 25 years. Overall, Williams assures us that American society in comparative terms is in good shape as far as racial and ethnic relations go and there is much to be proud of.

That important changes have taken place no one can deny. How these changes are interpreted, however, is likely to vary with the interpreter's perspective. It may seem impressive to a white liberal that black income is now 12 percentage points higher, relative to whites, than it was in the forties. To many blacks the 37 percent remaining difference is still a source of outrage. White liberals may wish to celebrate the abolition of segregation; blacks are likely to see it as the removal of an abomination which was a century overdue.

More important than these differences in perspective, however, is the fact that the changes themselves may well mean far less in real terms for blacks than they appear to do at first sight. Dan Lacy has observed that "the halfheartedness of Southern resistance to the later civil-rights acts measured not so much growing tolerance and moderation as indifference to a group no longer important enough to the Southern economy to justify the effort to confine them to subsistence-rewarded labor."[63] And while the number of black officeholders has increased considerably, the proportion of all officeholders who are black is still minuscule. The Joint Center for Political Studies estimates that at the present rate of increase only 3 percent of all officeholders will be black by the year 2000.[64] What is more, the vast majority of these officeholders are in minor and politically powerless positions.[65]

Without doubt the most significant development during this period has been the rise of the black middle class. A large number of analysts are in agreement that the black middle class has been the main beneficiary of recent changes. Freeman has summarized the gains as follows:

> In education, the average educational attainment of blacks moved closer to that of whites, with the proportion of high school and college graduates increasing significantly among the young.
>
> In the job market, ratios of black to white incomes rose substantially for most groups of workers. Black women enjoyed exceptionally great advances which brought them economic parity with white women having comparable education or job skills.
>
> Black and white occupational distributions tended to converge, as black women moved from domestic service to factory and clerical jobs and as black men increased their representation in craft, professional and managerial jobs.
>
> In each region of the country, but notably in the South, income differences by race declined, although sizeable gaps remained, especially in the South.[66]

On the other side of this seemingly bright picture, however, we find certain disturbing developments with respect to the black lower class. According to Levitan et al., "The poor and the near poor represented a staggering 42 percent of all blacks, and blacks were more than three times as likely to be poor as whites"; this is so in spite of "substantial income gains since 1960."[67] Blacks earn substantially less than whites in the same occupations. "The better paid the occupation, the less likely blacks are to be well represented."[68]

On the severe unemployment problem, Levitan et al. found that for 1972, 10.8 percent of black males over 16 were unemployed compared with 8.2 percent of white males, and that 57.2 percent of white males were full-time workers compared with 47 percent of black males. However, employment means something quite different for whites. Blacks were disproportionately concentrated in dead-end jobs: "A large minority are trapped in a secondary labor market where there is no reward for tenure and where wages and working conditions are barely preferable to street life and welfare."[69] That was in 1972. Since then the situation has grown considerably worse. According to the *Wall Street Journal* (November 28, 1977), "In September [1977] President Carter ordered a new look at the problem after being jolted by August figures showing a rise in the black unemployment rate to 14.5 percent, or double the overall jobless rate of 7.1 percent, with 40 percent of black teenagers out of work." Two months later the situation had grown still worse. The *U. S. News and World Report* (December 5, 1977) reported: "In October [1977] 15 percent of the black labor force was jobless, compared with 6.1 percent of the white. For black teenagers, the rate was a towering 40 percent, against 14.8 percent for the white teenagers." And as if this is not deplorable enough, the unemployment figures, because they measure only those who are still actively in search of a job, and take no account of those who have given up looking, actually underestimate the extent of the problem.

Because of their lower income and the exorbitant expense of health care in the United States, blacks are far more unhealthy than whites. This is reflected in the higher mortality rates of blacks, and in particular, their higher infant mortality rate which is twice that of whites. Blacks also have lower life expectancies at every age level. "Black people not only die younger, they live lives that are less healthy: they have more days of disability, of illness and of work loss; greater unmet dental needs; almost twice as much likelihood of being in poor or only fair health."[70]

It is in housing that the least progress has been made. Zoning laws and real estate practices such as block-busting are nakedly racist in their motivation and effects.[71] Levitan et al. found that *"black housing is now (1975) more segregated than it was a decade ago—a fourth of all* blacks still live in homes which are severely deteriorated. . . . a fifth contain more than one person per room. . . . black homes are older and have fewer amenities on the average, yet may cost more than those occupied by whites. Worst of all, blacks do not have equal opportunity to choose where and how they want to live."[72] An important difference between the black poor and the white poor, which has a direct impact on their life chances, is the fact that whereas the former are over-whelmingly concentrated in desperately poor ghetto areas, the latter are largely dispersed among the more affluent whites. Thus the poor white child constantly has the demonstration of successful whites around him or her, and has access to the personal contacts, social networks, and educational facilities that ensure and reinforce upward mobility. The black poor child, on the other hand, lives in conditions in which he or she constantly sees failure, has very few, if any, role models of success, has no access to the social networks that are crucial for mobility, and experiences educational and other facilities that reinforce and ensure failure.[73]

Discrimination against blacks at the primary, secondary, and college levels has been largely eliminated and, as we have seen, college education has been the main vehicle of mobility for the expanding black middle class. The situation is different for the underclass. The quality of education received by ghetto blacks is still a matter of some controversy, but the issue is really secondary to another: the social capacity of lower-class blacks to take advantage of the opportunity offered by higher enrollment and, just as important, the questionable social and economic benefits of greater numbers of years schooling. Indeed, among the underclass, studies have shown "that dropouts did as well or better than their high school graduate counterparts."[74]

These opposing developments among the black middle and lower classes have led a large number of analysts to argue that the major division that blacks now face is not that between blacks and whites but the intraracial division between the black middle class and the black underclass. The most recent statement of this thesis is that of Wilson. According to this scholar, race is a rapidly declining issue in the fate of black Americans. Equal employment legislation has paved the way for the entry of the educated blacks into "the mainstream of American occupations." These government programs, however, are unable "to deal with the new barriers imposed by structural changes in the economy" that result in the exclusion of the black underclass from the economy. Thus, "the very attempts of the government to eliminate traditional racial barriers through such programs as affirmative action have had the unintentional effect of contributing to the growing economic class divisions within the black community."[75]

To emphasize the growing gulf between the black lower and middle classes is one thing. To argue, however, that race has declined significantly as a causal factor in the status of black Americans is quite

another. While it is true that ultimately the problem of the black underclass is due to economic marginality, the fact remains that blacks are
disproportionately represented in the underclass as a result of both
historical as well as current racial discrimination. The black working
poor—the great majority of the black poor—still earn far less than their
white counterparts for the same jobs. And there can be no doubt that the
considerably higher incidence of black unemployment relative to whites
is directly attributable to racism. Ultimately, the solution to the problem of the black poor will be the same as that for the white poor—a
significant reduction in the structurally determined inequality of America—but until such major changes come about much can be done to
relieve the problem by at least equalizing the life chances of blacks and
whites who must suffer the frustrations of economic marginalization.

Nor is it true that racism is no longer operative with respect to the
black middle class. This view is primarily the result of a statistical
illusion created by the overwhelming emphasis on the median income
as the measure of relative black progress. However, in an important
paper, the economists Wohlstetter and Coleman have shown that a far
different conclusion is arrived at if we concentrate not on a single point
in the income distribution, but on the entire income distribution.[76]
Using what they call the "income ratio at quintile curve," which is
derived by "taking non-white to white income ratio at selected percentiles and plotting the ratio against the percentiles," they found that the
curve has three distinct segments. The bottom segment (0 to 21st percentile) shows marked improvement in the relative status of blacks due
largely to income transfers and other welfare programs. While the
relative status of the black poor to the white poor has improved, however, their absolute position still remains desperate for reasons mentioned earlier. And the remaining gap is still significant. It is in the
middle segment of the curve (the 21st to 83rd percentile) that the
celebrated improvements have been made. While the gap between
white and black income has narrowed substantially at this segment the
reasons for the narrowing are worth noting. Perhaps the most important of these is the improvement in the economic position of black
women. Middle-class black family income equates with that of white
families because of the much greater tendency of black middle-class
women to work. What is more, the income of black wives is positively
associated with the income of black husbands, unlike the white family
situation where the relationship is inverse.

When we move to the top segment of the income ratio-at-quintile curve, we immediately see how rash it is to claim that race has declined in significance, for at this level (the 83rd to 100th percentile of incomes) the black presence rapidly slopes down to zero. There is an income ceiling above the black middle class, which almost all optimistic analysts choose to neglect. As Wohlstetter and Coleman observe, "To focus only on the lowest quintiles is to neglect the fact that there is a lower statistical ceiling over non-white income, one that is hard to penetrate."[77] In response to this interpretation, it has been argued that blacks have only just begun to penetrate the lower rungs of the professional elite and that it will take some time to move up the ladder into the top income categories. Freeman tried to get at this problem by examining cohort income differentials and found them to be "generally stable." It is questionable, however, whether an analysis of cohort income differentials really gets to the issue since such analyses are still based on median income differentials and it is precisely this statistical measure which grossly understates the problem. Freeman himself was forced to admit that "serious danger of future discrimination in promotion decisions cannot be denied," and he added: "Two-thirds of the placement directors in the *Black Elite* survey expressed concern that at least some black graduates being offered jobs in 1970 could face dead-end careers ten years hence."[78]

Another issue is the fact that it is not only the number of middle- or upper-class jobs that require attention, but the kinds of jobs the black middle class do. Real power in American society lies not in the public sector—where most black middle-class persons find employment—but in the private sector. Furthermore, within the private sector, power is wielded by a relatively small elite of top management and by those who own disproportionately large amounts of the country's wealth. Blacks are almost totally unrepresented in this power elite and there is not the slightest hint that they will have any presence worth mentioning in this all-important segment of American society anytime in the near or middle future. Indeed, one can state quite confidently that there is no hope of an improvement of the black community by means of the black elite gaining access to the levers of power in American society. It need hardly be added that even if the improbable were to happen and the black elite gained some hold on the levers of power, it might be naive to expect such a group to behave any differently from its white counterpart.

Finally, it should be pointed out that important cultural changes have accompanied the emergence of the black elite and the widening gulf between it and the black underclass. The situation that existed in the earlier period of this century wherein cultural patterns cut across income lines no longer pertains, at least not to any significant degree. Class and status groups have now largely merged in the black community, thereby reinforcing the gulf between the two groups.[79] Because education is now the major means of individual mobility and because there has been an increasing tendency for educational success to be related to family background, there has been a strong intergenerational reinforcement of blacks who belong to the two cultures. Increasingly, it is from the ranks of the "acculturated" blacks that the newly expanded elite is coming, and increasingly the "externally adapted" blacks are being left behind in the ghetto. Although he did not interpret it quite in these terms, this is perhaps the most important finding of Freeman:

> The relation between family background and educational and labor market achievement, traditionally quite weak among black Americans, was greatly strengthened for young persons in the new market, to approach that found among whites. Because of the enhanced curvature of the background-achievement locus for blacks and declines in discriminatory differentials, differences in family background resources became the chief deterrent to attainment of educational and economic equality among the young. While even young black men from the poorest backgrounds, those born in the rural South, progressed in the new market, persons from higher socioeconomic backgrounds made the most rapid improvements, creating greater "class" cleavages in black America.[80]

What Bernard calls the "externally adapted" cultural response has now hardened into a life-style that has been well documented and is currently most frequently referred to as the "street culture" of the ghetto.[81] There still remains in the ghetto patterns of survival other than the dominant street culture. What McCord calls the "achievers" can still be found in the ghetto; these still hope to make it in the white world which is, in spite of formidable obstacles to entry, their primary mode of reference. There are also the "exploiters"—black landlords, shopkeepers, and small-time capitalists—who make middle-class incomes by exploiting those trapped in the ghetto no less ruthlessly than their white counterparts. And among those who reject the white world or no longer aspire to enter it, not all are street people. There are still the other-worldly fundamentalists of the store-front churches who withdraw into religious ecstasy and, at the other extreme of religious reaction, this-world cultists and others such as the Black Muslims who puritanically adjust to the present world though one that excludes whites.[82]

On the whole, however, the range and variety of black ghetto styles are rapidly declining. Black Muslim membership, never very high even at its height in the late sixties, has declined precipitously in recent years. The "achievers" have almost all left or are scrambling to leave. The activists and revolutionaries of the sixties are now almost nonexistent. The Black Panthers and other such groups are spent forces. What remains, therefore, as the dominant pattern of response, are what Mc-Cord calls the "defeated," the "rebels without causes" or criminal elements, and most pervasive of all, the "street people." The three types of responses overlap, for often the same persons may shift from one strategy to the next and the boundaries between the response patterns themselves are blurred. Even so, it is useful to distinguish the major foci of these three main ways of dealing with economic marginalization.

The "defeated" refers to those who seek escape from their miseries in drugs, alcohol, and psychotic delusions. Self-destructive withdrawal is the dominant theme of this pathological strategy. McCord et al. observe that 60 percent of all identified drug addicts are urban blacks; that the alcoholic rate of urban blacks is two to four times greater than the white rate; and that black psychosis, especially schizophrenia, "exceeds white rates by about 200 percent."[83]

Direct criminal activity is seen by many young ghetto blacks as the only path to survival. Given the small risks involved in committing many crimes, the low probability of ever getting a steady job and, in the event of getting a job, the low and unrewarding wages likely to be received, resorting to a life of crime is, in terms of pure economic choice, highly rational behavior. Fellow blacks, as is well known, constitute the overwhelming majority of the victims of black crime. So what makes economic sense in individualistic terms turns out to be disaster for the black group as a whole.[84] With respect to crimes of violence, one bleak statistic that speaks volumes by itself is the simple fact that the single most important cause of death among black males between the ages of 15 and 25 is homicide, by other blacks. In general, apart from "personal larceny without contact," blacks suffer to a greater degree than whites in every category of personal crimes with almost all the offenders being other blacks (see Figure 1).

Fig. 1
Victimization Rates for Personal Crimes, by Type of Crime and Race, 1976

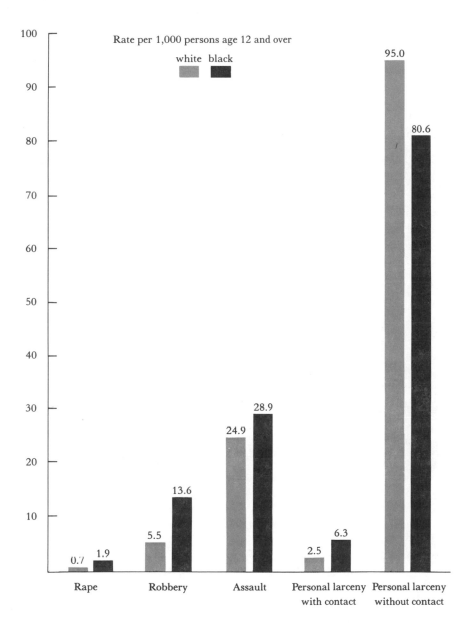

Rate per 1,000 persons age 12 and over

white black

SOURCE: *Criminal Victimization in the United States,* National Crime Survey Report, U.S. Dept. of Justice, Nov. 1977, p. 15.

It is the street culture that has become the dominant response pattern of the black underclass. "Street people are known," according to Horton, "by their activities . . . 'duking' (fighting or at least looking tough), 'hustling' (any way of making money outside of the 'legitimate' world of work), 'gigging' (partying)—and by their apparent nonactivity, 'hanging' on the corner." The central activity is hustling, i.e., "conning, stealing, gambling and selling dope." The street people live constantly on the margin of the law and getting in and out of trouble is a "major theme" in their lives.[85]

Liebow has given us one of the best accounts of the street culture of the underclass. Failure to achieve economic security, he concludes, is carried over into the home, resulting in failed marriages.

> The streetcorner is, among other things, a sanctuary for those who can no longer endure the experience or prospect of failure. There . . . public fictions support a system of values which, together with the value system of society at large, make for a world of ambivalence, contradiction and paradox, where failures are rationalized into phantom successes and weaknesses magically transformed into strengths.[86]

The sexual exploitation of women is one of the main forms of psychological compensation among the street people, and this is true of both wives and lovers. "Where women are concerned, he says, a man should take what he can when he can get it."[87] What this means, of course, is that women bear the major psychological as well as economic burdens of black poverty. As Abbey Lincoln, speaking for the black underclass woman observes:

> . . . to be a black woman is to operate almost totally as a physical body without the inducements offered her white counterpart. While white females are sexual objects, black women are sexual laborers. . . . Although black women are frequently described by the white agency in terms that suggest power, such as "strong," "domineering," "matriarchal" and "emasculating" . . . the domination of the kitchen and the welfare department are hardly powerful vantage points.[88]

The pathetic and ruthless exploitation of women becomes the model of all human relationships among the street people. Friendships are important, but like their love affairs they quickly reach a peak of intensity then collapse. The fluidity and fragility of relationships is reflected also in the absence of any neighborhood ties. In spite of all the rhetoric of community pride there is no sense of neighborhood solidarity among the street people. Indeed, the neighborhood is ripped off more than any other area.[89]

For the underclass youth, excluded from the economy, alienated from political life, deprived of all hope of a decent future, obliged to live in a squalid ghetto that is more like a concentration camp without walls and in which daily indignities chip away at his soul, in which "yesterday merges into today, and tomorrow is an emptiness to be filled in through the pursuit of bread and excitement,"[90] for such youths it is both tragic and understandable that the model of the successful "dude" should be the pimp or "mackman."

> Both terms describe a person of considerable status in the street hierarchy, who, by his lively and persuasive rapping . . . has acquired a stable of girls to hustle for him and give him money. For most street men and many teenagers he is the model whom they try to emulate. Thus within the community you have a pimp walk, pimp style boots and clothes, and perhaps most of all "pimp talk."[91]

Used, abused, and discarded like spent whores, the underclass youths desperately try to get back by idealizing and playing the pimp. Symbolically, the pimp style is a sociological metaphor, a statement about the system, that is, it is a way of denying the economic status of a discarded whore by assuming the status of the person who does the discarding, the capitalist pimp. Thus the pimp style is a way of assimilating the role of the powerful white economic marginalizer and discarder. But of course, the pimp style is not just symbol; it is real, and as such, is another one of the many self-destructive mechanisms that sustains degradation.[92]

THE THIRD MOVEMENT: BLACKS AS A RADICAL CATALYST IN POST-INDUSTRIAL SOCIETY

The remaining decades of the twentieth century and the early decades of the twenty-first will be critical times for black Americans and, just as surely, for American society at large. On the national level

American society is moving toward what Daniel Bell calls a post-industrial phase in which the economy increasingly shifts toward a high technology base reflected, in socioeconomic terms, in an occupational restructuring that focuses increasingly on the technical and professional groups. There will be an increasing tendency to move from a "goods-producing to a service economy" with over 70 percent of the work force in services by 1980. The new service sector, however, will refer primarily to jobs in "health, education, research and government" resulting in "the expansion of a new intelligentsia—in the universities, research organizations, professions, and government."[93]

Although Bell has relatively little to say in specific terms about the fate of the black and other poor in post-industrial society, he is shrewd enough to recognize that in his proposed techno-meritocratic future the "central question" will be "the relation of technocratic decisions to politics."[94]

For those who are ready for the coming meritocracy the future must be bright indeed. Ever-increasing "marginal productivity," ever-increasing earnings, ever-increasing work satisfaction, and, for the technocrats and professionals, ever-increasing power, ever-increasing movement to wider and wider rings of exurbia or else to closely guarded luxury apartments in refashioned "renaissance centers" in the cities of the future.

For the mass of the black poor, and for the poor generally, this scenario must seem—if the seeming were either possible or comprehensible—like the closest thing to a social nightmare. For if the industrial world already has little use for them, what in the world will the post-industrial world do with them? Until a solution can be found the immediate future must mean less and less chance of securing any of the declining factory jobs, more concentration in abandoned inner cities or equally segregated metropolitan ring suburbs, greater alienation from the mainstream, a heightened feeling of meaninglessness and irrelevance—total degradation.[95]

For those who cannot compete for a place in the new meritocracy the answer would seem to be painfully simple: tough! There is only one problem here. It is not possible to say "tough" to 20 million people, a conservative estimate of the number of blacks who would not be able to participate meaningfully in post-industrial society as it is currently forecast by current analysts. And when one adds to these 20 millions the greater millions of poor whites from Appalachia and elsewhere, many of whom are now behind the blacks in terms of structural involvement with the economy, and the further millions of the nonblack minorities, it would not only be foolish but downright madness to adopt such a stance.

And yet, American society has reached the limits of reformism in its handling of the problem of the black poor.[96] The partly artificial creation of a black bourgeoisie cannot continue. For not only is it not solving the problems of the group as a whole, but the public sector as it is currently conceived within the capitalist free enterprise framework has been thoroughly saturated. What is more, the professional organizations and schools as well as the business community are in open revolt against what they consider a clear breach of the rules of the capitalist and meritocratic game in the political pressure for affirmative action.[97] Yet if the poor, especially the black poor, are to catch up it is not enough simply to eliminate racial discrimination. As Andrew Brimmer and others have noted, they must "be able to acquire skills at an accelerated rate," one faster than the rate at which whites acquire such skills. Christopher Jencks has neatly summarized the problem:

> Unfortunately . . . skills are not absolute but relative—and hence, competitive. If the least adept students are given slightly better instruction, while instruction of the most adept gets substantially better, the competitive position of the least adept will deteriorate rather than improve. If that happens, poverty will grow more widespread. If the schools want to end poverty, they must not only improve the position of the poor pupils; *they must improve it faster than they improve the position of the rest of the pupils.* (emphasis added)[98]

So what is to be done? Clearly, if the problem is not just to be neglected, which it cannot be, then only one or two courses are possible: one is proto-fascist repression, the other a radical restructuring of the society in a manner that goes beyond the limits of reformism.

For many segments of the ruling class in post-industrial society the proto-fascist response must seem enormously tempting. Black Americans, even more than the Jews of Nazi Europe, are now highly concentrated in segregated ghettos. Because they are nonwhite it would be much easier to identify pockets of them in nonghetto areas. Strategically placed paramilitary stations combined with an efficient intelligence network could easily maintain what in effect would be highly contained concentration camps with tight surveillance on egress and entry while maintaining the appearance of freedom of movement. Unlike the concentration camps of Nazi Germany or present-day South Africa, a pass system would not be necessary to maintain blacks in de facto concentration camps.[99] In the first place most young blacks in the ghetto already live out their lives within the boundaries of the ghetto. There is nowhere else to go. Jobs are not to be found outside the central cities.[100] Friends and relations are also not to be found anywhere else except the ghetto. The illusion of freedom of movement could be maintained further by deemphasizing exit from the ghetto while emphasizing restraint or constraint on movement into nonblack areas. Already, as a result of purely legal and economic means, blacks are largely prevented from living in nonblack areas. Police patrol of white areas and vigilante type citizens groups already prevent blacks from entering many all-white neighborhoods. Areas such as Cicero, in metropolitan Chicago, and South Boston are already effectively closed to blacks.

In recent years the ideological support for such exclusion has come in the form of community control of neighborhoods. The American government has actually given the seal of approval to such neighborhood protection movements by voting funds for the promotion of ethnic heritages and the development of community based organizations. The so-called revival of ethnicity closely dovetails with this development.[101]

The proto-fascist solution would not necessarily involve anything so drastic as the liquidation of the black community. Any such attempt would clearly be met with worldwide condemnation and the ideology of democracy would be irretrievably damaged by the very hint of such a strategy.[102] To liquidate the black community, in any case, would not only be impractical and counterproductive but wasteful. Ideally the proto-fascist scenario calls for the containment of the black poor in concentrated areas and the use of their labor for the menial but still essential tasks that will remain even in the most highly advanced, post-industrial utopia: street cleaning and general sanitation, sewage disposal, hospital attendants, the less technical aspects of the transportation industry, and the filthier and more hazardous types of blue collar jobs.

The proto-fascist scenario can obviously not be dismissed as a paranoid fantasy. As we have seen, many of the essential elements of such a development already exist as a result of unplanned structural changes affecting the masses of the black poor. All that it requires is a policy that would make intentional what has already unintentionally evolved and that systemizes, rationalizes, and reinforces these unplanned developments. Much of the law and order rhetoric of the Nixon-Agnew years had a clear proto-fascist ring and, as is well known, was aimed mainly at the urban black poor.

A proto-fascist response, however, will not work and while it might be attempted in certain metropolitan areas—Houston, Chicago, and Pittsburgh are the most likely cities (note, for example, the recent scandal in Houston where death-squad-like police murders have gone largely unpunished with the strong support of the white community)—this will almost certainly fail. The proto-fascist scenario will not work primarily because of what I have called elsewhere the counter-leviathan power of the urban poor.[103] The urban poor, being a minority, may not possess the power to force through positive programs in their own interests, but they do possess the power to undermine the urban industrial base of American society. We may list here four main counter-leviathan powers: political terror, economic sabotage, criminality, and cultural sabotage. The use of political terror in the advanced West European societies has become a commonplace in recent years. If such developments are possible in more egalitarian and homogeneous societies such as West Germany, it would seem obvious that they are even more likely in the United States where inequities are not only more pronounced but are associated with racial differentiation. The amazing thing indeed is that America has so far been spared such acts of terror. There is every reason to believe, however, that terrorism or other forms of violence are quite a distinct possibility in America. Certainly this possibility is taken seriously by the Congress of the United States. The Ribicoff Committee, for example, tried to get Congress to approve an omnibus anti-terrorist bill. Both the FBI and the army have recently given the matter special priority and have set up special units to deal with it. Some time ago Project Delta was set up by the army, the so-called "D" detachment of the army special forces, with the objective of training an elite core of army officers in anti-terrorist strategy.[104] The political establishment has every reason to be concerned. The American poor is not a passive group. One major achievement of the activism of the sixties has been the politicization of the economically deprived and the demonstration of the fact that violence can be a useful means of promoting group interest. It is generally felt among the politically conscious poor that the more legitimate means of mass protest have been exhausted, including that of spontaneous riots.[105] Clearly then, if legitimate political action fails, or worse, if the established forces respond by engaging in more repressive action, the resort to the counter-leviathan of terror will be a near certainty. Almost all students of violence in all students of violence in modern societies have reached the same conclusion that the MIT scholar Douglas A. Hibbs arrived at in his comparative study of violence, namely that "the dominant causal sequence that indirectly relates to the dimensions of violence is one in which protest is met with repression by elites which produces in turn an escalated response of internal war from its recipients."[106]

American cities are also obviously highly vulnerable to economic sabotage. As H.L. Nieburg, another distinguished student of political violence has observed, "highly organized societies, for all their power and magnificence, are delicately balanced organisms."[107] It would take little technical expertise or organizational skill to disrupt the transportation of any of the major urban areas of America. Major health hazards could result from a disruption of the sanitation system before National Guard or paramilitary forces could be mobilized. Equally vulnerable are the electricity generating power plants of the major urban areas.

Crime, especially violent crime, is already a major social problem in urban America. Recent studies indicate that violent crimes are on the increase in suburban and rural areas. The trend indeed is ominous.[108] As crime levels off or decreases in the central ghettos it increases in the suburban areas. Increasingly, the victims become the affluent instead of other residents of the ghetto. While most crime is still intraracial, there is an increasing tendency toward interracial crime, and a significant development in recent years has been the fact that "when interracial assaults do occur, they usually involve black offenders and white victims."[109]

Unplanned cultural sabotage is already rampant in American society. I refer to the debasement of the quality of life, the rapid vulgarization of the cultural products,[110] the low standard of public intercourse and discourse that the presence of a large minority of culturally debased human beings partly imposes on their society. Ironically, the mass media and those who control the production of public culture by operating on the principle of defining standards so as to include the most deprived are the primary agents of lower-class cultural influence.[111] Television violence and its deleterious consequences are obviously not unrelated to the pervasive presence of crime in U.S. life and national consciousness.

There is also, however, a more subtle, upward diffusion of lumpenproletarian values, which constantly corrodes the bourgeois culture of the affluent majority. We indicated that there was a basic division in the black community between the acculturated middle-class culture and the externally adapted or street culture. The street culture, now exclusively identified with the ghetto segment of the black community, still cuts across class lines. Only now, ironically, it is middle-class white youths who seem more inclined to adopt it than the newly expanded black middle class. To take one example, the destructive use of hard drugs is now almost entirely a problem of the black ghetto and the white suburbs.[112] Middle-class blacks have made a strict avoidance of drug abuse almost a sine qua non of their new-found status.

To summarize, it is not possible to neglect the 20 million blacks who reside in America's urban ghettos, nor is it possible to respond to their demands by the use of proto-fascist or other repressive measures. At any rate, such responses are likely to be counterproductive. If the limits of reformism have been reached, so have the limits of repressive law-and-order strategy. There is clearly then only one long-term alternative, a fundamental change in social policy involving a restructuring of the American occupational structure. The restructuring required to include the black and nonblack poor falls well short of any revolutionary change. However, it does involve the adoption of policies that are currently viewed with horror by large segments of the establishment. We are thinking here of such policies as a positive shift toward a full-employment strategy, even if this involves lowering the present high priority on inflation control; a much greater expansion of the public sector, especially into permanent labor-intensive programs, similar to but more sophisticated than the New Deal experiments; a much greater control of the employment practices of the private sector by the expanded and more effective use of government contracts against discriminating firms; and above all an emphasis on the minimization of the human costs of blind industrial change. No romantic limits on growth per se will be necessary (since any such limits are bound to affect the poor more adversely than any other group), but limits on the direction of growth will be needed to ensure that no segment of the population is to be made marginal or structurally irrelevant.

The likelihood of such choices being made may seem remote at the present time given the current drift toward neoconservatism among both the political and intellectual establishment. The problem, however, is that the alternatives of not making such decisions are horrendous. If such choices are not voluntarily made they will be made under pressure from the poor, pressure of the counter-leviathan sort we briefly discussed above. Dorothy K. Newman et al. have observed that:

What has redounded to the benefit of blacks in good times has not
been eagerly handed over; it had to be wrested from an unwilling
white majority. What has been retained during downturns has been
fiercely contested. That has been central to much of the struggle in
every area of life.[113]

We expect this pattern of struggle and grudging response to continue during the remaining decades of the present century and onward
in the twenty-first until black Americans are truly equal. In the coming
years, however, the stakes will be much higher and as such the struggle
more intense and the threat to American tranquility all the greater.
Collective violence will be a near certainty and for much the same
reasons as those suggested by Charles Tilly in his analysis of the role of
violence in modern Western societies, namely: "(1) its frequent success
as a tactic, (2) its effectiveness in establishing or maintaining a group's
political identity, (3) its normative order, (4) its frequent recruitment of
ordinary people, and (5) its tendency to evolve in cadence with peaceful
political action."[114] We are confident that the outcome will be salutary
and that American democracy will survive this process of conflict.
However, before conditions get any better they will certainly get much
worse, for the black poor in particular and for American race and class
relations in general.

Western industrialization was built partly on black slavery. The
exploitation of black labor made the American South possible. The
American South as an internal dependency partly made the American
North possible. Internal migrant black labor further supported the
rise of American industry to world hegemony. In these so-called post-
industrial times, one great civilizing role remains for the black Americans. Because their problems can only be solved by a restructuring of
the American economy and social order and a humanizing of its domestic priorities, and because their problems cannot be solved in a repressive manner, or be neglected, it follows that in struggling for their own
equality, black Americans are struggling for the equality of all Americans and for the humanization of a post-industrial order that, left to its
own devices without this radical catalyst, could so easily become not a
servant of democratic mankind but a monstrous dehumanizing master.
On the shoulders of black Americans then, in this their last epic struggle
for equality, largely rests the burden of avoiding such a catastrophe.

The Future of Women in America's Third Century

Sheila K. Johnson

M'GUINNESS

12 It is a daunting task to make any predictions about society a hundred years hence. Had I been a 40 year-old woman a century ago (instead of, as I am now), would I have foreseen the passage of the Nineteenth Amendment in 1920, the multitude of inventions and household appliances we now have, or the sexual mores of the Jazz Age and the present? Probably not. In any event, a good part of my insight would have derived from my station in life. Had I been born Louisa May Alcott (who was 42 in 1874), I would have been supporting a mother, father, and three sisters with my writing of children's books and thrillers. Or had I been born Lola Montez or Marie Duplessis (the latter of whom inspired both *La Dame aux camélias* and *La Traviata*), I would have had a brief but interesting career as a *grande horizontale*. Had I been born in Europe and emigrated to America during the 1870s I would probably—depending on my country of origin—have settled on a farm or worked in one of the new sweatshops in a northern city. None of these positions might have prepared me very well to foresee American women's next hundred years, but at least even a century ago I would have been no stranger to hard work and sex.

I begin with these two concepts because like Freud, I take it that the two great tasks of all adults—women as well as men—are to love and to work. What does the future hold for American women in these two realms, and how have they changed in the recent past? One reason why it is useful to begin by looking back a hundred years is that it provides some perspective on the problem of looking ahead. Translated into human terms, a hundred years actually does not seem very long: it means approximately three generations. That is to say, we are speaking about someone born this year plus his or her children and grandchildren. And while none of us can feel very confident when it comes to predicting what sort of government these three generations will live under, fortunately there is somewhat greater continuity in the realm of biology. I think it safe to say, for example, that men and women—

whatever they may be wearing in the 2070s—will still look like men and women and will still be attracted to one another. I even think that women will continue to exist in approximate numerical parity with men, although given the likelihood that we shall soon be able to choose the sex of a child, this now becomes an open question rather than a fixed assumption, and one to which I shall return.

In contemplating the future of love and work in the lives of American women, it seems to me that one of the first observations one can make is that there is some connection between these two things. It is often argued today that modern marriage has been made brittle primarily because of its dependence on sexual attraction and notions of romantic love. But it is also the increasing ability and tendency of women to work outside the home that renders divorce possible. Until recently, many men and women put up with unhappy marriages simply because there was no viable alternative. Today a woman who wants a divorce knows she can go out and support herself, and a man need not feel he is abandoning his wife to destitution or prostitution if he leaves her.

Of course, in real life things seldom work as neatly as they do in theory. In the late 1960s, when these so-called "modern" attitudes began to be codified into "no-fault" divorce laws, it was argued that since both partners in a marriage were equal, a husband should no longer be required to pay alimony to his ex-wife. Women are now having some second thoughts about this. It is clear, for example, that a woman who has spent twenty years married to a $40,000-a-year businessman experiences a radical drop in income if she must all of a sudden support herself as a salesperson or an office worker. And if she has never held an outside job during her married life, she may not be able to find work at all. Many women are therefore suggesting that housewifely tasks should be compensated by a regular salary, complete with social security withholding tax, so that every wife will have savings and a retirement income of her own.

I do not happen to think that this particular proposal will be adopted, although it contains some features that most certainly will come to dominate our lives: namely, increasing bureaucratization and interference by the state. But forcing every husband to pay his wife a salary would probably be the swiftest way imaginable to do away altogether with marriage and the family. One reason why the family exists in all societies from the most simple to the most complex is that it is so extraordinarily flexible and adaptable: for example, it can function as a hereditary nobility, or a lendlease bank in times of hardship and rapid social change, or a welfare office for the young, ill, and elderly. In a fascinating article, anthropologist Burton Benedict once argued that family firms were a common feature of developing economies precisely because they could afford to take long-term risks without paying strict attention to union wages, dividends, and the like.[1] The same techniques have often been used by upwardly mobile families in our own society: a wife works to put her husband through law or medical school, or she cooks, sews, and economizes until his income is established. If such couples were forced, by law, to operate on the basis of strict accounting methods and "what's mine is mine, and what's yours is yours," they would never make it. It is, of course, grossly unfair if a husband exploits his wife's labor until he has reached the economic "take-off" stage and then divorces her. This is one of the situations alimony was designed to redress.

Some women today believe that instead of asking for housewife's compensation they should simply enter the labor force and remain there throughout their married lives, as a form of social insurance. Certainly, the statistics show that since 1900, an ever-increasing percentage of married women do work outside the home. Many do so because it is the only way to bring in an adequate income for the family—that is, like a member of a family firm they are contributing to the welfare of a joint enterprise. But those who do so merely as a form of marriage insurance are probably insuring, instead, that they will one day be divorced. Isabel Sawhill, for example, has observed, "There is now fairly convincing evidence that the higher a wife's earnings, other things being equal, the more likely it is that a couple will separate. We suspect that changing attitudes about women's roles and the fact that more married women are participating in the labor market have combined to create new tensions within marriage while simultaneously decreasing the social and economic constraints which once bound many women to relatively unsatisfactory marriages."[2] It is a bit like the dilemma faced by some businesses that want to be insured against terrorist attacks and ransom demands: if you have the insurance you become instantly more vulnerable since, in fact, you can now afford to pay.

Regardless of the reasons, however, the number of women entering the workforce is likely to increase. It has been increasing steadily since the turn of this century, with neither the depression nor the post-World

War II baby boom having cut into that trend. As of the end of 1976, 55.6 percent of all adult women in the United States had paying jobs. During the next hundred years, female participation in the labor force may well rise to 75 or 80 percent. It will probably never go higher than that because some women will always be at least temporarily at home having babies and because there will always be some high-status women who either do not want to work or would be criticized for taking jobs. For example, one cannot easily visualize some future president's wife leaving the White House every morning for her law office. (Just to be even-handed about this, if and when we elect a female president, I rather doubt that her husband will be allowed to do anything more than engage in ceremonial functions. The likelihood of conflicts of interest and charges of nepotism is simply too great: one has only to recall Marion Javits's brief stint as a "flak" for the Iranian government or the dubious business entanglements of Holland's Prince Bernhard.)

So let us assume that in the future 75 or 80 percent of all women will be employed outside the home. One can anticipate a host of accompanying social changes, many of them already much more than straws in the wind. As the labor force becomes more heavily concentrated in tertiary industries, fewer jobs require great physical strength, and the distinction between strictly male and female occupations will disappear. This distinction is, of course, already disappearing thanks to the efforts of the women's movement; but one has only to look at such relatively new fields as computer programming to see that the structural impetus is also there. As more men and women work together at identical jobs, the principle of equal pay for equal work will become firmly entrenched. The problem of whether men get promoted more frequently than women remains, but here too the trend is toward promotions based strictly on merit. During the next few decades we can expect to see in the realm of women's work the same process that we have seen occur during the past few decades with regard to blacks: they will become more fully dispersed throughout the labor structure instead of having their jobs clustered in certain occupations at one end of the economic scale.

However, many of these changes, which are being hastened by shifts in the industrial structure, are also eliminating jobs formerly done by human beings and replacing them with machines. Both men and women in the labor force are therefore likely to experience certain other changes in their working lives. The average work week will probably be reduced from five to four days, and the average workday may go down to six hours instead of eight. Shorter workdays and work weeks will contribute to a blurring of traditional male-female roles in the household—a process that is already underway. Men will be more likely to do the marketing, collect children from school, and become avid gardeners or gourmet cooks. This growing together of male-female domestic roles has long been observed among retired couples and it is also evident among couples where the husband does not hold a traditional 9 to 5 job—for example, among writers and professors. In other words, in the future we shall not need elaborate marriage contracts specifying who will make the beds on alternate Thursdays, since flexible household arrangements will develop as a natural response to greater amounts of leisure for both men and women.

In the future, large numbers of women will also come to face the problems of formal retirement. Gerontological research has established that many men experience serious emotional, and often health, problems shortly after they retire. Up until recently, if there has been a similar crisis point for women it was thought to be the menopause or the time when the last child leaves the family home—the so-called "empty-nest" stage. (However, some researchers are now beginning to challenge this finding and argue that most women are in fact relieved when their children are finally launched.)

But until recently few women have experienced retirement crises because even if they worked, their working career was probably intermittent and their identity was not so exclusively invested in this single role. Anyone who has interviewed elderly men and women soon discovers that the women still take pleasure in being—and identify themselves as—good cooks, clever seamstresses, helpful grandmothers, or competent housekeepers, whereas the men chiefly identify themselves in terms of the jobs they used to hold. Even when retired men develop hobbies, they very seldom identify strongly enough with these new pursuits to say, for example, "I am a damned good golfer." It will therefore be interesting to see whether the working women of the future feel as bereft of purpose and identity as many men do now when they retire.

It should be added that one of the great mysteries of the next one hundred years is the direction that retirement will take. There has been a long-term trend toward early retirement, which continues to be a goal of most labor unions; and some researchers predict that this trend will continue, with voluntary retirement dropping to 60 and even 55 years of age.[3] At the same time, Congress has recently passed a law prohibiting forcible retirement at age 65, and many analysts foresee that by the year 2010, when the large cohort born during the post-World War II "baby boom" begins to reach retirement age, a genuine labor shortage will develop. They also point out that even without early retirements, the labor force of the year 2030 and beyond will have a dependency ratio of 2 to 1 (compared to 3.2 to 1 at the present time).

By the year 2020, there will be approximately twice as many people over 65 as there are today (40 million instead of 20 million). So in addition to visualizing a society in which most adult men and women hold down paying jobs, and most couples probably have no more than two children, we must project a very large leisured class—a group of elderly citizens who are being supported by these working adults and who will occupy (dare I say it) roughly the same status formerly held by nonworking wives. There are several ways of looking at this eventuality. Dyed-in-the-wool Marxists will probably argue that capitalist societies cannot function without an exploited substratum and that as women and blacks cease to occupy this position the elderly will be forced to take their place. Some students of revolution confidently predict that the next major social movement will occur among the aged. Others fear that it may be just the other way around: that the real revolt will occur among the hard-pressed young people working to support this large contingent of nonproductive citizens which will use its voting power to protect its pensions, free health care, and state-supported housing. These analysts argue that the current taxpayer revolt may seem mild compared to the outcry of workers who see half their salary docked to maintain Social Security or private pension systems.

I tend to take a somewhat median position, since I see the elderly of the future as a neither wholly exploited nor exploiting class. I do find it intriguing that they may come to play certain roles recently abandoned by women—for example, they may come to dominate volunteer work. They may also help solve that most difficult and tragic problem of aging—the case of the truly dependent, physically disabled individual. As the number of older people grows, there are more and more individuals in their sixties whose own parents are still alive. Based on what I have seen in a number of families (including, most recently, my own) I think that children in their sixties (or younger brothers and sisters of that age) may revert to home care for relatives in their eighties rather than abandoning them to impersonal nursing homes. These sixty-year-olds will, after all, have the leisure to undertake such tasks while the rest of the adult population is out earning money in factories and offices; and they will also have the requisite compassion, since they can clearly foresee their own needs twenty years hence. What I am suggesting is similar to British sociologist Peter Townsend's observations that, "the four generations of surviving relatives may tend to separate into two semi-independent groupings—each of two generations"; and "the rapid relative increase in importance of the third generation, with its younger age-span, will result in much greater emphasis being placed in the future than formerly on reciprocal relations between the third and fourth generations."[4]

However, aside from the possibility of this one salutary move back toward familial, ad hoc relationships, the new roles of women will produce an increase in bureaucratized, depersonalized institutions. As more women work outside of the home, they will earn and be expected to draw their own pensions. I suspect that an already hard-pressed Social Security Administration will soon abandon the rule that a woman is entitled to either her own or her husband's pension, whichever is larger, and simply force any formerly employed woman to draw her own. Thus only full-time housewives would still be covered by their husbands' pensions. At the same time, there will probably be a decline (or, at any rate, a slower growth) in the size of all pensions, since the assumption will become that a pension merely provides for an individual instead of a family or a couple.

I also foresee an increase in the number of preschool and after-school nurseries, both public and private. As more women take advantage of the maternity leaves that are being negotiated into union contracts, fewer of them will leave the labor force for periods of five years or more to look after their preschool children. Those with high-status jobs may opt for full-time housekeepers (that is, lower status women who probably have children of their own), but low-status women with low-paying jobs will send their children to state or privately financed nurseries. These nurseries, of course, will be staffed by still other women working away from their own homes, who are also sending their children to nurseries. I do not mean to suggest that all of this is necessarily bad for society. Given the increase in child-abuse by parents who do not know how to raise their children, a case can be made for professionalizing child-care. But it is also possible that we may be witnessing a social fad akin to the use of wet nurses in eighteenth-century Europe.

Edward Shorter estimates that in the late 1700s, something like a sixth of all infants in the Paris region were boarded out, even though "the wet nurses, drawn from the agricultural laborers, marginal peasants, and unwed mothers (who often got pregnant in order to lactate and thus market themselves) were desperately poor, harried creatures who generally lived in rural hovels." These nurses generally "would not have enough milk for all the nurslings, giving their own children first go (in the event that they hadn't abandoned them), and then supplementing the milk remaining to the outsiders with hand food. Or even worse, the more destitute nurses, who had neither a cow nor a goat, would have to offer their charges 'pap'—a mixture of flour, water, and sugar which, devoid of protein and vitamins, gave them starches far too soon and in general deprived them of any natural immunities they might have received from human milk." No wonder that whereas the normal mortality of infants who stayed with their mothers was 19 percent, it was double that for infants sent to rural wet nurses.[5]

The point is not that I expect the widespread use of preschool nurseries to have a similar deadly effect, but that their champions may be just as misguided and naive as those eighteenth-century parents.[6] For example, few people in this society have given much thought to the fact that institutions devoted to child care do not operate on the basis of familial values but develop bureaucratic interests and ideologies of their own. Kibbutz nurseries instill the values of the kibbutz; Soviet and Chinese nurseries instill the values of the state. It will therefore be interesting to see what sort of ideology—perhaps the work of some latter-day Dr. Spock—American nurseries develop.

In addition to individual pension plans and child-care centers, many other activities formerly performed by families (and, more specifically, by women) will move out of the home. More meals will be prepared and eaten in restaurants—a trend that is already well underway. More women will attempt to hire maids to clean their homes, but unless there is a vast influx of unskilled labor into the country, few individuals will want to take these low-paying, low-status jobs. The result will probably be a rise in various kinds of businesses designed to perform specific tasks: floor-waxing, drapery- and rug-cleaning, house-painting, window-cleaning, clothes-cleaning and mending, dog-walking, plant-watering, tree-trimming, party-catering, house-watching, telephone-answering, interior-decorating. There will even be services designed to relieve the working woman of contacting and supervising these other services. In fact, all of these businesses already exist, and I am merely predicting their future success and expansion.

I would be less than honest if I did not admit that the thought of walking other people's dogs or watering other people's plants for a living does not appeal to me nearly as much as looking after my own. But this is an old-fashioned attitude. After all, we no longer make our own soap, charcoal, butter, or furniture; we no longer spin our own wool; and I can't say that I miss those chores. The future holds increasing specialization for all of us—at work as well as at home. Indeed, in one sense the women's movement and the tendency for women to go to work outside the home can be viewed as a fine way to stimulate the economy. For the tasks that housewives used to perform for free will have to continue being done—only now by others and for money. In addition, every woman who leaves her home to go to work (even if she goes to work in someone else's home) greatly expands her use of consumer goods: hosiery, clothes of all kinds, second cars, gasoline, frozen foods, cosmetics, to name only some of the obvious items.

So far, however, I have assumed that the "home" or "nuclear family" will remain a constant in this sea of changing roles and habits. But we already know that some of the greatest social changes today are taking place in the realm of sex and marriage, and I began by suggesting that work and love do not exist in water-tight compartments. Women who work are more likely to get divorced. On the other hand, women who devote themselves to being housewives may also wind up divorced and, as a result of their initial choice to remain at home, in worse emotional and financial straits than their more pragmatic sisters. What is the answer, or perhaps—as Gertrude Stein is supposed to have said on her deathbed after asking that and getting no reply—what is the question?

The question, it seems to me, is what has happened to the modern family and why. Edward Shorter, in his intriguing book *The Making of the Modern Family,* argues that a profound change in the relations and roles of the sexes occurred back in about 1800. This change altered marriage from an alliance between two families in which property and economic concerns were paramount into the union of two individuals drawn together by romantic love and sex. The result, since romance and sexual attraction are notoriously evanescent, has been a great increase in family instability. Shorter argues that another major change occurred in the 1960s: namely, what he calls the "unlinking of 'coitus' and 'life-long' monogamy."[7] It is important to note that Shorter does not believe the change of the 1960s consisted of the unlinking of coitus and romance; in other words, he does not believe we have entered an era of total promiscuity and licentiousness. His survey data convince him that most young girls and women still insist on going to bed only with men they "love." But this love does not necessarily lead to marriage, whereas in earlier days most extramarital intercourse occurred between two people who subsequently did get married.

Shorter is aware that his two revolutions in male-female relations can be viewed as either two cyclical waves of sexual concern or a straight-line increase caused by a variety of changes in the rest of society. He favors the latter view—the notion that permanent change, or progress, if you will, has occurred. I am not going to argue the opposite—that *plus ça change, plus c'est la même chose*—although the romantic lives of some late eighteenth- and early nineteenth-century figures (for example, George Sand, Mary and Percy Shelley, Lord Byron, or Mary Wollstonecraft) certainly do not suffer by comparison with our own times. But I think it is possible that there is a position somewhere between the cyclical view and the straight-line progression: call it the corkscrew or two-steps-forward-one-step-back point of view, in which certain periods, such as the present, witness a surge of social change and are followed by periods in which there is either consolidation or social reaction.

It is also questionable whether this process, either straight-line or corkscrew-like, can be called "progress." If anthropologists have anything to teach the world it is that every social arrangement has its plusses and minuses; and even Edward Shorter sums up the costs of our modern emphasis on individual choice and sexual freedom by noting that "one price paid for this new capacity to explore one's sensory responses has been the abandonment of a meaningful emotional life outside the home. Another price is a vastly increased instability in marital relations. A final price of the eroticization of the couple's life, both before marriage and after, is the disintegration of a sense of the lineage of the family. Nothing is free in this world."[8]

Shorter argues that the first sexual revolution was probably caused by the rise of market capitalism. "The principal link here is the increased participation of young unmarried people, especially women, in the free-market labor force. The logic of the marketplace positively demands individualism: the system will succeed only if each participant ruthlessly pursues his own self-interest, buying cheap, selling dear, and enhancing his own interests at the cost of his competitors (i.e., his fellow citizens). . . . In the domain of men-women relations, the wish to be free emerges as romantic love."[9] But he is frank to admit that he has found no similar large-scale change in social organization that produced the 1960s revolution in the family. "What master variable is at work today though, I must say, is unclear."[10]

It may be that we are simply too close to these events in time to spot any deep underlying causes. There is one thing that Shorter does not mention, however, which I think has had a major impact on today's sexual mores. This is the advent of the birth control pill. Whatever second thoughts some scientists and women may now be having about the dangers and side-effects of the pill, it brought something totally new into women's lives: a virtually fool-proof, self-administered method of controlling the fertility of their own bodies. No man can really understand what sort of impact it has on a woman's psyche to spend several days every month wondering whether or not she is pregnant: whether all of her plans—be they to finish school, take a vacation, or write a book—are about to be blown out of the water. The tendency for women always to hold themselves in abeyance for the contingency of motherhood is, incidentally, one reason why many creative women in previous times either were spinsters or did not reach their peak of creativity until after the menopause. I find it entirely plausible that the great upsurge in women going to graduate school, making career plans, and asserting themselves in the women's movement is largely caused by the powerful sense of freedom they derive from knowing that they can now choose when to get pregnant.

Of course the pill has also produced some less desirable results. The fear of pregnancy acted as a powerful brake on female promiscuity, and what Shorter calls the unlinking of coitus and life-long monogamy is one logical outcome of the pill. In previous times, women often risked premarital intercourse with someone they were "engaged" to knowing that if they "got caught" marriage was not far off. But with the pill, a woman can jump into bed with any number of men to whom she is attracted knowing that she cannot be trapped into a permanent commitment.

The pill has also been instrumental in cutting the American birthrate to below replacement level. The result is that as women have fewer children there is a growing emphasis on the recreational aspects of sexual intercourse. In other words, it ought to be fun for both partners, or else why bother? Interestingly enough, Sarah B. Pomeroy found a similar increase in erotic preoccupations linked to a drop in the birthrate in Hellenistic Greece. Only in this instance the birthrate was kept down by means of abortion and the "exposure" (usually leading to death) of female infants.[11] Again, one is forced to observe that social change is never an all-good or all-bad proposition. A few years ago Club of Rome experts, ecologists, bird-lovers, and others were urging zero population growth on us lest we all perish due to overcrowding or lack of food. Now that we have obliged by limiting our fertility, still other experts are wringing their hands because the family is disintegrating. What did they expect? That we would continue to build nests even though there is no one to occupy them?

As a matter of fact, however, nest-building remains a strongly atavistic urge in most Americans. Demographers have recently calculated that although from 25 to 30 percent of all women now in their thirties have ended or will end their first marriage in divorce, about four-fifths of these divorced women have remarried or will probably do so. And some 5 to 10 percent will probably marry and divorce more than twice.[12] This would seem to indicate that people may get fed up with a particular marriage, but they are not ready to forswear marriage altogether. Similarly, the current decline in the birthrate cannot be attributed to a growing disinclination to have any children. In the 1930s—the last time there was a substantial dip in the birthrate—the decline was caused by a sizable percentage of women remaining unmarried or childless. But many depression couples that had families continued to have large ones of five or six children. Today the decline in the birthrate is caused by neither widespread spinsterhood nor voluntary childlessness but by a generalized decline in the size of families: two, or at the most three, children seems to be the ideal.[13]

The ability we will soon have to choose the sex of a child should, if anything, reinforce this trend. In many societies the desire for sons is so strong that actually being able to choose the sex of a child would lead to a large surplus of males being born. But in the United States, attitude surveys going back to the 1930s show that while Americans have long had a slight preference for sons as the first-born, most couples want a balance of the sexes among their children. When large families were popular, couples wanted two or three of each sex; now that the two-child family is popular, most people want both a boy and a girl. If sexual engineering becomes available, therefore, it is likely that it will be used by couples who already have one child and who want to ensure that their second (and presumably last) child will be of the opposite sex.[14]

But what sort of future do these children face if at least a third of them can expect to grow up living with only one parent, or with a newly acquired step-parent? According to sociologist Mary Jo Bane, such a situation is actually not as recent a development as many of us think. For example, "Among children born between 1911 and 1920, about 22 per cent lost a parent through death and 5 per cent had parents divorce sometime before their eighteenth birthday."[15] Thus the total percentage of children who "lose" a parent has remained virtually the same. Only the proportion between the causes has changed, and one can plausibly argue that the death of a parent is much more traumatic for a child than a parent's departure for another house or city.

It may be that the real brunt of all these new marital arrangements falls not on the children but on the parents themselves. Take, for example, the practical matter of paying for college educations. It is often hard enough for parents to support two or three closely spaced children when they are all in college simultaneously, but I know of at least one couple that is currently struggling to keep *six* children in college—three of hers and three of his.

Well, even if there are financial drawbacks, there is always sex to bring one solace and distraction. We are living, after all, in the age of what Erica Jong has called "the zipless fuck," open marriage, multiple orgasms, and other modern improvements. Again, however, some recent research makes one wonder whether the sexual revolution is an unalloyed blessing for women. *The Hite Report,* a 1977 best-seller that surveyed the sexual practices and attitudes of over 3,000 women, contains some scathing comments on this subject. For example, one woman writes: "The sexual revolution is the biggest farce of the century for females. Before at least she had the right to say 'no.' Now she is a prude or worse if she doesn't put out whenever asked. And if she does have many short-term sexual encounters, she is considered a whore. The sexual revolution is a male production, its principles still concentrated on male values, e.g., Why get married any more, since we have our pick of slick chicks."[16] And another woman says, "To me, the sexual revolution is just a simple reversal of the pressure I grew up with to be chaste—now there is another one path for all to follow, and it makes just as little sense. Both enforced sex and enforced abstinence are bad."[17]

Among the most disillusioned women quoted in *The Hite Report* are those who appear to have had many sexual encounters. Some of the responses to the question "How have most men had sex with you?" are enough to shrivel the soul of any male. One woman writes, "There is a pattern but it's too boring to tell about." Another observes, "The only pattern I can discern is one of brevity. Men arrive and depart as if they had a round-trip ticket. It has reached a point that I almost know it is no use starting any more." Still a third notes, "How most men have tried to have sex with me can be summed up as Insert A into B. Dull-dulldulldull."[18]

Much of *The Hite Report* is devoted to documenting in great detail the rather old and banal saying that there are no frigid women, there are only clumsy men. In fact, one might conclude from reading the first two-thirds of the book that women would prefer to dispense with men altogether. It therefore comes as a surprise to learn (on page 284) that 87 percent of the women who answered the questionnaires actually said that they enjoyed sexual intercourse with men. Some lyrical descriptions of husbands and lovers can be found in this chapter, which Ms. Hite has chosen to call "Sexual Slavery." "My entire marriage revolves around making love to my husband," one woman writes. "It makes me feel loved and wanted." Another says, "It is the ultimate of physical and psychological fulfillment. . . only God could have imagined [something] that is so beautiful." And, a very interesting response not easily assimilated by Ms. Hite: "The greatest thing is the security I feel when I'm in bed with a man. I feel loved and wanted and *powerful*."[19] Ms. Hite, a loyal feminist, dismisses all of those responses as evidence of sexual slavery because "the role of women in sex, as in every other aspect of life, has been to serve the needs of others. . . . And just as women did not recognize their oppression in a general sense until recently, just so sexual slavery has been an almost unconscious way of life for most women."[20]

My own interpretation is that women are probably more exploited in the current climate of sexual freedom than they were during previous periods of greater inhibition. It is interesting, for example, that some women recall with nostalgia the sexual mores of the 1950s, when girls were allowed to neck but were not supposed to "go all the way": "No sexual experience has probably ever quite equalled those old high school days in the back seat of a parked car when arousal was an end in itself."[21] And one woman goes so far as to say, "My feeling is, 'whatever happened to the good night kiss?' "[22]

Given this climate of opinion, I think it very likely that we will soon enter a period of backtracking, when sex will be much less free and easy to come by. I agree with Edward Shorter that a complete turning back of the clock is probably not possible. But regardless of whether the impetus comes first from disillusioned divorcees, or self-reliant single women, or cold-eyed college girls, the promiscuous part of the sexual revolution is probably over.

It may even be that the high divorce rate will level off. The most recent statistics indicate that the percentage of the population aged 25 to 29 who have never been married increased substantially between 1970 and 1976—from 19.1 percent to 24.9 percent among men, and from 10.5 percent to 14.8 percent among women.[23] This would lead one to suspect that instead of entering early marriages that end in divorce, some young couples are simply living together instead. If such an interpretation is correct, one might expect to see something of a swing toward monogamous marriages contracted by couples in their late twenties or early thirties—even though these statistics would disguise a fair amount of premarital experimentation.

I am aware that some famous social scientists—including Margaret Mead—find it irrational, given our extended lifespan, to imagine men and women living with the same partner for fifty or more years. All sorts of fanciful arrangements are being proposed instead—for example, the notion that everyone should marry three times: once for youthful sex, once to raise a family, and once for comfort in old age. (According to a variation on this scheme, moreover, the first match would consist of young women and older men, the second of middle-aged individuals, and the third of older women and young men. Presumably that way everyone would get his or her heart's desire!) I am doubtful, however, that even a dictator could legislate such an arrangement, let alone enforce it.

In short, I do not foresee any radical changes in the roles of American women over the next hundred years. More of them will work outside the home, for paychecks commensurate with those of men. The size of the family will remain small, I suspect, unless there is a major cataclysm such as a world war.[24] The divorce rate will probably level off but not decline. The Equal Rights Amendment will finally be ;ratified and become what one political scientist I know has called a "Constitutional excrescence." That is to say, it will not provide women with a single thing to which they are not already entitled, except perhaps make them subject to the draft, should we ever abandon the volunteer army.

Will there be a woman president sometime during the next hundred years? That seems rather likely, although if one bears in mind that most presidents nowadays serve eight years, we are actually talking about one out of the next twelve individuals to occupy the White House. I would expect that among those twelve there will also be a Jewish president, a black president, a Polish-American president, and an Italian-American president, as well as several other "firsts." I imagine that the first woman to become president of the United States will be smart, dedicated, and tough. She may or may not be married; she will almost surely not be beautiful, resembling, in that respect, Eleanor Roosevelt and Golda Meir rather than Jacqueline Onassis or Gloria Steinem. Whether the advent of a female president will also inaugurate a renaissance for America's body politic is something I am happy to leave to star-gazers and historians of our fourth century to decide.

The Future of the University

Robert Nisbet

M GUINNESS

13 Let us begin by assuming the continuing reality of post-industrial society, with its dependence upon the growth of organized knowledge. What, then, is the role of the university to be? It will not do, I suggest, to assume as a number of scholars have, that the place of the university is automatically assured by virtue of its historic association with research, with the quest for knowledge.[1] For the university is far from being today the only institution in our society dedicated to the pursuit of knowledge.

Few changes have done more to distinguish present-day society in America from that of a half-century ago than the astonishing proliferation of institutes and centers, public and private alike, the prime purpose of which is the discovery or advancement of the kind of knowledge our society is dependent upon. One may love the university and believe, as I do, that it has a unique and necessary function, now and in the decades ahead. But one is obliged by the evidence to recognize, academic loyalties notwithstanding, that our post-industrial society could survive, could indeed advance, without the universities. Hundreds of nonacademic research centers make this possible.

Of course it can be said that such centers are made possible only by the *educations* supplied by universities. As I shall note momentarily, I think this emphasis upon teaching, the kind of teaching historically associated with the university, teaching rooted in ongoing research by scholar-teachers, and with a substantial diversity of teaching fields in close, even communal union, offers more hope to the university in the future than does any single-minded emphasis upon research alone. But even here, a sense of reality obliges us to recognize that teaching, at a very high level, can be carried on outside university walls. Apprenticeship is the very heart of such teaching. In many a nonacademic institute or center, in industry, in the arts, and professions, excellent teaching is going on—the result of junior scholars, artists, or scientists working closely with seniors. Think only of a Sloan-Kettering Institute, a Juilliard School, the Eastman Laboratories, and the New York City

Ballet! No, like it or not, a university is not indispensable to a post-industrial society either by virtue of its research or its teaching.

I predict that external, nonacademic institutes and centers offering full-time appointments to scholars and scientists will increase during the years ahead and thus offer the university increasing competition for first-rate minds. Already we witness a growing number of scholars and scientists departing the university for the nonacademic institute or laboratory. The number is bound to increase, for such an organization offers respite from conventional academic duties. Once there was no place for the scholar-scientist but a university, unless of course one enjoyed (as a number of major scholars did) private means with which to support one's research. Without the universities, however, it is a fair statement that Western scholarship and science would have remained at a rather low level. And that is especially true of the United States through the greater part of its history. But it is not true today, and there are ample opportunities, with ample salaries and research funds, for those gifted minds that crave research but do not take happily to the conventional paraphernalia of the academic community, including students, regular courses, service on faculty committees, and the like.

Even so, I choose to believe that the university will survive, will continue to attract the first-rate scholarly and scientific mind, just as it has in the past, though, as noted, with much more formidable competition from other agencies. To begin with there is the sheer institutional age, strength, and prestige of the university in the West. An Oxford or Cambridge, a Harvard, Columbia, Michigan, or Stanford does not blow away easily. Despite everything I have said about the rivalry offered universities by research institutes, it would be blindness not to recognize the attraction of the great university to even the greatest of our scientists and scholars. Not easily or quickly does an intellectual community achieve the luster that goes with our greatest universities, and their presence cannot help but have a supporting, a reinforcing effect upon universities of lesser renown.

There is, moreover, the fact that in all but a tiny few of the external, nonacademic institutes and laboratories—and foundations as well—there is a degree of single-mindedness of objective, a kind of discipline that proceeds from the specialized aim of the institute itself, and oftentimes a genteel factory-like emphasis upon an eight-to-five schedule that is inimical to the leeway and individual autonomy the university can offer. What F. A. Hayek has written is pertinent:

The reason why it still seems probable that institutions like the old universities, devoted to research *and* teaching at the boundaries of knowledge, will continue to remain the chief sources of new knowledge is that only such institutions can offer that freedom in the choice of problems and those contacts between representatives of the different disciplines that provide the best conditions for the conception and pursuit of new ideas. However greatly progress in a *known* direction may be accelerated by the deliberate organization of work aiming at some known goal, the decisive and unforeseeable steps in the general advance usually occur not in the pursuit of specific ends but in the exploitation of those opportunities which the accidental combination of particular knowledge and gifts and special circumstances and contacts have placed in the way of some individual.[2]

I find Hayek's words admirable in their illumination of what has been central to the university throughout most of its long history even though, as I shall indicate presently, the contemporary university has come to be shorn, through well-meant political restriction, of much of that freedom of inquiry Hayek marks. But we are still left with the question of the *function* or *mission* of the university in present-day, post-industrial society. Once the mission could have been described simply in terms of its unique orientation toward the discovery and dissemination of knowledge. But for reasons I have just given, that is no longer the case. The university competes with many organizations today along this line.

It may be said, indeed has been widely said in recent years, that the function of the university is to enable the individual "to achieve or upgrade his potential." But I find that characterization as repugnant in its egocentrism as it is irrelevant.[3] There are many contexts in which one "realizes his potential," and the educationists responsible for this preposterous definition would do well to consider them. It is also said by many that the university is the necessary, indispensable shaper of extraordinary talent or genius. But this characterization also misses the mark. On the evidence of history it is possible to be a great leader, a great artist, or great philosopher and not have ever been near a university. I do not say the university is necessarily inclement to genius; there may indeed be geniuses on faculties. The larger truth, though, remains: genius has its own multiple sources (which we know little about), and although, as I have just noted, there is no absolute incompatibility between the university and individual genius—in certain fields at least—it cannot be said that the university is in any way vital to the eruptions of genius in the arts and sciences. I will go farther. There are, I think, fields of imagination and creation where presence in the university is probably harmful, made so by the more or less corporate, regulation-ridden, curriculum-dominated atmosphere. One shudders at the thought of a Mozart obliged to complete an A.B. in the liberal arts and then to present, say, a master's degree in musical composition. True, there are not many Mozarts in history, but I believe my proposition stands. There is much reason to believe that among the reasons for the general enfeeblement of our novels, poems, paintings, and musical compositions during the last half-century has been the tenured presence of so many writers, painters, and composers on university faculties. Such presence is, I believe, demonstrably cloistering, fettering to creative faculty.

What, then, is the mission of the university? It is, I suggest, remarkably close to what Saul Bellow, in his recent Nobel address in Stockholm, has described as the mission of literature, of great literature: that of speaking to what Bellow refers to as "the main human enterprise." It is Bellow's contention that the bond that once existed between writers and the public, between such minds as Tolstoy, Dickens, and Tennyson and the people who read them avidly, has become dissolved in our age. Speaking of our own contemporary writers and artists, Bellow says: "The intelligent public is wonderfully patient with them, continues to read them and endures disappointment after disappointment, waiting to hear from art what it does not hear from theology, philosophy, social theory, and what it cannot hear from pure science."[1] The vast number of those writers and artists who may be considered "serious," write, compose, and paint for each other, or under the stimulus of some abstract concept, or to gratify the impulse to perform as a virtuoso would, or merely to divert a handful of critics. The immense public that serious artists and writers once had exists no more. There has been, as Bellow emphasizes, a disappearance of the desire—so obvious in a Tolstoy, Dickens, Conrad, or James—to speak at the highest possible level of art to the public. We are left with darlings of coteries on the one hand and mass producers of pap on the other.

Now, I find Saul Bellow's words valuable in their own right but also suggestive of the problem the contemporary university faces. I believe that the bond that once existed between university and public has also been allowed to weaken as the result of a spreading misconception during the past quarter-century or more of what the university's function is. Too many scholars, scientists, teachers in our universities have, in effect, closeted themselves from any due regard for public obligation, have come increasingly to perform for each other or for gratification of egoistic purpose. From being a community once closely related to the larger community that is the nation, the university has become, or threatened to become, a mere aggregate of academic-individual particles.

If the university is to have a lasting and creative future, it will, I suggest, have to gain, or rather regain, a distinctive mission, one that is turned, as all true missions are, to the public. And here I should like to quote some wonderfully illuminating words from Newman's *The Idea of a University*. Newman, as we know, was a devout, converted Roman Catholic, but when he gave his lectures in Dublin, largely to Roman Catholic clergy and laity, he made it clear at the outset that the university's true function was not spiritual or moral. Neither, he said, is the university to be regarded solely as the setting for discovery of knowledge, for if that were the case, students would not be needed. The university's mission, Newman tells us, is strictly intellectual, but beyond this it is a mission of disseminating intellectual values to the widest possible audience, to the largest possible public. Let me quote him in full on this point:

> It [the university] does not promise a generation of Aristotles or Newtons, of Napoleons or Washingtons, of Raphaels or Shakespeares, though such miracles of nature it has before now contained within its precincts. Nor is it content on the other hand with forming the critic or the experimentalist, the economist or the engineer, though such too it includes within its scope. But a University training is the great ordinary means to a great but ordinary end; it aims at raising the intellectual tone of society, at cultivating the public mind, at purifying the national taste, at supplying true principles to popular enthusiasm and fixed aims to popular aspiration, at giving enlargement and sobriety to the ideas of the age, at facilitating the exercise of political power, and refining the intercourse of private life. It is the education which gives a man a clear conscious view of his own opinions and judgments, a truth in developing them, an eloquence in expressing them, and a force in urging them. It teaches him to see things as they are, to go right to the point, to disentangle a skein of thought, to detect what is sophistical, and to discard what is irrelevant. It prepares him to fill any post with credit, and to master

any subject with facility. It shows him how to accommodate himself to others, how to throw himself into their state of mind, how to bring before them his own, how to influence them, how to come to an understanding with them, how to bear with them.[5]

Newman's eloquent definition of the university is not only apposite today; it is, I would argue, even more apposite than when he was lecturing in Dublin. For we live, as Newman did not, in a society that has become profoundly lowered, at times debased, in its intellectual and cultural values. I charge this lowering, this debasement, to two main causes: first, the decline of the ethic of equality to what is mere egalitarianism and leveling, with all merit going to the lowest common denominator; and second to the immense power and impact in our day of the media—newspaper, magazine, radio, television, motion picture—all of them designed largely for the purpose of diverting, gratifying, pleasing popular taste, and at the lowest possible level of intellect. The consequences of egalitarianism and "mediacracy" have been, on the record, almost totally destructive of culture and civility.

It is, I believe, the university alone that has the power left in it to offset the barbarizing tendencies of our age, to reassert and to disseminate widely the central ideas, values, and perspectives of Western civilization. Beleaguered and, as I shall emphasize momentarily, beset by its own self-inflicted wounds, though the American university is, it is nonetheless our last great hope for, in Newman's words, "raising the intellectual tone of society, cultivating the public mind, [and] purifying the national taste." The public schools can no longer help us. The toll of "progressivism" there is only too plainly to be seen: in loss of intellectual discipline (or discipline in any form), in impoverishment of curriculum, and in enslavement to the mammoth bureaucracy that today governs primary and secondary education in the United States. There is no point in relying upon press or television, for, as I have just stated, the decline in quality there is patent, looking back only a few years; and it is a decline that we may confidently expect to continue, to accelerate. The arts will not help us, for ours is by general agreement a period of decadence and sterility, and, as Saul Bellow has stressed, of nearly total separation between serious artist and the public. Nor, finally, can the church help us. For today, not only has much religion come to seem futile and irrelevant, but all too often the voice of the religionary is that of either the politician-reformer manqué, or else that of a self-proclaimed messiah.

We must ask the university to do what it did earlier, when, building on what the monastery had begun, it rescued Europe from the intellectual drought that had existed for several centuries. It was the university alone that, in characteristically medieval-communal fashion, revived, reinterpreted, and added to the classics which had come down from the ancient world. It was the university indeed—the fabled humanists of the Italian Renaissance to the contrary notwithstanding—that made the classics household words, and has continued to do this right to down to the present. Great as were Aeschylus, Plato, Cicero, Augustine, Abelard, Rabelais, Shakespeare, Goethe, Wordsworth, and Dickens in their own right, I doubt very much that they or any of the other greats in the Western literary-humanist tradition would have stood the test of time had it not been for the place given them (sometimes reluctantly, it has to be admitted) in university curricula and, as a consequence of this, in the curricula and courses of schools.[6]

Only today are we in serious danger of losing our classics, our lamps of culture, which stretch from Homer to the present. First it was the ancient classics that eroded away under the acids of modernity. There were those then who predicted the same forces of erosion would in time work against the very modern classics that were offered by reformers in place of the Greeks and Romans. Today I am told that it becomes an increasingly arduous chore to arouse interest in English classes in Eliot, Joyce, Yeats, and Pound, much less Dickens, Thackeray, and George Eliot, so distant and "irrelevant" have these been made by the media and their incessant drive toward the new, however trivial, and the journalistically arresting. A half-century of mass production of books and magazines, with never a week passing but what some new book, article, or author is duly pronounced "brilliant" and "deathless," only to be forgotten utterly a month later, its or his place taken by some new book, article, or author with weeks of immortality ahead, has made precarious indeed the place of those works that, stretching from Homer to the present day, have over and over again demonstrated their true power and their capacity to communicate something vital and life-giving to those put in touch with them. I do not say for a moment that the mission of the university is that of keeping classics alive. I have said, drawing from Newman, that its mission is that of elevating, cultivating, and purifying the public mind. This is its distinctive, its unique mission. There are many and diverse ways in the university by which this mission can be, and is, achieved.

The sciences and their objectives and techniques have just as much right to university status as do the humanities, and these necessarily have a somewhat different relationship to classics than do the humanities. In the end, what is vital is not the classic, the "great book" as such. It is instead the bringing of students, young or old, into direct experience with the major ideas, values, perspectives, and visions that have been the stuff of Western culture. How else can the university play its vital role in seeking to immunize a substantial part of the population against the dross, the trivia, the banality, oftentimes the downright evil which thrive currently in our mediacracy? It is said that under Gresham's Law the bad inevitably drives out the good—but only when all other things are equal. It is, I suggest, the role of the university and of university teaching to prevent all other things from being equal, to so successfully inculcate the perspectives of reason, logic, civility, and culture that the good will not be driven out, or at least not wholly.

If, however, the university in America is to serve as it is uniquely qualified to do, to do in the future what it has managed to do in the past, there are certain binding obligations to be faced. The first of these is an accurate sense of what the university is and is not. At the risk of dogmatism I must be firm and terse here. The university is, first and last, a setting for teaching, the kind of teaching that requires as its foundation active research, in whatever field. I stress this even though to many here it will seem obvious. George Orwell once wrote: "We are now at a depth at which restatement of the obvious is the first duty of intelligent man." I repeat, therefore: the primary function of the university is that of teaching, but teaching at a level, whether for the undergraduate, the graduate, or the continuing student, that requires active cultivation of the teaching mind, best represented by visible evidence of scholarship and research. There is room in the university for the titan of research, the eminent scholar-scientist, but only on condition that such individual recognize that his primary obligation is to teaching. There are many gifted, valuable minds for whom teaching in any form is an annoyance, a distraction. Fortunately, contemporary society is not lacking in lustrous centers and institutes where such minds may go, with profit to all.

It would not have been necessary to stress the foregoing prior to World War II. Then, no matter how illustrious the scientist or scholar, how prolific in publication a faculty member might be, it was understood universally that teaching had the highest priority. And what is interesting to recall is the eagerness with which even the greatest of scientists and scholars took to teaching, in whatever form, at whatever level. At Berkeley in the 1930s I saw eminent scientists and scholars almost literally fight for what was regarded as the privilege of teaching a given course, introductory included, as I remember full well. That great variation of quality existed in teaching from one individual to another is of far less importance than the fact that *teaching as a value* weighed heavily, mattered a great deal.

World War II began the change. As a result of the atom bomb and related achievements the belief became widespread that science, university science, had in effect won the war for the United States. Never before had scientists known the esteem, the mass popularity, they did during the decade or two following the war. Affluence of unprecedented extent followed, of course, and the university in America reached the point where it could do no wrong. The eminence of the physical scientist came to include the social scientist and the humanist so far as the lawmakers, foundations, and the public were concerned.

I will not go into detail here, as I have elsewhere, on this transformation of the American university.[7] Its structure, its unique form of community, and pattern of authority began to change as traditional entities—departments, faculties, and colleges—were forced to live with, indeed compete with, the vast number of new organizations that appeared in the universities—the centers, bureaus, and institutes consecrated to research alone. All essential structures and lines of authority in the traditional university had flowed from the priority, the essentiality, of teaching in the universe. But now, all of a sudden, the unity of the university, its accustomed hierarchy, authority, and community were violated, by the new hierarchy, authority, and forms of relationship that emerged directly on the campus by reason of the massive funding from the federal government and the great foundations, nearly all of which had been granted to, not the university as such, but to one or other of the thousands of new institutes, centers, and bureaus that were springing up on campuses.

Side by side with this form of politicization of the university went another. I refer to the entry on a large scale in the universities of ideological blocs, which drew their identities, not so much from internal-academic issues as from national and international loyalties. Inevitably it was the radical-liberal blocs that assumed control, given the historic tendency of faculty members, especially in the social sciences and humanities, to identify with the left. The radicalization of university faculties was well along by the end of the fifties. (It has not ended yet!)[8]

The way was thus made easy for the student riots, so-called, in the sixties. The faculty's own radicalization of the campus, coming on top of the breakdown of traditional spheres of hierarchy, authority, and community, made the way easy for student revolutionaries. Looking back, it was really quite easy for the students, especially with forceful, guilt-ridden, hand-wringing pleas in their behalf by faculty members and the ardent cooperation of the media.

Thus, what we saw during the quarter-century following World War II was the conversion of the American university from an institution of finite aspiration, anchored in the sacredness of the teaching function and of the kind of scholarship that went with teaching, to an institution of Faustian ambition. The dreadful phrase "knowledge industry" came into being, and everywhere in the academic world there were those to declare that the university must be the capstone of this industry, with professors as entrepreneurs, capitalists of higher order. Then came the concept of "multiversity," with its implications of university involvement in a host of functions—political, economic, social, humanitarian, even therapeutic. It was all very intoxicating. We, the universities, had won World War II with our atom bomb, and we, the universities, would now win wars against poverty, city blight, ethnic tensions, international conflicts, middle-class alienation, even crises of ego-identity. As I say, it was all very exciting and a New Class assumed a hegemony that has not been ended even yet: a New Class consecrated to research entrepreneurialism and in closest league with government, especially federal government.

The greatest single *consequence,* I would argue, of the hubris that overtook the American university during the years following World War II was politicization of the academy. I firmly believe that the greatest single *objective* of the university during the years immediately ahead is that of somehow regaining the autonomy that we once knew from political power and caprice. The university is one of the favorite targets of those who really operate the American government, the permanent employees of the large federal regulatory agencies. They form what I have called the New Despotism in this country, and their appetites are very great indeed, as is their effective freedom from either Congress or the executive branch of government—or, I think it can be shown, the judiciary.

We didn't often think of it as politicization in the glorious days when the federal government rained money on us in the universities and when little was said about quid pro quo or tit for tat. Who then would have given respect to the ancient maxim: "Who pays the piper calls the tunes." And of course the whole vast politicization of the American university justifies itself in the sweet name of humanitarianism. If a division of the Department of Health, Education, and Welfare (HEW) "counsels" our medical schools to accept forthwith second-year students from foreign medical schools, the division expects to be respected, that is, obeyed. It is, of course, in the same sweet name that HEW, Justice, and other major departments of the federal government regularly require reports on university employment, academic and nonacademic, and, although, as I understand it, federal bureaucracy and judiciary have not yet promulgated guidelines on ethnic composition of student enrollment, we know that many a college and university, only too eager to please, has found itself setting what can only be called ethnic quotas. Who can doubt that the collective autonomy once taken for granted by universities in this country, even in substantial degree public universities, has been jeopardized—not by malevolence but— much more dangerous—benevolence that manifests itself through rules and regulations that daily increase in number and become ever more constricting. Such rules and regulations (and I paraphrase Tocqueville here) do not so much bend, coerce, or repress the academic will as they simply extinguish it. Government covers the surface of university life with a network of small, complicated rules, minute and uniform, through which the most energetic characters and original minds find difficulty penetrating. Such a power does not destroy but it prevents existence; it does not tyrannize but it compresses, enervates, extinguishes, and stupefies a univerity administration and faculty, till each university is reduced to nothing better than a flock of timid and industrious sheep of which the government is the shepherd.[9]

That an adversary relation between the federal government and the universities now exists is hardly to be doubted. It was the subject of an unusually revealing article in the *Chronicle of Higher Education* in its issue of September 27, 1976. Reporting a national meeting of academic administrators, the article quoted the respected Earl F. Cheit, Dean of the School of Business Administration at Berkeley. Dean Cheit pointed out that the federal government had begun to extend its role as controller of higher education in the mid-1960s. By 1976, he went on, "the process has reached a new stage. The psychological set of enforcement and control is extending through the whole range of federal relationships with colleges and universities. Now, even without a change in statutory requirements, such as in administration of research grants by H.E.W., there is a new posture of regulation and control."

Anyone who thinks this is but a tempest in a teapot, something that will shortly blow itself out, is myopic, to say the least.[10] Even federal officials, who by philosophic conviction and long-established records support private enterprise and its freedoms, are increasingly taking the point of view of government. Thus at a conference in early December at Georgetown University sponsored by University Centers for Rational Alternatives, a meeting devoted to the problem of the government's proper relation to the universities, the Solicitor General of the United States, Robert H. Bork, himself a scholar and former university professor, and a mind profoundly dedicated to academic freedom, was obliged by present circumstances to say:

> What is not correct and what I have heard in the pronouncements of university presidents, is the thought that the Federal Government makes a unique kind of error when it undertakes to regulate universities, or that universities are so different and more subtly complex than other institutions that regulation is bound to be uniquely destructive when applied to them. None of these things are true.
>
> Authority is deeply resented in any form. . . . [But] There is pleasure nonetheless real, even if perverse, in seeing elitist institutions scream when the remedies they have prescribed for others are applied to them.[11]

As I say, Robert Bork is incontestably devoted to the ideal of the autonomous university and to academic freedom, but he is also incontestably correct, I would argue, in his assessment of the relation between governmental power and the kind of university we have allowed to develop since World War II in this country.

Nevertheless, while I hope that in the long run government will pull back from present bureaucratic despotism in all areas of society where initiative and creativeness are vital—and I stress here the business, financial, and professional areas as well as others—my immediate and chief concern is the university and its present relation to the federal government. Modern Western history has not been kind to the great intermediate structures of society. Beginning with aristocracy, the guilds, monasteries, urban communes, and other medieval groups, of which the university is of course one—we have seen political processes of centralization and leveling take a large toll from those associations that are intermediate to individual and state.[12] True, new forms of intermediate association have arisen during the centuries—chartered companies, learned societies, cooperatives, labor unions, corporations, and others—but it is questionable how deep are the loyalties in human beings that have been created by these newer structures. Suffice it to say the university is almost unique in the degree to which it has, ever since medieval times, continued and even developed a set of values and a network of authorities, which first came into being nearly a thousand years ago.

The university has, let us concede cheerfully, weathered many a storm. But I am skeptical that it has ever been confronted by the kind of political power that currently threatens to envelop it and its historical autonomies. Threatening power in past times has almost always been malign, in substance and aspect. The political power that penetrates the academic world at the present time is not malign in intent or premise. Quite the contrary. Whether through disbursing large grants of money to scientists and scholars, to tens of thousands of students, making possible tuition and subsistence, and to university administrations, or whether through an effort to give effect to such morally commendable ideals as ethnic opportunity and integration, the state's power has almost invariably rested upon humanitarian foundations. But as Mr. Justice Brandeis wrote many years ago: "Experience should teach us to be most on guard to protect liberty when the government's purposes are beneficent. Men born to freedom are natually alert to repel invasion of their liberty by evil-minded rulers. The greatest dangers to liberty lurk in insidious encroachments by men of zeal, well-meaning but without understanding."[13]

I do not know what the outcome will be for the university in its relation to the federal government, its great money and its great bureaucracy and perhaps its representation of a New Populism among the people that will not take kindly to anything as historically elitist as universities have been. I know only that local and associative and communal liberties are the very hardest to preserve in those mass societies that are surmounted by monoliths of power and periodically swept by storms of mass egalitarianism and hedonism. It will take a great deal of thought, effort, and courage to restore to the university in America the kind of autonomy from political power it once had. We shall be beset at every hand by taunts of elitism, special privilege, and arrogance. Make no mistake about the sheer force that has accumulated in those agencies of HEW (and other departments as well) which are concerned in any way with the universities. At the risk of imposing an individual political philosophy upon my readers, I have to say that I think our largest hope lies in joining the ranks of *all* libertarians who believe in free private enterprise, whether in the world of the university or that of business and the professions.

Now I want to turn to a few requirements of our reform of the university. I shall begin with a few fairly concrete prescriptions, saving until the final section the more general and inclusive. Let us assume we can abandon the hubris, the Faustianism of recent decades in academe. What else must we do?

First, modify as best we can the present system of iron tenure. I respect those who, though deploring its defects, justify it on the ground of academic freedom. But I am not persuaded that tenure is in fact a guarantee of academic freedom, though it may once have been. And what I am deeply concerned by is tenure's protection of the mediocre and its prevention of the rise of the buoyant and eager minds fresh from the graduate schools, minds that would gladly teach at all levels and that are just coming into their prime of creativeness.

How, in present circumstances, can very many of these talented and trained young minds be given jobs in colleges and universities where, as the result of profligate, wanton granting of quick tenure in the fifties and sixties, few if any tenured positions exist that the young might aspire to? There are faculties in this country where up to 75 to 80 percent of all positions are occupied by tenured individuals, many of whom are barely at middle age. We are, I believe, going to have to be more discerning and courageous in this matter than we have been in the past. If administrations and faculty committees have the wisdom to appoint and promote, they have, I would argue, the wisdom to dislodge the inept, the mediocre, and the exploitative.[14] And do this without diminishing academic freedom!

Second, with the same objective in mind, I recommend strong consideration of an early lowering of the present average age of academic retirement in this country. It has been going down, very slowly, for years. When I began teaching, 70 was the common age for academic retirement; today, the average is, I believe, around 67. I think it should be substantially lower. In the first place, the age of retirement is dropping steadily in other professions and in the business world. Post-industrial society surely makes possible, makes desirable, a retirement age substantially lower than was once the case. And I believe this is just as applicable to the universities as to professions and industries.

I would like to think that before many more years, age 60, at very most, will be standard for academic retirement. I have two reasons for this hope. In the first place, a lowered retirement age will assist, as will a more enlightened doctrine of tenure, in creating places in the universities for the younger scholars and scientists emerging from the graduate schools. But, in my judgment, there is another, at least equally important ground for earlier academic retirement. I think the intellectual level, on the average, of university faculties will be enhanced. Several decades of experience in American universities have taught me that, with rarest exceptions, scholars and scientists tend to lose a great deal of their creativeness, buoyancy, sheer energy, and dedication to teaching and research after age 55 to 60. The commonly claimed "wisdom" inherent in those who stay on after reaching this age does not seem to me real enough, or useful enough, to offset what has been lost. There will of course be exceptions. But let them be so dealt with.

Third, we must somehow gain, or regain, a higher degree of *academic pluralism*.[15] The Ph.D. brought on academic standardization, just as William James predicted early in the century, and the rise of the American Association of Universities (AAU) meant an inevitable drive toward uniformity of the type who went in for teaching. I do not say this was entirely without value, looking back on some of the peculiar institutions that had arrogated to themselves the status of colleges and universities in the nineteenth century. But the unhappy and counter-productive result was for two or three prestige-laden universities in the East to become, wittingly or unwittingly, iron models of what the Ph.D. and for that matter graduate education should be. One Harvard, or Columbia, was without doubt good for the country. A plethora of imitations of either or both was not so often good. I am old enough to remember the almost talismanic effect reference to Harvard could have at faculty meetings at Berkeley even as late as the 1930s.

Today, as I intimated above, we have a new and infinitely more powerful source of standardization of universities and colleges at all levels. I refer of course to the federal government, operating through HEW and other departments and through the courts. There is no evidence that such agencies care much about academic quality, only the literal meeting of national standards based upon nonacademic norms. It was, I believe, Sidney Hook who testified memorably before a congressional subcommittee on this kind of standardization and its baneful effects, citing the case of a department of graduate religious studies (if I remember correctly) in which there were no women on the faculty. Why was this, a representative of HEW sternly asked? Because, the chairman of the department answered—laying out for the HEW representative all applications of the past twenty years—no woman applicant thus far has happened to have in her academic background the languages we require: Hebrew, Greek, Latin, among others. "Then drop the language requirements" enjoined the HEW commissar. I doubt that the requirements were dropped, but it takes no great imagination to conceive the pressure that can be exerted in a great variety of ways upon universities so dependent upon federal grants of money, so responsive by this time to executive or judicial mandate, that compliance in some degree will become in time almost automatic.

Pluralism, regionalism, and localism have ever been marks of the universities of the Western world. It was the striking differences among a Bologna, a Paris, a Salamanca that led to what Helen Waddell, in her great study, has referred to as "the wandering scholars" of the Middle Ages. The nationalization of American universities began, as I have said, with the instituting of the Ph.D. It acquired a new dimension in World War I when, through the blandishments and sheer absolute executive power of Woodrow Wilson, himself of course an academic man, the faculties of the universities were brought, *as faculties,* into the war effort. Nationalization went a long step further in World War II when the military actually occupied campuses, through direct war research and such things as ASTP. And now, as noted, we have, under the name of humanitarianism and equality, the source present of a still greater nationalization and standardization of universities. When one looks at what Congress can come up with in the way of income tax law—requiring huge volumes to cover all the details—it is easy to imagine what it could come up with as a program for higher education for the United States—with the power of the purse and of judicial activism there to give it effect.

I do not know how or even whether we shall find ways of arresting nationalization of education and of setting reverse processes of diversity, regionalism, pluralism into motion, but I believe we somehow must, and before too many more years pass. My nightmare is one of a single University of the United States with branches at Cambridge, Mass., Morningside Heights, Ann Arbor, Reno, Tucson, Berkeley, and Stanford, and a few thousand other places, with a Secretary of Higher Education in Washington able to note proudly to any visitor or questioner that, it being Tuesday, March 16, 2:00 P.M., he can report accurately on what is being studied by a given age group throughout the country. This is, I iterate, at the moment only a nightmare, but there is much we are doing, indeed have already done, to make the establishment and work of such a secretary much easier than could once have been the case in this country. The universities' quest for, acceptance of, and now in so many instances acute dependence upon, large federal grants or other subventions, has inevitably helped along the possibility. For, as I have already stressed, there never has been and never will be in America any disbursement of large sums of money by Congress, or departments heavily funded by Congress, without ever more inquisitorial means of following up on such disbursements. The result is, cannot help but be, accelerated centralization and an increasingly blurred line between private and public universities.

There is still another force on the academic landscape, one now no larger than a man's hand but surely destined to grow rapidly unless strong currents of faculty opposition appear. I refer to the labor union and its ultimate powers of strike and collective bargaining. In an important article on the subject John H. Bunzel has noted that the unionization movement is now confined pretty much to three or four geographic centers and to the less important colleges and universities.[16] He writes that of

> the roughly 2500 accredited institutions of higher learning in the United States, about 160 were estimated in 1972 to have been covered by collective-bargaining contracts, though not all conform to the conventional model of such contracts in nonacademic organizations. As an educated guess, some forty-five to fifty thousand members of college and university faculties are included in established and recognized collective-bargaining units—approximately 10 percent of the total teaching faculty across the country.

Now, it is quite possible that there have been instances in which formation of a faculty union has been constructive: not only a protection of economic and other rights but even a means of raising intellectual and academic standards. But I know of no evidence to suggest that very many, if any, such instances have existed. What we have been able to see of the effects of labor unions on elementary and secondary school teachers, and upon the standards of instruction and fidelity to profession, has not, I am frank in saying, been very encouraging. I know of nothing that will more quickly convert what is left of academic community into mere academic business enterprise than widespread unionization of university faculties. In the beginning, doubtless, individuals of attested academic-intellectual commitment assume key roles in the unions. But this does not last long. Their places are soon taken by the hard-eyed for whom wages, hours, vacations, and other material benefits become overriding in significance. Nor is this all. Think only of the widened opportunity for that wonderful structure of bureaucracy known as the AFL-CIO Council to penetrate academic walls. Nor is *this* all. Reflect a moment on the spirit of satisfaction that will spread through the NLRB in Washington once it is known that cases coming before them will henceforth include Columbia and Princeton and Stanford as well as ITT, General Motors, and National Paper Products. To suppose that unionization of faculty will leave intact present structures of academic-faculty authority is to suppose nonsense. "The *union* makes us strong!" *Not* the Faculty Committee on Courses.

With unionization and automatic assimilation of the universities into the vast and complex sphere of labor law in the United States, it is inevitable that present tendencies of intrusion of law, lawyers, and the courts into academic life will be greatly accelerated. Nathan Glazer, in a perceptive essay, has written of the grave problems already posed to universities by the increasing use of lawyers and mechanisms of adjudication peculiar to the adversary procedures of law in academic matters.[17] The role of the lawyer has become much larger in academic affairs since Glazer wrote his essay in 1970. Affirmative action has seen to that. But all that has happened in this respect is small by comparison with the condition that will exist once university faculties have become major elements of the American labor movement.

Now, reaching conclusion, let us suppose that we in the universities succeed in halting, in reversing the currents of politicization which now threaten to bring on federal management of the universities. Let us suppose that a fair and equitable relation with government is worked out, giving the universities the autonomy they must have if they are to fulfill their mission. Let us further suppose we abolish or sharply modify academic tenure and its baneful consequences to academic creativeness, that we do in fact lower substantially the retirement age of faculty members, and manage somehow to keep the AFL-CIO, its shop stewards, hiring halls, and grievance committees out of academe. Will there be, given these salvations, a university worthy of the name in America, as there once was?

Not, I would argue, until we restore to the American university some sense of intellectual community. This will not be done by incantation or college or department cocktail parties each term. Recitations of the spirit of togetherness will not help. All that will help is facing up to the dreadful fragmentation, the atomization, of academic culture that may, historically, be traced back, I think, to Harvard's adoption under President Eliot of the elective system. The ordinary university today in this country resembles, in its organization, nothing so much as a department store with students free to shop where and as they see fit, even indeed to order custom-made goods of their own individual design. This movement toward academic atomization, which, as I say, really began with Harvard's adoption of the free elective system long ago and that spread almost continuously thereafter, with curricula and requirements in inevitable process of erosion, reached its height in the 1960s. Who will soon forget the charges from students of intolerable coerciveness when a given history, or language, or science requirement was held before them? And who will soon forget the spectacle in that decade of students fashioning their own courses, aided all too often by faculty members eager to avoid any teaching, the familiar pattern proving to be: course designed by students Monday, approved by dean or committee on Tuesday, found wanting by selfsame students on Wednesday, accused of reactionary tendencies on Thursday, and dead on Friday. Solomon Grundy!

But we are out of that dark decade, and signs exist that point to a reversal of decades-old tendencies. All one can say is, high time! For if the university is indeed to raise the intellectual tone of society, cultivate the public mind, and purify the national taste, as Newman proposed, to supply prophylaxis, so to speak, against the barbarisms of our media and other parts of our culture, it must begin to move, and quickly.

But the university cannot move, cannot accomplish these vital objectives, unless it works from a true culture of its own, a culture that has, as does any culture worthy of the name, its central core, its identifiable themes, and its means of acculturation, its assimilation of those young or otherwise alien by background. Needless to say, I am not proposing any return to the iron classical curricula of the nineteenth century, still to be found until a few years ago in certain religious colleges and universities. Such return would be an enterprise in antiquarianism.

But I *am* proposing that the *liberal arts,* general education, call it what we will, be made once again the heart of university culture and that, moreover, the liberal arts be regarded as coterminous with the entirety of the university. I believe it is an invitation to futility to force down the throats of freshmen and sophomores the central ideas, values, and works of Western civilization and then pronounce them, so to speak, liberated, free to plunge into whatever specialization or bizarre complex of studies they desire. Nothing has been more hurtful to the unity and meaning of the modern university than the rigorous separation we have established between liberal education and professional. I find it heartening, if somewhat chastening (speaking as a humanist myself), that in recent years some of the most clarion calls for a reinstituting of the liberal arts have come from the deans and faculties of professional schools; not, I hasten to emphasize, a reinstituting of genuine liberal arts courses and values in our present so-called liberal arts colleges alone, *but in the professional schools themselves.* At the present moment, medical, law, engineering, and other professional schools are asking for, at times almost begging for, teaching *in* the professional schools of a kind heretofore associated with the liberal arts colleges alone. Increasingly, ethical problems—the kinds of problems historically associated with the humanities in the West—confront our professionals in their dealings with patients, clients, and the social order as a whole. I could wish that our liberal arts colleges were stronger than they currently are along these lines, that they had not been atomized by specialization and also given rising vocational character during recent decades. But we are not wholly without resources of humanistic nature, and I foresee a closer and closer liaison between the liberal arts and the professional schools.[18]

In many places at this moment—Columbia University, where, it is a pleasure to emphasize, required courses in the humanities have not been allowed to languish, Harvard, Yale, Chicago, and others—there is a renewed interest in achieving some kind of genuine liberal, intellectual community, and in endowing the liberal arts with a vitality, with a sense of relevance, that will reach *all* students in the university. I pray that this continues, that it does not wash away as did the old classical curriculum under the relentless pressures of free electives for students, with all courses given equal value, and of increasingly rampant specialized, consuming, research by the faculty. We cannot be certain in these matters. This, however, I know. If the university is to fulfill its mission of elevating, cultivating, and purifying the public mind, of insulating it from the currents of banality, triviality, and vulgarity, which now threaten to engulf it as the result of media-dominance, and of making us aware of the intellectual tissues with which we are, so to speak, born—tissues ancient, medieval, and modern—it will have to be on the basis of a thorough reordering of the university's present raddled, fragmented, and so often atomized, intellectual offerings. The university was born as a form of community and it will survive only to the degree that it remains a community. And beyond this we must see to it that this community of intellect is oriented toward what Saul Bellow has so well called "the main human enterprise."

I have one final hope, prescription, for the university. This is its increasing participation in what has come so widely to be called *continuing education.* I mean education populated by men and women in their thirties and forties, even older. For a long time we in the universities have taken a rather aloof view of these age groups, consigning them to second- and third-class divisions of the universities, or otherwise making them feel inferior to the young who alone, it is argued, belong in the undergraduate college or graduate school. We have, in effect, *driven* these age groups to the barbarisms of Hollywood, the tube, and the annual inundation of best-sellers that tend to expire within weeks of publication. Charles Frankel of Columbia is one of the scholars of our time who has come to appreciate the importance of this. "If we rearranged scholarship programs, living arrangements and curricula to provide, say, one-third of the places in residential universities to people of twenty-five, thirty, and older, might we not achieve a fairer distribution of educational opportunity, a more efficient and economical use of expensive resources, as well as a stabilizing and energizing change in the compositions of student bodies?"[19]

We must rid ourselves of the delusion that only that education is good which is, as we say, full-time, and centered on those just out of high school. The often-dangerous segregation of the young and the old in the academic world—with a gulf never so manifest as in the 1960s—

could, I think, be greatly reduced if we conceived the university as a place for intellectually qualified, yes (there must be no dilution of intellectual standards, no matter how widely we wish the university to reach into society), but the intellectually qualified of all ages and of varying time and capacity for residence and continuity. What little experience I have had so far persuades me that the young enjoy the presence of the older as students in undergraduate and graduate classes.

In conclusion: ways, means, techniques, and structures will and should vary widely across the academic landscape in the decades ahead. But if the dangerous restriction or closeting of the artist, described so ably by Saul Bellow in his Nobel address, is to end, if the arts are once again to have the relation to society they had at an earlier time, if the fateful domination of culture by the media, with the terrible consequences of such domination already evident, is to terminate, there is really no other institution in society but the university to make these ends achievable. It alone has, still has, the means of that raising, cultivating, and purifying of the public mind Cardinal Newman gave to the university as its prime and unique function.

The Adversary Culture of Intellectuals

Irving Kristol

M'GUINNESS

14 No sooner did the late Lionel Trilling coin the phrase "adversary culture" than it became part of the common vocabulary. This is because it so neatly summed up a phenomenon that all of us, vaguely or acutely, had observed. It is hardly to be denied that the culture that educates us—the patterns of perception and thought our children absorb in their schools, at every level—is unfriendly (at the least) to the commercial civilization, the bourgeois civilization, within which most of us live and work. When we send our sons and daughters to college, we may expect that by the time they are graduated they are likely to have a lower opinion of our social and economic order than when they entered. We know this from opinion poll data; we know it from our own experience.

We are so used to this fact of our lives, we take it so for granted, that we fail to realize how extraordinary it is. Has there ever been, in all of recorded history, a civilization whose culture was at odds with the values and ideals of that civilization itself? It is not uncommon that a culture will be critical of the civilization that sustains it—critical, however and always, of the failure of this civilization to realize perfectly the ideals that it claims as inspiration. Such criticism is implicit or explicit in Aristophanes and Euripides, Dante and Shakespeare. But to take an adversary posture toward the ideals themselves? That is unprecedented. A few writers and thinkers of a heretical bent, dispersed at the margins of the culture, might do so. But culture as a whole has always been assigned the task of, and invariably accepted responsibility for, sustaining and celebrating those values. Indeed, it is a premise of modern sociological and anthropological theory that it is the essence of culture to be "functional" in this way.

Yet ours is not. The more "cultivated" a person is in our society, the more disaffected and malcontent he is likely to be—a disaffection, moreover, directed not only at the actuality of our society but at the ideality as well. Indeed, the ideality may be more strenuously opposed than the actuality. It was, I think, Oscar Wilde who observed that, while he rather liked the average American, he found the ideal American contemptible. Our contemporary culture is considerably less tolerant of actuality than was Oscar Wilde. But there is little doubt that if it had to choose between the two, it would prefer the actual to the ideal.

The average "less cultivated" American, of course, feels no great uneasiness with either the actual or the ideal. This explains why the Marxist vision of a radicalized working class erupting into rebellion against capitalist society has turned out to be so erroneous. Radicalism, in our day, finds more fertile ground among the college educated than among the high-school graduates, the former having experienced more exposure to some kind of "adversary culture," the latter—until recently, at least—having its own kind of "popular" culture that is more accommodating to the bourgeois world that working people inhabit. But this very disjunction of those two cultures is itself a unique phenomenon of the bourgeois era, and represents, as we shall see, a response to the emergence, in the nineteenth century, of an "avant-garde," which laid the basis for our "adversary culture."

Bourgeois society is without a doubt the most prosaic of all possible societies. It is prosaic in the literal sense. The novel written in prose, dealing with the (only somewhat) extraordinary adventures of ordinary people, is its original and characteristic art form, replacing the epic poem, the lyric poem, the poetic drama, the religious hymn. These latter were appropriate to societies formally and officially committed to transcendent ideals of excellence—ideals that could be realized only by those few of exceptional nobility of character—or to transcendent visions of the universe wherein human existence on earth is accorded only a provisional significance. But bourgeois society is uninterested in such transcendence, which at best it tolerates as a private affair, a matter for individual taste and individual consumption as it were. It is prosaic, not only in form, but in essence. It is a society organized for the convenience and comfort of common men and common women, not for the production of heroic, memorable figures. It is a society interested in making the best of this world, not in any kind of transfiguration, whether through tragedy or piety.

Because this society proposes to make the best of this world, for the benefit of ordinary men and women, it roots itself in the most worldly and common of human motivations: self-interest. It assumes that, though only a few are capable of pursuing excellence, everyone is capable of recognizing and pursuing his own self-interest. This "democratic" assumption about the equal potential of human nature, in this limited respect, in turn justifies a market economy in which each individual defines his own well-being, and illegitimates all the paternalistic economic theories of previous eras. One should emphasize, however, that the pursuit of excellence by the few—whether defined in religious, moral, or intellectual terms—is neither prohibited nor inhibited. Such an activity is merely interpreted as a special form of self-interest, which may be freely pursued but can claim no official status. Bourgeois society also assumes that the average individual's conception of his own self-interest will be sufficiently "enlightened"—i.e., sufficiently farsighted and prudent—to permit other human passions (the desire for community, the sense of human sympathy, the moral conscience, etc.) to find expression, albeit always in a voluntarist form.

It is characteristic of a bourgeois culture, when it exists in concord with bourgeois principles, that we are permitted to take "happy endings" seriously (". . . and they lived happily ever after"). From classical antiquity through the Renaissance, happy endings—worldly happy endings—were consigned to the genre of Comedy. "Serious" art focused on a meaningful death, in the context of heroism in battle, passion in love, ambition in politics, or piety in religion. Such high seriousness ran counter to the bourgeois grain, which perceived human fulfillment—human authenticity, if you will—in terms of becoming a good citizen, a good husband, a good provider. It is, in contrast to both pre-bourgeois and post-bourgeois *Weltanschauungen,* a *domestic* conception of the universe and of man's place therein.

This bourgeois ideal is much closer to the Old Testament than to the New—which is, perhaps, why Jews have felt more at home in the bourgeois world than in any other. That God created this world and affirmed its goodness; that men ought confidently to be fruitful and multiply; that work (including that kind of work we call commerce) is elevating rather than demeaning; that the impulse to "better one's condition" (to use a favorite phrase of Adam Smith's) is good because natural—these beliefs were almost perfectly congruent with the world view of post-exilic Judaism. In this world view, there was no trace of aristocratic bias: Everyman was no allegorical figure but, literally, every common person.

So it is not surprising that the bourgeois world view—placing the needs and desires of ordinary men and women at its center—was (and still is) also popular among the common people. Nor is it surprising that, almost from the beginning, it was an unstable world view, evoking active contempt in a minority, and a pervasive disquiet among those who, more successful than others in having bettered their condition, had the leisure to wonder if life did not, perhaps, have more interesting and remote possibilities to offer.

The emergence of romanticism in the middle of the eighteenth century provided an early warning signal that, within the middle class itself, a kind of nonbourgeois spiritual impulse was at work. Not anti-bourgeois; not yet. For romanticism—with its celebration of noble savages, *Weltschmerz,* passionate love, aristocratic heroes and heroines, savage terrors confronted with haughty boldness and courage—was mainly an escapist aesthetic mode as distinct from a rebellious one. It provided a kind of counter-culture that was, on the whole, safely insulated from bourgeois reality, and could even be tolerated (though always uneasily) as a temporary therapeutic distraction from the serious business of living. A clear sign of this self-limitation of the romantic impulse was the degree to which it was generated, and consumed, by a particular section of the middle class: women.

One of the less happy consequences of the women's liberation movement of the past couple of decades is the distorted view it has encouraged of the history of women under capitalism. This history is interpreted in terms of repression—sexual repression above all. That repression was real enough, of course; but it is absurd to regard it as nothing but an expression of masculine possessiveness, even vindictiveness. Sexual repression—and that whole code of feminine conduct we have come to call Victorian—was imposed and enforced by women, not men (who stand to gain very little if *all* women are chaste). And women insisted on this code because, while sexually repressive, it was also liberating in all sorts of other ways. Specifically, it liberated women, ideally if not always actually, from their previous condition as sex objects or work objects. To put it another way: all women were now elevated to the aristocratic status of *ladies,* entitled to a formal deference, respect, consideration. (Even today, some of those habits survive, if weakly—taking off one's hat when greeting a female acquaintance, standing up when a woman enters the room, etc.). The "wench," as had been portrayed in Shakespeare's plays, was not dead. She was still very much to be found in the working and lower classes. But her condition was not immutable; she, too, could become a lady—through marriage, education, or sheer force of will.

The price for this remarkable elevation of the status of women was sexual self-restraint and self-denial, which made them, in a sense, owners of valuable (if intangible) property. It is reasonable to think that this change in actual sexual mores had something to do with the rise of romanticism, with its strong erotic component, in literature—the return of the repressed, as Freud was later to call it. For most of those who purchased romantic novels, or borrowed them (for a fee) from the newly established circulating libraries, were women. Indeed they still are, even today, two centuries later, though the romantic novel is now an exclusively popular art form, which flourishes outside the world of "serious" writing.

This extraordinary and ironical transformation of the novel from a prosaic art form—a tradition that reached its apogee in Jane Austen— to something radically different was itself a bourgeois accomplishment. It was made possible by the growing affluence of the middle classes that provided not only the purchasing power but also the leisure and the solitude ("a room of one's own"). This last point is worth especial notice. It is a peculiarity of the novel that, unlike all previous art forms, it gains rather than loses from becoming a private experience. Though novels were still occasionally read aloud all during the romantic era, they need not be and gradually ceased to be. Whereas Shakespeare or Racine are most "enchanting" as part of a public experience—on a stage, in daylight—the novel gains its greatest power over us when we "consume" it (or it "consumes" us) in silence and privacy. Reading a novel then becomes something like surrendering oneself to an especially powerful daydream. The bourgeois ethos, oriented toward prosaic actualities, strongly disapproves of such daydreaming (which is why, even today, a businessman will prefer not to be known as an avid reader of novels, and few in fact are). But bourgeois women very soon discovered that living simultaneously in the two worlds of nonbourgeois "romance" and bourgeois "reality" was superior to living in either one.

The men and women who wrote such novels (or poems—one thinks of Byron) were not, however, simply responding to a market incentive. Writers and artists may have originally been receptive to a bourgeois society because of the far greater individual freedoms that it offered them; and because, too, they could not help but be exhilarated by the heightened vitality and quickened vivacity of a capitalist order with its emphasis on progress, economic growth, and liberation from age-old constraints. But, very quickly, disillusionment and dissent set in, and the urge to escape became compelling.

From the point of view of artists and of those whom we have come to call "intellectuals"—a category itself created by bourgeois society, which converted philosophers into *philosophes* engaged in the task of critical enlightenment—there were three great flaws in the new order of things.

First of all, it threatened to be very boring. Though the idea of *ennui* did not become a prominent theme in literature until the nineteenth century, there can be little doubt that the experience is considerably older than its literary expression. One can say this with some confidence because, throughout history, artists and writers have been so candidly contemptuous of commercial activity between consenting adults, regarding it as an activity that tends to coarsen and trivialize the human spirit. And since bourgeois society was above all else a commercial society—the first in all of recorded history in which the commercial ethos was sovereign over all others—their exasperation was bound to be all the more acute. Later on, the term "philistinism" would emerge to encapsulate this sentiment.

Second, though a commercial society may offer artists and writers all sorts of desirable things—freedom of expression especially, popularity and affluence occasionally—it did (and does) deprive them of the status that they naturally feel themselves entitled to. Artists and writers and thinkers always have taken themselves to be Very Important People, and they are outraged by a society that merely tolerates them, no matter how generously. Bertolt Brecht was once asked how he could justify his Communist loyalties when his plays could neither be published nor performed in the USSR, while his royalties in the West made him a wealthy man. His quick rejoinder was: "Well, there at least they take me seriously!" Artists and intellectuals are always more respectful of a regime that takes their work and ideas "seriously." To be placed at a far distance from social and political power is, for such people, a deprivation.

Third, a commercial society, a society whose civilization is shaped by market transactions, is always likely to reflect the appetites and preferences of common men and women. Each may not have much money, but there are so many of them that their tastes are decisive. Artists and intellectuals see this as an inversion of the natural order of things, since it gives "vulgarity" the power to dominate where and when it can. By their very nature "elitists" (as one now says), they believe that a civilization should be shaped by an *aristoi* to which they will be organically attached, no matter how perilously. The consumerist and environmentalist movements of our own day reflect this aristocratic impulse, albeit in a distorted way: because the democratic idea is the only legitimating political idea of our era, it is claimed that the market does not truly reflect people's preferences, which are deformed by the power of advertising. A minority, however, is presumed to have the education and the will to avoid such deformation. And this minority then claims the paternalist authority to represent "the people" in some more authentic sense. It is this minority, which is so appalled by America's "automobile civilization," in which everyone owns a car, while it is not appalled at all by the fact that in the Soviet Union only a privileged few are able to do so.

In sum, intellectuals and artists will be (as they have been) restive in a bourgeois-capitalist society. The popularity of romanticism in the century after 1750 testifies to this fact, as the artists led an "inner emigration" of the spirit—which, however, left the actual world unchanged. But not all such restiveness found refuge in escapism. Rebellion was an alternative route, as the emergence of various socialist philosophies and movements early in the nineteenth century demonstrated.

Socialism (of whatever kind) is a romantic passion that operates within a rationalist framework. It aims to construct a human community in which *everyone* places the common good—as defined, necessarily, by an intellectual and moral elite—before his own individual interests and appetites. The intention was not new—there isn't a religion in the world that has failed to preach and expound it. What was new was the belief that such self-denial could be realized, not through a voluntary circumscription of individual appetites (as Rousseau had, for example, argued in his *Social Contract)* but even while the aggregate of human appetites was being increasingly satisfied by ever-growing material prosperity. What Marx called "utopian" socialism was frequently defined by the notion that human appetites were insatiable, and that a self-limitation on such appetites was a precondition for a socialist community. The trouble with this notion, from a political point of view, was that it was not likely to appeal to more than a small minority of men and women at any one time. Marxian "scientific" socialism, in contrast, promised to remove this conflict between actual and potentially ideal human nature by creating an economy of such abundance that appetite as a social force would, as it were, wither away.

Behind this promise, of course, was the profound belief that modern science—including the social sciences, and especially including scientific economics—would gradually but ineluctably provide humanity with modes of control over nature (and human nature, too) that would permit the modern world radically to transcend all those previous limitations of the human condition previously taken to be "natural." The trouble with implementing this belief, however, was that the majority of men and women were no more capable of comprehending a "science of society," and of developing a "consciousness" appropriate to it, than they were of practicing austere self-denial. A socialist elite, therefore, was indispensable to mobilize the masses for their own ultimate self-transformation. And the techniques of such mobilization would themselves of necessity be "scientific"—what moralists would call "Machiavellian"—in that they had to treat the masses as objects of manipulation so that eventually they would achieve a condition where they could properly be subjects of their own history making.

Michael Polanyi has described this "dynamic coupling" of a romantic moral passion with a ruthlessly "scientific" conception of man, his world, and his history, as a case of "moral inversion." That is to say, it is the moral passion that legitimates the claims of "scientific" socialism to absolute truth, while it is the "scientific" necessities that legitimate every possible form of political immorality. Such a "dynamic coupling" characterized, in the past, only certain religious movements. In the nineteenth and twentieth centuries, it became the property of secular political movements that sought the universal regeneration of mankind in the here and now.

The appeal of any such movement to intellectuals is clear enough. As intellectuals, they are qualified candidates for membership in the elite that leads such movements, and they can thus give free expression to their natural impulse for authority and power. They can do so, moreover, within an ideological context, which reassures them that, any superficial evidence to the contrary notwithstanding, they are disinterestedly serving the "true" interests of the people.

But the reality principle—*la force des choses*—will, in the end, always prevail over utopian passions. The fate of intellectuals under socialism is disillusionment, dissent, exile, silence. In politics, means determine ends, and socialism everywhere finds its incarnation in coercive bureaucracies that are contemptuously dismissive of the ideals that presumably legitimize them, even while establishing these ideals as a petrified orthodoxy. The most interesting fact of contemporary intellec-

tual life is the utter incapacity of so-called "socialist" countries to produce socialist intellectuals—or even, for that matter, to tolerate socialist
intellectuals. If you want to meet active socialist intellectuals, you can
go to Oxford or Berkeley or Paris or Rome. There is no point in going to
Moscow or Peking or Belgrade or Bucharest or Havana. Socialism
today is a dead end for the very intellectuals who have played so significant a role in moving the modern world down that street.

In addition to that romantic-rationalist rebellion we call socialism,
there is another mode of "alienation" and rebellion that may be, in the
longer run, more important. This is romantic antirationalism, which
takes a cultural rather than political form. It is this movement specifically that Trilling had in mind when he referred to "the adversary
culture."

Taking its inspiration from literary romanticism, this rebellion first
created a new kind of "inner emigration"—physical as well as spiritual—in the form of "bohemia." In Paris, in the 1820s and 1830s,
there formed enclaves of (mostly) young people who displayed *in nuce*
all the symptoms of the counter-culture of the 1960s. Drugs, sexual
promiscuity, long hair for men and short hair for women, working-class
dress (the "jeans" of the day), a high suicide rate—anything and everything that would separate them from the bourgeois order. The one
striking difference between this bohemia and its heirs of a century and a
quarter later is that to claim membership in bohemia one had to be (or
pretend to be) a producer of "art," while in the 1960s to be a consumer
was sufficient. For this transition to occur, the attitudes and values of
bohemia had to permeate a vast area of bourgeois society itself. The
engine and vehicle of this transition was the "modernist" movement in
the arts, which in the century after 1850 gradually displaced the traditional, the established, the "academic."

The history and meaning of this movement are amply described
and brilliantly analyzed by Daniel Bell in his *The Cultural Contradictions of Capitalism*. Suffice it to say here that modernism in the arts can
best be understood as a quasi-religious rebellion against bourgeois so-
briety, rather than simply as a series of aesthetic innovations. The very
structure of this movement bears a striking resemblance to that of the
various gnostic-heretical sects within Judaism and Christianity. There
is an "elect"—the artists themselves—who possess the esoteric and
redeeming knowledge *(gnosis)*; then there are the "critics," whose task
it is to convey this gnosis, as a vehicle of conversion, to potential ad-

herents to the movement. And then there is the outer layer of "sympathizers" and "fellow travelers"—mainly bourgeois "consumers" of the modernist arts—who help popularize and legitimate the movement within the wider realms of public opinion.

One can even press the analogy further. It is striking, for instance, that modernist movements in the arts no longer claim to create "beauty" but to reveal the "truth" about humanity in its present condition. Beauty is defined by an aesthetic tradition that finds expression in the public's "taste." But the modern artist rejects the sovereignty of public taste, since truth can never be a matter of taste. This truth always involves an indictment of the existing order of things, while holding out the promise, for those whose sensibilities have been suitably reformed, of a redemption of the spirit (now called "the self"). Moreover, the artist himself now becomes the central figure in the artistic enterprise—he is the hero of his own work, the sacrificial redeemer of us all, the only person capable of that transcendence that gives a liberating meaning to our lives. The artist—painter, poet, novelist, composer—who lives to a ripe old age of contentment with fame and fortune strikes us as having abandoned, if not betrayed, his "mission." We think it more appropriate that artists should die young and tormented. The extraordinarily high suicide rate among modern artists would have baffled our ancestors, who assumed that the artist—like any other *secular* person—aimed to achieve recognition and prosperity in this world.

Our ancestors would have been baffled, too, by the enormous importance of critics and of criticism in modern culture. It is fascinating to pick up a standard college anthology in the history of literary criticism and to observe that, prior to 1800, there is very little that we would designate as literary criticism, as distinct from philosophical tracts on aesthetics. Shakespeare had no contemporary critics to explain his plays to the audience; nor did the Greek tragedians, or Dante, Racine, etc. Yet we desperately feel the need of critics to understand, not only the modern artist, but, by retrospective reevaluation, all artists. The reason for this odd state of affairs is that we are looking for something in these artists—a redeeming knowledge of ourselves and our human condition—which in previous eras was felt to lie elsewhere, in religious traditions especially.

The modernist movement in the arts gathered momentum slowly, and the first visible sign of its success was the gradual acceptance of the fact that bourgeois society had within it two cultures: the "avant-garde" culture of modernism, and the "popular culture" of the majority. The self-designation of modernism as "avant-garde" is itself illuminating. The term is of military origin, and means not, as we are now inclined to think, merely the latest in cultural or intellectual fashion, but the foremost assault troops in a military attack. It was a term popularized by Saint-Simon to describe the role of his utopian-socialist sect vis-à-vis the bourgeois order, and was then taken over by modernist innovators in the arts. The avant-garde is, and always has been, fully self-conscious of its hostile intentions toward the bourgeois world. This is, as has been noted, a cultural phenomenon without historical precedent.

And so is the "popular culture" of the bourgeois era, though here again we are so familiar with the phenomenon that we fail to perceive its originality. It is hard to think of a single historical instance where a society presents us with two cultures, a "high" and a "low," whose values are in opposition to one another. We are certainly familiar with the fact that any culture has its more sophisticated and its more popular aspects, differentiated by the level of education needed to move from the one to the other. But the values embodied in these two aspects were basically homogeneous: the sophisticated expression did not *shock* the popular, nor did the popular incite feelings of revulsion among the sophisticated. Indeed, it was taken as the mark of true artistic greatness for a writer or artist to encompass both aspects of his culture. The Greek tragedies were performed before all the citizens of Athens; Dante's *Divine Comedy* was read aloud in the squares of Florence to a large and motley assemblage; and Shakespeare's plays were enacted before a similarly mixed audience.

The popular culture of the bourgeois era, after 1870 or so, tended to be a culture that educated people despised, or tolerated contemptuously. The age of Richardson, Jane Austen, Walter Scott, and Dickens—an age in which excellence and popularity needed not to contradict one another, in which the distinction between "highbrow" and "lowbrow" made no sense—was over. The spiritual energy that made for artistic excellence was absorbed by the modernist, highbrow movement, while popular culture degenerated into a banal reiteration—almost purely commercial in intent—of "wholesome" bourgeois themes. In this popular literature of romance and adventure, the "happy ending" not only survived but became a standard cliché. The occasional unhappy ending, involving a sinful action (e.g., adultery) as its effectual cause, always concluded on a note of repentance, and was the occasion for a cathartic "good cry." In "serious" works of literature in the twentieth century, of course, the happy ending is under an almost total prohibition. It is also worth making mention of the fact that popular literature remained very much a commodity consumed by women, whose commitment to the bourgeois order (a "domestic" order, remember) has always been stronger than men's. This is why the women's liberation movement of the past two decades, which is so powerfully moving the female sensibility in an antibourgeois direction, is such a significant cultural event.

In the last century, the modernist movement in the arts made constant progress at the expense of the popular. It was, after all, the only serious art available to young men and women who were inclined to address themselves to solemn questions about the meaning of life (or "the meaning of it all"). The contemporaneous evolution of liberal capitalism itself encouraged modernism in its quest for moral and spiritual hegemony. It did this in three ways.

First, the increasing affluence that capitalism provided to so many individuals made it possible for them (or, more often, for their children) to relax their energetic pursuit of money, and of the goods that money can buy, in favor of an attention to those nonmaterial goods that used to be called "the higher things in life." The antibourgeois arts in the twentieth century soon came to be quite generously financed by restless, uneasy, and vaguely discontented bourgeois money.

Second, that spirit of worldly rationalism so characteristic of a commercial society and its business civilization (and so well described by Max Weber and Joseph Schumpeter) had the effect of delegitimizing all merely traditional beliefs, tasks, and attitudes. The "new," constructed by design or out of the passion of a moment, came to seem inherently superior to the old and established, this latter having emerged "blindly" out of the interaction of generations. This mode of thinking vindicated the socialist ideal of a planned society. But it also vindicated an anarchic, antinomian, "expressionist" impulse in matters cultural and spiritual.

Third, the tremendous expansion—especially after World War II—of post-secondary education provided a powerful institutional milieu for modernist tastes and attitudes among the mass of both teachers and students. Lionel Trilling, in *Beyond Culture*, poignantly describes the spiritual vitality with which this process began in the humanities—

the professors were "liberated" to teach the books that most profoundly moved and interested them—and the vulgarized version of modernism that soon became the mass counter-culture among their students who, as consumers, converted it into a pseudo-bohemian life-style.

Simultaneously, and more obviously, in the social sciences, the anti-bourgeois socialist traditions were absorbed as a matter of course, with "the study of society" coming quickly and surely to mean the management of social change by an elite who understood the verities of social structure and social trends. Economics, as the science of making the best choices in a hard world of inevitable scarcity, resisted for a long while; but the Keynesian revolution—with its promise of permanent prosperity through government management of fiscal and monetary policy—eventually brought much of the economics profession in line with the other social sciences.

So utopian rationalism and utopian romanticism have, between them, established their hegemony as "adversary cultures" over the modern consciousness and the modern sensibility. But, inevitably, such victories are accompanied by failure and disillusionment. As socialist reality disappoints, socialist thought fragments into heterogeneous conflicting sects, all of them trying to keep the utopian spark alive while devising explanations for the squalid nature of socialist reality. One is reminded of the experience of Christianity in the first and second centuries, but with this crucial difference: Christianity, as a religion of transcendence, of *other-worldly* hope, of faith not belief, was not really utopian, and the Church Fathers were able to transform the Christian rebellion against the ancient world into a new, vital Christian orthodoxy, teaching its adherents how to live virtuously, i.e., how to seek human fulfillment in this world even while waiting for their eventual migration into a better one. Socialism, lacking this transcendent dimension, is purely and simply trapped in this world, whose realities are for it nothing more than an endless series of frustrations. It is no accident, as the Marxists would say, that there is no credible doctrine of "socialist virtue"—a doctrine informing individuals how to live "in authenticity"—in any nation (and there are so many!) now calling itself "socialist." It is paradoxically true that other-worldly religions are more capable of providing authoritative guidance for life in this world than are secular religions.

The utopian romanticism that is the impulse behind modernism in the arts is in a not dissimilar situation. It differs in that it seeks transcendence—all of twentieth-century art is such a quest—but it seeks such transcendence within the secular self. This endeavor can generate that peculiar spiritual intensity that characterizes the antibourgeois culture of our bourgeois era, but in the end it is mired in self-contradiction. The deeper one explores into the self, without any transcendental frame of reference, the clearer it becomes that nothing is there. One can then, of course, try to construct a metaphysics of nothingness as an absolute truth of the human condition. But this, too, is self-contradictory: if nothingness is the ultimate reality, those somethings called books, or poems, or paintings, or music are mere evasions of truth rather than expressions of it. Suicide is the only appropriate response to this vision of reality (as Dostoevski saw long ago) and in the twentieth century it has in fact become the fate of many of our artists: self-sacrificial martyrs to a hopeless metaphysical enterprise. Those who stop short of this ultimate gesture experience that *tedium vitae,* already mentioned, which has made the "boringness" of human life a recurrent theme, since Baudelaire at least, among our artists. This modern association of culture and culture heroes with self-annihilation and *ennui* has no parallel in human history. We are so familiar with it that most of us think of it as natural. It is, in truth, unnatural and cannot endure. Philosophy may, with some justice, be regarded as a preparation for dying, as Plato said—but he assumed that there would never be more than a handful of philosophers at any time. The arts, in contrast, have always been life-affirming, even when dealing with the theme of death. It is only when the arts usurp the role of religion, but without the transcendence that assures us of the meaning of apparent meaninglessness, that we reach our present absurd (and *absurdiste)* condition.

Moreover, though utopian rationalism and utopian romanticism are both hostile to bourgeois society, they turn out to be, in the longer run, equally hostile to one another. In all socialist nations, of whatever kind, modernism in the arts is repressed—for, as we have seen, this modernism breeds a spirit of nihilism and antinomianism that is subversive of *any* established order. But this repression is never entirely effective, because the pseudo-orthodoxies of socialism can offer no satisfying spiritual alternatives. It turns out that a reading of Franz Kafka can alienate from socialist reality just as easily as from bourgeois reality, and there is no socialist Richardson or Fielding or Jane Austen or Dickens to provide an original equipoise. Who are the "classic" socialist authors or artists worthy of the name? There are none. And so young people in socialist lands naturally turn either to the high modernist culture of the twentieth century or to its debased, popularized version in the counter-culture. Picasso and Kafka, blue jeans and rock-and-roll may yet turn out to be the major internal enemies of socialist bureaucracies, uniting intellectuals and the young in an incorrigible hostility to the *status quo*. Not only do socialism and modernism end up in blind allies—their blind allies are pointed in radically different directions.

Meanwhile, liberal capitalism survives and staggers on. It survives because the market economics of capitalism does work—does promote economic growth and permits the individual to better his condition while enjoying an unprecedented degree of individual freedom. But there is something joyless, even somnambulistic about this survival. For it was the Judeo-Christian tradition, which, as it were, acted as the Old Testament to the new evangel of liberal, individualistic capitalism—which supplied it with a moral code for the individual to live by, and which also enabled the free individual to find a transcendental meaning in life, to cope joyfully or sadly with all the *rites de passage* that define the human condition. Just as a victorious Christianity needed the Old Testament in its canon because the Ten Commandments were there—along with the assurance that God created the world *"and it was good,"* and along, too, with its corollary that it made sense to be fruitful and multiply on this earth—so liberal capitalism needed the Judeo-Christian tradition to inform it authoritatively about the use and abuse of the individual's newly won freedom. But the "adversary culture," in both its utopian-rationalist and utopian-romantic aspects, turns this Judeo-Christian tradition into a mere anachronism. And the churches, now themselves a species of voluntary private enterprise, bereft of all public support and sanction, are increasingly ineffectual in coping with its antagonists.

Is it possible to restore the spiritual base of bourgeois society to something approaching a healthy condition? One is tempted to answer: no, it is not possible to turn back the clock of history. But this answer itself derives from the romantic-rationalist conception of history, as elaborated by Saint-Simon and Hegel and Marx. In fact, human history, read in a certain way, can be seen as full of critical moments when human beings deliberately turned the clock back. The Reformation, properly understood, was just such a moment, and so was the codification of the Talmud in post-exile Judaism. What we call the "new" in intellectual and spiritual history is often nothing more than a novel way of turning the clock back. The history of science and technology is a cumulative history, in which new ways of seeing and doing effectively displace old ones. But the histories of religion and culture are not at all cumulative in this way, which is why one cannot study religion and culture without studying their histories, while scientists need not study the history of science to understand what they are up to.

So the possibility is open to us—but, for better or worse, it is not the only possibility. All we can say with some certainty, at this time, is that the future of liberal capitalism may be more significantly shaped by the ideas now germinating in the mind of some young, unknown philosopher or theologian than by any vagaries in annual GNP statistics. Those statistics are not unimportant, but to think they are all-important is to indulge in the silly kind of capitalist idolatry that is subversive of capitalism itself. It is the ethos of capitalism that is in gross disrepair, not the economics of capitalism—which is, indeed, its saving grace. But salvation through this grace alone will not suffice.

The Mass Media in Post-Industrial Society

Stanley Rothman

15 Sometime during the late 1950s or early 1960s the United States turned a corner in its social and cultural life in some very key respects, as a whole series of changes ushered in the beginnings of a new cultural, social, and political dynamic. The changes included a tremendous growth in the college population and those who taught them. They also included the emergence of national television, and communication and transportation networks, which guaranteed that most Americans, to an historically unprecedented extent, would be subject to much the same image of reality, whether they lived in Podunk or New York.[1]

Daniel Bell and others coined the term "post-industrial society" to describe these changes, and the phrase was widely disseminated, especially during the 1960s. Whether or not one accepts it as a short-hand description of what is happening to American life, it is clear that quantitative changes have—to paraphrase Engels—yielded changes in quality.[2]

In this paper, I plan to emphasize changes in one area: the media. I will concentrate on television and newspapers, with a short nod at the motion picture industry. The changes that have taken place in this realm have indeed had a profound impact upon American politics in ways that are just beginning to become clear.

It is the argument of this essay that during the past thirty years a national media network has emerged in the United States, and that first, key individuals working for this media network (the national media "elite") share a common perspective (paradigm) as to the nature of social reality; second, this perspective strongly influences the manner in which they portray reality to other Americans; and third, the national media have had a significant impact on political behavior and social attitudes. Most significantly they have contributed to the decay of traditional political and social institutions.

Each of these propositions is controversial and none of the evidence that I can offer will be conclusive. I hope only to make a plausible preliminary case. To do so, however, some background is necessary.

THE BACKGROUND AND THE CONTEXT

The first newspapers began to appear in Europe in the 1500s. The mass media, however, date from about the turn of the twentieth century. It was not until then that technology, literacy, and (relative) freedom permitted the emergence of an industry that could transmit both domestic and foreign news to large numbers of people in a relatively short period of time.[3] The emergence of the mass media also required the institutionalization of commitment to popular participation in the political process[4] and, in the capitalist West, the development of mass consumption societies in which business relies heavily upon advertising.

It is perhaps no accident that journalism for the masses first developed in the United States, followed closely by England and other Western European countries. By 1910, some 24 million issues of daily newspapers were being published in this country, as against about 2 million in England. The economic and technological infrastructure for the mass production of news was uniquely present in the West at that time, as was the social and political commitment.[5]

Western countries were relatively unique in another respect. In many it had been established that newspapers should be free and uncensored; that within certain broadly defined boundaries, editors and publishers should be permitted to write what they wanted to write. Western European countries (and by no means all of them) are still relatively unique in this regard. The nations in the world today outside of Europe or the United States that boast even moderately free media (and I speak here of newspapers, television, and motion pictures) are relatively few and show little sign of increasing. Indeed, the trend seems to be in the other direction. In an increasing number of third-world nations restrictions upon the press are becoming more rigid.[6] Even in European countries associated with a relatively long history of freedom, governments still regularly attempt to control the organs of public opinion. For example, between 1955 and 1962 some 269 individual issues of newspapers were confiscated by the French government, most of them for articles about the Algerian conflict. De Gaulle was quite open in his (at least partially successful) efforts to control French television as a counterfoil to a press he considered hostile.[7]

While Europe and America have been the home of a free, i.e., freely competitive press, the American media (both newspapers and television) have always differed from the Western European and English for reasons having to do with cultural, economic, and political variables as well as with the sheer size of the United States. Although some of these differences are of diminishing importance, it is necessary to describe them before undertaking an examination of the changes that have taken place in the United States during the past fifteen years. Such a description will help place recent changes in historical and comparative context.

First, the mass media in the United States have been and still are primarily privately owned businesses, even though radio and television operate within the framework of public regulation of a sort.[8] In most European countries, on the other hand, both radio and television have been primarily public enterprises. Even where private enterprise has recently come to play a more significant role, it is far less important than in this country.[9]

Second, while newspapers in the United States and Europe are privately owned commercial enterprises, the historical tradition in the United States has been quite different from that of Europe. On the European continent a great many newspapers and magazines began as the organs of political parties and remained closely affiliated with them. Others began as organs of the Catholic church, especially in countries such as Germany, where Catholics considered themselves an embattled minority, or France, where the church felt that it was crucial to protect its flock from the secularizing and anticlerical tendencies of much of the political left's party press. As late as 1930, for example, about half the newspapers in Germany were essentially party newspapers. The Catholic church and the Catholic Center Party together published 312 newspapers and the Socialist Party (SPD), 169. In England this was not true, although the British Labour Party did maintain a mass circulation newspaper of its own for many years. It should be noted that the Continental pattern described above has changed considerably since World War II in both France and Germany. Today fewer than 20 percent of the newspapers in Germany are formally affiliated with a political party. In terms of circulation the figure is only 4 or 5 percent.[10]

The American pattern was quite different. To be sure, some newspapers were party affiliated, and the Catholic press in this country (as well as papers produced by other religious groups) played some role. At least since the middle of the nineteenth century, however, most publishers have considered themselves free of any attachments other than those of profitability, the personal biases of their editors, and the desire to report the news.*

The reasons for the differences between the European and the American press are quite obvious and tell us a good deal about the nature of the American mass media. As Louis Hartz pointed out in *The Liberal Tradition in America,* the United States was characterized by a broad ideological consensus during the nineteenth and early twentieth centuries.[11] It was assumed that both liberalism (a democratic republic) and capitalism had been handed down from on high. America did not develop a mass socialist party; nor did it develop a conservative party. For some of the same reasons, the country lacked explicitly ethnic or religious political movements.[12]

It is no accident that the whole notion of objective news reportage was first fully institutionalized in the United States at a time when most European newspapers still emphasized interpretive commentary. Living within the framework of a liberal consensus, American newsmen, like most other Americans, found it difficult to recognize that their view of the world might be shaped by a particular set of premises, a paradigm or *Weltanschauung,* which strongly influenced their views of social causation and hence their view of what the "facts" were. Under such circumstances the "facts" were merely the facts. On the other hand the more self-conscious European journalist was more aware that perceptions of social action were at least partly a function of the assumptions that were brought to them. These historical differences still influence the manner in which American and European newspapermen approach the news. And this lack of awareness helps explain the very inconclusive debate in America over questions of television and newspaper bias.

Of course, European countries cannot all be lumped together. In their relative freedom from censorship and belief in the possibility of

---

*It is important to remember that identification with a political party in the United States generally meant just that. Party affiliation in Europe, however, often implied that a newspaper was under more or less direct policy control by the party.

objective reportage of the news, British journalists more closely resembled American than they did those of Continental countries. On the other hand, there have always been important differences between England and the United States, aside from some of those already mentioned.

Political reporting in England was, until quite recently, very much influenced by the fact that politics in England was the preserve of "gentlemen" with "proper" educations from upper-class families, while most reporters came from lower middle-class backgrounds and had usually left school at age fifteen. In the United States, on the other hand, neither class nor educational differences between these two groups were pronounced.* Thus American newspapermen were never as deferential to bureaucrats or even politicians as their British counterparts tended to be. Indeed, Americans have always been more than willing to criticize, expose, and denounce "political malefactors," though less likely to develop fundamental criticisms of the political system.

The American propensity for (and enjoyment of) exposing and denouncing political leaders stems from a powerful populist strain in American liberalism. Americans may have felt a strong attachment to their sociopolitical system, but they were wary of those to whom they delegated political power.

To the above must be added elements of our legal and political structure. In England, the cabinet, since the end of the nineteenth century, has consisted of a team in which the prime minister has been *primus inter pares.* And Parliament as well as the bureaucracy have been dominated by the prime minister, the cabinet, and his party. Whatever disagreements might exist, say, within the Labour Party, it remained united on certain key issues. In the United States, on the other hand, the political fragmentation of Congress and its localism tended to result in a variety of centrifugal pressures, which encouraged bureaucrats or congressmen to leak to the press information designed to counter policies desired by others in the government. Further, even before Supreme Court decisions made it all but impossible for a public figure to sue a journalist, libel laws were far less rigorous in this country than in England. And we have had no Official Secrets Act. In England, the

---

*Of course, the relative fluidity of class lines also played a role.

publication of the Pentagon papers could have (and probably would have) led to very long jail sentences for the staff of any newspaper that had dared to publish them. Indeed it is very unlikely that the material would have been published.[13]

Finally, in England, until very recently, those elected to office were supposed to govern. They might be turned out eventually, but while governing they were given fairly wide leeway. This was far less true on the Continent, given the sharpness of ideological divisions, but even there the gap in status between newsmen and leading political figures was always considerable, and the leeway permitted to government in preventing the publication of items "essential to the national security" much greater. Though the pattern is changing quite rapidly, many European commentators still regard American political life as taking place in a fishbowl.

One other unique quality of the American media deserves mention, before turning to the changes of the 1950s and 1960s. Unlike most Western European countries, America has lacked a national press. To be sure there were magazines with national circulations (by the 1930s this included *Time* and *Life* magazines), growing newspaper chains, and, even before World War II, a very few prestigious newspapers such as the *New York Times,* which boasted a broader influence. However, localism was the dominant theme. The roaring twenties may have roared in some cosmopolitan centers like New York and (to a lesser extent) Chicago, but Babbitt dominated Main Street in most cities around the country, including the ethnic enclaves of metropolitan areas. In the short run, at least, most Americans remained relatively unaffected by the middle and upper-class culture of the few large cities that counted.

All these features of the American media predominated until the post-World War II period. Even in the midst of the Great Depression, most Americans were not especially conscious of New York or even Washington. Most also accepted the basic cultural and social parameters of their society as good and right and thought that those who wished to radically change them were either odd or evil.* This world view was reinforced by the images obtained from the newspapers, ra-

---

*None of this was incompatible with a generalized hostility to big business, and a desire for social reform of a certain kind—a desire which brought the New Deal to power. However, as European Marxists observed at the time, Roosevelt was merely a "bourgeois reformer."

dio, and Hollywood. Most publishers were relatively conservative, as were those who controlled the airwaves and motion pictures.[14] Especially in the radio and movie industries, executives were primarily concerned with entertaining the public and making profits. They were not by any means all Republicans. Many supported FDR and the New Deal, but their aim was to reform and save capitalism, and their products by and large reinforced the American Liberal Protestant consensus.

The working press was probably more liberal than were publishers, and some newsmen were even radicals. But the reins of authority were in the hands of the publishers, and reporters who wanted their jobs stayed in line. Publishers and network officials also actively catered to the preferences of their advertisers. After all, many if not all radio programs were directly controlled by the advertisers who sponsored them. For the most part, however, the threat of economic pressure was not the major force behind the media's conservatism. News and entertainment took the hue they did largely because publishers and most reporters believed that that was the way it was and should be. Key elites in American society accepted the broad framework of the American liberal consensus, and most did not even realize that there might be other ways to look at the world.

To be sure, in New York and a few other places, small groups of radicals were publishing journals, organizing workers, and with the onset of the New Deal, even entering government. For the most part, however, their influence on the broader social, cultural, and political underpinnings of society was marginal. Even when some of these people found themselves in positions in the culture where they might have an impact, a sense of limits (and fear) held them back. Historically the most interesting thing about the investigations of Hollywood in the late 1940s, and the blacklisting that followed, was how little had been done, even by those who considered themselves radical, to try to get their political or cultural message across. The second most interesting thing was how quickly Hollywood producers and New York television executives collapsed in the face of investigations.[15]

Paradoxically, the investigations of the late 1940s and early 1950s were something of a last gasp. For in the midst of them both America and its communications media were changing very rapidly, and the pace of change was accelerating.

THE NEW ELITES AND THE NEW SENSIBILITY

As noted in the introduction, the changes were those associated with the development of an advanced industrial society or, more precisely, an advanced industrial capitalist society of a certain kind. For our purposes two changes are significant: the development of national media, and the emergence of a stratum in the society some of whose members were to be producers and consumers of the products of the media.

Eric Goldman has called this stratum the "metro-Americans."[16] The term encompasses both socioeconomic status and cultural style. These people were members of minorities (especially Jews) raised in metropolitan areas, who had received college educations, were liberal-cosmopolitan in orientation, and had chosen the professions rather than traditional business careers. Their emergence as a power in the society was influenced by a number of variables. One of these, certainly, was the great expansion in college and graduate education that peaked after World War II, though it had started much earlier. By 1967, over 7 million students were attending institutions of higher learning: of these almost 1 million were obtaining advanced degrees. They were being taught by some 500,000 faculty members.[17]

During the immediate postwar period, American colleges and universities moved sharply in the direction of meritocracy in both the hiring of staff and admission of students. To be sure certain groups were still under-represented, but whole new segments of the population were being educated, and many were being educated at those elite universities that had once been the bastions of the Protestant middle and upper-middle class. In the social sciences and humanities, they were being educated by a faculty whose world view was increasingly liberal, or to put it another way, an academic community that was increasingly critical of traditional American social, cultural, and political institutions. All of this has been well documented by Everett Ladd, Martin Lipset, and others, and one need not go into detail.[18] Suffice to say that those being educated were being introduced to new ways of looking at social causation and social life in general. Faculty and students at elite institutions were even more liberal than those at lesser colleges and universities, and attitudes tended to "trickle down" from elite institutions to the backwaters.[19]

We do not have very good evidence from the period before the advent of scientific polling, but since then the trend has been clear. In the 1944 presidential election, college faculties voted only 3 percent more Democratic than did the general public; in 1952, they voted 12 percent more Democratic; and in 1972, they gave McGovern 18 percent more votes than did the general public. While only 39 percent of the faculty at non-elite schools described themselves as liberal or very liberal in Lipset's study, the figure for elite schools was 55 percent.[20]

As one might expect, those in the social sciences and humanities were even more liberal than academics as a whole. In 1972, 76 percent of social science faculty voted for McGovern, and 64 percent of social scientists described themselves as "liberal" or "very liberal." Various attitudinal measures used by Ladd and Lipset indicate that this self-description is not inaccurate.[21] Unfortunately Ladd and Lipset do not offer data on attitudes by specialty within various fields. However, Moynihan indicates that the proportion of "liberal to very liberal" professors is probably higher among those specializing in areas of current public interest such as race relations.[22]

Many of those graduating from colleges and universities were quite upwardly mobile, for the size of the American middle class was increasing. And many were entering professions that they perceived as not particularly dependent upon traditional economic and social institutions—the "knowledge industries," including teaching and the media. Nor is it surprising that those who picked careers in teaching, social work, and journalism tended to be more to the left than those who chose engineering or business.[23] Even those entering upon more traditional professional or business careers during the 1960s were undoubtedly changing. But one suspects that the metro-Americans contributed most heavily to the declining correlation of social class with party vote during the 1960s and early 1970s. Thus, while only 33 percent of those with college educations voted for Democratic congressional candidates in 1948, the figures for 1968 and 1974 were 55 percent and 69 percent, respectively. If one takes socioeconomic status as the criterion, the shift is not quite as dramatic. Dividing the population into three groups by socioeconomic status, Ladd found that while only 33 percent of those classified as high socioeconomic status voters supported Democratic candidates in 1948, the percentage had risen to 57 by 1974. Comparable figures for voters under age 30 (those most likely to be college educated) were 42 percent and 69 percent.[24]

The new metro-Americans were still a relatively small portion of the population of the 1960s; the total number of technical and professional employees (occupations requiring at least some college education) had grown from about 3.8 million in 1941 to over 8.5 million in 1964.[25] Nonetheless, their values and attitudes were beginning to have an impact on newspapers, magazines, and even television. For one thing, their numbers were now large enough to provide an audience for more sophisticated films and periodicals, as well as for journals that took a less parochial and narrowly patriotic view of American institutions.

The *New York Review of Books*, for example, was founded in the 1960s and, to the surprise of most, became an almost instant success. Movies as well as television programs were able to make profits while presenting themes that would not have been profitable in previous decades if, indeed, they had not been banned.

And so the new class emerged, increasingly cosmopolitan, eschewing simple-minded patriotism and faith in the American dream, and seeking to "actualize" themselves through the consumption of "meaningful" experiences. Education was, of course, not the only variable in the equation. As Bell points out, Liberal Capitalism in America, with its emphasis on consumption, contributed a good deal to this developing orientation.[26]

At the same time, the United States was gradually developing a national media network. That is, a relatively small group of media outlets was increasingly determining the manner in which the world was being presented to Americans. And this group of media was largely centered in New York and (secondarily) Washington.

Perhaps the major reason for this development was the emergence of television and its domination by three major networks in New York. Given the expense of producing programs, including news programs and television specials, local network affiliates increasingly came to depend upon the networks for their programs. Edward Epstein demonstrates this in *News From Nowhere*,[27] and corroboration can be found in the works of the British sociologist Malcolm Warner and others.[28] This relatively small group of people received their own world view from the *New York Times, Time Magazine, Newsweek,* and to a lesser extent, the *Washington Post* and the *Wall Street Journal*.[29]

Television also contributed to major changes in the motion picture industry. Previously the studio had been central to the business, controlling the artists through a quasi-monopolistic arrangement that included domination of distribution and exhibition. Now, as Robert Sobel points out, the artist was set free from the studio.[30] The studios continued to turn out films, but increasingly they concentrated on renting space to independents producing television shows, and working out arrangements for ancillary activities. When movies had been purely business, the product was safe, sensible, and above all salable. Now, however, the artists, many of them highly critical of American values and freed by court decisions and changes in public mood from fears of political authorities, could move ahead on their own. They also had a potential audience. By the mid 1970s the pattern had changed again as fairly giant conglomerates came to play a larger and larger role in the movie industry. However, while their aim, like that of the old tycoons, was to create smash hits, they did not exercise control over the industry comparable to that of the moguls of the 1930s and 1940s. Besides, their tastes and attitudes had been partly formed by the 1960s, as had that of the moviegoing public. The counter-culture had been absorbed, but it had also partially triumphed in the cultural sphere.[31]

Thus movies increasingly began to picture small-town America not as a place of virtue but rather as evidence of the sickness of American culture. As Stanley Kramer put it: "Of course, they're reactionary, extremely reactionary. They pursue the clichés of America so strictly that they endanger America."[32]

In *The Apartment* (1960) and *One, Two, Three* (1961) Billy Wilder took advantage of every opportunity to portray the moral ambivalence of business executives. His aim was, in his own words, to show: "How corrupt we are, how money-mad we are! How shaky all our convictions are." Similarly, Kubrick satirized the military in *Dr. Strangelove,* and Frankenheimer viewed *Seven Days in May* as an opportunity "to illustrate what a tremendous force the military-industrial complex is." Similarly, the approach of traditional films to the conflict between settlers and Indians was inverted. In such movies as *Little Big Man* and *Soldier Blue,* settlers and soldiers appeared, with some exceptions, as the clear villains of the story.

The misfit became the new American hero, and the forces of law (or convention) were pictured as either ludicrous or evil.[33] Charles T. Samuels's description of *Bonnie and Clyde* is quite accurate here:

In Bonnie and Clyde the Cops and Robbers are literal, but the latter are portrayed as cryptorevolutionaries against a society in the throes of economic collapse. . . . The Cops, on the other hand, are imbecile sadists who submit the heroes to an overkill familiar from American foreign policy.[34]

Samuels's criticism is from a radical perspective. His argument is that, rather than developing an intelligent critique of American society, the movies of the 1960s replayed the 1950s with different "good guys" and different "bad guys"; "each film plays to stock responses, and reflects audience prejudices as shamelessly as the discredited old models."

Actually, he is wrong about at least some of the movies of the 1950s. For example, many American Westerns had begun to attempt to portray American Indians with some dignity, and as morally superior to many whites, and to present the driving of the Indians from their land as a tragedy. In that sense the portrayals were perhaps somewhat more complex than those of *Little Big Man* or *Soldier Blue*.

The ultimate result was, as Elliot Gould expressively put it, a series of motion pictures whose theme was "Screw God Bless America"; in the words of Paul Newman these films suggested that society itself was the real enemy.[35]

What television had done, of course, was to *nationalize* and *standardize* communications to an extent never before achieved in the United States. New York and Washington styles and modes now became national styles and modes. And if the *New York Times* was read by the New York and Washington elites, it would also be read elsewhere. Again, one must not exaggerate. *Time, Life,* and other journals had already established a national constituency, but the difference by the early 1960s was significant enough to constitute a change in kind.

For example, a study completed by the American Institute of Political Communication in 1972 reported that 96.9 percent of members of the Washington press corps read the *New York Times* and the *Washington Post;* 83 percent of a national sample of newspaper editors read the *New York Times.* The figure for a sample of broadcast news executives was 56.3 percent.[36] Sampling congressmen and senators, Allen Barton of the Bureau of Applied Social Research found that 67 percent read the *New York Times* and 82 percent read the *Washington Post.* The percentage of those reading the *Times,* especially, was equally high for other elites. In fact the *Times* was read more widely than any other publication in all elite groups except for business elites and "owners of large wealth," who tended to rely somewhat more heavily on the *Wall Street Journal*. The same study found that *Time* and *Newsweek* received similar rankings among such groups.[37]

The influence of the elite media extended to foreign affairs. American diplomats, like their European counterparts, increasingly obtained their information about the world from these media, supplemented by diplomatic or intelligence channels.[38] As Leonard Sigal notes in his *Reporters and Officials:*

> The news media, but especially the *Times* and the *Post,* constitute one network in the central nervous system of the U.S. government. This network, unlike almost any other, transmits information throughout government, and often with greater speed than internal channels of communication. News organizations select the sights and sounds that Washingtonians will sense the next day. They thereby shape perceptions in their environment.[39]

Patterson and Abeles, in describing a major research project sponsored by the Social Sciences Research Council on the 1976 elections, sum up the change nicely: "Decisions about what the public will know rest increasingly upon the beliefs of the small elite which determines what the public should know."[40]

Most studies seem to agree, then, that the key national media consist of the three national television networks, the *New York Times,* the *Washington Post,* the *Wall Street Journal, Time, Newsweek,* and when the Barton et al. study was completed a few years back, the *Washington Star,* primarily because of its location.

The people who work for these publications are relatively highly educated. My reanalysis of the data from a major study of television and newspaper personnel, conducted by Johnstone et al., yields the following information:[41] 88 percent have graduated from college, of whom 43 percent have completed at least some graduate work. Less than 6 percent have not received at least some college education. According to the Columbia study, they claim to read intellectual or semi-intellectual journals such as the *New Yorker* (56 percent); *Harper's* (51 percent); and the *New York Review of Books* (25 percent). *Commentary* was read by 15 percent of Barton's respondents, *Esquire* by 22 percent, and the *Reader's Digest* by a mere 8 percent.[42] It is on this basis that Charles Kadushin suggests, in the *American Intellectual Elite,* that intellectuals now have a greater influence on public policy than ever before through a trickle-down effect of their ideas to the national media elite.[43] Of course some of these figures are exaggerated. Epstein, for example, suggests that very few television producers or reporters do more than read the *New York Times,* but that would move the trickle-down effect only one step further up or down the line.[44]

What of the political and social attitudes of this elite? According to Johnstone's data, 14 percent of respondents working for elite media classified themselves as "far left," and 56 percent classified themselves as "a little to the left," for a total of 70.1 percent in about 1970. In contrast, 37 percent of the non-elite portion of Johnstone's sample classified themselves as "left" or "far left."* Among the general population at the time the comparable figure was 3 percent.[45] Of course one question proves very little. However, Barton asked a far wider range of questions to a somewhat broader group of media leaders from 30 relatively large cities, with much the same results. The national media elite, as he defined it, is among the most liberal in the country, especially on cultural issues, but also on social reform and economic redistribution issues, despite their relatively high salaries.[46] A more recent study, sponsored jointly by Harvard University and the *Washington Post,* reveals much the same pattern among the Washington press corps. Approximately 61 percent of the group voted for McGovern in 1972 while only 22 percent supported Nixon. (Among the population at large, Nixon received 61 percent of the vote to McGovern's 38 percent.) About 59 percent classify themselves as liberal or "radical."[47]

Why are those who comprise the national media elite liberal or liberal left? A number of factors are involved. The first is that many of them turned to journalism as a career initially because of a disenchantment with the dominant economic institutions of the society (witness Eric Sevareid's autobiography, *Not So Wild a Dream*).[48] These early proclivities were undoubtedly strengthened by their education and, finally, by their location in communities such as New York, which involved them in reinforcing associations with like-minded people.

As Epstein points out:

> Producers (of television programs) who tend to read the same newspapers (particularly the *New York Times*) and news magazines, commute to the same area of the City (New York), and discuss with

---

*Again, this figure is based on a reanalysis of the Johnstone et al. data.

friends the same agenda of problems can be expected to share a similar perspective on the critical themes of the day.[49]

Several caveats should be offered at this point. First, we are discussing averages. Obviously the media elite includes numbers of conservatives who read the *National Review* and neoconservatives (as they are now called) who read the *Public Interest.*

Second, I am aware that what I am saying seems contrary to arguments by respected critics of the press like Ben Bagdikian, who points out that more newspapers in the country endorse Republican than Democratic candidates, and that many very conservative publishers are all about us.[50] Bagdikian also argues that, because of newspaper concentration and the declining number of journals, such newspapers are often the only source of news in one-paper towns and cities.[51]

Editorial endorsement, however, says little about the daily content of newspapers. Such content, as regards national news at least, is obtained largely from the press services or such opinion leaders as the *New York Times.*[52] Further, despite the lament about newspaper concentration, it is not true that people are the victims of small-town newspaper backwardness simply because their communities publish only one paper. The *Manchester Union Leader* may be New Hampshire's leading paper, but citizens still watch Walter Cronkite and Eric Sevareid, among others, on the evening news, and they can and do buy the *Boston Globe, Time, Newsweek* and/or the *New York Times.*

Furthermore, the power of publishers is not what it was even twenty years ago. Even relatively conservative publishers have become convinced that liberals may be correct. In addition, they are committed to hiring according to merit criteria if only because they need good writers. For these and other reasons they have lost a good deal of control over their staffs. Rodney Stark described the process on a metropolitan newspaper he called the *Express,* which was owned by a conservative publisher. No matter how hard he tried, the publisher was unable to hire the kind of staff he wanted. His best reporters (the educated, experienced "pros," as the author calls them) tended to be liberal. As a result, he lamented:

When I think of all the new dealing, liberal propaganda that gets into this newspaper, I'm ashamed and angry. It's almost impossible to print the kind of newspaper America needs today, because of the kind of people we have to hire. I'd like to fire about half of them.[53]

Nor were the publishers the only ones at a loss. Even editors found that they could no longer fully control their staffs as much as they would have liked. The bright younger reporters saw things in certain ways and insisted on reporting them as they saw them. And the young reporters were, by and large, more likely to view events from a liberal to radical perspective.

All this had been happening rather quietly during the 1950s, supposedly a time of reaction, but had been concealed by the Cold War consensus and the lack of sharp polarizing domestic issues. The 1960s changed all that. The emergence of the civil rights issue and the Vietnam War revealed very quickly how weak the traditional establishment was. The new metro-Americans were not the conformist mass in split-level suburbs pictured in the 1950s. And the old elites, not outnumbered by them, but less and less sure of their own values, and often confronting offspring whose education was critical of those values, did not know how to react.

The result was the rapid breakdown of the 1950s consensus; a distinct shift to the left by liberals who suddenly found themselves to be radical; and increased influence for a whole group of individuals who, it had been thought, were marginal to the culture. It was only then that conservatives (and some of those who had become conservatives or "neoconservatives") began to raise the question of liberal bias in the national media.

PARADIGMS AND "REALITY"

This, of course, brings us to the main issue. Do the liberal cosmopolitan attitudes of the media elite affect the manner in which they report the news? In a broad sense, the answer is clearly yes. After all, reporters and editors are human beings. Whatever efforts they may make to be objective, there is bound to be some slippage.*

---

*Media personnel (radicals, liberals, and conservatives) are not exceptional in this regard. The same slippage occurs with all of us including the most "objective" social scientists.

This is a very difficult issue, for one's view of whether the presentation of reality has been distorted depends very much on one's view of reality. Thus "radical" critics of the media argue that the *New York Times* and the television networks are basically conservative, and that their presentation of the world reflects this bias, even as conservatives argue an alternate position. Many of those in key positions in the national media, of course, maintain that they are merely describing reality as it is and that the fact that they are simultaneously criticized from the right and the left demonstrates this. The issues are far too complex to fully resolve here. I shall argue that the manner in which "reality" is presented by the national media is strongly influenced by a (largely unconscious) paradigm. Given the very few extant systematic studies of this issue (some of which are discussed below), it is impossible to offer fully persuasive evidence at this time. Rather, I will rely largely on a series of examples.[54] I expect to publish more systematic data in the future. Before I do, an explanation of my terms and some caveats are in order.

The paradigm concept was first popularized by Thomas Kuhn and has been widely used by social scientists (especially those on the left) to criticize what they consider to be the dominant and "distorting" assumptions of the American academic community.[55] Kuhn had argued that natural scientists generally operate within the framework of assumptions about the universe which determine what shall be regarded as a fact, and that these only change during periods of scientific revolutions.

At least some of those who attempt to apply this notion to social life are persuaded that our perceptions of "reality" are so permeated by preexisting value commitments that objectivity is impossible to achieve. My own view is that while paradigms change slowly and are often supported by all kinds of unconscious and irrational needs, they do change. We can improve our understanding of the social world by a process of criticism and self-criticism.

Now for the caveats.

First, newspapers such as the *New York Times,* and television networks are pluralistic organizations.[56] Thus, news stories reflect a number of perspectives. Second, I must agree with E.J. Epstein, Paul Weaver, and Michael Robinson that many of the complaints registered against television and even newspapers have much to do with structural imperatives of time, money, opportunities, and competition.[57] However, beyond these, I would argue that pivotal members of the elite media do share a "paradigm," which tells them what the world should be like and which leads them to deal with events in certain ways. In fact (as I shall argue later) the paradigm is so much a part of their conventional wisdom that its assumptions often seem to merely constitute common sense, that instinct for truth which, as Tom Wicker argues, all reporters must rely upon when they attempt to make some sense out of the world around them.[58] Unfortunately, one person's instinct for truth is another's ideology. As Tunstall puts it:

> Along with the more blatant censorship by others . . . goes the more important "self-censorship" of the journalist as he systematically attempts to fit events into a particular world view whose basic premises he sees as embodying a faithful portrayal of society. So-called "objectivity" becomes a matter of interpreting and analyzing the event dispassionately in the light of the accepted paradigm of "how things happen" and "what the social universe looks like." That the paradigm itself may be false is a question which occurs on very rare occasions.[59]

Let me suggest the content of the paradigm that, I suspect, pivotal groups among the media elite accept as obviously true. However, it should be stressed that journalists are not unique in accepting this paradigm. It is a paradigm of choice among pivotal elements in the knowledge stratum of the society:

1. While the ideas that people hold may influence the manner in which a society functions to a certain extent, the key variables are socioeconomic and, among these, class and group interests are key determinants of behavior.

2. Social disorganization in any society is to blamed on its underlying sociopolitical structure. Thus in seeking the causes of crime, political discontent, or general alienation one should examine flaws in the social underpinnings of the society.

3. Groups calling for change in a radical direction to correct what are defined as societal abuses are generally humanitarian, even if misguided. The way to deal with them and their constituency is to counsel patience and promote reform.

4. Groups calling for change in a conservative direction are generally behaving on the basis of narrow self-interest or psychological malfunctions.

5. As long as it cannot be demonstrated that they harm others, individuals should be allowed as much freedom to "actualize" themselves as fully as possible. No limits should be placed on the kind of experiences they want to undergo.

6. Societal problems are inherently soluble by a combination of good will and rational management. If a situation of injustice continues to persist, it must be because self-interested powerful individuals and groups are preventing the development and implementation of reasonable policies.

7. All institutions in the society should be subject to rational scrutiny. Any institution that cannot be defended rationally and which imposes restrictions on the individual should be reformed or eliminated.

8. People are pretty much alike in terms of their basic needs. Among these needs is full democratic participation. However, one can excuse (or explain away) the authoritarian controls of radical political orders, because they are dedicated to improving the lot of the poor.

Along with these assumptions go a generalized distrust of the American military, of people who are "overly patriotic," of the police, and of working-class and lower middle-class Americans who do not share cosmopolitan life-styles.

The list is not complete; it is something of a caricature, and certainly not all members of the media elite hold to all these views. Nor am I convinced that all of the propositions are false. I am persuaded, however, that they are accepted too uncritically by too many, with results that are distortive. And, all too often, people who do not see things exactly the way they do are considered to be blind, prejudiced, or inhumane.

As Walter Cronkite put it in an interview: "As far as the leftist thing is concerned, that I think is something that comes from the nature of a journalist's work. . . . I think that they're inclined to side with humanity rather than with authority and institutions."[60]

It is clear, incidentally, that the paradigm I have described is not totally antisystem. It is liberal-cosmopolitan, which involves taking a rather more benign view of those opposed to the system than to unsophisticated ardent supporters of it. It is also still peculiarly American in its emphasis on self-actualization and self-realization (the belief that if, somehow, everyone "does one's thing," an invisible hand will take care of community interests) and in its anti-Puritanism.

And the paradigm does define the content of common sense for those who share it. More than that, it helps define what is news, whose reports of the facts shall be accepted as likely to be true, and whose views can be ignored, or at least must be checked. I am not suggesting that the view of the world presented by the media is simply a matter of the paradigm chosen. Much reporting is largely factual and even paradigm-influenced reporting is usually related in some causal manner to the facts.

For example, for several months in 1969, respectable newspapers around the country, including the *New York Times* and the *Washington Post*, printed story after story asserting that 28 Black Panthers had been killed by the police. The charge had originally been made by Charles Gary, general counsel for the Panthers, and was widely accepted among intellectuals as indicative of a police campaign to get the Panthers. It was not until two years later that Edward J. Epstein, in a lengthy *New Yorker* article, traced the alleged killings and discovered that, aside from the shootings of Fred Hampton and Mark Clark in the Chicago raid, there was no evidence of concerted action against the Panthers.[61] Some of those listed by Gary had been killed by each other; others had been killed in the course of robberies (of other black people) during which the police could not possibly have known that they had shot Black Panthers.

To its credit the *Washington Post* had appointed an ombudsman to catch errors like this, and Richard Harward apologized, in an editorial, for the gaffe. One can find his piece in a volume of office memos from the *Washington Post,* edited by Laura Langley Babb and entitled *Of the Press, By the Press, and For the Press, and Others, Too.*[62] As one examines the various articles in the book, however, one notes that the gaffes caught are largely ones in which conservative figures or institutions have been treated badly. The fairly uniform directionality suggests that other such errors, sins of commission and omission, may have gone unnoticed.

Why did it happen? It is not necessary to argue that either Mr. Gary or reporters were being dishonest or conspiring. They simply were emotionally prepared to believe that the police and the FBI were engaged in a concerted effort to kill the Black Panthers, and, given the press of time (it took Epstein sixteen months full time to track down the facts) they followed their instinct. (Their suspicions were, of course, not completely without foundation.)

In 1964, during the presidential nominating convention, CBS televised a program from Germany strongly suggesting that Barry Goldwater was planning to link up with German rightwingers. The story was picked up by the *New York Times* along with additional information about interviews Goldwater had supposedly given to extreme right-wing publications, and his planned attendance at a school that was supposedly a gathering place for neo-Nazis. Goldwater protested that all this was untrue, and five days later a clarification by Daniel Schorr appeared in the *Times*. "In speaking the other day of a move by Senator Goldwater to link up with these forces, I did not mean to suggest conscious effort on his part, of which there is no proof here, but rather a process of gravitation which is visible here."[63]

Again, one need not believe that Mr. Schorr or the *Times* were consciously lying. In those days most liberals believed that Goldwater was an incipient fascist, and it was simply common sense to accept what seemed to be good evidence, even if it could not be fully verified. Schorr, incidentally, still does not understand why Goldwater was so angry that he refused to accept an apology. In his recent book, Schorr suggests that, given Goldwater's politics, the senator should have known better than to plan to visit Germany just after having been nominated for the presidency.[64]

Some myths perpetuated by the press and television are far more serious, and have never been even partially corrected. Let us take, as an example, the treatment by the *New York Times* of just one aspect of the Pentagon papers, which is still widely accepted as fact.

In establishing the sources of the "credibility" gap, the *Times* claimed that the papers proved conclusively that a general consensus to bomb North Vietnam was reached at a White House strategy meeting on September 7, 1964. In fact, Epstein again demonstrates, these papers provide no evidence that such consensus was reached.[65] Epstein suggests that the *Times's* inference was based *not* on a bias against the war but rather on the need for a hinge around which to frame the story. But another interpretation is equally plausible. I believe that the papers were read—again without conscious malice—as proving certain points because some *Times* staffers were already convinced that Johnson had decided to escalate the war and wanted to conceal this from the American people.

There is considerable reason to believe that even earlier the credibility gap derived almost as much from the preconceptions of at least
some media personnel as it did from Lyndon Johnson's style. As Professor Guenter Lewy has demonstrated in a recently published volume,
we now know that the State Department was correct in asserting that
North Vietnamese infiltration into South Vietnam began long before
the United States began to escalate its involvement and that, from the
beginning, the "revolutionary" effort in South Vietnam was dominated
by the North.[66] Yet newsmen on the *Times* and elsewhere accepted I.F.
Stone's contrary analysis of the situation simply because they regarded
him as a more reliable source. If Stone was correct, it followed that the
Administration was lying.

Reportage of the war itself was at least as filled with distortions as
were military communiqués on the other side, as Professor Lewy amply
documents. For example, there is evidence that reporters and television
cameramen may have concocted horror stories because they believed
that this was the way the war was being conducted and that the war was
wrong. Certainly many atrocity stories were accepted as fact without
adequate checking of sources.

Professor Lewy documents one case in which a CBS television
cameraman photographed a young GI cutting off the ears of a dead
Vietcong soldier. This was broadcast in the United States as an example of the way the war was being fought. However, there is evidence
indicating that the soldier may have been responding to a dare by the
cameraman, who even provided him with the necessary knife.[67] In
another widely publicized case, both the *Chicago Sun Times* and the
Washington Post published a photograph purportedly showing Americans pushing a Vietcong captive out of a helicopter in order to frighten
other prisoners into providing information. Again, there is reason to
believe that the incident was staged with a dead body. In this instance
reporters were not directly involved, but the willingness to accept dubious evidence by editors in Washington and Chicago without detailed
checking clearly indicates certain kinds of expectations.[68] Reporters
also photographed marines setting fire to huts in a village, without
informing their audience that these had been the source of enemy fire.[69]
There were legitimate horror stories in Vietnam, which Professor
Lewy also documents. The point is that these were very much exaggerated by the media.

Perhaps the most outstanding example of misleading reporting from

Vietnam was press and television coverage of the Tet offensive of 1968, which for a long time was treated as a Vietcong victory. Peter Braestrup has published a massive study of the reporting of that event in which he describes the behavior of reporters in detail.[70] While he denies that ideology played a role, he does speak of an adversary attitude on the part of reporters. One can legitimately ask from whence such an attitude was derived. It certainly did not characterize World War II or the Korean War. But these wars were regarded as legitimate. Thus, during World War II, errors resulting in civilian casualties and genuine horror stories were not repeated lest they injure the war effort.[71]

By and large, too, the media tended to take at face value the statements of individuals who claimed to have seen horrors that were being covered up by the "big brass." For example, Lt. Col. Anthony Herbert's accounts of his relations with the army and his "hounding out of the service" was accepted by most of the media for a long time, until investigations by CBS raised important questions about his credibility. However, the exposé on "60 Minutes" came too late to rectify the damage that had already been done.[72]

An even more important example of reporter's attitudes toward the war and their effect on reportage is revealed by reports in the *New York Times,* the *Washington Post,* and NBC on the effects of defoliants used in Vietnam. With some dissent, an international panel of experts found that, although damage had resulted, the extent was difficult to estimate; that it was probably less than had been alleged by critics of the war; that damage from defoliation was only a very small part of the destruction that resulted from shelling, etc.

The *New York Times* summary of this report contained a good many inaccuracies: its headline was misleading; the story attempted to impugn the objectivity of the report; and far greater attention was given to dissenters than was warranted by their number or arguments.[73] Indeed, the National News Council censored the *Times* for its reporting in this area. Bernard Rubin summarizes the findings of the council, which has tended to be very cautious in criticizing the press:

> The Council found that the article "relied heavily on information obtained from those who disagreed in part with the majority conclusions." Therefore, "the *Times* had a special obligation to its readers . . . to disclose any differences between its original article and the official version." Further criticism was leveled at the newspaper for

its failure to print the text of a letter of complaint by Dr. Anton Lang of the National Academy of Sciences and its failure to state, in a fuller article ". . . that the original article was incomplete."[74]

NBC's discussion of the report was similarly inaccurate. Although the *Washington Post's* coverage was better, it too stressed dissent,[75] a ritualized way of seeming to be objective (perhaps even to oneself) while leaning in one direction.[76]

The same pattern of reporting holds true for treatments of the CIA. Although some of the organization's behavior is subject to serious reproach, it often seems that the press is (as George Crile notes) more anxious to "get" the CIA than to provide a balanced assessment of it.[77] Crile provides an excellent example of the pattern of television coverage. ABC wanted to "review the record of the Central Intelligence Agency." For this purpose they decided to make use of one Frank Sturgis but:

> Sturgis presented the documentarians with a dilemma: off camera he alluded to involvement in all sorts of CIA ventures, but on camera he wouldn't say that he had participated in CIA assassination plots; worse he wouldn't even say that he was a CIA agent. ABC solved the problem by saying it for him. ABC reporter David Schoumacher: "Frank Sturgis first came to our attention when he was arrested in the Watergate break-in. He first came to the CIA's attention many years before, one of Fidel Castro's trusted security men, but an agent working for the CIA. Did you, Frank, ever participate in any plots to kill Castro?" Sturgis: "Yes, I participated in several plots in Havana. Yes."

As Crile points out, statements by the CIA to the effect that Sturgis had never worked for the agency were simply ignored.

The continuing impact of the Vietnam War is indicated by a story that appeared in the *New York Times* on January 2, 1977. The headline in the Sunday edition reads: "Anti-War Teachers of the 1960's Are Now at Peace with Honor."[78] The thrust of the story suggests that teachers who were opposed to the war were treated badly during the 1960s but are now, for the most part, back in harness. Four cases of academics "punished" for their opposition to the war are discussed, including those of Eugene Genovese and H. Bruce Franklin. Eugene Genovese is an important scholar, perhaps the most original and provocative Marxist scholar in the United States. He *may* have been forced out of Rutgers for a statement he made about his hope for a Vietcong victory. On the other hand, H. Bruce Franklin was dismissed from Stanford (where many other faculty opposed the war) not because of his antiwar stand, but because, after lengthy and complex investigation, it was decided that he had incited students to violence. Franklin was not *merely* antiwar. Genovese, of course, was strongly opposed to any campus disruption of the type supposedly engaged in by Franklin, and to couple these scholars in this context is like lumping Hubert Humphrey and Joseph McCarthy together as "anti-Communists." The author of the story does admit it was "alleged" that Franklin had incited to violence, but the article gives the impression that this charge was merely an excuse to fire him.

The story just cited is not exactly inaccurate. The *Times* does mention all the facts, and thus can claim objectivity or fairness. However, the story's headline and choice of words yield a tilt that is quite clear.

The same tilt permeates other apparently objective reporting. For example, a recent front page *Times* story was headlined "Gulf Aides Admit Cartel Increased Price of Uranium: Testimony Apparently Weakens Defense."[79] The *Times* followed the story some weeks later with an editorial criticism of the company's actions. Without going into too much detail, the key issue concerned the possible illegality of Gulf entering into a cartel through arrangements with other uranium producing countries. Under American law, their action was not illegal unless such arrangements affected prices in the United States. The tenor of the article on page 1 was to the same effect as the headline. The *Times* quoted Gulf's supposedly damning testimony only toward the end of the article, on an inside page: " 'They [American companies] would probably pay a higher price,' Mr. Zagnoli [the Gulf official testifying] replied, adding that, 'I would say that the impact was insignificant.' " Whatever the merits of the case, this was hardly the damaging admission that both the headline and thrust of the story made it appear to be.

The influence of paradigms in reporting can also be seen quite clearly in media coverage of the American Indian movement. The *Times* invariably pointed out that those on the reservation who opposed the more radical groups were middle class (successful), and hence conservative. The clear implication of many of the stories was that those who had "made it" abstained from protest out of narrow self-interest.

Consider, however, how the same material might have been dealt with thirty years ago. To most newsmen at that time, the fact that the militants often were persons with criminal backgrounds who had not held steady jobs, would probably have been interpreted to mean that the "troublemakers" were "riff-raff," who were using ideology as a cover for their personal failings and an opportunity to engage in aggressive behavior behind the mask of a moral cause.[80]

The same orientation permeates treatment of crime or other forms of violence in the black ghetto. When Fred Freed decided to develop a special on the ghetto, he needed an angle. Seeing an alley full of garbage, the proper approach suddenly hit him:

> The people living in this alley were the people who rioted, who looted, and who threw some of the fire bombs. The people who lived in this alley, in this slum, were what Gunnar Myrdal called "an underclass." They were the lost, the dispossessed people outside our society. And what did this alley say about our society? Didn't we have our priorities mixed up, making too many automobiles, too many washing machines, and letting people rot all around them?[81]

Freed's flash of inspiration obviously did not come out of nowhere. Rather, it reflected a certain view of the social process. It seems obvious that the angle would have been quite different thirty years ago. And even today, it is at least possible to argue that the issues are not *merely* the use of more resources and/or the selfishness of the white middle class, but are rather more complicated.

One would never recognize that such is the case, however, from the predominant pattern of reporting both on television and in the *New York Times* concerning the widespread looting that accompanied the 1977 New York City blackout.

The looting was perceived by reporters as a cry of despair at the refusal of middle-class white society to provide funds to solve urban problems, including housing and employment.[82] Nowhere was it indicated that between 1950 and 1970 alone, federal, state, and local governments had spent more than $200 billion on housing;[83] that between 1950 and 1975, national, state, and city expenditures for education, health, welfare, etc., had risen from $23.5 billion annually to $286.5 billion annually;[84] that welfare expenditures alone had risen from $1.3 billion in 1950 to $21.6 billion in 1976.[85]

The issues are obviously quite complex, and reporters were certainly not more biased in their perceptions than were those who saw the looters as merely "animals." Nevertheless reporters for the national media were quite clearly operating within the framework of a paradigm that led them to at least partially ignore some of the facts.[86] Indeed, one black businessman argued on the op. ed. page, the very manner in which the *Times* (and other newspapers) have described looting over the years (including the implicit blame placed on businessmen) may have served to legitimize it in the eyes of a segment of the black community, thus exacerbating the difficulties of the ghetto.[87] Certainly neither day-to-day nor interpretative reporting in the *Times* or in other national media searched for facts that would portray ghetto crime other than as a response to racism and poverty. Nonetheless, more complex explanations do exist. Some serious scholars have suggested that current racism is sometimes no more important to the black ghetto's problems than a pattern of personal and social disorganization that builds on itself, a pattern not easily dealt with merely by continuing policies of the kind that the *Times* has supported in recent years.

For example, it is difficult to find any recognition in the *Times* of the fact that some of New York's economic problems may stem from legitimate fears of violence that are contributing to the flight of businessmen from the area; that housing stock for lower class residents is superior in quality, amenities, and space to that of working class populations in France and England, not to say the Soviet Union, and that some of the problems of teen-age black youth have to do with problems of personal disorganization rather than merely lack of jobs.[88]

None of the examples offered so far is intended to demonstrate systematic bias. They are, after all, merely examples. We lack a sufficient number of systematic studies of media treatment of events. We do, however, have a few. I think that Edith Efron has demonstrated beyond a reasonable doubt that television coverage of the news in the period just before the 1968 election was characterized by a liberal tilt.[89] I am also persuaded that Ernest Lefever is essentially correct in arguing that CBS's coverage of national defense tended to support dovish positions on defense spending.[90] And the American Institute of Political Communication's study of the 1972 primaries clearly demonstrates a tilt toward McGovern by the television networks.[91]

We do need more systematic studies. Unfortunately, although Vanderbilt University has established a television news archive (after a long fight with the networks), we still lack the material to analyze the paradigms that infuse television specials and general programming.

Our further study is of particular interest, because it does not deal with actual events, and because its results were quite the opposite of the author's hypotheses, but he could not quite bring himself to recognize this. In an effort to demonstrate that authoritarian editors would *overemphasize* stories that portrayed antiwar demonstrators unfavorably from the point of view of middle-class audiences, i.e., stories involving the use of violence or drugs or general descriptions of "scruffiness," T.J. Madden administered an "authoritarianism scale" to a selection of editors on the *Philadelphia Inquirer*.[92] As with most such scales, the one used was actually a measure of views on a conservative-liberal continuum.[93] Before being given the scale, the editors were asked to rank a series of stories having to do with student demonstrations in terms of the play they would be given in the paper.

To Madden's surprise, the more authoritarian editors (read "conservative") were not influenced by the favorable or unfavorable treatment of the demonstrators in assigning importance to the story. On the other hand, less authoritarian editors (read more liberal) consistently played up protest stories, especially those that, from Madden's view, portrayed demonstrators unfavorably.

Madden concludes that less authoritarian editors must not have realized that they were encouraging a backlash against demonstrators. He admits, only as a possibility, that the tendency of more liberal demonstrators to focus on the protestors' deviance might have reflected empathy with such deviance. I would suggest that this possibility is the more likely explanation.

Some network executives are not unaware of the overall slant of TV news, although one may question the sophistication of their understanding. Av Westin, when brought to ABC in 1970, decided to shift the station's perspective in an effort to enhance its ratings. In a television interview he quite candidly admitted what he was doing. He would replace the "Eastern Liberal Way" with a middle American perspective. For example, on the question of abortion:

> On the other networks, there is a clichéd formula for doing abortion stories. This might be called the Eastern Liberal syndrome. You begin by showing a film of unwanted children in a hospital; a voice-over narration gives essentially the liberal position: "These un-

wanted children exist because we don't have liberalized abortion laws." An advocate of abortion reform is then put on to reinforce this position. Finally a balancing interview with an old fogey is put on, who says "Abortion is wrong," and a correspondent sums it up by saying, "A controversy still exists."

To reverse perspectives I order the correspondent to start with pictures of destroyed fetuses, with a voice-over narration saying that "abortion has resulted in these deaths."[94]

And, of course, the rest follows, including the balancing statement.

Westin is unusual in this regard. Most network people and reporters seem unaware of the influence of their paradigms, as do most students of the media.

This lack of self-awareness applies to even as sophisticated a participant observer as Fred Friendly. In an article written for the *New York Times,* Friendly suggested that the fairness doctrine be revised so as not to discourage the "probing hard-hitting journalism that. . . the public interest demands."[95] However, all the television specials he cites as serving this public interest take a somewhat "anti-system" perspective.

In his book *The Good Guys, The Bad Guys, and the First Amendment,* Friendly admits that an NBC special on pensions was inaccurate and biased in important dimensions (to the extent *at least* that it cited as fact propositions that are debatable). Given the evidence he offers, his own defense of the program is rather weak. "Its makers were muckrakers with their eyes and hearts open, not blind disciples of justice." More revealing is the fact that NBC officials were not even aware that they had produced a controversial show, and that many of the facts might be in dispute.[96]

Once again some caveats are needed. First, as noted earlier, the *New York Times* as well as the other media are often collections of feudalities with conflicting perspectives. Further, countervailing forces exist. Television, for example, does cater to mass audiences and needs to sell to advertisers, as do newspapers. Thus a considerable amount of television programming (including advertising itself) is very supportive of more traditional perspectives, though less so than it once was.[97] However, the vaunted power of advertisers sharply diminished in the 1960s and 1970s.[98] Again, one can cite counter-examples, especially in the provinces, and there are still limits beyond which the commercial media will not go. Increasingly, however, advertisers feel that they cannot and should not interfere with news content. Indeed, they will even advertise in counter-culture journals quite hostile to business, in order to reach the youth and metro-American market. The same pattern largely prevails on television. In the early days, advertising agencies and sponsors sometimes directly controlled much of the content and produced many of the programs. However, the networks now control programming and, within broad parameters; "advertisers must use television on whatever terms they can get it, for television is the most potent vehicle ever devised. . . . As one agency man said once, 'Bad television is better than no television.' "[99]

Thus, Ralph Nader could for many years achieve full media coverage despite business hostility and less than full factual support for some of his charges. As Charles McCarry notes: "From the instant of his birth as a public figure Ralph Nader enjoyed a great measure of tolerance from the press. No Kennedy was ever held in higher regard or quoted more freely. Nader was perceived by reporters to be what, in fact, he was, the enemy of their enemies."[100]

In fact, as we now know, newspapers from the very first headlined his charges without checking the facts. For example, while General Motors executives played some role in Nader's rise by the immoral and illegal manner in which they dealt with his allegations, the Corvair was not the horror it was widely assumed to be. The interesting fact is that more balanced assessments by responsible sources like Consumers Union were available at the time.

In 1970, Senator Ribicoff, an early Nader supporter, assigned the staff of the Senate Subcommittee on Executive Reorganization to investigate charges by Nader that GM executives had lied when they told the committee they felt the Corvair to be safe. After two and one half years the investigators issued a report in which they concluded that the committee had *not* been misled by GM. While the staff members did not pass judgment on the safety of the car, claiming lack of technical expertise, they pointed out that GM officials widely used the car themselves. However, the 119 pages of the report reproduced in the *Congressional Record* make it clear that the Corvair was considered by most experts to be no less safe than other cars on the road at the time. (The assessment by Consumers Union is included in the report.)

Nader, and the press, had accepted the testimony of the relatively few technically competent persons who thought otherwise and had discounted or ignored the majority view. By 1973 the Corvair was no longer news. Incidentally, after the report was published Nader charged Ribicoff with having sold out to the automobile companies.[101]

Nader, and the groups created by him, have undoubtedly made a number of important contributions to the public welfare. It is clear, however, that many of the reports issued under his name have lacked a solid evidential base. It is also fairly clear that Nader often dictated the conclusions of reports without regard to the facts.[102] Nevertheless newspapers and television gave his charges conspicuous attention. And replies by members of the business community were regarded as suspect.

One of the major issues in Nader's work has always been the problem of acceptable risk. Many things we do involve some danger, from consuming sugar or salt to building bridges. The key problem is to balance risks against other costs, including other risks.[103] The media have usually accepted Nader's absolute standards without any attempt to deal with the somewhat more subtle issues involved. In the 1950s they probably would have ignored Nader or, at least, been careful to present the other side, for the conventional wisdom perceived the American business community as relatively responsible and trustworthy. By the late 1960s this had all changed. The burden of proof was now on the business community and other social institutions. Attacks on these institutions were accepted at face value, and attempts by corporations, the military, or the Atomic Energy Commission to respond to critics tended to be discounted by the elite media as merely reflections of self-interest.

I shall turn to this issue shortly with further examples and documentation. However, it might be well to do so in a rather different context. The paradigms subscribed to by pivotal groups in the elite media were not simply created by them. To understand why these paradigms have become so much part of the conventional wisdom among these and other elite groups we need a more complex analysis.

THE MEDIA ELITE AND PUBLIC OPINION

Let us assume for the moment that the three propositions for which I have argued are correct, namely that: a national media elite has developed in the United States; pivotal individuals in this elite are "liberal-cosmopolitans"; and the paradigms that (unconsciously) guide members of this elite influence the manner in which they view reality and present it to the larger community.

What does all of this prove? If the views of reality held by all of us (including social scientists) are influenced by paradigms, does not the public receive messages with a kind of selective perception? That is, do not audiences primarily listen to or read what is supportive of their views? Barring this, are not even media messages that challenge these views perceived selectively? Certainly the power Lippmann attributed to the media has been demonstrated as false by many studies, and by the electorate's responses to media coverage of individual television programs or presidential campaigns.[104]

Such undoubtedly was the case before the era of television, when traditional institutions such as political parties, churches, and the family, as well as face-to-face communication, played a much larger role in transmitting images about reality, and when the national media's impact was not so powerful. The impact of television is, however, of a unique kind. It personalizes and dramatizes events in a manner that lends inherent plausibility to its message.[105] Thus, as Table 1 indicates, during the whole period when television was coming under increasing criticism (by both radicals and conservatives) the faith in its probity of those who watched it was increasing.

The impact of the media might also be less significant if it were

TABLE 1

PUBLIC ATTITUDES TOWARD THE MEDIA (PERCENTAGES)

"Now, I would like to get your opinions about how radio, newspapers, television, and magazines compare. Generally speaking, which of these would you say. . ."	*Television* 1960–1970		*Magazines* 1960–1970		*Newspapers* 1960–1970		*Radio* 1960–1970		*None/NA* 1960–1970	
Gives the most complete news coverage?	19		4	3	4	59	39	18	14	1	2
Presents things most intelligently?	27	38	27	18	33	28	8	9	5	8
Is the most educational?	32	46	31	20	31	26	3	4	3	5
Brings you the latest news most quickly?	36	54	0	0	5	6	57	39	2	1
Does the most for the public?	34	48	3	2	44	28	11	13	8	10
Presents the fairest, most unbiased news?	29	33	9	9	31	23	22	19	9	16
Gives you the clearest understanding of the candidates and issues in national elections?	42	59	10	8	36	21	5	3	7	9

SOURCE: Adapted from Robert T. Bower, *Television and the Public* (New York: Holt, Rinehart and Winston, 1973), p. 100. The percentages are based on a national probability sample.

more pluralistic. However, when most national outlets share more or less the same paradigm it is quite another matter. Selective perception does, of course, take place, but there is some evidence that the general outlines of the paradigm begin to take on the quality of reality for viewers. Of course, the fact (for middle-class, college-educated audiences at least) that this same paradigm is shared by those who taught them in college merely increases the influence of what they read in newspapers and see on television.

Most studies of a single program or an election campaign really miss the point. It is the changes in perspective that take place over a period of ten or fifteen years that are potentially most significant. And there is evidence that these changes have been important. Studies of Soviet defectors in the 1940s and 1950s, for example, revealed that, despite their hostility to the regime and their suspicion of all its messages, they had absorbed many of them.[106] It is true that no comparable monopoly exists or ever has existed in the United States. Yet, for example, it is clear that on the Vietnam War and the race issue, the media played a key role in producing changes in the attitudes of the middle-class and eventually the working class public.[107] Indeed, increasing numbers of social scientists are now persuaded that the media in this regard have at least an agenda-setting function. They determine the questions that will be discussed, even if not the answers.[108] I would suggest they do more than that.

The national media are part of an elite and sub-elite stratum of the population that includes academics, activist bureaucrats, foundation presidents, activist lawyers, and others. Members of the stratum read the same newspapers and magazines, review each other's books, and share a common perception of the world, which has had a tremendous influence on public policy.[109]

Nathan Glazer describes the process very well in dealing with certain aspects of judicial activism:

> The judges follow the weight of judicial analysis and opinion. They are affected by it because, in these complex cases, they must be guided by what is set before them in lengthy briefs and analyses of complex facts. These analyses are then digested by other lawyers. . . . But this entire process is guided by the weight of educated opinion, an educated opinion which is convinced that morality and progress lie on the side of the broadest possible measures of intervention to equalize the employment of members of minority groups

in every sphere, and to evenly distribute students and teachers and administrators through school districts. . . . How is this educated opinion made?

. . . facts are assumed—they are the facts that are presented in textbooks, presented by professors and journalists in the mass media.[110]

Thus national media personnel are remarkably immune from the kind of criticism that might make them rethink some of their assumptions. They are part of a self-contained world that defines out of existence those perspectives that are considered conservative and hence not humane. The attitude permeates more than news stories. It determines which books shall be brought to the attention of the public in reviews and who shall review them. For example, the *New York Times,* not to mention the *New York Review of Books,* regularly assigns books on the women's issue to at least moderate feminists; on law to legal reformers; on radical approaches to psychology to those sympathetic with the approach; and on race to those whose position is liberal-cosmopolitan. Studies that run counter to the conventional wisdom are usually sharply criticized, or, more importantly, ignored.[111]

I've already mentioned several volumes that have not been reviewed by the *Times.* There are many others that have been completely ignored. For example, Thomas Sowell, an economist who happens to be black, has written several volumes on the race issue which run counter to the conventional wisdom of the *New York Times.* They have never been reviewed.[112] Most studies of multinational corporations reviewed by the *New York Times* have suggested that these companies represent an almost unmitigated evil, and that the oil companies in particular have been reaping huge and unwarranted profits over the past twenty years as the result of their monopolistic positions. One would never know from reading the *Times* that many very reputable scholars dispute all of these points of conventional wisdom. Their books are not reviewed, nor are they asked to review books for the *Times.*[113]

Many of the volumes taking an alternative view are fairly technical. However not all of them are. In any event, as regards the oil industry, there is a general consensus among economists to the effect that while large multinational oil companies may have constituted a monopoly in the 1950s and earlier this is no longer the case. They also agree that the profits of the industry were rather depressed during the 1960s, given the risks involved in oil exploration. Even the Ford Foundation studies (which were not overly sympathetic to the industry) did not maintain that the industry was characterized by excessive concentration, although concern was expressed as to the future.[114]

Until the late 1970s when the tide began to turn somewhat, the pattern of reporting and book reviewing (or nonreviewing) characteristic of the *Times* was shared by the other media. For example, the 1974 "primer" by ABC on the oil crisis repeated all the conventional wisdom on this question, prompting the National News Council to suggest that ABC might have misled the public in suggesting that the documentary was "striving conscientiously for balance and fairness."[115]

To take another area, the *Times* has never reviewed any of the fairly large number of books written by Americans who were captives of the Vietcong. Some of these are fairly good and describe in some detail the torture inflicted on American prisoners by the North Vietnamese, despite Ramsey Clark's disclaimers.[116]

Again, one could offer numerous additional examples, but I will present just one more. For the past ten years Americans have been deluged with articles and books suggesting that they are being injured by the chemicals added to their food, chemicals that are cancer inducing, among other things. Indeed the FDA has probably been pushed into taking a rather more conservative stance in approving additives than it might have if this conventional wisdom had not come to dominate the media. Ralph Nader has been quite active in this area, and *The Chemical Feast,* first published in 1970, by one of his staff, was received well by *New York Times* reviewers, despite some caveats.[117] Actually, the author builds a case largely on innuendo. He tells us that cancer rates are on the rise. At the same time the use of food additives has risen. Thus, food additives are responsible. In fact no evidence exists that cancer rate increases are the result of food additives. The largest increases that have occurred (taking into account changes in the age of populations and better diagnosis) are in lung cancer and most probably are the result of smoking. The rate of some cancers that might most plausibly be related to additives (stomach and liver cancer) have, in fact, either remained the same or have fallen.

Describing in some detail the chemicals that have been added to our food, the author fails to note that: all foods are composed of chemicals; the fact that rats develop tumors as the result of massive injections of a substance does not prove that the substance is carcinogenic to human beings in moderate doses; massive doses of many foods, including salt, can produce tumors in white rats, even though we know that in moderate amounts they are not particularly harmful to human beings.[118]

Nor is it mentioned in *The Chemical Feast* that many additives are useful preservatives, and that the use of additives has undoubtedly resulted in a decline of botulism in Western countries. There are now many books on the subject by reputable scholars, which make these and other points. None of these has been reviewed in the *New York Times*. It is true that some of them are highly technical, but at least two are popularly written.[119]

Television has been equally at fault in all these areas. An NBC special, "The American Way of Cancer," was quite poor on the issue of additives, and a CBS program on this "crisis" repeated all of the conventional clichés in this area.[120] Little wonder that the mass public, in poll after poll, increasingly assumes that American business routinely ignores consumer needs in order to increase its profits.

These cases are not isolated examples, for the perspective that dominates them tends to be characteristic of the national media as a whole. The predominance of this perspective derives in part from the fact that pivotal segments of the academic community and, increasingly, the government bureaucracy, share the media elite paradigms. As indicated earlier, the academic community is itself liberal-cosmopolitan, especially that portion of it that writes on current issues. And of course, those editing journalism reviews are, on the whole, rather more liberal than the media managers themselves, and serve as their liberal conscience. Finally, there seems little question but that, even within the group writing on public policy issues, the more liberal-cosmopolitan types write more frequently and are probably more likely to write for the general literate public.[121] In short, they more closely resemble media personnel themselves and partake of the same social milieu.

The pattern is self-reinforcing. As in academia itself, books are considered important and reviewers are chosen on the basis of shared perceptions of reality.* It is thus that a conventional wisdom has

---

*I suggest that the same criteria operate in academic hiring procedures, and that many of the most prestigious foundations operate in the same manner. These are staffed by many of the same people even though often financed by the business community. There are, of course, conservative foundations supported by conservative businessmen. On the whole, however, such foundations tend to be distrustful of social science, and regard the role of ideas developed by academics as relatively unimportant. Thus, by and large, most foundations tend to support social science research by liberal cosmopolitans.

emerged, which has been at least partially accepted by elites who stand outside this milieu but who obtain their perceptions of the world from it. And it is not implausible to suggest that this conventional wisdom has had an important impact upon key areas of public policy.

And what of the effect of the media on the non-elites; the great mass of ordinary lower middle-class and working class citizens? Elizabeth Noelle-Neumann argues that the media affect public perception of the extent to which ideas are held in a society.[122] Following the course of several political issues in Germany, she concluded that, given nearly universal support for a position by the media, it is possible to *create* a majority opinion for that position. Those in the oppositional majority begin to feel that they are isolated, and perhaps wrong, for near media unanimity begins to persuade them that they are either a minority or soon to become one. Thus the number of "don't knows" among this segment of the population begins to grow; they become less and less willing to argue about the issues publicly and, finally, they change their minds, especially on issues removed from their immediate personal experience.

More broadly, in the long run images projected by the media do affect perceptions of the causes of personal and social events, and conceptions of appropriate or "moral" responses to them. They also affect the public's perception of moral or at least permissible personal behavior. The power of the media is often underestimated because the long-term effect is to establish a new conventional wisdom, which passes for social truth.

Even those who resist the new conventional wisdom for a variety of reasons are adversely affected. As Michael Robinson points out, those who watch television, especially, have become more confused and more alienated from the American political system in recent years.

These people, tied to neighborhood and jobs, are in Gabriel Almond's terminology, parochials.[123] It is difficult to mobilize them except for issues directly related to their work, for they are essentially nonpolitical. And as much as they may distrust those on top (especially intellectuals), they eventually absorb some of the culture, which trickles down from the knowledge strata even when it seems, at least initially, to run counter to their personal experience. The result is a turning inward to personal concerns in a world that they find increasingly confusing.[124]

Both Robinson and Epstein suggest that the nature of television itself is responsible. The feeling on the part of those in charge of television that they must deal with news as high drama and create pseudo events (and, especially, both personalize the news and emphasize conflict) plays a key role. Even were that not so, television would be a potent force for activating large groups of people and exacerbating discontents. With the best will in the world, the mass media (and especially television) now do have the capacity to spread any contagion further and more rapidly than ever before.

Epstein and Robinson are certainly correct in part, but only in part, for they ignore the directionality of the conflict emphasized and the manner in which issues are personalized. NBC, for example, in a typical news special on radioactive waste, personalized the dangers to individuals without placing the matter in any broader context.[125] The overwhelming impression of the script was to accept the views of such dangers being pressed by some groups, while largely ignoring alternative views by responsible and competent people.[126] On the other hand, in the 1960s, none of the networks personalized crime in urban areas to the extent of following through on the effects on victims and their families. Producers argued that such coverage would only inflame public passions.[127]

Overall, then, the messages received by ordinary people during the past fifteen years have tended to give the impression that the country's institutions are corrupt and that modern technology is leading us into a *cul-de-sac.* During the 1960s the media also contributed in significant ways to the emergence of the counter-culture. To be sure the emergence of that culture and its ability to obtain publicity had other sources, but television and the print media did provide important support.

Beyond this, white Americans have seen themselves constantly described as racists because they supposedly refuse to appropriate adequate funds for black schools, or do not wish to bus their children in order to bring about integration. Little attention is paid in the academic community or in the media to the fact that predominantly black schools probably now receive more money per student than the schools in *white working class* areas or that many white and black parents are probably more concerned with the prevalence of violence in ghetto schools (or public housing) than with the color of the students or tenants.[128]

The issue of black violence in the schools and its relation to integration is one that the media and the academic community have dealt with very gingerly and then primarily to deny that it is a problem. However, we do know that rates of violent crime among black ghetto youth are very high, and we do know that parents of both black and white youth (and young people themselves) are fearful about will happen to them in ghetto schools.[129]

This is not to deny that racism continues to permeate American life and that black Americans have historically been (and still are) victims of considerable oppression. It is to suggest that the tendency to turn such matters into a morality play may obscure the nature of the problems and hamper rather than further humane solutions.

Liberal-cosmopolitan media personnel often fail to recognize their inconsistencies in these areas, as witness the following exchange between Tom Wicker and an interviewer from *People* magazine:

> He (Wicker) has been tagged a limousine liberal by critics who point out that although he advocates bussing editorially, he sends his own children to private schools. "It gives me a lot of intellectual discomfort," he admits. "But I am not going to disadvantage my children to win more support for my views."[130]

Let me conclude this section of the essay with two final pieces of conventional wisdom that distort the problems we face as a nation. I use them because they illustrate the interrelationship between the media and the academic community.

The first has to do with the issue of crime and punishment. It has been widely assumed in academic circles and the media that homicides by blacks committed against whites are punished more severely than are homicides with black victims. This was undoubtedly true in the past, and yet evidence exists that it may no longer be the case, especially as regards the death penalty. The conventional wisdom obtains plausibility because intraracial homicides are much more likely to occur among people who know each other, and to be the result of sudden outbursts of passion than are interracial homicides. The latter (usually black on white homicides) are likely (in a largely segregated society) to be directed against strangers during the course of a robbery, an offense that, under the law (and for understandable reasons), is punished more harshly.[131]

The statistics cited in most articles to demonstrate bias in sentencing have often been inadequate, because the investigators failed to hold constant both the nature of the crime and the previous record of the accused, or relied upon the dubious use of statistics. In an article published in *The Law and Society Review* in 1975, Professor John Hagen reviewed all the major studies in this area and recalculated the data. He demonstrates that, holding the nature of the crime and previous record constant, the great bulk of these studies show *no* statistically significant differences in sentencing patterns. In those few cases where they do, race explains no more than 5 percent of the variance.[132] Hagen's article was published in a very respectable journal, but has been almost totally ignored. In the meantime, *Times* articles and editorials have continued to cite academic studies that make the same errors Hagen pointed out, and the conventional wisdom continues to predominate.

My final example involves the question of hunger and malnutrition. It is now fairly widely accepted among metro-Americans that millions of Americans suffer from malnutrition if not starvation as the result of poverty and government indifference. Some of the credit must go to CBS. Its famous documentary *Hunger in America,* produced in 1968, is regarded as a prime example of courageous reporting.[133]

CBS decided to do the program, it seems, on a suggestion from Senator Edward Kennedy, and relied very heavily for information on a group called the Citizens Crusade Against Poverty. To illustrate the effects of malnutrition, CBS began the program with a picture of a newly born child who had supposedly died of malnutrition. It was subsequently determined that the child had been born prematurely as the result of an automobile accident, and that its death in fact had nothing to do with the issues at hand.

If one reads through the many pages of the congressional investigation of the program, it becomes clear that the opening sequence was not untypical of CBS's treatment of the subject. Indeed the evidence is fairly clear from those hearings and other studies that malnutrition is not nearly as widespread as implied and that, for the most part, it results less from lack of income than from personal disorganization and a lack of knowledge of proper dietary habits.[134] Nor was CBS alone in this type of distortion. A *New York Times* story on October 14, 1970, began: "The first results of a Federal study of malnutrition in New York City show that nearly half of a sample of low income children under 7 years old suffer from low levels of vitamin A." Only later in the story did one discover, among other things, that there was only a 2 percent difference in vitamin A deficiency between lower- and upper-income children.

The point is not that all is well, or that nothing should be done to help those who do so suffer. However, aside from the impact on the public of the distortions involved, such reporting is not necessarily conducive to the formulation of intelligent policy. The response to malnutrition, for example, was an expansion of the Food Stamp Program, but studies indicate that most people receiving food stamps increase their purchase of food by no more than 20 cents for every dollar received. Nor is there any indication that the increased expenditure actually results in dietary improvement.[135]

Again, there is little need to look for conspiracies. The CBS staff undoubtedly felt that, in remodeling examples that did not quite fit its preconceived notions, it was fulfilling the spirit if not the letter of the truth. The same is undoubtedly true of those in the academic community who provided it with data.

THE MEDIA ELITE AND SOCIAL COHESION

The pattern I have been describing has held for at least the past fifteen years, and its effects have been very serious. Middle-class youth are now by and large convinced that America is a seriously flawed society, and their reaction has been a shift to the left or, most recently, a withdrawal from political activity into personal concerns. The same has been true of the working class population. The demoralization Robinson discovered is, I would suggest, partly a function of a loss of faith in American political and social institutions.[136]

For working-class and lower middle-class ethnics the situation is compounded by the gap between their personal experience and the dominant messages on television. They know that discrimination is wrong, for example, and they do not want to be racists. On the other hand, their own experience convinces them that the violence in schools that contain a substantial portion of lower class ghetto children is real.

Unlike the citizenry of most countries Americans have, in the past, been held together not by a common sense of ethnic identity, but rather by a common ideology, by a sense that their institutions and their way of life represented something new and better. Thus, a loss of faith in the country's institutions is far more traumatic for Americans than it would be (or has been) for Frenchmen or Englishmen who have a very long "tribal" historical experience on which to fall back.[137]

To summarize: the national media have exacerbated the feelings of discontent of many groups; they have made various strata more aware of the issues that divide them; they have weakened traditional sources of political and social authority including political parties; they have made it possible to mobilize relatively small groups in the population that can secure their ends in the face of a larger but more parochial majority. In short they have given "true believers" a tremendous advantage in the political process; and they oversimplify and personalize complex problems, thus reducing our ability to understand and cope with them.

All of this is not particularly conducive to stable democratic politics. When, to all of the above, is added a commitment to the kind of paradigm I have outlined, the results could be a kind of stasis and decay.

I am not attempting to set forth a monocausal analysis. The emergence of liberal-capitalism in Europe was the product of a unique configuration of political and cultural forces, including Protestantism. As Daniel Bell has pointed out in his recent work, the dialectics of its own development have contributed to the erosion of both its religious and motivational base.[138] The crisis has been exacerbated both by international crisis and the new problems of an advanced industrial society.[139]

It may be, then, that the decay, to be followed, it is hoped, by the institutionalization of new political and cultural patterns, was inevitable in the long run. Whether or not this is so, the knowledge stratum has quite clearly contributed significantly to its pace.

As cosmopolitan intellectuals, most of us have been somewhat pleased by the decline of the "Yahoos" in America and the elimination of some of the simple-minded inanities that characterized much of American life until well into midcentury. However, it is at least possible that the weakening of simple patriotism and the other general myths that have upheld the society in the past may lead to something else. Freud certainly believed that any form of authority was problematic and Rousseau felt, despite his general image as a radical, that a democracy could survive only if intellectuals remained silent, and the simple virtues were maintained.

If they were right, then the growth of the knowledge strata and of a media elite may yield something other than what we anticipated. Rather than a sophisticated social democracy of cosmopolitan men and women who hold to a rational and humane perspective and are capable of acting upon it, the contradictions in our society and the character of its intellectual class may yield quite the opposite.

Most human beings for most of history have lived under one form of tyranny or another, and the new bureaucratic empires of China and the

Soviet Union, with their rigid control of intellectuals, may turn out to have more staying power precisely because of their authoritarian qualities.

The above analysis will probably sound too pessimistic to most. America has passed through periods of crisis before only to achieve a new equilibrium. While pivotal members of the media elite probably fit the model I have outlined, a good many probably do not. Their reactions to events are largely determined (like those of most of us) by the ethos of a given time and place.

There are some signs that this ethos is changing, that with the end of the Vietnam War and the recognition that some of our social problems are not merely melodrama, a more sober attitude is developing. It is to be hoped that this attitude will lead to a reassessment of some of the over-simplifications that have guided the actions of the knowledge stratum during the past fifteen years—over-simplifications which were, in part, a reaction to an earlier and even more naive conventional wisdom. If this does occur we may witness the emergence of a new balance of forces and, perhaps, a perspective that will enable us to deal more intelligently with the myriad problems with which America is likely to be faced in the third century of her history.

Alex Inkeles

Continuity and Change in the American National Character

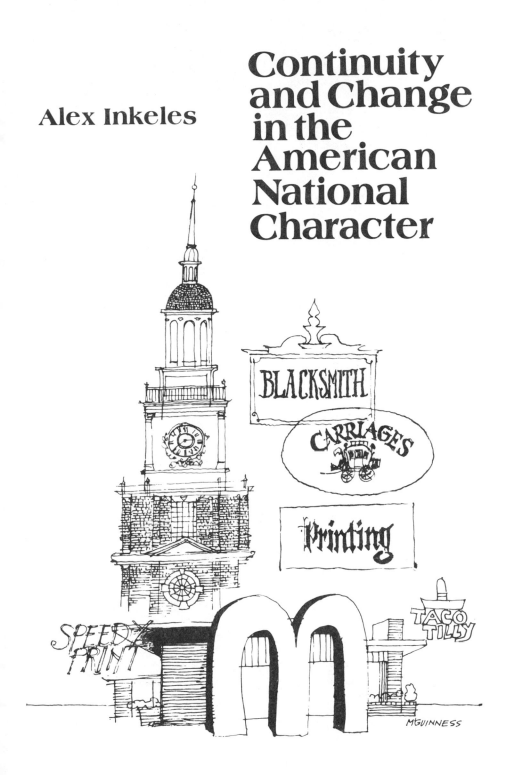

MGUINNESS

16 On committing myself to a study of continuity and change in the American national character, I began to revisit the classics that have long dominated our thinking about the early Americans. Inevitably I turned again to Harriet Martineau's sensitive and perceptive *Society in America*. Feeling a bit insecure about relying on shortened and adapted versions available on my own bookshelf, I sought an unabridged text. To my delight, the Stanford University Library yielded up the first edition, published in London in 1837. But on opening this edition I received a rude shock. On the very first page, set off in special type, I encountered a paralyzing statement, which I had previously either not seen or not noticed. It read as follows:

> To seize a character, even that of one man, in its life and secret mechanism, requires a philosopher; to delineate it with truth and impressiveness is work for a poet. How then shall one or two sleek clerical tutors, with here and there a tedium-stricken esquire, or speculative half-pay captain, give us views on such a subject? How shall a man, to whom all characters of individual men are like sealed books, of which he sees only the title and the covers, decipher from his four-wheeled vehicle, and depict to us, the character of a nation? He courageously depicts his own optical delusions . . . and so, with a few flowing strokes, completes a picture, which, though it may not resemble any possible object, his countrymen are to take for a national portrait. Nor is the fraud so readily detected: for the character of a people has such a complexity of aspect, that even the honest observer knows not always, not perhaps after long inspection, what to determine regarding it. From his, only accidental, point of view, the figure stands before him like the tracings on veined marble—a mass of mere random lines, and tints, and entangled strokes, out of which a lively fancy may shape almost *any* image . . . . Thus each repeats his precursor; the hundred-times-repeated comes in the end to be believed; the foreign nation is now once for all understood, decided on, and registered accordingly; and dunce the thousandth writes of it like dunce the first.[1]

The words were not Martineau's, but rather were quoted by her from a piece in the *Edinburgh Review*. Nevertheless, they were, as Martineau noted, calculated to strike fear into the heart of the likes of me. As she said, who will consciously choose to be "dunce the thousandth?"

Like Martineau, however, I managed to allay my anxiety. A skeptic might convincingly argue that 50 years of effort had yielded slight progress in building theory, and only modest advances in the precision and refinement of our concepts, but he could not shake my conviction that we now have a much broader and firmer empirical basis for judging the American national character. So I pressed on.

The task proved more tractable and the expedition more rewarding than I had anticipated. For example, I had been concerned that the psychological terms in which the classical description of the American character had been couched would prove so archaic, so idiosyncratic, or so vague and imprecise as to render impossible any systematic comparison of the great commentaries of the past with the evidence gathered by contemporary social psychologists. This fear proved unfounded. With some modest adjustments the statements of the former could quite readily be translated into the language of the latter, and vice versa.

As the translation progressed I was increasingly struck by the apparent consistency of the description that had been given in the classic commentaries with that which gradually emerged from my compilation of the available evidence from contemporary sociopsychological studies. Indeed, as the evidence accumulated, its thrust was unmistakable. It indicated that over a span of at least 200 years there has been a marked, indeed one must say a remarkable, degree of continuity in the American national character.

This continuity has been noted before.[2] And it has been challenged, as our Edinburgh writer long ago challenged Harriet Martineau, as proving little more than the continuity of a shared delusion. What will be different, perhaps even distinctive, about my reiteration of this continuity is that I can test this shared "delusion" against some objective facts. The statements I shall make about the contemporary American character rest not on what our Scotch friend labeled "an accidental point of view," but rather derive from the direct, systematic, and, if I may use the term, "scientific" testing of the attitudes, values, beliefs, and psychic dispositions of the real individuals who make up the American people. At which point we are obliged to take a slight methodological detour.

WAYS OF LOOKING
AT NATIONAL CHARACTER

There is a widespread belief that if you ask a sociologist to describe or explain some social phenomenon he will respond immediately—not with the description or explanation, but rather with a treatise on the problems of methodology raised by your request. I shall not disappoint this expectation. The subject of national character is so complex and sensitive, and it has been approached in such diverse manner and spirit, as to make it indispensable for me to specify the meaning of my terms, to delineate the types of evidence I consider relevant, and to propose some appropriate rules for evaluating that evidence and for reaching conclusions from it.

National character has been conventionally derived from a variety of sources. Some prefer to look at a nation's typical institutions, political and social. If we followed this path, we might be examining the U.S. Constitution and the organization of the local school board, the inner workings of IBM and the operations of the Teamsters' Union, the Sunday meeting in the local church and the proceedings of the district family court. Others find constitutions and organizational charts misleading, and prefer to look at a nation's public and collective action. If we followed that path, we should be seeking to find what is common to the presence of the Peace Corps in India and the Air Corps in Vietnam, in turn relating the activities of those groups to the investigations of the Un-American Activities Committee and the ruling of the Supreme Court in the Miranda case, then fitting all that together with our nation's readiness to finance the Defense Department and starve the public transportation system. A third approach emphasizes both the "high" and "common" culture of a people as the best indicators of their national character. Following that line would challenge us to find the common thread running from American primitive painting, through Mary Cassatt to Diebenkorn, in turn to relate the painting to the cult of Babe Ruth, Joe Louis, and Janis Joplin, and to fit all that together with the architecture of Louis Sullivan and Frank Lloyd Wright, of Levittown, and of the World Trade Center.

In *The Handbook of Social Psychology*, D. J. Levinson and I argued that all three of these approaches are less appropriate than the alternative of treating national character as "the relatively enduring personality characteristics and patterns that are modal among the adult members of the society." As we went on to say in that review, "This is a

purely definitional statement, not an empirical one. It describes a hypothetical entity that may or may not exist."[3] It does not prove the existence of national character; it only proposes how we should look for it.

My emphasis on personal attributes, on individual attitudes, values, opinions, beliefs, and personality dispositions is not at odds with
the position taken by the classical commentaries. Some translation is, of
course, necessary, because our vocabulary has changed. Thus de Tocqueville was wont to talk not about personality, but rather about manners. Yet it is clear that he was referring to the same range of
phenomena as I do; indeed, he explicitly included in the category of
"manners" the peoples' "practical experience, habits, [and] opinions."
Moreover, de Tocqueville explicitly stated that elucidating the importance of these manners was "the principal object" of his work.[4]

To ascertain the manners of Americans de Tocqueville had to rely
on what he could see for himself. For one person he proved to have an
extraordinary range of observation and an awesome depth of perception. Nevertheless, there was then and is now no "objective" method for
verifying what de Tocqueville says he saw. Even in the early nineteenth
century the United States was large and diverse, making it almost
certain that different observers were often looking at different things
and talking to different people.

Matters of sampling aside, however, we are still left with disagreements and outright contradictions between and among different observers. Thus, de Tocqueville felt that the Americans showed such
"astonishing gravity" that they had displaced the English as "the most
serious nation on the face of the earth," but Lord Bryce thought we
were a humorous people![5] And Anthony Trollope found American
babies "an unhappy race" whereas Harriet Martineau felt that only in
America was the tremendous suffering of children lessened, if not totally obviated.

To resolve such contradictions in the historical record we may ask
which view more agrees with what *most* observers saw. Beyond that,
however, we cannot turn to any record of actual personal qualities that
would permit us to decide for ourselves what was the character of the
early American. In assessing the nature of the *contemporary* American
character, however, we are put at a great advantage by the extensive
development and application of modern measures for recording individual opinion, habit, belief, behavior, and psychological disposition.
These permit us to base our assessment of the American national character on the direct study of representative samples of the population of

the United States. Moreover, these studies have often been undertaken simultaneously in a number of countries. Consequently we can now assess the American character not only in its own terms, but in the perspective of what is known about the character of other national groups.

Although the existence of this new type of evidence puts us at a great advantage, it still leaves a number of major issues unresolved. I must limit myself to five points, which, I hope, deal with the most fundamental issues.

Is it not true that one gets quite different responses depending on which question one asks, how one asks it, and when it is put to people? The answer must be: "Yes, indeed!" Nevertheless it is also true that on many topics one gets essentially the same pattern of response even when there is a great deal of variation in how and when one asks the question. We can thus identify those elements of the national character that merit classification as relatively pervasive and enduring personality dispositions. Unfortunately, the space available does not permit me to go into any detail in presenting and assessing the facts. I can only offer assurances that I have screened the data, and have presented only those conclusions that I believe rest on substantial evidence. Of course, this does not guarantee that there are no exceptions to the examples I cite, or that all experts in the field would support each and every conclusion I have reached.

Does not the existence of religious, racial, ethnic, and class differences in most national societies render invalid the expectation that there can be "a" or "one" national character in any large-scale society? There are indeed such internal differences visible on every hand, and they may be quite substantial. For example, in the United States almost three times as many white collar as blue collar workers consider the most important quality of a job to be how important the work is and how much of a feeling of accomplishment it gives.[6] This sort of question probably reflects situational pressures more than it does basic values. Nevertheless, the challenge is obvious. Statements about national character should, therefore, be based mainly on responses cutting across class and ethnic lines to thus define a commonly held set of dispositions. As we shall see, such widely shared characteristics do exist. Indeed, it can be shown that on the most fundamental values, and in the more basic psychological dispositions, minorities such as blacks and Catholics share the general American national character.[7]

Is it not arbitrary to insist that nothing is part of the national character unless it is shared by most people in the country? It is, which is why we introduce the concept of *modal* patterns. If one nation shows a great deal more of an unusual characteristic than does any other national population, we are quite prepared to consider it an element of the national character, even if the characteristic is not shared by the majority. Such distinctive modes can be very important in distinguishing one national group from another.

Is it necessary, then, that a characteristic be distinctive, even unique, to be considered part of the national character? I think not. Indeed, that seems an almost impossible requirement, since it is so often the case that several nations share the same cultural tradition. Even more important, processes like industrialization, urbanization, and mass education may serve to inculcate similar psychological dispositions in otherwise diverse groups. The national character is the set of psychosocial characteristics manifested by a given national population. Some of those characteristics will inevitably be shared with some other populations. The total profile, however, is much more likely to be distinctive, if not unique. In any event, it would not invalidate the concept of national character if Australia and New Zealand shared the same profile, or if some of those characteristics were also shared with the American people.

Do not most of the tests and questions used in attitude and value studies reflect mainly momentary pressures and situational forces that are highly variable? Some do indeed. However, long experience in working with this sort of material enables us to distinguish between those questions that seem to tap "situation-bound" attitudes, and those that reflect more stable and deeper lying sentiments and dispositions. Obviously, those responses that come through repeatedly despite situational variability have the greatest claim to a place in any given national character profile.

These methodological reservations being duly noted, we may return to our assessment of continuity and change in the character of the American people.

CONTINUITY IN THE AMERICAN CHARACTER

In 1782, when J. Hector Saint John de Crèvecoeur first put his famous question, What then is the American? he emphasized the idea

of the American as "this *new* man." In this he spoke directly to the
sentiments of Europeans who, in the late eighteenth and early nineteenth centuries, assumed the American was profoundly different from
the kind of man common to Europe; indeed they took him to be almost
as distinctive as the native Indian. De Crèvecoeur was a settler, but he
was followed by a great succession of shorter term visitors all drawn by
the challenge of capturing the essence of this new country. Many wrote
at length about the vastness, the richness, and the virginity of the territory. Most also gave a full account of the distinctive institutions that a
great frontier and a profound revolution had generated.

But for some, among whom we must give first place to de
Tocqueville, the most remarkable quality of the country lay in the
nature of the men and women it produced. Indeed, he criticized the
preoccupation with the country's physical characteristics and its laws,
arguing that "the real cause" of our democracy, our order, and our
prosperity lay in our character.[8]

De Tocqueville's description of the American character emphasized
a set of traits that appeared over and over again in the descriptions of
early visitors and indeed in later accounts as well. Within that set of
qualities, noted as early as the eighteenth century, there are at least ten
concerning which we have substantial psychological test results and
public opinion data derived from studies of the contemporary adult
population of the United States. The space available permits me to
discuss in even modest detail no more than four of these. Given the
opportunity, however, I could present an equally convincing case for
the continuity of the other six personal qualities.

The United States as the Promised Land

De Crèvecoeur no doubt assumed he was speaking for most of the
settlers in America when he wrote in 1782: "We are the most perfect
society existing in the world." Here in America, he continued, a people
of "original genius" had been "incorporated into one of the finest systems of population which have ever appeared."[9]

De Toqueville never met de Crèvecoeur, but he gives testimony to
the fact that such pride was not exceptional for he reports: "If I say to
an American that the country he lives in is a fine one, 'Ay,' he replies,
'there is not its fellow in the world!' "[10]

Of course, we are all used to the patriotic panegyrics that are generated for great public occasions and from the production of which some writers derive their regular livelihood. As de Tocqueville noted, "All free nations are vainglorious," but, as he went on to say, "national pride is not displayed in the same manner in all countries."[11] What so impressed the early visitors to the United States was, first, the broad diffusion among the common people of this conviction about America's virtue and uniqueness, and, second, the vigor and firmness with which they held that conviction. Indeed de Tocqueville complained that: "It is impossible to conceive a more troublesome or more garrulous patriotism; it wearies even those disposed to respect it."[12] And Martineau echoed his sentiments, observing that "no peculiarity in [the Americans] is more remarkable than their national contentment . . . this contentment will live down all contempt, and even all wonder."[13]

The conviction that the Lord meant to relocate the Garden of Eden in America and to establish here the one best system humankind might hope to enjoy on earth seems to have persisted remarkably intact over the 150 years since de Tocqueville first visited our shores. Moreover, its manifestations are not limited to the Fourth of July celebrations, though I would urge one not to discount the significance of the solemnity with which those parades and speeches are approached in high school stadiums and on the steps of town halls all over the country. Indeed, one can seriously argue that a special brand of patriotism is the true American religion whose rituals are celebrated on these occasions.

Numerous studies give evidence that into the 1970s residents of the United States continued to be outstanding in the intensity and pervasiveness of their belief in the special qualities of the American system and the virtues of American life.

Asked in 1971 "If you were free to do so, would you like to go and settle down in another country?" many fewer people in America expressed an interest than did those from eight other countries. Indeed, the proportion of Americans who said yes, at 12 percent, was half the average rate for the others, which included a high of 41 percent in Great Britain. We should keep in mind, moreover, that by 1971 we were deeply involved in Vietnam, and much of the emigration sentiment evidently reflected opposition to the war among the young and well educated.[14]

It would be a mistake to assume that the advantage that the United States showed in this competition could be readily explained as merely reflecting the obvious attraction of the greater wealth that American citizens enjoy. On the contrary, the American's pride in his system has in modern times focused first and foremost on the special character of American government and political institutions. Asked in the late fifties "What are the things about this country that you are most proud of?" an astonishing 85 percent of Americans pointed to the Constitution, or noted their experience of freedom, or cited the virtues of our democracy, and so on. This is especially noteworthy because the questions were not precoded. These topics were not listed as alternative answers; they were mentioned spontaneously in answer to an "open-ended" question.

Even among those who live under the Mother of Parliaments in Great Britain, only 46 percent showed comparable pride in their governmental system, while in Germany and Italy a mere 7 percent and 3 percent, respectively, followed this pattern. Germans were most proud of the characteristics of their people, and Italians of the beauty of their country, but in each of these cases only about a third of the commentaries focused on any one category. Nowhere else was there the extraordinary unanimity displayed by the Americans in singling out their political and governmental institutions as special objects of pride.[15]

Self-Reliance, Autonomy, and Independence

Homely virtues of persistence, initiative, self-reliance, and independence are continuously extolled in Franklin's *Autobiography* and in *Poor Richard's Almanac*. We cannot say whether Franklin was only reflecting tendencies already deeply rooted in the American character, or whether his writings themselves produced that outcome. In any event, by 1830 it was evident to de Tocqueville that individualism and self-reliance were distinctive expressions of the American character. He said of us, "They owe nothing to any man; they expect nothing from any man. They acquire the habit of always considering themselves as standing alone."[16] Some seventy years later the same qualities were evidently still salient, and they led James Bryce to comment that in America "everything tends to make the individual independent and self-reliant."[17]

Numerous surveys have repeatedly shown the belief that fate or luck significantly determines what happens to us is not a salient idea among the American people. We may, for example, note the experience of James Morgan, who, in 1964, described to a national sample two people having the same skill and training, one of whom had succeeded in life and the other not, and then asked his respondents to explain that outcome. A mere 1 percent volunteered either God's will or fate as an explanation.[18] By way of contrast, when I asked a comparable question in six developing countries, the proportion who attributed a man's success to luck or fate averaged about 30 percent and went to a high of 53 percent in Bangladesh.[19]

Instead of God or luck, the great majority of Americans still believe that it is a person's own efforts that account for success or failure in life. If it were only the business and professional classes that expressed such sentiments we might discount their response as an obvious justification of their special privileges, and as a camouflage of the harsh realities of life for the disadvantaged rank and file. It is therefore striking, indeed extraordinary, how regularly something like two-thirds, or even three-fourths, of American blue collar workers affirm the very same principles.

Seventy percent of American blue collar workers asserted in 1971–1972 that people who work hard have the same chance as anyone else, even if their parents are poor, and 69 percent felt that most unemployed people had failed to make use of the opportunities that had come their way.[20]

Some might argue that there is a catch in these questions. Since the failures judged were those of other people rather than those of the self, the respondents may have found it easier to put the blame on the individual and thus avoid criticizing the system. It follows from this argument that when individuals come to explain what has happened to themselves personally, they should be much more likely to deny that their failures are their own fault. But the data do not support this expectation.

Given a chance to put their own personal failures down to bad health or accidents, more than 90 percent of American blue collar workers denied that such factors accounted for their condition in life. More than 80 percent of these same workers specifically denied the role of bad luck, of growing up poor, or even of being discriminated against!

If neither discrimination, nor poor parents, nor bad luck are used by Americans to explain their failure to get ahead in life, how do they explain it? Evidently mainly by reference to a series of homely virtues. Of these the most important are persistence, hard work, and initiative.[21]

What is notable in these spontaneously offered explanations for personal success and failure is that they do not put blame outside, on the society or on social conditions, but rather place blame inside the person, indeed inside the very person answering the question. Nothing sums up this tendency more sharply than the fact that an astonishing 75 percent of blue collar workers in the United States affirmed the proposition that "What happens to me is my own doing!"[22] One cannot help but be struck by the congruence between this assertion by a representative sample of American workers in 1972 and de Tocqueville's observation, in 1835, that Americans "are apt to imagine that their whole destiny is in their own hands."[23]

Unfortunately, these questions seem not to have been asked, at least in the same form, of individuals in Europe, let alone in the less developed countries. Such evidence as is available, however, indicates that in Western Europe changes in one's economic fortunes are mainly attributed either to the actions of others, or to the government, or to the intervention of the trade unions. It seems that the tendency to attribute the improvement or decline of one's economic condition to one's own effort and accomplishment is a distinctive American characteristic, reflecting our general disposition to feel self-reliant.[24]

Communal Action, Voluntarism, and Cooperation with Neighbors

On coming ashore in the 1830s de Tocqueville was struck by a phenomenon he said "must be seen in order to be understood." What so vigorously caught his attention was the Americans' propensity to form themselves into organizations and thus participate in local affairs. In an oft-quoted passage he wrote:

> Americans of all ages, all conditions and all dispositions constantly form associations. They have not only commercial and manufacturing companies, in which all take part, but associations of a thousand other kinds—religious, moral, serious, futile, extensive or restricted, enormous or diminutive.[25]

The tidal wave of voluntary associations that de Tocqueville ran into had, in fact, been rising and swelling for almost a hundred years. The first ripples were set in motion by men like Benjamin Franklin. Not finding any good bookseller in Philadelphia after he settled there, Franklin suggested that he and his friends in the Junto bring their individually owned books together in their clubroom "where they would not only be ready to consult in our conferences, but become a common benefit, each of us being at liberty to borrow such as he wish'd to read at home."[26] In 1730 Franklin extended the idea by setting up a subscription library on a city-wide basis, and as he wrote later in his *Autobiography,* this was "the mother of all the North American subscription libraries . . . become a great thing in itself and continually increasing."[27]

Franklin applied the same principles to ensure that there should be constables to guard property and a fire-fighting company. These voluntary companies were instruments not only for the more ready extinguishing of fires but were also for "discoursing and communicating such ideas . . . upon the subject of fires as might be useful on our conduct on such occasions." Again the concept spread, and new companies were rapidly formed.[28]

Except for those living in a few small towns Americans no longer rely on volunteer companies to provide their fire protection. Nevertheless, the American people continue to be outstanding in their commitment to the value of community participation and in the extent to which they carry this principle into action.

Our best data come from the five-nation study by Almond and Verba. They found that more Americans, by a wide margin, assert the obligation of the ordinary man to be active in local affairs. In this respect the United States was well ahead even of Great Britain. Americans affirmed this obligation more than twice as often as did Germans, and more than five times more frequently than Italians. Moreover, Americans are much more likely to actually join organizations, and, as a manifestation both of organizational democracy and individual earnestness, many more Americans have held office in the organizations to which they belong. Around 1960 one of every four adult Americans reported having held office in an organization—double the rate for even Great Britain and four times the rate for Germany and Italy.[29]

Trust

Individuals may come together under great pressure of need, but they cannot work together effectively nor will they stay together for very long if they lack basic trust in the motives and the reliability of those with whom they are joined. Anthropologists and sociologists trying to understand why it is so difficult to establish and maintain cooperative programs in many of the countries in which they seem so desperately needed, have repeatedly identified the lack of interpersonal trust as one of the chief obstacles.

A typical example comes to us from a classic on modernization, Manning Nash's *Machine Age Maya*. In the highland Guatemala community of Cantel, which had long been industrialized, Nash noted that among the traditional peasants and the industrial workers both, there was a pervasive quality of suspiciousness that permeated social interaction. Nash described the average person in Cantel as secretive, acting as if the revelation of any private purpose or plan would lay him open to interference by a hostile neighbor. If anyone asks a question as part of even a casual encounter, he is open to suspicion as to the motives behind the question. If anyone should be bold enough to ask "Where are you going?" the Cantel citizen will offer the stock enigmatic answer "Well, I have my errand to do," and immediately move on.[30]

No greater contrast with the ideal and the actual in the American character can be found. Ben Franklin made *sincerity* one of his thirteen basic precepts, urging himself and others: "Use no hurtful deceit; think innocently and justly; and if you speak, speak accordingly."[31] Martineau was struck by "the frank, confiding character of . . . private intercourse . . . the extraordinary mutual respect and kindness of the American people . . . their cheerful and generous helpfulness."[32] Numerous other visitors, then and later, noted the Americans' qualities of openness and friendliness, their quick readiness to share preferences and confidences, their casualness and spontaneousness in stray encounters with mere acquaintances and even strangers.

The confidence that people can be trusted, the feeling that they care and will fulfill their obligations to you, the readiness to extend the benefit of doubt to other people even when they are your nominal opponents, the respect for the mutual rights of others, all seem to have been transmitted to the majority of Americans over the generations down to the present time.

Confronted with the statement "Most People Can Be Trusted," a mere 7 percent in Italy and 19 percent in Germany agreed, whereas the Americans were first with 55 percent.[33] On the summary scale, of which this question is a part, a score indicating little faith in people was earned by 56 percent of the Italians, as against a mere 16 percent of Americans. These differences, moreover, applied across all educational levels from grade school to college.[34] Equally striking, in this connection, is the American's openness to having intimate relations with his nominal political opponents. Close to three-fourths of all Americans would not oppose having a son or daughter marry someone from the opposition party. Indeed, 74 percent of Americans explicitly dismissed such considerations as irrelevant in marriage. They did so three times as often as Germans and five times as often as Italians.[35]

These findings are in accord with those from a number of other studies. We may point, for example, to Gordon's scale measuring the anticipation of personal support, that is, the feeling that you will be approached with understanding, will receive encouragement from others, and will be treated with kindness and consideration. In comparisons with people from nine other countries Americans were not only first in expressing their confidence that they could count on others for support, but they had a commanding lead over the representatives of all countries represented.[36] Taken all together, the evidence indicating a high degree of interpersonal trust to be an outstanding characteristic of the contemporary American is quite extensive and notably consistent.

Other Themes

The space available does not permit me to deal at the same length with the continuity of any of the other attributes that merit our attention. If it did permit, I could demonstrate that the following attitudes, values, and psychic dispositions, earlier identified as part of the American national character by perceptive visitors at the time the nation was founded, are today widely distributed in the contemporary American population.

A Sense of Efficacy This may be thought of simply as the opposite of fatalism. Americans have always been, and remain, convinced that they can transform the physical and social world, and even human nature itself, if necessary, to make things over the way they want them to be. They resonate to the boast, "The difficult we do right away; the impossible takes a bit longer."

Optimism is Closely Linked to Efficacy Efficacy leads to trying. Optimism gives the confidence that one will succeed. Even in the depth of the 1974 recession, 68 percent of all Americans said they had quite a lot "of confidence" in the future of the country, and the question was worded so that no greater expression of enthusiasm was possible.[37]

The same confidence applies to one's purely personal prospects. For example, George Katona notes that despite the superior performance of the German and the Dutch economies in recent years, Americans continue to approach their personal economic future with a degree of optimism which is so different as to be distinctive.

Innovativeness and Openness to New Experience   These terms used to be called being "progressive." The readiness to try the new and to experiment, especially in the realm of the technical and mechanical, goes back a long way in the American experience. It now extends to many other realms as well, including especially new forms of organization, and new sensate experiences. Servan-Schreiber expressed it well when he said: "We Europeans continue to suffer progress rather than to pursue it. Americans pursue it, welcome it, and adapt to it."[38]

Anti-Authoritarianism   De Crèvecoeur declared that one of the things that was new about the American was his total rejection of any servile dependence. De Tocqueville wrote at considerable length about the cautious, almost mistrustful attitude of the early American to the authority of the state. Today the American seems more like Laocoön, getting wrapped ever more firmly in the coils of the government's laws and regulations even as he struggles to escape their control. Nevertheless, numerous studies of political psychology show Americans to be still outstanding in their anti-authoritarianism, with no deep psychic need to submit themselves to higher political authority, and a continuing propensity to assert their rights to personal autonomy over public control.

Equality   The sense of one's intrinsic worth, and the feeling that one is equal to all others in rights before the law, have long been linked to the quality of anti-authoritarianism, and the two are often treated interchangeably. Americans have always been described as notable in this quality. As de Tocqueville long ago observed, even within the covenant of master and servant Americans are yet but "two citizens of the commonwealth—two men—and the precise limits of authority and obedience are clearly settled in the mind of the one as in that of the other."[39] This sense of basic equality with all other individuals can be shown to be still almost universal in America today.

Beyond these qualities we should also at least list: individualism;

restless energy; pragmatism; a tendency toward brashness or boastfulness; this-worldliness; a preference for the concrete; and a certain discomfort in coping with aesthetic and emotional expression. As in the case of the qualities previously more fully documented, each of these was regularly noted in the classical accounts of the American character, and can be documented by recent empirical psychosocial tests to still be part of that syndrome that makes up the modal personality pattern of the current population of the United States.

EXPLAINING THE CONTINUITY

As we have seen, the available evidence indicates a high, indeed one may say a striking, degree of continuity in the American national character over a period of some 200 years. The attitudes, values, sentiments, and psychic dispositions of the people inhabiting the country at the Bicentenary seem remarkably like those eulogized by Franklin and de Crèvecoeur around the time of the Revolution, and then so vividly described by observers such as de Tocqueville and Martineau when they visited the country around 1830. The portrait they drew, moreover, agrees very closely with that sketched later by James Bryce in 1888 and Frederick Jackson Turner in 1893, suggesting that a more or less unbroken line connects the earlier period with the latest.

If the facts are real, they would seem to be most singular. Even by 1900, let alone by 1970, the country that Franklin and de Crèvecoeur knew and that de Tocqueville and Martineau later visited had in its physical and social form been profoundly, one is tempted to say totally, transformed. The general dimensions of this transformation are well known, but the details merit emphasis.

From the first census in 1790 to the last in 1970 the territory of the country increased four times, and the population by a staggering 52 times. From a sparsely populated land having only 4.5 persons per square mile the density increased by 13 times.

Whereas only 5 percent of the population had lived in cities and large towns, more than 75 percent are now urban dwellers, and in large part live in cities of such magnitude as to have been literally inconceivable in colonial times.

Infant mortality fell to one-tenth of its former rate and life expectancy at birth doubled.

Whereas less than 1 percent had received secondary education, now 76 percent are graduating from high school. And whereas at least 80 percent of those employed in colonial times worked in agriculture, the proportion of farm owners and workers in the civilian labor force is down to a mere 3 percent.[40]

How can it be that a basic personality structure should remain fundamentally unchanged while the successive generations experience such profoundly different conditions of life?

Under other circumstances some anthropologist might come forward to explain to us that basic personality structures are, after all, only another manifestation of deep-lying culture patterns. These culture patterns, he might further advise us, are very persistent in tribes, clans, and other closed populations, which can effectively transmit them through the family and other primary groups from generation to generation across long spans of time.

In the case of the United States, however, this anthropological argument runs afoul of the great cultural discontinuity that the American population experienced as a result of successive and massive waves of immigration. The three million Americans in the country at the time of the Revolution got to be 203 million in 1970 not mainly by reproducing themselves, but rather by being greatly augmented by a tremendous influx from abroad. In the 45 years from the Revolution to 1820 only 250,000 people are estimated to have entered the country. By 1847 that many were coming in, on the average, *every year,* and by 1905 five times that number, actually more than a million people, were coming to settle here each year. From being overwhelmingly white, Anglo-Saxon, and Protestant, the country became significantly Catholic and Jewish, more German, Irish, Scandinavian, Slavic, and Italian—significantly black and Spanish speaking. By 1920, about 36 percent, more than one in three Americans, was either foreign born or was the child of a couple one or both of whom were foreign born. Add the Negroes and almost half of the population in 1920 came from outside the mainstream, which had accounted for the original settlement.

Even if the settlers had in their own line been transmitting unimpaired a heritage of the personal qualities carried forward from colonial times, how could these masses of latecomers possibly have acquired the attitudes, values, and basic dispositions we have identified as making up the typical American character structure? In this realm there exists little or no firm evidence. Among numerous explanations frequently mentioned three are most substantial.

First, we should consider differential recruitment. This theory holds that the migrants to the United States were self-selected, and assumes that those who chose to come were precisely those whose personality was already in tune with the character predominant in American life.

This theory has considerable appeal for its simplicity, and there seems every reason to grant it some validity. For example, people who were timid, who were not open to new experience, or reasonably self-reliant, would not cross the ocean under the conditions that prevailed or volunteer for the uncertainty of immigrant status. On other counts, however, the situation is much more ambiguous. Persons escaping persecution might well be more tolerant, but we know that often they were not. People who challenge received authority are, nevertheless, themselves often authoritarian. Moreover, there is no reason to associate any particular personality characteristic with the accident of experiencing drought, famine, landlessness, and unemployment, all great winds of change, which drove masses of immigrants before them across the oceans to the shores of the United States.

The second theory assumes the immigrants were initially not at all like Americans, but argues that once here they were transformed under the impact of their contact with the unique American political, cultural, and psychological ambience. This might be called "learning on the job."

De Tocqueville again and again emphasized the importance of our democratic institutions—especially the institutionalization of equality before the law and in the governance of society—as critical factors in shaping the American character. Turner saw the frontier as "the line of most rapid and effective Americanization." He called it a "crucible" in which diverse elements were fused to create a composite nationality embodying the distinctive personal traits of the American character.[41] In his turn Potter explained the shaping of American character as due to the abundance that people enjoyed in this country.[42] No doubt millions of immigrants crammed into New York, Pittsburgh, and Chicago never saw the frontier, except in a very special sense. And while they may have experienced much better conditions here than they had known in "the old country," most of them probably did not feel that they were enjoying great abundance. Nevertheless, there seems good reason to believe that the responsiveness of government, the experience of equality, the availability of opportunity, the openness of the land and system, the active practice of democracy, and the relative abundance of the material means of existence all exerted considerable influence on the values, opinions, beliefs, and psychic dispositions of very large numbers of new Americans.

A third and serious contender for primacy in explaining the continuity of the American character is the theory that it was inculcated in the successive immigrant generations predominantly through the impact of the American public school on its young charges. Certainly it was the intention of most of the country's leading educators that the school should achieve this purpose, which led to those educators being dubbed the "Americanizers."

Whether the process actually worked as we imagine is difficult to prove objectively, but there certainly is impressionistic evidence to support the assumption. For example, Adele Marie Shaw, a reporter who visited 25 classrooms in New York in 1903, thought that even over the span of a few days she could observe children losing their foreign look, so that by the time they reached the upper grades Ms. Shaw could report that the initial melange of ethnic types had been transformed into what she called an "extraordinary homogeneousness."[43]

To go beyond the anecdotal I should note that my own research in developing countries, some of which are now at the stage of development the United States was in around 1890, shows clearly that attendance at a modern school is the most powerful single factor in inculcating in young people a sense of personal efficacy and of openness to new experience, a spirit of self-reliance, and a striving for independence from traditional authority—all of which we have identified as elements of the American national character. If this happens in less developed countries now, it very likely happened in American schools earlier. Moreover, if one takes account of the more distinctive features of the American school one can readily imagine how it might also have inculcated other values especially associated with the American character, such as readiness for voluntary action, individualism, trust, equalitarianism, tolerance, and faith in democratic principles.

CHANGING ORIENTATIONS

Although the basic character of Americans has manifested remarkable continuity, it has certainly not been completely stable. On the contrary, in a number of respects it seems to manifest major change and to be currently undergoing further rather rapid, indeed sometimes precipitous, shifts. Some of these can be well documented. Others are more speculative. All may be related to a long-term process of social and structural change, which is frequently taken to herald the arrival of the post-industrial society.[44] Unfortunately those trends that have been precisely measured can be followed for at most 20 or 25 years, leaving us quite uncertain as to whether we are observing really fundamental long-term trends or only short-term and possibly cyclical fluctuations.

Space is available to discuss only three such shifts, one of which will probably be looked on as positive, one perhaps unfortunate, and one quite ambiguous in its import.

Increasing Tolerance of Diversity

Freedom of religion in the Colonies was granted only very slowly and generally grudgingly. No matter how noble an expression of the democratic spirit our Constitution was, it did accept slavery as the law of the land. De Tocqueville said, "I know of no country in which there is so little true independence of mind . . . as in America."[45] Martineau agreed with him, charging the early Americans with a "deficiency of moral independence." Moreover, with explicit regard to religion, she noted with disapproval our "laws against speculative atheists; [the] opprobrium directed upon such as embrace natural religion otherwise than through Christianity; and yet more bitter oppression exercised by those who view Christianity in one way, over those who view it in another."[46]

De Tocqueville and Martineau were not alone in expressing such views. Of all the many virtues that the classic commentaries saw in the American character, tolerance was seldom cited.[47] This tendency persisted over time. Thus, in his review of the observations made by foreign visitors to the United States after 1880, Lipset notes that "a number were startled to find overt signs of anti-Semitism such as placards barring Jews from hotels . . . and social clubs which denied them membership."[48] In the same period many of those who stressed the Americanizing role of the schools took little pain to cover up their disdain, even repugnance, for the diverse cultural characteristics of the immigrant children. Thus, in 1889 a member of the Boston School Committee proposed that corporal punishment be instituted specifically in those schools in which immigrants were concentrated on the ground that "many of these children come from homes of vice and crime." According to him these children had "in their blood generations of iniquity . . . they hate restraint or obedience to law. They know nothing of the feelings which are inherited by those who were born on our shores."[49]

It was this spirit that caused the children of the Chinese in San Francisco and the blacks in many other places to be confined to special, and often completely segregated, schools. Later on we had the dogs in Selma, the incident at Kent State, the mass arrests in Washington, and the complex relations with all the "gooks" in Vietnam, which culminated in My Lai. Finally, CBS struck the final blow at those of us who wanted to believe that more, if not all, of these events were aberrations, not expressing the true sentiments of the American people.

CBS accomplished this mischief by conducting a poll with questions designed to test the American people's adherence to the principles set forth in the Bill of Rights. For example, to test our allegiance to the right of peaceable assembly and petition they asked: "As long as there appears to be no clear danger of violence, do you think any group, no matter how extreme, should be allowed to organize protests against the government?" Seventy-six percent said such protests should not be allowed, in flat contradiction of the guarantees provided by Article I.[50]

Despite this doleful preface, I believe that tolerance of religious, sexual, and racial differences in the United States has been quite substantially and steadily increasing over the last 25 years. Survey data on relevant questions over that span of time is extremely hard to come by. I limit myself to one city, Detroit, because it has been the subject of an unusual series of continuous researches sponsored by the University of Michigan. There is, however, good reason to assert that these tendencies are not limited to Detroit, but rather are nationwide and go back some 40 years.[51]

Those studies provide numerous indicators of declining intolerance. For example, in 1958, 46 percent of Catholics felt Jews were less than fair in business dealings with them; by 1971 the proportion saying that, at 27 percent, was down to almost half. In 1956 only 40 percent of whites thought their young daughter's Negro playmate should be permitted to come into the home. By 1971 the figure was almost double at 79 percent. Some might seek to dismiss these findings by asserting they show no more than that the whites have learned to give more socially acceptable answers while nothing has changed in real attitudes or behavior. No one would be better able to judge that than the blacks of Detroit, and in 1971, 73 percent declared that there had indeed been "lots of progress" in getting rid of social discrimination in the last ten or fifteen years.[52] In other words, the blacks' response is a challenge to the theory that whites only *talk* a better line now.

I myself am convinced the change is real. Moreover, I feel that the change in racial attitudes is only one manifestation of a general transformation of American values, moving us toward greater tolerance of diversity and deviant behavior, at least so far as that deviant behavior has no victims. Americans have broken the grip of the absolute moral principles that so rigidly divided right from wrong, and that so amply broadened the definition of public wrong to include all manner of private acts among consenting adults. There has been a pervasive and marked increase in tolerance for largely individual actions, many of which were formerly treated as crimes—even if without victims—such as divorce, abortion, premarital sex, interracial sex, homosexuality, smoking pot, and a number of similar personal indulgences.

Of course, pendulums swing, and there may soon be a massive swing back. But one intriguing item in the Detroit Area Study suggests the trend may, if anything, be intensified in the next generation, at least if we judge by how mothers there say they are bringing up their children. After being told about a situation in which a child found that the other children just did not interest the central character of this little drama, the mothers were asked what they would urge the child to do. From 1953 to 1971 the percent who said the child had nevertheless better continue to play with the others fell from 33 to a mere 10 percent. The proportion who urged the child to continue with his or her own interests rose a resounding twenty points, so that by 1971, 73 percent of the mothers favored that course of action. Contrary to David Riesman's thesis, Americans seem to have not become more other-oriented but rather now overwhelmingly favor the inner-directed style.[53] It is equally encouraging that the proportion of U.S. citizens who support specific applications of the Bill of Rights has risen steadily, year in, year out, since 1970.[54]

The Ethic of Hard Work, Temperance, Frugality

In his writings Benjamin Franklin elaborated a set of precepts so striking that Max Weber later used the material as the basis for his famous sketch of the Protestant Ethic, which Weber considered the ethos underlying the development of modern capitalism.[55] Franklin's *Autobiography* describes the thirteen principles according to which he sought to guide his own personal conduct. Among these, *industry* was featured, with the admonition that we "lose no time: be always employed in something useful; cut off unnecessary actions."[56] According to Arthur Schlesinger, the original settlers were indeed "the hardest working people on earth." He considered the "habit of work" to be the most salient feature of the American character inherited from the experience of colonial agriculture.[57]

To *industry* Franklin added the goal of *temperance,* meaning "Eat not to dullness; drink not to elevation," and requiring one to moderate "every other pleasure, appetite, inclination or passion, bodily or mental." On top of this he proposed *frugality,* requiring that we "waste nothing."[58]

According to his own account Franklin lived according to these precepts even as he prospered. Thus, he took his breakfast "out of a twopenny porringer, with a pewter spoon." But on coming to the table one morning he found there a china bowl and a spoon of silver, bought by his wife without his knowledge for what he called "the enormous sum" of three-and-twenty shillings. Therefore "mark," says Franklin, "how luxury will enter families, and make a progress, in spite of principle."[59]

Franklin's little parable seems to have foreshadowed the fate of the American values of hard work, frugality, and temperance. Thus, from 1958 to 1971 the number of people who considered the most important attribute of a job to be either its intrinsic importance or its promise of advancement fell steadily, whereas the importance of high income and shorter hours became markedly more attractive.[60]

A more dramatic statistic comes from the responses of a national sample who were asked what accounted for getting ahead in their line of work. Well over one-third said it depends mainly on sheer seniority or experience. Only 18 percent mentioned hard work and persistence, and a mere 1 percent cited qualities such as taking on tough tasks, being aggressive, or showing initiative and enterprise.[61] We have evidently come a long way from de Crèvecoeur's America of 1782 where, he claimed, "We are all animated with the spirit of an industry which is unfettered and unrestrained because each person works for himself."[62]

Americans once accumulated to save and invest. Today the consumption ethic has replaced the Protestant Ethic. The annual personal saving rate of Americans, expressed as a proportion of disposable income, is a mere 6 percent, less than half that in Germany and Holland, possibly only a third that in Japan. In the United States the checking account, the credit card, and the installment loan now largely overshadow the savings book. The "put away" society has become the "throw away" society. In virtually every year since World War II the new consumer debts Americans incurred greatly exceeded the amounts they paid off.[63] In simultaneous studies of nine European countries this pattern of consumer behavior was found not to be common to other affluent nations. In other words, it is distinctively American. American ingenuity has been extended to the point where a whole nation has learned how to "buy goods we don't need with money we don't have."[64] How far we have come from Franklin's urging that we pursue frugality and industry to attain the even higher goal of freedom from debt.[65]

Planfulness is very much part of a syndrome of qualities, which includes industry, temperance, and frugality. Franklin called it the precept of "order" requiring that "all your things have their places, and each part of your business have its time," all arranged on the basis of an advanced plan. Franklin acknowledges that of all his precepts this one gave him personally the most trouble. Yet there is no doubt that for much of American history this principle was one of the almost universally acknowledged Golden Rules. We must be struck, therefore, to find that in the 1970s almost half the American people identify themselves as the kind who do not plan ahead, but instead merely live from day to day.[66]

Erosion of Political Confidence

During the last 25 years the typical American seems to have experienced a very sharp, indeed one might say a precipitous, decline in his confidence as a political being. This malaise takes two closely related forms.

First, there has been a steady erosion of the belief that our institutions are capable of doing their respective jobs. Year by year they are increasingly seen as working less well, as failing to perform adequately, as not deserving trust and confidence. The disenchantment seems to extend to almost all our major institutions, the presidency, the Congress, the courts, industry, and the universities. By 1976 only 20 percent of the American people could muster "a great deal of confidence" in the executive branch, an all-time low. Lest this be assumed to somehow reflect the peculiar influence of the Nixon debacle, note that confidence in major companies was down to 16 percent, and in our Congress to a mere 9 percent! In all cases these figures represented a striking decline in confidence over the years.[67]

This sense that our institutions are failing is linked to a second malaise, namely, the feeling that one has lost control over the political system. For example, in the late fifties the proportion of people who said, "public officials don't care what people like me think" was only about 20 percent. By the mid seventies over half of all Americans were voicing this complaint.[68] The discontent with particular aspects of the system's functioning leads to a more general disillusionment. Asked in 1973 to pull everything together to assess the state of the nation, almost two-thirds thought it poor or, at best, only fair.[69] It is especially interesting for us to note that this view was highly uniform across all social groups.[70]

The explanation for our crisis of confidence, for this loss of faith in our system and its capacity to produce the wonders it has always been assumed capable of producing, obviously demands attention. It also requires explanation. I have elsewhere noted a series of changes in the composition and location of the American population, which seems to go some distance in explaining the despair we have noted.[71] Others have suggested this response may be endemic to modern large-scale societies, pointing to similar developments in Europe.[72] Still others argue that the phenomenon is only a cyclical manifestation, linked to a set of historical circumstances that are already changing.[73]

Whatever interpretation is put on it, there seems no denying the fact. The Americans' previously exceptional pride in their governmental institutions and their vibrant confidence in their personal political efficacy have vastly declined. What was previously a great, almost deadening, "hurrah" has now shrunk to a barely audible whisper.

CONCLUSIONS

Earlier I argued that there was a striking degree of continuity in the tendency of Americans to be exceptionally proud of their governmental institutions. Yet in these last pages I have been at pains to show that over the last quarter century confidence in these institutions has been sinking steadily and rapidly, reaching all-time lows.

I could say, in my defense, that the contradiction is more apparent than real. Americans might be increasingly disappointed in the way their institutions have been working, while still considering them to be the best available the world over. There is considerable substance in that argument.[74] I prefer, however, to use this seeming contradiction to make a quite different, and, I believe, much more important point.

The American character was not cast in concrete in 1776. It was not transmitted from generation to generation through the genes. It had to be taught, learned, and developed anew in each generation. Moreover, the fact of continuity does not constitute evidence for lack of flexibility or adaptability, any more than the continuity of an individual personality over time precludes growth and development in personal skills and qualities. The American national character is a dynamic entity, the elements of which interact both with their institutional environment and with the other qualities constituting the character.

If the American character has been notably continuous in certain respects, that must be because the necessary conditions existed that made possible its continuous renewal. Yet we have seen that the American character remained the same in many respects despite massive changes in the size and composition of the population, its level of education, its patterns of residence, and its forms of work.

Here, in this apparent paradox lies a great challenge, both to our common sense and to our scientific curiosity. Why should trust persist undiminished in the American people, while the old strict, unrelenting punitive morality, which so long fought against the temptations of the flesh as against the very devil, seems to have been so largely relinquished?

One possibility is that the elements of the social structure vary greatly in their relevance for character structure, so that certain types of institutional change support or undercut some personal qualities and not others. If so, our task is to determine which institutions most influence which qualities, and to learn how they produce their impact. An alternative explanation might be that some personal qualities are more resistant to change than others. If so, we will want to know which are resistant, which malleable, and why.

Because both character and social structure are changing, we face the prospect of increasing inconsistency, and the strain and conflict that inhere in such inconsistency. The qualities Ben Franklin eulogized were psychologically all of a piece; they cohered as a meaningful syndrome. They also fit quite well with the institutional structure and the fabric of everyday life in America in the nineteenth and early twentieth centuries. But we must wonder how peacefully self-reliance, on the one hand, and on the other, today's distaste for hard work, can coexist in the same personality system? We may equally wonder how long we can preserve our trust in others, and our spirit of cooperation, when everyone is so preoccupied with discovering his or her own true "unique" personality through the relentless pursuit of what Maslow called the need for self-actualization?

Moreover, the continuing and emergent American character must meet the test of relevance. It must somehow be consistent with the array of institutions and the patterns of living that will prevail in America's third century. Daniel Bell, for one, perceives a profound disjunction between the role demands set by our increasingly technological institutional structure and the expressive style characteristic of our latest cultural tendencies.[75] I take a more sanguine view. I consider the elements of the American character structure that have been most persistent to be those most essential to the continued functioning of a modern democratic policy governing a large-scale, industrial, technological society. The mounting clamor for equality, and the more relaxed attitude about personal indulgence, seem to me not incongruent with such institutional changes in our social system as are emerging. Neither of these two tendencies seems to me to strike at the core, or to undermine the foundations.

Bell may have been too quick to generalize the trends of the sixties, now largely contained and rechanneled by those of the seventies. Of course, my reading of the seventies may be proved to have been wide of the mark when we get into the eighties. Martin Lipset may be right in asserting that we cannot predict the future. But we can monitor it as it emerges. Our ability to do that with increasing perceptiveness and accuracy is one small element in the promise of the next century.

Notes

CHAPTER 1/Lipset

1. Ruldolf Klein, "Growth and Its Enemies," *Commentary* 53 (January 1972): 38–39.
2. Henry C. Wallich, "Economic Growth in America," in Chester L. Cooper, ed., *Growth in America* (Westport, Conn.: Greenwood, 1976), p.62.
3. Arthur M. Okun, "What's Wrong with the U.S. Economy? Diagnosis and Prescription," *Quarterly Review of Economics and Business* (Summer 1975), p. 26.
4. George Katona, "Behavioral Economics," *Challenge* 21 (September–October 1978): 17–18; see also Milton Friedman, "Nobel Lecture: Inflation and Unemployment," *Journal of Political Economy* 85 (June 1977): 451–71.
5. Norman Macrae, "The Future of International Business," *Economist,* January 22, 1972, p. v.
6. Robert L. Heilbroner, "The Missing Link(s)," *Challenge* 21 (March–April 1978): 17
7. Wassily Leontief, "Theoretical Assumptions and Nonobserved Facts," *American Economic Review* 61 (1971): 3.
8. Robert M. Solow, "The Public Discussion of Economics: Some Pitfalls," *Challenge* 21 (March–April 1978): 39.
9. Dudley Kirk, "The Field of Demography," in David L. Sills, ed., *International Encyclopedia of the Social Sciences* 12 (New York: Macmillan and The Free Press, 1968): 345.
10. Kenneth E. Boulding, "The Shadow of the Stationary State," *Daedalus* 102 (Fall 1973): 93.
11. "Population Drop Worries Australia," *New York Times,* October 3, 1976, p. 16; Donald J. Bogue and Amy Ung Tsui, "Zero World Population Growth?" *The Public Interest*, No. 55 (Spring 1979): 100, and Peter C. Stuart, "Undoing Malthus: Developing Asia's Countryside," *The New Leader* 62 (March 12, 1979): 8–10.
12. Charles F. Westoff, "Marriage and Fertility in the Developed Countries," *Scientific American* 239 (December 1978): 51–52.
13. For a review of the evidence on social mobility, see S.M. Lipset, "Equality and Inequality," in Robert K. Merton and Robert Nisbet, eds., *Contemporary Social Problems,* 4th ed. (New York: Harcourt Brace, Jovanovich, 1976), pp. 305–53.

14. Nathan Glazer and Daniel P. Moynihan, "Introduction" to their *Ethnicity: Theory and Experience* (Cambridge, Mass.: Harvard University Press, 1975), pp. 6–7 (emphasis in original).

15. Eugene B. Skolnikoff, "The Governability of Complexity," in Cooper, ed., *Growth in America*, p. 78. For a sophisticated critique of scholars who failed to anticipate the renewed importance of ethnicity, see Walker Connor, "Nation-Building or Nation-Destroying?" *World Politics* 24 (April 1972): 319–55. See also S. M. Lipset, Racial and Ethnic Tensions in the Third World," in W. S. Thompson, ed., *The Third World* (San Francisco: Institute for Contemporary Studies, 1978) pp. 123–48.

16. See the essays in Daniel Bell, ed., *The Radical Right* (Garden City: N.Y.: Doubleday-Anchor Books, 1963).

17. I still find it a useful analytic concept. See S. M. Lipset and Earl Raab, *The Politics of Unreason: Right-Wing Extremism in America, 1970–1977* (Chicago: University of Chicago Press, Phoenix Edition, 1978).

18. For a review of the original writings and various critical commentaries see S. M. Lipset, "The End of Ideology and the Ideology of the Intellectuals," in Joseph Ben David and Terry Clark, eds., *Culture and Its Creators* (Chicago: University of Chicago Press, 1977), pp. 15–42.

19. For a discussion of the literature seeking to explain the student revolt, see S.M. Lipset, *Rebellion in the University* (Chicago: University of Chicago Press, Phoenix Edition, 1976), pp. 3–38.

20. Gabriel A. Almond and Stephen J. Genco, "Clouds, Clocks, and the Study of Politics," *World Politics* 29 (July 1977): 494.

21. Ida R. Hoos, *Systems Analysis in Social Policy* (London: The Institute of Economic Affairs, 1969), pp. 20–24.

22. Alvin Gouldner, "Toward a Radical Reconstruction of Sociology," *Social Policy* 1 (May–June, 1970): 21.

23. S.M. Lipset, "Why No Socialism in the United States?" in S. Bialer and S. Sluzar, eds., *Sources of Contemporary Radicalism* (Boulder, Co.: Westview Press, 1977), pp. 31–149, 346–63.

24. Robert K. Merton, *Social Theory and Social Structure* (New York: The Free Press, 1957), pp. 9–10, 280, 328.

25. Lee J. Cronbach, "Beyond the Two Disciplines of Scientific Psychology," *American Psychologist* 30 (February 1975): 122–23.

26. S.M. Lipset, *Political Man* (Garden City, N.Y.: Doubleday, 1960), pp. 100–101.

27. Robert E. Lane, "The Politics of Consensus in an Age of Affluence," *American Political Science Review* 59 (1965): 874–95, and "The Decline of Politics and Ideology in a Knowledgeable Society," *American Sociological Review* 31 (1966): 649–62.

28. See James D. Wright, *The Dissent of the Governed* (New York: Academic Press, 1976), pp. 168–200; S.M. Lipset and William Schneider, "How's Business? What the Public Thinks," *Public Opinion* 1 (July–August 1978): 41–47.

29. Lester Milbrath and M.L. Goel, *Political Participation* (Chicago: Rand McNally, 1977), pp. 90–106; S.M. Lipset, *Political Man*, pp. 182–84, 190–200, 214–15.

30. President's Commission, *Registration and Voting Participation* (Washington, D.C.: Government Printing Office, 1963).

31. James Q. Wilson, "On Pettigrew and Armor: An Afterword," *The Public Interest* No. 30 (Winter 1973): 133.

32. Donella H. Meadows et al., *The Limits to Growth* (New York: Universe Books, 1972); E.P. Schumacher, *Small is Beautiful* (London: Blond and Briggs, 1973). A comprehensive summary of the growth and no-growth positions as well as a detailed presentation of various scenarios related to different assumptions can be found in Edison Electric Institute, *Economic Growth in the Future* (New York: McGraw-Hill, 1976).

33. Macrae, "Future of International Business," pp. v–vi, x.

34. Herman Kahn, William Brown, and Leon Martel, *The Next 200 Years: A Scenario for America and the World* (New York: William Morrow, 1976), p. 1.

35. Lester R. Brown, *World Population Trends* (Washington, D.C.: Worldwatch Institute, 1976) and Bogue and Tsui, "Zero World Population Growth?" pp. 99–113.

36. U.S. Bureau of the Census, *World Population: 1977—Recent Demographic Estimates for the Countries and Regions of the World* (Washington, D.C.: 1978); Patrice Wingert, "Chinese Birthrate for '78 Down, Says Population Expert," *Houston Chronicle,* December 13, 1978, p. 8, Section 7; "Study Shows Drop in Mexico's Growth," *San Francisco Chronicle,* December 14, 1978, p. 11; Westoff, "Marriage and Fertility," pp. 51–57; "Indonesia Stressing a Lower Birth Rate," *New York Times,* February 18, 1979, p. 31.

37. Peter Grose, "Report at U.N. Says Rich-Poor Gap Can Be Narrowed by the Year 2000," *New York Times,* October 14, 1976, p.1; Wassily Leontief et al., *The Future of the World Economy* (New York: Oxford University Press, 1977).

38. Daniel Aaron, "Reflections on Growth and Literature in America," in Cooper, ed., *Growth in America,* pp. 152–53.

39. E.J. Mishan, "Ills, Bads, and Disamenities: The Wages of Growth," *Daedalus* 102 (Fall 1973): 74–75.

40. Willard R. Johnson, "Should the Poor Buy No Growth?" *Daedalus* 102 (Fall 1973): 165.

41. As quoted ibid.

42. David Potter, *People of Plenty: Economic Abundance and the American Character* (Chicago: University of Chicago Press, 1954).

43. Werner Sombart, *Why Is There No Socialism in the United States of America?* (White Plains, N.Y.: International Arts and Sciences Press, 1976).

44. Potter, *People of Plenty,* p. 102.

45. Malcolm Sawyer, "Income Distribution in OECD Countries," *OECD Economic Outlook* (July 1976): pp. 3–36.

46. Gunnar Myrdal, *An International Economy* (New York: Harper, 1956), p. 133. See Simon Kuznets, *Modern Economic Growth* (New Haven, Conn.: Yale University Press, 1966), p. 207.

47. See particularly the essays in Hollis Chenery et al., *Redistribution with Growth* (London: Oxford University Press, 1974).

48. For a review of the findings relevant to different aspects of inequality in the United States, see S.M. Lipset "Equality and Inequality," in Merton and Nisbet, eds., *Contemporary Social Problems,* pp. 305-53.

49. "Where the Grass Is Greener," *Economist,* December 25, 1971, p. 15.

50. Gideon Sjoberg, "Are Social Classes in America Becoming More Rigid?" *American Sociological Review* 16 (December 1951): 775-83.

51. Boulding, "Shadow of the Stationary State," p.95.

52. Robert L. Heilbroner, "Middle-Class Myths, Middle-Class Realities," *Atlantic* 238 (October 1976): 41.

53. Richard Zeckhauser, "The Risks of Growth," *Daedalus* 102 (Fall 1973): 103.

54. Lipset, *Political Man,* pp. 66-67.

55. Leon Trotsky, *The Revolution Betrayed* (Garden City, N.Y.: Doubleday, 1937).

56. Friedrich Engels, "On Authority," in Karl Marx and Friedrich Engels, *Basic Writings in Politics and Philosophy,* Lewis S. Feuer, ed. (Garden City, N.Y.: Doubleday, 1959), pp. 482-84.

57. Karl Marx and Friedrich Engels, *The German Ideology* (New York: International Publishers, 1947), p. 22.

58. See Joachim Israel, *Alienation from Marx to Modern Sociology* (Boston: Allyn & Bacon, 1971), p. 25.

59. For discussion of the Communist attitude to American productivity, see Lipset, "Why No Socialism in the United States?" pp. 78-79; Warren L. Susman, "Comment 1," in J.H.M. Laslett and S.M. Lipset, eds., *Failure of a Dream? Essays in the History of American Socialism* (Garden City, N.Y.: Anchor Press/Doubleday, 1974), pp. 450-51.

60. G.R. Barker, "La femme en Union Soviétique," *Sociologie et Sociétés,* 4 (November 1972): 180-81.

61. Trotsky, *Revolution Betrayed,* esp. p. 56.

62. Karl Wittfogel, *Oriental Despotism* (New Haven, Conn.: Yale University Press, 1957).

63. Mancur Olson, "Introduction," *Daedalus* 102 (Fall 1973): 8-9.

64. Klein, "Growth and its Enemies," p. 43.

65. Nathan Keyfitz, "World Resources and the World Middle Class," *Scientific American* 235 (July 1976): 32, 34.

CHAPTER 2/Davis

1. Calculated from data in Michael Drake, *Population and Society in Norway 1735-1865* (Cambridge: Cambridge University Press, 1969), pp. 195ff.

2. See my chapter on "The World's Population Crisis" in Robert K. Merton and Robert Nisbet, *Contemporary Social Problems,* 4th ed. (New York: Harcourt Brace Jovanovich, 1976).

3. The actual life expectancy in 1975 was 73.2 years; under the hypothesis stated, it would be 76.2.

4. For a more extended treatment of this topic, see my paper, "The Changing Family in Industrial Societies," in R.C. Jackson and J. Morton, eds., *Family Health Care* (Berkeley: School of Public Health, University of California, 1976).

5. See Eduardo E. Arriaga, *Mortality Decline and its Demographic Effects in Latin America* (Berkeley: Institute of International Studies, University of California, 1970).

6. United Nations, *World Population Prospects, 1970–2000, as Assessed in 1973* (New York, March 10, 1975), p. 12.

7. See my paper, "Asia's Cities: Problems and Options," *Population and Development Review*, vol. 1 (September 1975), pp. 71–86.

8. Ansley J. Coale and Melvin Zelnik, *New Estimates of Fertility and Population in the United States* (Princeton, N.J.: Princeton University Press, 1963), p. 36.

9. U.S. Bureau of the Census, "Demographic Aspects of Aging and the Older Population in the United States," *Current Population Reports*, Special Studies, Series P-23, No. 59 (May 1976), p. 51.

10. See Robert D. Retherford, *The Changing Sex Differential in Mortality* (Westport, Conn.: Greenwood Press, 1975): Samuel H. Preston, *Older Male Mortality and Cigarette Smoking: A Demographic Analysis* (Berkeley: Institute of International Studies, University of California, 1970).

CHAPTER 4/Elazar

1. See, for example, "Federal Government," *Encyclopedia of the Social Sciences* (New York: Macmillan, 1931); and *Fédéralisme Révolutionnaire*, issues 190–92 of *L'Europe en Formation* (1976).

2. See Perry Miller, *The American Puritans* (Garden City, N.Y.: Doubleday, 1956).

3. Alexis de Tocqueville, *Democracy in America* (V 835), vol. 1, part I, chap. 5 (New York: Knopf, 1963 [c1945]).

4. James Sundquist, *Making Federalism Work* (Washington, D.C.: Brookings Institution, 1969): and Daniel J. Elazar, *Toward a Generational Theory of American Politics* (Philadelphia, Pa.: Center for the Study of Federalism, 1970).

5. Daniel J. Elazar, *American Federalism: A View From the States*, 2nd ed. rev., (New York: Crowell, 1972); and "Federalism vs. Decentralization: The Drift from Authenticity," in Jeffrey Mayer, ed., *Dialogues on Decentralization, Publius*, vol. 6, no. 4 (Fall 1976), pp. 9–19.

6. Vincent Ostrom, *The Political Theory of a Compound Republic: A Reconstruction of the Logical Foundations of an American Democracy as Presented in The Federalist* (Blacksburg, Va.: Public Choice VPI, 1971).

7. Morton Grodzins, "The Federal System," in *Goals for America* (Englewood Cliffs, N.J.: Prentice-Hall, 1960), chap. 12.

8. See the Penguin series on the history of Great Britain.

9. Richard Rose, *The Politics in England Today; An Interpretation*, 2nd ed. (Boston: Little, Brown; London: Faber and Faber, 1974).

10. Morton Grodzins, *The American System* (Chicago: Rand McNally 1974), p. 277.

11. The position of the Nixon administration was made clear in the "New Federalist Papers" circulated within it and later published as "The Publius Symposium on the Future of American Federalism," *Publius,* vol. 2, no. 1 (Spring 1972).

12. See William Anderson, *The Nation and the States: Rivals or Partners?* (Minneapolis, Minn.: University of Minnesota Press, 1953); Jane Perry Clark, *The Rise of a New Federalism* (New York: Russell and Russell, 1965 [c1938]); Edward Corwin, *The Twilight of the Supreme Court* (New Haven: Yale University Press; London: H. Milford, Oxford University Press; 1934); Morton Grodzins, *The American System*; V. O. Key, Jr., *The Administration of Federal Grants to States* (Chicago: Public Administration Service, 1937).

13. See Daniel J. Elazar, *The American Partnership* (Chicago: University of Chicago Press, 1962).

14. For an attempt to differentiate between kinds of "cooperation," see James Sundquist, *Making Federalism Work;* and A. Lee Fritschler and Morley Segal, "Intergovernmental Relations and Contemporary Political Science: Developing an Integrative Typology," *Publius,* vol. 1, no. 2 (Winter 1972), pp. 95–122.

15. Walter Lippmann discusses the conflict between Jacobin and Anglo-American democracy in *The Public Philosophy* (Boston: Atlantic–Little, Brown, 1955), see particularly ch. 7.

16. Martin Diamond has developed a comprehensive view of federal democracy in "Democracy and the Federalist—A Reconsideration of the Framers' Intent," *American Political Science Review,* vol. 53 (March 1959), pp. 52–68; and in Martin Diamond, "The Ends of Federalism," in *The Federal Polity, Publius,* vol. 3, no. 2 (Fall 1973), and Martin Diamond, "The Forgotten Doctrine of Enumerated Powers," in *Publius,* vol. 6, no. 4 (Fall 1976), pp. 187–93.

17. To cite three exemplary opinion-molders of the time: for J. Allen Smith, the Progressive historian who wrote *The Spirit of American Government* (London: Macmillan, 1970), the checks and balances of federal democracy seemed to be no more than convenient barriers to the assertion of popular control over the governmental system. For Edward Bellamy, the utopian visionary, the advantages of a fully articulated technocratic hierarchy made the old system seem to be a dreadful device for wasting resources, *Looking Backward* (Cambridge, Mass.: Belknap Press, 1967). For Herbert Croly, the liberal attempting to turn bigness to public advantage, the federal system's opposition to unmitigated bigness was anachronistic, see his *The Promise of American Life* (Cambridge, Mass.: Harvard University Press, 1965).

18. See, for example, Edward Corwin, *The Commerce Clause of the Constitution* (Princeton, N.J.: Princeton University Press; London: H. Milford, Oxford University Press, 1936); and William W. Crosskey, *Politics and the Constitution* (Chicago: University of Chicago Press, 1953), particularly vol. II.

19. Harold Underwood Faulkner, *American Economic History,* 8th ed. (New York: Harper, 1960).

20. Daniel J. Elazar, *The American Partnership.*

21. Milton Kotler, *Neighborhood Government: The Local Foundations of Political Life* (Indianapolis and New York: Bobbs-Merrill, 1969).

22. See Arthur J. Viditch and Joseph Bensman, *Small Town in Mass Society*

(Princeton, N.J.: Princeton University Press, 1958); Daniel J. Elazar, "Constitutional Change in a Long-Depressed Civil Community: A Case Study of Duluth, Minnesota," *Proceedings of the Minnesota Academy of Science* 33 (1965); and Benjamin R. Schuster, "The Relationship Between Economic and Political Power in Three Midwestern Communities" (Ph.D. dissertation, Temple University, Department of Political Science, 1977).

23. See de Tocqueville's comments on this in vol. 1 of *Democracy in America;* also Russell Kirk, "The Prospects for Territorial Democracy," in Robert A. Goldwin, ed., *A Nation of States* (Chicago: Rand McNally, 1962).

24. G. Theodore Mitau, *Decade of Decision: The Supreme Court and the Constitutional Revolution 1954–1964* (New York: Scribner, 1967).

25. See Henry J. Abraham, *The Judiciary: The Supreme Court in the Governmental Process,* 4th ed. (Boston: Allyn and Bacon, 1977), chs. II and III; and Alexander Bickel, *The Supreme Court and the Idea of Progress* (New York: Harper and Row, 1970).

26. Marshall McLuhan, *The Medium is the Message* (New York: Random House, 1967).

27. *The Condition of Education: 1970 Edition, A Statistical Report on the Condition of Education in the United States,* vol. 3 part I. Compiled by Mary Golladay (Washington, D.C.: National Center for Educational Statistics, HEW, 1977).

28. See *Newsweek,* January 10, 1977, p. 49, and February 28, 1977, p. 98.

29. Norton Long has discussed this phenomenon as a factor in local politics in "The Local Community as an Ecology of Games," *American Journal of Sociology,* 64, no. 3 (November 1958). Morton Grodzins identifies and describes the ecology of complexes in the local community in some detail in Part Three of *The American System.*

30. This, indeed, is the thrust of so much of *The Federalist.* See Ostrom, *The Political Theory of a Compound Republic,* and Martin Diamond, "Notes on the Political Theory of the Founding Fathers" (Philadelphia, Pa.: Center for the Study of Federalism, 1971).

31. See Diamond, "Notes."

32. Peter Woll, *American Bureaucracy* (New York: Norton, 1963).

33. *National League of Cities v. Usery,* 96 Supreme Court 2465 (1976).

34. See Martin Landau, "Federalism, Redundancy and System Reliability," in *Publius,* vol. 3, no. 2 (Fall 1973), pp. 173–96; and Vincent Ostrom, *The Intellectual Crisis in American Public Administration* (University, Ala.: University of Alabama Press, 1974).

CHAPTER 5/Shapiro

1. See e.g., Arthur Von Mehren, *The Civil Law System* (Boston: Little, Brown, 1957), pp. 250–414.

2. Ibid.,: pp. 22–30, 63–70.

3. See particularly F. Geny, *Méthode d' interpretation et sources en droit privé*

positif (Paris: F. Pichon et Durand-Auzias, 1899); E. Ehrlich, *Freie Rechstfindung* (Leipzig: Hirschfield, 1903).

4. See Joseph Schacht, *The Origins of Muhammadan Jurisprudence* (Oxford: Clarendon Press, 1950).

5. See Thomas Metzger, *The Internal Organization of the Ching Bureaucracy* (Cambridge, Mass.: Harvard University Press, 1973).

6. See H.W.R. Wade, *Administrative Law*, 4th ed. (Oxford: Clarendon Press, 1977); M. Letourneur, J. Bauchet, J. Meric, *Le Conseil d'Etat et les Tribunaux Administratifs* (Paris: Armand Colin, 1970).

7. See Martin Shapiro, *The Supreme Court and Administrative Agencies* (New York: Free Press, 1968).

8. *United States v. Caroline Products,* 304 U.S. 144, fn. 4 (1937).

9. See Robert G. McCloskey, "Economic Due Process and the Supreme Court: An Exhumation and Reburial" in Phillip Kurland, ed., *1962 Supreme Court Review* 34 (1962); Frank R. Strong, "The Economic Philosophy of Lochner: Emergence, Embrasure and Emasculation," 15 *Arizona Law Review* 419 (1973); John Schmidhauser, *The Supreme Court As Final Arbiter in Federal-State Relations* (Chapel Hill N.C.: University of North Carolina Press, 1958).

10. See Martin Shapiro, *Freedom of Speech, The Supreme Court and Judicial Review* (Englewood Cliffs, N.J.: Prentice-Hall, 1966), pp. 58–59.

11. See Ralph S. Brown, *Loyalty and Security* (New Haven: Yale University Press, 1958).

12. See Norman Dorsen, Paul Bender, and Burt Neuborne, *Political and Civil Rights in the United States* 4th ed. (Boston: Little, Brown, 1976), 1:133–52.

13. Eventually, however, the Supreme Court did give them decisions somewhat limiting the offensive intrusions of the Immigration and Naturalization Service, and a landmark decision holding that citizenship once acquired could not be taken away again by legislative action.

14. See Gerald Gunther, "In Search of Evolving Doctrine on a Changing Court: A Model for a Newer Equal Protection," 86 *Harvard Law Review* 1, 8–10 (1972).

15. See Robert L. Rabin, "Job Security and Due Process," 44 *University of Chicago Law Review* 60 (1976). I have treated the continuity of the Supreme Court's concern for economic rights at greater length in Shapiro, "The Supreme Court and Economic Rights," in M. Judd Harmon, ed., *Essays on the Constitution of the United States* (Port Washington, N.Y.: Kennikat Press, 1978).

16. Cf. *Mass. Board of Retirement v. Murgia,* 96 S. Ct. 2562 (1976) with *City of New Orleans v. Dukes,* 96 S. Ct. 2513 (1976).

17. 424 U.S. 1 (1976).

18. 347 U.S. 483 (1954).

19. 411 U.S. 1 (1973).

20. *Miller v. California,* 413 U.S. 5 (1973).

21. *Lemon v. Kurtzman,* 403 U.S. 602 (1972); *Tilton v. Richardson,* 403 U.S. 672 (1971).

22. *Roe v. Wade,* 410 U.S. 113 (1973).

23. *Buckley v. Valeo,* 424 U.S. 1 (1976).

24. See Roscoe Pound, *Social Control Through Law* (Hamden, Conn.: Anchor Books, 1968).

25. *Government and Science* (New York: New York University Press, 1954).

26. See Robert Stevens, "Two Cheers for 1870: The American Law School," in Donald Fleming and Bernard Bailyn, eds., *Law in American History* (Boston: Little, Brown, 1971), pp. 435–41.

27. For an early linkage of law to science see Barbara Shapiro, "Law and Science in Seventeenth-Century England," 21 *Stanford Law Review* 727 (1969). For an interesting attempt to recapture the name science for law see Harold Berman, "The Origins of Western Legal Science," 90 *Harvard Law Review* 894 (1977).

28. See e.g., Louis Jaffee, *Judicial Control of Administrative Action* (Boston: Little, Brown, 1965).

29. See James March and Herbert Simon, *Organizations* (New York: John Wiley, 1958); Michel Crozier, *The Bureaucratic Phenomenon* (Chicago: University of Chicago Press, 1964); Anthony Downs, *Inside Bureaucracy* (Boston: Little, Brown, 1967); James Q. Wilson, *Political Organizations* (New York: Basic Books, 1973).

30. A major sign of the change of mood was the widely cited K.C. Davis, *Discretionary Justice: A Preliminary Inquiry* (Baton Rouge, La.: Louisiana State University Press, 1969).

31. See Shapiro, *Supreme Court and Administrative Agencies,* pp. 52–54.

32. While the general current has been toward a broader and broader conception of standing, there has been some retrenchment from the most extreme position. See K.C. Davis, *Administrative Law of the Seventies* (Rochester, N.Y.: Lawyers Cooperative, 1976).

33. On the importance of taking transaction costs of litigation into account see Jerome Posner, *Economic Analysis of Law* (Boston: Little, Brown, 1972).

CHAPTER 7/Ladd

1. Alexis de Tocqueville, *Democracy in America* (New York: Doubleday Anchor Books edition, 1969), p. 177.

2. Ibid. The emphasis is mine.

3. Clinton Rossiter, *Parties and Politics in America* (Ithaca, N.Y.: Cornell University Press, 1960), p. 1.

4. I should emphasize that my commentary here on party functions and on the requisite capabilities for such functions is intended to apply only to the United States. Some of the observations may fit other polities, but many clearly do not. My discussion of "planning," for example, presupposes a party system in which there are at least two—and scarcely if ever more than two—major parties, each pursuing an absolute electoral majority.

5. Everett Carll Ladd, Jr. and Seymour Martin Lipset, "How Faculty Members Expect to Vote," *The Chronicle of Higher Education,* November 1, 1976, pp. 4–6.

6. Everett Carll Ladd, Jr., with Charles D. Hadley, *Transformations of the American Party System* (New York: Norton, 1975), p. 273.

7. For the full text of the recommendations, see *Mandate for Reform: A Report of the Commission on Party Structure and Delegate Selection to the Democratic National Committee,* 1970.

8. The conference was held in Kansas City, Missouri, December 6–8, 1974, and was attended by some 2,000 delegates. This off-year meeting had been mandated by the 1972 Democratic Convention.

9. See "Delegate Selection Rules for the 1976 Democratic National Convention," adopted by the Democratic National Committee, March 1, 1974.

10. James Reston, "Does it Really Matter," *New York Times,* October 20, 1976.

11. "What Will Sway Voters when Election Day Comes; Interview with Richard M. Scammon, Director, Elections Research Center," *U.S. News and World Report,* October 25, 1976, p. 30.

12. Jeane Kirkpatrick, *The New Presidential Elite* (New York: Russell Sage Foundation and the Twentieth Century Fund, 1976), esp. pp. 281–331.

13. Myra MacPherson, "They Came with the Accents of Home," *Washington Post,* July 12, 1976. For comparable data on Democrats in the general population, I have drawn on April to October 1976 surveys of Yankelovich, Skelly, and White.

14. Barry Sussman, "Electorate More Moderate than Poles-Apart Party Workers," *Washington Post,* September 27, 1976, pp. A–1, A–2.

15. Sidney Verba and Norman H. Nie, *Participation in America: Political Democracy and Social Equality* (New York: Harper and Row, 1972). Verba and Nie note that "If participants came proportionately from all parts of society. . . then political leaders who respond to participation will be responding to an accurate representation of the needs, desires, and preferences of the public at large" (p. 12). But in fact, they quickly observe, "the participants are by no means representative of the public as a whole but come disproportionately from particular—especially upper-status—groups. . . ." The most highly participant Americans, whom Verba and Nie label "complete activists," manifest an extraordinary overrepresentation of the college educated and the above average in income (p.100). In general, the correlation between participation rate and socioeconomic status is exceptionally high, dwarfing the relationship between participation and any other aspect of social status. When we examine the social standing of 1976 presidential primary voters, we find the expected skewing toward the higher socioeconomic classes. In every state, NBC and CBS–New York Times survey data show, the primary voters come disproportionately from the ranks of these overlapping groups: the college trained, the professional middle class, and those of upper-middle to high income.

16. Yankelovich, Skelly, and White, Survey No. 8510, April 1976; and Survey No. 8520, June 1976.

17. *The Harris Report,* March 18, 1976; April 29, 1976; June 3, 1976; and August 2, 1976.

18. The analysis of Jeane Kirkpatrick, while confined to 1972 national convention delegates, supports this general line of interpretation. Kirkpatrick, *New Presidential Elite,* esp. chs. 4 and 5.

19. A number of studies have confirmed the general outlines of the above description. See Aaron Wildavsky, "The Goldwater Phenomenon: Purists, Politicians, and the Two-Party System," *Review of Politics* 27 (July 1965): 386–413; Wildavsky, "The Meaning of 'Youth' in the Struggle for Control of the Democratic

Party," in his collected essays, *The Revolt Against the Masses* (New York: Basic Books, 1971), pp. 270–87; and James Q. Wilson, *The Amateur Democrat* (Chicago: The University of Chicago Press, 1962).

20. I have shifted usage here, for the Republican weakness to which I refer is primarily of the "party in the electorate," rather than of party organization.

21. The data are from American Institute of Public Opinion (Gallup) surveys 430, 431, 432, and 433.

22. Gallup surveys 697, 699, 701, and 702 for 1964; 915 and 916 for 1974.

23. Robert Reinhold, "Carter Victory Laid to Democrats Back in Fold, Plus Independents," *New York Times,* November 4, 1976, p. 25.

24. For discussion of the polls of Harvard student preference, see S.M. Lipset, "Political Controversies at Harvard," in Lipset and Riesman, *Education and Politics at Harvard* (New York: McGraw-Hill, 1975), ch. 8.

25. For supporting data, see Lipset and Ladd, "College Generations: From the 1930's to the 1960's," *Public Interest* 25, Fall 1971, pp. 105–9.

26. *The Gallup Opinion Index,* no. 109, July 1974, p. 15.

27. Ibid.

28. CBS News Election Day Survey, data made available to the Social Science Data Center, University of Connecticut, courtesy of CBS News.

29. *The Gallup Opinion Index,* no. 88, October 1972, p. 3.

30. For supporting data and analysis, see Ladd and Lipset, *The Divided Academy: Professors and Politics* (New York: McGraw-Hill, 1975), chs. 5 and 9.

31. Samuel Beer, "Liberalism and the National Idea," *Public Interest,* Fall 1966, pp. 70–82.

32. See, for example, Kevin Phillips, *Mediacracy: American Parties and Politics in the Communications Age* (Garden City, N.Y.: Doubleday, 1975), esp. pp. 95–101.

CHAPTER 8/Dunlop

1. *Socialism and the Social Movement,* translated from the sixth "enlarged" German edition with introduction and notes by M. Epstein (New York: Dutton, 1909), pp. 267–78.

2. *Misleaders of Labor,* Trade Union Educational League (1927), p. 334.

3. "American Trade Unionism and Social Insurance," *American Economic Review* (March 1933); 1–8.

4. Paul Jacobs, *The State of the Unions* (New York: Atheneum, 1963). The last chapter is a reprinting of "Old Before Its Time: Collective Bargaining at Twenty-Eight," p. 292. See many others on similar negative themes: Irving Kristol, "Writing About Unions," *New York Times Book Review,* February 1, 1970; Daniel Bell, *The End of Ideology* (Glencoe, Ill.: The Free Press, 1960), pp. 208–21.

5. E. Levasseur, *The American Workman,* Theodore Marburg, ed. (Baltimore: Johns Hopkins Press, 1900), pp. 490–509. He is particularly interesting in the contrasts drawn between European and American workers.

6. See John T. Dunlop, "The American Industrial Relations System in 1975," in Jack Stieber, ed., *U. S. Industrial Relations: The Next Twenty Years* (East Lansing: Michigan State University Press, 1958), pp. 27–48; "The Development of Labor Organization: A Theoretical Framework" in Richard A. Lester and Joseph Shister, eds., *Insight into Labor Issues* (New York: Macmillan, 1948), pp.163–93.

7. Selig Perlman, *A Theory of the Labor Movement* (New York: Macmillan, 1928), pp. ix, 5–6.

8. One is reminded of Lenin's comment, "The spontaneous labour movement is able by itself to create (and inevitably will create) only trade unionism, and working class trade-union politics are precisely working-class bourgeois politics" (V.I. Lenin, *What Is To Be Done? Burning Questions of Our Movement* [New York: International Publishers, 1929], p. 92).

9. Harold L. Wilensky, *Intellectuals in Labor Unions, Organizational Pressures on Professional Roles* (Glencoe, Ill.: The Free Press, 1956).

10. George Meany accepted the Eugene V. Debs award on March 31, 1977. In an acceptance speech he said, "Yes, we have come a long, long way since Debs's day. Many of his ideas did not stand the test of time and have fallen by the wayside. Many of his visions for the labor movement have been fulfilled, even if not in ways he expected. Much more remains to be done on the road to achieving a more democratic, a more just and a more equalitarian society."

11. Louis Adamic, *Dynamite, The Story of Class Violence in America,* rev. ed. (New York: Viking, 1934), pp. 194–5.

12. William Z. Foster, *Misleaders of Labor* (Trade Union Educational League, 1927), p. 9.

13. This list generally corresponds to the headings of the chapters in *Misleaders of Labor,* ibid.

14. *Trade Unions in the New Society* (New York: Viking, 1949), p. 41. (The substance of this book derives from The Sidney Hillman Lectures for 1949.)

15. Leo Troy, Trade Union Membership, 1897–1962, Occasional Paper 92 (New York: National Bureau of Economic Research, 1965), p. 8. There were 1.8 million union members in 1955 unaffiliated with the AFL or CIO federations for a total of 17 million.

16. See, The *UAW Administrative Letters* for 1966–68 and *To Clear the Record, AFL-CIO Executive Council Report on the Disaffiliation of the UAW,* 1969.

17. Derek C. Bok and John T. Dunlop, *Labor and The American Community* (New York: Simon and Schuster, 1970), pp. 30–34.

18. Selig Perlman, *A Theory of the Labor Movement,* p. 281.

19. Morris Hillquit, Samuel Gompers, and Max J. Hayes, *The Double Edge of Labor's Sword, Discussion and Testimony on Socialism and Trade-Unionism Before the Commission on Industrial Relations* (New York: Socialist Literature Company, 1914), p. 134.

20. A National Conference to Examine American Labor's Stake and Voice in a Changing World Economy (Port Chester, N.Y., December 15, 1976).

21. Nick Kotz, "Oilcan Eddie Takes On the Old Guard," *New York Times Magazine,* December 19, 1976, p. 32. The subtitle is instructive: "A rebel candidate for president of the steelworkers wants to move his union—and the whole labor movement—back to the class struggle."

22. See, Walter Galenson, *The CIO Challenge to the AFL* (Cambridge, Mass.: Harvard University Press, 1960).

23. Charles E. Lindblom, *Unions and Capitalism* (New Haven: Yale University Press, 1949), p. 139. Also see Philip D. Bradley, ed., *The Public Stake in Union Power* (Charlottesville: University of Virginia Press, 1959). For a substantive discussion of this full range of issues, see Bok and Dunlop, *Labor and the American Community,* pp. 207–360.

24. It is, of course, an appropriate intellectual exercise to explain the character of American workers and their political behavior in American society. See, for example, the interesting paper by S.M. Lipset, "Radicalism in North America: A Comparative View of the Party Systems in Canada and the United States," 1976, in *Transactions of The Royal Society of Canada,* Series iv, v, xiv (1976), pp. 19–55.

25. Daniel Bell, *The End of Ideology* (Glencoe, Ill.: The Free Press, 1960), p. 213.

26. Sumner H. Slichter, "The American System of Industrial Relations: Contrasts with Foreign Systems," January 1955, reprinted in *Potentials of the American Economy, Selected Essays in Honor of Sumner H. Slichter,* ed. by John T. Dunlop (Cambridge, Mass.: Harvard University Press, 1961), pp. 285–6.

27. The present discussion makes no attempt to describe and to explain the structure and operation of American unions and collective bargaining. For these topics, see Bok and Dunlop, *Labor and the American Community;* John T. Dunlop, "Past and Future Tendencies in American Labor Organization," *Daedalus,* Winter 1978; Lloyd Ulman, *The Rise of the National Trade Union* (Cambridge, Mass.: Harvard University Press, 1955).

28. Solomon Barkin, "A New Agenda for Labor," *Fortune,* November 1960.

29. George Strauss, "Workers: Attitudes and Adjustments," in *The Worker and the Job, Coping With Change,* Jerome M. Rosow, ed., The American Assembly (Englewood Cliffs, N.J.: Prentice-Hall, 1974), pp. 74–75. (There are technical difficulties with the Gallup Poll. See Robert Quinn, Thomas Mangione, and Martha Mandilovitch, "Evaluating Working Conditions in America," *Monthly Labor Review,* November 1973, p. 39.) Also see, in the same American Assembly volume, Peter Henle, "Economic Effects: Reviewing the Evidence," pp. 119–44.

30. Robert J. Flanagan, George Strauss, and Lloyd Ulman, "Worker Discontent and Work Place Behavior" *Industrial Relations* (May 1974); 101–23.

31. See Quinn, Mangione, and Mandilovitch, "Evaluating Working Conditions in America."

32. See *Employment and Training Report of the President,* U.S. Department of Labor (Washington, D.C., 1976), pp. 147–57 ("The Changing Nature of Work").

33. Arnold S. Tanenbaum, "Systems of Formal Participation," in *Organizational Behavior, Research and Issues,* Industrial Relations Research Association Series (1974), p. 78.

34. *Report of the Committee on Inquiry on Industrial Democracy,* Cmnd. 6706; *TUC Guide to the Bullock Report on Industrial Democracy,* The Trades Union Congress (London, February 1977); B.C. Roberts, "Participation by Agreement," *Lloyds Bank Review,* no. 125 (July 1977), pp. 12–23; *The Economist* 13–19 (November 1976): 105.

35. Report, p. 160.

36. Thomas R. Donohue, "The Future of Collective Bargaining," *AFL-CIO Free Trade Union News* (September 1976), p. 6.

37. John T. Dunlop, "The Settlement of Emergency Disputes," *Proceedings of the Fifth Annual Meeting, Industrial Relations Research Association,* December 28–29, 1952: "I believe that in twenty-five years the emergency dispute will have ceased to be a serious question."

38. Alfred Marshall, *Elements of Economics of Industry* (London: Macmillan, 1893), ch. XIII, "Trade Unions," pp. 374–411.

39. National Center for Productivity and Quality of Working Life, *Directory of Labor-Management Committees* (Washington, D.C., October 1976); William Gomberg, "Special Study Committees," in *Frontiers of Collective Bargaining,* John T. Dunlop and Neil W. Chamberlain, eds. (New York: Harper and Row, 1967), pp. 235–51.

40. Arthur Okun, "Conflicting National Goals," in *Jobs for Americans,* The American Assembly (Englewood Cliffs, N.J. 1976), p. 81.

41. John T. Dunlop, "Wage and Price Controls as Seen By a Controller," Industrial Relations Research Association, *Proceedings of the 1975 Annual Spring Meeting,* May 8–10, 1975, pp. 457–63. See Committee for Economic Development, *Fighting Inflation and Promoting Growth,* August 1976, pp. 62–67.

42. Benjamin Aaron, "The Impact of Public Employment Grievance Settlement on the Labor Arbitration Process," in Benjamin Aaron, et al., *The Future of Labor Arbitration* (New York: American Arbitration Association, 1976), p. 48.
    Also see Harry T. Edwards, "Labor Arbitration at the Crossroad: The 'Common Law of the Shop' versus External Law," *Arbitration Journal,* June 1977.

43. Michael J. Piore, "The 'New Immigration' and the Presumptions of Social Policy," Industrial Relations Research Association, *Proceedings of the Twenty-Seventh Annual Winter Meeting,* December 28–29, 1974, pp. 350–8.

44. On several occasions, I have sought to outline the future course of development of American unions and collective bargaining. See John T. Dunlop, "The American Industrial Relations System in 1975," *U. S. Industrial Relations: The Next Twenty Years,* Jack Stieber, ed. (East Lansing, Mich., 1958), pp. 1–24; "Future Trends in Industrial Relations in the United States" (paper presented to the Third World Congress, International Industrial Relations Association, London, December 1973. Unpublished).

45. A.H. Raskin, "The Obsolescent Unions," *Commentary* (July 1963): 18.

CHAPTER 9/Greeley

1. Andrew M. Greeley, *Crisis in the Church* (Chicago: Thomas More Press, to be published 1979).

2. Andrew M. Greeley, with William C. McCready and Kathleen McCourt, *Catholic Schools in a Declining Church* (Mission, Ka.: Sheed and Ward, 1976).

3. Charles Westoff and Larry Bumpass, "Revolution in Birth Control Practices of United States Roman Catholics," *Science* 179 (January 1973): 41–44.

4. Andrew M. Greeley, *The Catholic Experience: A Sociologist's Interpretation of the History of American Catholicism* (New York: Doubleday, 1967).

5. Kenneth R. Hardy, "Social Origins of American Scientists and Scholars," *Science* (August 9, 1975): 497–506.

6. Andrew M. Greeley, *The American Catholic: A Social Portrait* (New York: Basic Books, 1977).

CHAPTER 11/Patterson

1. See my paper, "Toward a Future That Has No Past: On the Fate of Blacks in the Americas," *Public Interest*, no. 27 (Spring 1972): 25–62.

2. See Eric R. Wolf and Sid W. Mintz, "Hacienda and Plantations in Middle America and the Antilles," *Social and Economic Studies* 6 (September 1957): 380–412.

3. See Eric Foner, *Free Soil, Free Labor, Free Men* (New York, 1970).

4. See Winthrop Jordan, *White Over Black* (Chapel Hill, N.C., 1968); idem, "Modern Tensions and the Origins of American Slavery," *Journal of Southern History* 28 (February 1962). See also Gary B. Nash, *Red, White and Black* (Englewood Cliffs, N.J., 1974); Edgar J. McManus, *Black Bondage in the North* (Syracuse, 1973); Leon Litwak, *North of Slavery* (Chicago, 1961); and Mervyn Ratekin, "The Early Sugar Industry in Espanola," *Hispanic American Historical Review* 34 (1954).

5. See Rolando Mellaje, *Negro Slavery in Latin America* (Berkeley, 1975); chap. 4; Colin A. Palmer, *Slaves of the White God: Blacks in Mexico, 1570–1650,* esp. chaps. 2 and 3.

6. It is not being suggested that this was the sole reason for the decline. See Woodrow Borah, *New Spain's Century of Depression* (Berkeley, 1954); Earl J. Hamilton, "The Decline of Spain," in E.M. Carus-Wilson, ed., *Essays in Economic History* (London, 1958), pp. 215–26; for a review of recent studies and general interpretation, see Immanuel Wallerstein, *The Modern World System* (New York, 1974), pp. 191–6.

7. On which, see Arturo Morales-Carrión, *Puerto Rico and the Non-Hispanic Caribbean* (Rio Piedras, 1952); and Franklyn Knight, *Slave Society in Cuba During the Nineteenth Century* (Madison, Wis., 1970).

8. See Marian Malowist, "Les Débuts du système des plantations dans la période des grandes découvertes," *Africana Bulletin* 10 (1969); for a useful recent review and assessment see Sidney W. Mintz, "The So-Called World System: Local Initiative and Local Response," *Dialectical Anthropology* 2, 4 (1977). For an excellent discussion of the nature of the plantation system see Jay R. Mandle, "The Plantation: An Essay in Definition," *Science and Society* 36 (Spring 1972).

9. For a good example of this ambivalence and its effects, see the case of seventeenth-century Jamaica, in Orlando Patterson, *The Sociology of Slavery* (Rutherford, N.J., 1969), pp. 15–27.

10. See W.L. Westermann, *The Slave Systems of Greek and Roman Antiquity,* (New York, 1964), p. 58; Jules Toutain, *The Economic Life of the Ancient World* (New York, 1968), p. 192.

11. Of the vast literature on this subject, see in particular, W.E. Heitland, *Agricola* (Cambridge, England, 1921); P.A. Brunt, *Italian Manpower, 225 B.C.–A.D. 14* (Oxford, 1971); Cato and Varro, *De Re Rustica*, trans. W. D. Hooper and H. B. Ash (Cambridge, Mass., 1967); K.D. White, "Latifundia, A Critical Review of the Evidence on Large Estates in Italy and Sicily up to the End of the First Century A.D.," London University, Institute of Classical Studies, *Bulletin* 14 (1967).

12. See Mary L. Gordon, "The Nationality of Slaves Under the Early Roman Empire," in M.I. Finley, ed., *Slavery in Classical Antiquity* (Cambridge, England, 1964), pp. 131–89; A. Duff, *Freedmen in the Early Roman Empire* (Oxford, 1928).

13. See Jordan, *White Over Black* for a review of the literature on this problem.

14. For the definitive Marxist synthesis by a Western scholar see E.C. Welskopf, *Die Productionsverhältnisse im alten Orient und in der griechisch-römischen Antike* (Berlin, 1957).

15. M. Weber, "The Social Causes of the Decay of Ancient Civilization," in J.E. Eldridge, ed., *The Interpretation of Social Reality* (London, 1970).

16. See the papers on this thesis in *Revue Francaise d'histoire d'outre-mer*, tome 62, nos. 226–27 (1975); R.T. Anstey, "Capitalism and Slavery: A Critique," *Economic History Review* 2nd ser. 21 (1968): 307–20.

17. See A.E. Smith, *Colonists in Bondage: White Servitude and Convict Labor in America, 1607–1776* (Chapel Hill, 1947).

18. Roger Anstey, "The Volume and Profitability of the British Slave Trade, 1761–1807," in S.L. Engerman and E.D. Genovese, eds., *Race and Slavery in the Western Hemisphere* (Princeton, N.J., 1975), pp. 3–24.

19. Eric J. Hobsbawm, "The Seventeenth Century in the Development of Capitalism," reprinted in E.D. Genovese, ed., *The Slave Economies* (New York, 1973), vol. 1, pp. 145–60.

20. Ibid. p. 155.

21. Ibid. p. 156.

22. Ibid. p. 167.

23. See Philip Curtin, *The Atlantic Slave Trade: A Census* (Madison, Wis., 1969); and S.F. Cook and W. Borah, *Essays in Population History: Mexico and the Caribbean,* 2 vols. (Berkeley, 1971, 1974); see also Engerman and Genovese, eds., *Race and Slavery,* papers in part 2; R.W. Fogel and S.L. Engerman, *Time on the Cross* (Boston, 1974), ch. 1.

24. Fogel and Engerman, *Time on the Cross;* Cecil Gray, *History of Agriculture in the Southern United States to 1860* (Washington, 1933).

25. J.E. Eblen, "On the Natural Increase of Slave Populations: The Example of the Cuban Slave Population, 1775–1900," in S. Engerman and E.D. Genovese, eds., *Race and Slavery in the Western Hemisphere: Quantitative Studies* (Princeton, N.J., 1975); Knight, *Slave Society in Cuba.*

26. H.S. Klein, "The Trade in African Slaves to Rio de Janeiro, 1795–1811," in *Journal of African History* 10 (1969): 533–49.

27. See E.D. Genovese, *Roll, Jordan, Roll* (New York, 1974), pp 49–70.

28. S. Mintz, *Caribbean Transformation* (Chicago, 1974); O. Patterson, *Sociology of Slavery,* ch. 8.

29. Patterson, *Sociology of Slavery,* ch. 7. See also E. Brathwaite, *The Development of Creole Society in Jamaica, 1770–1820* (Oxford, 1971); S. Mintz and R. Price, *Anthropological Approach to the Afro-American Past: A Caribbean Perspective* (Philadelphia, 1976).

30. Genovese, *Roll, Jordan, Roll.*

31. S. Elkins, *Slavery* (Chicago, 1959).For criticisms, see A. Lane, ed., *The Debate Over Slavery* (Urbana, 1971).

32. "Quashie" was the West Indian counterpart of the "Sambo" stereotype. See Patterson, *Sociology of Slavery,* ch. 6.

33. On which, see David Lowenthal, *West Indian Societies* (New York, 1972), ch. 7; F. Henriques, *Family and Colour in Jamaica* (London, 1953).

34. The same, of course, is true of the black American middle classes. See John Dollard, *Caste and Class in a Southern Town* (New York, 1937); E.F. Frazier, *Black Bourgeoisie* (New York, 1962).

35. Genovese, *Roll, Jordan, Roll.*

36. Douglas F. Dowd, "A Comparative Analysis of Economic Development in the American West and South," reprinted in H.D. Woodman, ed., *Slavery and the Southern Economy* (New York, 1966), p. 244.

37. Ibid. p. 247.

38. M. Rothstein, "The Antebellum South as a Dual Economy: A Tentative Hypothesis," in Genovese, ed., *The Slave Economies,* vol. 2, pp. 157–70. For a review of the literature on the problem of Southern backwardness, see S. Engerman, "Marxist Economic Studies of the Slave South," in *Marxist Perspective,* vol. 1, no. 1 (Spring 1978): 148–64.

39. Dowd, "A Comparative Analysis," p. 252.

40. Ibid. p. 253.

41. For this discussion of the urbanization of the black population, I have drawn mainly on the following: R. Farley, "The Urbanization of Negroes in the United States," *Journal of Social History* (Spring 1968); 241–58; R. Farley, *Growth of the Black Population* (Chicago, 1970); Daniel O. Price, "Urbanization of the Blacks," in *The Milibank Memorial Fund Quarterly, Demographic Aspects of the Black Community* 48, 2 (April 1970), part 2, pp. 47–58. For the specific case of Chicago, see St. Clair Drake and Horace R. Cayton, *Black Metropolis* (New York, 1945), part 1.

42. I draw here on Price, "Urbanization of the Blacks."

43. Harold M. Rose, *Black Suburbanization* (Cambridge, Mass., 1976), p. 1.

44. Ibid, p. 8.

45. See August Meier and Elliott M. Rudwick, *From Plantation to Ghetto* (New York, 1969), ch. 6; for the standard work on black labor during this period see S.D. Spero and Abram L. Harris, *The Black Worker* (New York, 1968). See also Herman P. Miller, "Progress and Prospect for the Negro Worker," in R.J. Murphy and H. Elinson, eds., *Problems and Prospects for the Negro Movement* (Belmont, Ca., 1966), pp. 108–16. Still valuable is Drake and Cayton, *Black Metropolis,* chs. 9–12.

46. K. Arrow, "Models of Discrimination," in A.H. Pascal, ed., *Racial Discrimination in Economic Life* (Lexington, Mass., 1972), p. 100.

47. Fogel and Engerman, *Time on the Cross*; for criticisms of this thesis, see P. David et al., *Reckoning with Slavery* (New York, 1976). These criticisms do not, however, undermine the view that the slave worker was more efficient than the south European peasants.

48. On which, see Herbert Gutman, *The Black Family in Slavery and Freedom, 1750–1925* (New York, 1976).

49. See Martin Kilson, "The Political Status of American Negroes in the Twentieth Century," in M.L. Kilson and R.I. Rothberg, eds., *The African Diaspora* (Cambridge, Mass., 1976), pp. 459–84.

50. See J.R. Washington, *Black Religion* (Boston, 1964), ch. 2; E.F. Frazier, *The Negro Church in America* (New York, 1964); Gary T. Marx, "Religion, Opiate or Inspiration of Civil Rights Militancy Among Negroes?" *American Sociological Review* 32 (1967): 64–72. See also Drake and Cayton, *Black Metropolis*, pp. 412–29.

51. See E. David Cronon, *Black Moses: The Story of Marcus Garvey and the United Negro Improvement Association* (Madison, 1955). See also Harold Isaacs, *The New World of Negro Americans* (New York, 1964), pp. 114–72; and Theodore Draper, *The Rediscovery of Black Nationalism* (New York, 1969), pp. 48–56.

52. H. Gutman, *The Black Family;* Fogel and Engerman, *Time on the Cross*, vol. 1, pp. 126–44; John W. Blassingame, *The Slave Community* (New York, 1972), ch. 3.

53. Gutman, *The Black Family*, p. 433.

54. Jessie Bernard, *Marriage and Family Among Negroes* (Englewood Cliffs, N.J., 1966), p. 24.

55. Ibid., pp. 14, 24. For a more recent, and detailed analysis, see Farley, *Growth of the Black Population*, pp. 127–91.

56. Bernard, *Marriage and Family*, pp. 19–23.

57. Ibid, ch. 2.

58. On which see Oscar Lewis, *Anthropological Essays* (New York, 1970), ch. 4; Charles A. Valentine, *Culture and Poverty* (Chicago, 1968); Eleanor Burke Leacock, ed., *The Culture of Poverty: A Critique* (New York, 1971).

59. See, in particular, the classic study by Drake and Cayton, Black Metropolis, especially part iii; and more recently, St. Clair Drake, "The Social and Economic Status of the Negro in the United States," in T. Parsons and K.B. Clark, eds., *The Negro American* (Boston, 1965), pp. 13–46.

60. Robin Williams, *Mutual Accommodation: Ethnic Conflict and Cooperation* (Minneapolis, 1977), p. 5.

61. Ibid, p. 7.

62. Ibid, p. 23.

63. Dan Lacy, *The White Use of Blacks in America* (New York, 1972), pp. 230–1.

64. Cited in Dorothy K. Newman, et al., *Protest, Politics and Prosperity* (New York, 1977), p. 25.

65. On which see John R. Howard, *The Cutting Edge* (New York, 1974), pp. 67–87.

66. Richard B. Freeman, *Black Elite* (New York, 1976), p. 1.

67. Sar Levitan et al., *Still a Dream* (Cambridge, Mass. 1976), p. 41.

68. Ibid, p. 53.
69. Ibid, p. 69.
70. Newman, et al., *Protest,* p. 149.
71. Ibid, pp. 116–30.
72. Levitan et al., *Still a Dream,* p. 161.
73. For the standard demographic work on black segregation see Karl E. Taeuber and Alma F. Taeuber, *Negroes in Cities* (Chicago, 1965). On the social consequences of segregation see Lee Rainwater, *Behind Ghetto Walls* (Chicago, 1970), esp. Introduction and chs. 1, 11, 13, and 14. For a review of findings on the social and psychological consequences of segregation and desegregation, see Edward A. Suchman, et al., *Desegregation: Some Propositions and Research Suggestions* (New York, 1958), esp. pp. 47–75. And for the effects of segregation on interracial perceptions see Thomas F. Pettigrew, *Racially Separate or Together?* (New York, 1969).
74. Newman, et al., *Protest,* pp. 67, 60–75.
75. William Julius Wilson, *The Declining Significance of Race* (Chicago, 1978), p. 19.
76. A. Wohlstetter and S. Coleman, "Race Differences in Income," in A.H. Pascal, ed., *Racial Discrimination in Economic Life* (Lexington, Mass., 1972).
77. Ibid, p. 15.
78. Freeman, *Black Elite,* pp. 36–37.
79. This has been accompanied by a substantial degree of class segregation within the black group. See Taeuber and Taeuber, *Negroes in Cities,* pp. 180–4.
80. Freeman, *Black Elite,* p. 216.
81. Bernard, *Marriage and Family.* There is a large and growing literature on the subject. We cite here only those works we have consulted: Kenneth B. Clark, *Dark Ghetto* (New York, 1965); Lee Rainwater, *Behind Ghetto Walls;* Thomas Kochman, ed., *Rappin' and Stylin' Out* (Urbana, 1972); Elliot Liebow, *Tally's Corner* (Boston, 1967); Henry Etzkowitz and Gerald M. Schaflander, *Ghetto Crisis* (Boston, 1969); Ulf Hannerz, *Soulside: Inquiries Into Ghetto Culture and Community* (New York, 1969); E.B. Leacock, ed., *The Culture of Poverty: A Critique,* part 2; Roger Abrahams, *Deep Down in the Jungle* (Hartsboro, Pa., 1964); Charles Keil, *Urban Blues* (Chicago, 1966); Lee Rainwater, ed., *Soul* (New Brunswick, N.J., 1973); William McCord, John Howard, Bernard Friedberg, Edwin Harwood, *Life Styles in the Black Ghetto* (New York, 1969); Charles Valentine, *Culture and Poverty* (Chicago, 1968).
82. McCord, et al., *Life Styles,* part 2; for another discussion of typical ghetto roles and styles, see, H.C. Ellis and S.M. Newman, " 'Gowster,' 'Ivy-Leaguer,' 'Hustler,' 'Conservative,' 'Mackman,' and 'Continental,' A Functional Analysis of Six Ghetto Roles," in Leacock, ed., *Culture of Poverty,* pp. 299–314.
83. McCord, el al., *Life Styles,* pp. 146–63. In their study of opiate addiction in the slums, Glaser et al. found that the typical addict "came to the slum at an earlier age and stayed at home less." See D. Glaser, B. Lander, and W. Abbott, "Opiate Addiction in a Slum Area," in Lee Rainwater, ed., *Deviance and Liberty* (Chicago, 1974), p. 190.
84. For a grim catalog of the statistics on black crime, see Leonard D. Savitz, "Black Crime," in Kent S. Miller and Ralph Mason, eds., *Comparative Studies of*

Blacks and Whites in the U.S. (New York, 1973). Savitz finds a deliquency rate of 742 per 1000 blacks compared with 158 for whites. In Philadelphia, black men were 12 times more likely to be convicted of rape than whites and about 90 percent of all urban black men will acquire a police record sometime during their lives. For a psychosocial analysis see T.F. Pettigrew, *A Profile of the Negro American* (Princeton, N.J., 1964), pp. 136–56.

85. John Horton, "Time and Cool People," in Kochman, *Rappin,'* pp. 19–31.

86. Elliot Liebow, *Tally's Corner,* p. 214.

87. Ibid, p. 215.

88. Abbey Lincoln, "Who Will Revere the Black Woman?" in Toni Cade, ed., *The Black Woman* (New York, 1970), pp. 88–89.

89. Liebow, *Tally's Corner,* pp. 218–9.

90. Horton, "Time and Cool People," p. 25.

91. Thomas Kochman, "Toward an Ethnography of Black American Speech Behavior," in Kochman, ed., *Rappin,'* p. 243.

92. On the relationship between "economic disengagement" and personal debasement and feelings of worthlessness see Sidney M. Willhelm, *Who Needs the Negro?* (Cambridge, Mass. 1970), esp. pp. 164–73.

93. Daniel Bell, *The Coming of Post-Industrial Society* (New York, 1973), p. 15, and ch. 2.

94. Ibid, p. 337; see also pp. 451–75. For critiques of the Bell thesis, see the review essays in *Summation,* vol. 3, no. 2 (Fall 1973): 60–99. One weakness of the work, as Richard Hill notes, is Bell's failure to come to terms with the problems of disadvantaged groups, especially the racial minorities. See *Summation,* p. 72; and for Bell's response, pp. 99–103.

95. For a grim analysis of the social and economic implications of automation for the blacks, see Sidney M. Willhelm, *Who Needs the Negro?*

96. On the limits of reformism see S.M. Miller and Pamela Roby, *The Future of Inequality* (New York, 1970), esp. ch. 6; Christopher Jencks, et al., *Inequality* (New York, 1972), ch. 9; Jeremy Larner and Irving Howe, eds., *Poverty, Views from the Left* (New York, 1968), part 1, and pp. 293–314; Irving Krauss, *Stratification, Class and Conflict* (New York, 1976), chs. 15, 16, 17. Joan Huber, "The War on Poverty" and "Programs Against Poverty: Epilogue," in J. Huber and P. Chalfant, eds., *The Sociology of American Poverty,* pp. 300–323; 336–44. On the uses of reformism, especially the welfare system, to mute protest and to reinforce work norms, see Frances Fox Piven and Richard A. Cloward, *Regulating the Poor: The Functions of Public Welfare* (New York, 1971), esp. part 3. See also Robert M. Fogelson, *Violence and Protest* (Garden City, N.Y., 1971), pp. 145–77.

97. On which, see Nathan Glazer, *Affirmative Discrimination* (New York, 1975).

98. C. Jencks, "The Future of American Education," in I. Howe, ed., *The Radical Papers* (Magnolia, Me., n.d.).

99. For a brilliant analysis, using computer simulation models, of how American market forces and discrimination combine to create South African type reservation ghettos without the use of direct force, see Linton C. Freeman and Morris H. Sunshine, *Patterns of Segregation* (Cambridge, Mass., 1970). "With extremely high prejudice levels and consensus," they note, "apartheid type neighbourhoods can be maintained even without legislation" (pp. 66–9). They found,

further, that market forces are such that "even a small departure from the optimum condition of no prejudice results in a socially unacceptable ratio of Negroes to Whites and therefore to an appreciable degree of segregation" (p. 76).

100. Even where they exist, the transportation costs involved in taking these jobs are often prohibitive. See Dorothy K. Newman, "The Decentralization of Jobs," *Monthly Review* (May 1967); Miller and Roby, *The Future of Inequality*, pp. 103–8; Daniel R. Fusfeld, "The Basic Economics of the Urban Crisis," in Huber and Chalfant, eds., *Sociology of American Poverty*, pp. 51–55.

101. On the dangers of this development, especially for blacks, see Orlando Patterson, *Ethnic Chauvinism: The Reactionary Impulse* (New York, 1977), ch. 6. See also, O. Patterson, "Hidden Dangers of the Ethnic Revival," *New York Times,* February 20, 1978, op-ed page.

102. On fears of whites coming to view blacks as dispensable due to their economic irrelevance see Willhelm, *Who Needs the Negro?* chs. 5 and 8.

103. Orlando Patterson, "Inequality, Freedom, and the Equal Opportunity Doctrine," in W. Feinberg, *Human Equality* (Urbana, 1978).

104. See David Binder, "Antiterrorist Policy of U.S. Called Weak," *New York Times,* April 23, 1978, pp. 1, 14.

105. See *Report* of the National Advisory Commission on Civil Disorders, Otto Kerner, Chairman (Washington, 1968), pp. 91–93; and part 2 passim; Etzkowitz and Schaflander, *Ghetto Crisis.* For an anthropological perspective see Ulf Hannerz, *Soulside,* pp. 159–76. See also Robert M. Fogelson, *Violence as Protest* (Garden City, N.Y., 1971), esp. pp. 98–120.

106. Douglas H. Hibbs, *Mass Political Violence: A Cross National Analysis* (N.Y., 1973), p. 182.

107. H.L. Nieburg, *Political Violence: The Behavioral Process* (N.Y., 1969), p. 3.

108. See Richard Block and Franklin E. Zimburg, "Homicide in Chicago," in Rainwater, ed., *Deviance and Liberty,* pp. 198–205.

109. Christopher S. Dunn, coordinator, *The Patterns and Distribution of Assault Incident Characteristics Among Social Areas,* U.S. Department of Justice, Criminal Justice Research Center (1976), p. 25.

110. On which see Ernest Van Den Haag, "Of Happiness and of Despair We Have No Measure," in Bernard Rosenberg and David Manning White, eds., *Mass Culture,* (N.Y., 1957), esp. pp. 520–2.

111. As Rolf B. Meyersohn notes of TV, "Because the percentage of the total audience needed to 'break even' is so high, the medium has been forced to create as many lowest common denominators as possible," in Rosenberg and White, *Mass Culture,* p. 353.

112. Some upper-class liberal adults, while not directly adopting the street style, at least lend legitimacy to it in the eyes of their children by means of "radical chic." See Tom Wolfe, *Radical Chic and Mau-Mauing the Flak Catchers* (N.Y., 1970); Fred Davis and Laura Munoz, "Heads and Freaks: Patterns and Meanings of Drug Use Among Hippies," in Rainwater, ed., *Deviance and Liberty,* pp. 88–95.

113. Newman, et al., *Protest,* p. 10.

114. Charles Tilly, "The Chaos of the Living City," in Herbert Hirsch and David C. Perry, eds., *Violence as Politics* (N.Y., 1973), p. 103.

CHAPTER 12/Johnson

1. "Family Firms and Economic Development," *Southwestern Journal of Anthropology* 24, no. 1 (Spring 1968).

2. "Discrimination and Poverty Among Women Who Head Families," in Martha Blaxall and Barbara Reagan, eds., *Women and the Workplace* (Chicago: University of Chicago Press, 1976), p. 202.

3. Bernice L. Neugarten, "Age Groups in American Society and the Rise of the Young-Old," *The Annals,* vol. 415 (September 1974); 201.

4. Peter Townsend, "The Emergence of the Four-Generation Family in Industrial Society," in Bernice L. Neugarten, ed., *Middle Age and Aging: A Reader in Social Psychology* (Chicago: University of Chicago Press, 1968), pp. 257, 256.

5. *The Making of the Modern Family* (New York: Basic Books, 1975), pp. 178–81.

6. For a similar view, see Sheila M. Rothman, "Other People's Children: The Day Care Experience in America," *Public Interest,* no. 30 (Winter 1973): 11–27.

7. *The Making of the Modern Family,* p. 161.

8. Ibid., p. 254.

9. Ibid., pp. 258–9.

10. Ibid., p. 280.

11. *Goddesses, Whores, Wives, and Slaves: Women in Classical Antiquity* (New York: Shocken Books, 1975).

12. Paul C. Glick and Arthur J. Norton, "Perspectives on the Recent Upturn in Divorce and Remarriage," *Demography* 10 (1973): 301.

13. Mary Jo Bane, *Here to Stay: American Families in the Twentieth Century* (New York: Basic Books, 1976), pp. 8, 10.

14. Nancy E. Williamson, *Sons or Daughters: A Cross-Cultural Survey of Parental Preferences* (Beverly Hills: Sage Publications, 1976).

15. *Here to Stay,* p. 13.

16. Shere Hite, *The Hite Report* (New York: Macmillan, 1976), p. 320.

17. Ibid., p. 311.

18. Ibid., pp. 203, 204, 207.

19. Ibid., pp. 286, 287. Italics added.

20. Ibid., p. 281.

21. Ibid., p. 68.

22. Ibid., p. 311.

23. *New York Times,* February 20, 1977, Section 4, p. 16.

24. The birthrate usually rises during and immediately following a war, in order to compensate for those who were killed. In the event of a nuclear war, however, the birthrate might well plummet, if people were afraid of possible genetic defects.

CHAPTER 13/Nisbet

1. See, for example, Talcott Parsons and Gerald Platt, *The American University* (Cambridge, Mass.: Harvard University Press, 1975), esp. ch. 3. Also Daniel

Bell, *The Coming of Post-Industrial Society* (New York: Basic Books, 1973), esp. p. 423.

2. *The Constitution of Liberty* (Chicago: University of Chicago Press, 1960), p. 389.

3. It is this type of intellectual rubbish that has led to a near-disastrous abandonment of admissions standards and of genuine curricula.

4. Cited in the *New York Times,* December 13, 1976.

5. John Henry Cardinal Newman, *The Idea of a University* (London: Longmans, Green, 1923), pp. 177–8.

6. See my *Twilight of Authority* (New York: Oxford University Press, 1975), pp. 131–9, for extended discussion of this point.

7. In my *The Degradation of the Academic Dogma* (New York: Basic Books, 1971). The book is an enlargement of my John Dewey Lecture, Chicago, 1970.

8. See Everett C. Ladd and Seymour M. Lipset, *The Divided Academy* (New York: Worton Library, 1976) for the authoritative account of this.

9. See *Democracy in America,* vol. 2, pp. 318–19.

10. See Edward Shils's thoughtful and restrained analysis of the problem in *Newsletter,* International Council on the Future of the University (December 1976).

11. *New York Times,* December 13, 1976.

12. See my *Quest for Community* (New York: Oxford University Press, 1953), especially Part II.

13. In Chesterton's coruscating phrase: "Inverted Micawbers, always waiting for something to turn down."

14. See my "The Permanent Professors," *Public Interest* (Fall 1965). Also Nathan Glazer, "The Torment of Tenure," in *The Idea of a Modern University,* ed. Sidney Hook et al. (New York: Promethus Books, 1974).

15. See on this Christopher Jencks and David Riesman, *The Academic Revolution* (New York: Doubleday, 1968), especially Part IV.

16. "Collective Bargaining in Higher Education," in *The Idea of a Modern University,* ed. Sidney Hook et al., as cited, pp. 157–78.

17. See his *Remembering the Answers: Essays on the American Student Revolt* (New York: Basic Books, 1970), pp. 250–72.

18. It is a pleasure to salute here Wm. Theodore DeBary, Provost of Columbia University, for his active national leadership in this respect.

19. Harry D. Gideonse, review of Paul Seabury, ed., *Universities in the Western World* (New York: Free Press, 1975) in *Freedom at Issue,* a publication of Freedom House, New York (September-October 1976).

CHAPTER 15/Rothman

1. In 1952, 46.7 percent of all American homes included a television set: by 1965 the number had risen to 97.1 percent. By the middle 1960s as many as 41 million Americans were watching evening news programs presented by one of the three television networks.

2. For discussions see Daniel Bell, *The Coming of Post-Industrial Society* (New York: Basic Books, 1973) and *The Cultural Contradictions of Capitalism* (New

York: Basic Books, 1976). Other discussions of the same concept are legion but one may include the various articles in Leon Lindberg, ed., *Politics and the Future of Industrial Society* (New York: David McKay, 1976); Kenneth Keniston, *Young Radicals* (New York: Harcourt Brace Jovanovich, 1968); Robert Heilbronner, *An Inquiry into the Human Prospect* (New York: Norton, 1975), and A. Tourraine, *The Post-Industrial Society* (New York: Random House, 1971).

3. For a brief general discussion of the rise of the mass media in Europe and the United States see Stanley Rothman, *European Society and Politics* (Indianapolis: Bobbs Merrill, 1970), pp. 257–76 and the sources cited. John Tebbel's *The Media in America* (New York: New American Library, 1974), provides a rather breezily written overview of American developments.

4. See Fred S. Siebert, Theodore Peterson, and Wilbur Schramm, *Four Theories of the Press* (Urbana: University of Illinois Press, 1956).

5. Rothman, *European Society and Politics.*

6. International Press Institute Report 26 (February 1977).

7. Rothman, *European Society and Politics;* H.W. Ehrmann, *Politics in France,* 2nd ed. (Boston: Little Brown, 1971).

8. For general discussions of the American pattern see Tebbel, *Media in America;* Edwin Emery, *The Press and America,* 3rd ed. (Prentice Hall: Englewood Cliffs, N.J., 1972); B.H. Bagdikian, *The Information Machine* (New York: Harper and Row, 1971); Edward J. Epstein, *News from Nowhere* (New York: Random House, 1973); J.W. Johnstone, Edward J. Slawski, and Williams J. Bowman, *The News People* (Urbana: University of Illinois Press, 1976); William A. Rivers, *The Adversaries: Politics and the Press,* (Boston: Beacon Press, 1970); Leon V. Sigal, *Reporters and Officials: The Organization and Politics of Newsmaking* (Lexington, Mass.: D. C. Heath, 1973); Bernard Roshco, *The News-Making Process in the American Daily Press* (Chicago: University of Chicago Press, 1975); Erik Barnouw, *Tube of Plenty* (New York: Oxford University Press, 1975); Bernard Weisberger, *The American Newspaper Man* (Chicago: University of Chicago Press, 1971); and Michael C. Emmery and Ted Curtis Smythe, eds., *Readings in Mass Communications,* 3rd ed. (Dubuque, Iowa: William Brown, 1977).

9. For a general discussion and bibliography see Rothman, Scarrow, and Schain, *European Society and Politics,* 2nd ed. (Minneapolis: West Publishing, 1976). Additional material will be found in Arthur Williams, *Broadcasting and Democracy in West Germany* (London: Granada Publishing, 1976); Anthony Smith, *The Shadow in the Cave* (London: George Allen and Unwin, 1973); and Edward Ploman, *Broadcasting in Sweden* (London: Routledge and Kegan Paul, 1976).

10. The material and citations to the literature will be found in *European Society and Politcs,* and Rothman et al., ibid., 2nd ed.

11. (New York: Harcourt Brace, 1955).

12. In a "Lockean" individualistic society, only individuals were to be represented by political parties. The representation of group interests was considered illegitimate. For an interesting contrast between American and British attitudes, see Samuel Beer, *British Politics in the Collectivist Age* (New York: Knopf, 1965). For comparisons with France and Germany, see Rothman, *European Society and Politics.*

13. See James B. Christoph, "The Press and Politics in Britain and America," *Political Quarterly* 34 (April–June, 1963): 137–50.

14. For the radio and newspaper industry see footnote 8. For the movie industry see among others Philip French, *The Movie Moguls* (Chicago: Regnery, 1971); Jonas Mekes, *Movie Journal: The Rise of a New American Cinema, 1959–1971* (New York: Macmillan, 1972); Robert Sobel, *The Manipulators* (New York: Doubleday, 1976); Jerzy Toplitz, *Hollywood and After* (Chicago: Regnery, 1975); Michael Wood, *America in the Movies* (New York: Basic Books, 1975); and David Manning White and Richard Averson, *The Celluloid Weapon* (Boston: Beacon Press, 1972).

15. For a discussion of the Hollywood investigations see Murry Kempton, *Part of Our Time* (New York: Simon and Schuster, 1955), and Stefan Kanfer, *A Journal of the Plague Years* (New York: Atheneum, 1973).

16. In Eric Goldman, *The Tragedy of Lyndon Johnson* (New York: Knopf, 1969).

17. Bell, *The Coming of Post-Industrial Society.*

18. Everett Carll Ladd, Jr. and Seymour Martin Lipset, *The Divided Academy* (New York: Norton, 1976). See also S.M. Lipset, "Academia and Politics in America," in T.J. Nossiter, A.H. Hansen, and Stein Rokkan, eds., *Imagination and Precision in the Social Sciences* (London: Faber and Faber, 1972), pp. 211–89.

19. Ladd and Lipset, *Divided Academy,* pp. 25–148 and passim.

20. Ibid., p. 29.

21. Ibid., pp. 55–124, and Everett Carll Ladd, Jr. and S.M. Lipset, *Academics, Politics, and The 1972 Election* (Washington D.C.: American Enterprise Institute for Public Policy Research, 1973), Chs. 3 and 4.

22. Daniel P. Moynihan, *Maximum Feasible Misunderstanding* (New York: The Free Press, 1969), pp. 177–78.

23. Data on the relationship between political ideology and career choice is fairly extensive. Among other sources see S.M. Lipset, *Rebellion in the University* (Chicago: University of Chicago Press, Phoenix edition, 1976), pp. 82, 260; Lipset, "Academia and Politics in America," in Nossiter, et al., eds., *Imagination and Precision in The Social Sciences,* pp. 240–42; Joseph R. DeMartina, "Student Activists of the 1930's and 1960's," in *Youth and Society* 4 (June 1975): 395–422; James Fendrich and Alison T. Tarleau, "Marching to a Different Drummer: Occupational and Political Correlates of Former Student Activists," *Social Forces* 52 (December 1973): 245–53; and Richard G. Braungart, "Youth and Social Movements," in Sigmund E. Dragosten and Glen H. Elder, Jr., eds., *Adolescence in the Life Cycle* (New York: John Wiley, 1975), pp. 255–89.

24. Everett Carll Ladd, Jr. and Charles D. Hadley, *Transformations of the American Party System* (New York: Norton, 1975), pp. 237 and passim.

25. Bell, *The Coming of Post-Industrial Society,* p. 214.

26. Bell, *The Cultural Contradictions.*

27. (New York: Random House, 1973).

28. Malcolm Warner, "T.V. Coverage of International Affairs," *Television Quarterly* 7 (1968): 60–75; and "American Television Power Elite," *New Society* 13 (February 27, 1969): 320–22.

29. See Epstein, *News from Nowhere,* and Theodore White's "America's Two

Cultures," in Alfred Balk and James Boylan, eds., *Our Troubled Press: Ten Years of the Columbia Journalism Review* (Boston: Little, Brown, 1971), pp. 11–20. Of course one cannot ignore the increased role of government, and especially the national government's role in the economic life of the country, as a factor contributing to the development of a national media.

30. Sobel, *The Manipulators*. See also the other references cited in footnote 14.

31. See Robert Lindsey, "The New Tycoons of Hollywood," *New York Times Magazine,* August 7, 1977, pp. 12ff.

32. Benjamin Stein in *Public Interest* no. 46 (Winter 1977): 128. He offered the quotations in reply to Herbert Gans's criticism of his earlier essay on the treatment of American values by the movies. See Benjamin Stein, "Whatever Happened to Small Town America," in *Public Interest* no. 44 (Summer 1976): 17–26.

33. For a discussion see David Manning White and Richard Averson, *The Celluloid Weapon*. These authors, of course, see the new orientation as creative.

34. In S.G. Burke, ed., *Print Image and Sound: Essays on the Media* (Chicago: American Library Association, 1972), p. 112.

35. Emery and Smythe, *Readings in Mass Communications,* 1972 ed., p. 195.

36. The American Institue for Political Communication, *The Credibility Problem* (Washington, D.C., February 1972), p. 61.

37. Carol H. Weiss, "What America's Leaders Read," *Public Opinion Quarterly* 38 (Spring 1974): 6. In Barton's sample, 88 percent of the media elite read (or claim to read) the *New York Times,* and 51 percent read the *Washington Post.*

38. W. Phillips Davison, "News Media and International Negotiation," *Public Opinion* 38 (Summer 1974): 174–91.

39. Leonard V. Sigal, *Reporters and Officials* (Lexington, Mass.: D.C. Heath, 1973), pp. 185–86.

40. Thomas E. Patterson and Ronald P. Abeles, "Mass Communications and the 1976 Presidential Elections," *Items* 29 (June 1975): 1.

41. J.W. Johnstone, et al., *The News People* (Urbana, Ill.: University of Illinois Press, 1976).

42. Weiss, "What America's Leaders Read," p. 8. Of course, the sample in the Columbia study was broader than the one I used for my reanalysis of the Johnstone data.

43. Charles Kadushin, *The American Intellectual Elite* (Boston: Little, Brown, 1974).

44. Epstein, *News from Nowhere,* pp. 209–10.

45. Ladd and Lipset, *The Divided Academy,* p. 27. The wording of the Harris survey upon which Ladd and Lipset relied is somewhat different from the question used by Johnstone. My guess, however, is that no more than 10 to 15 percent of the public would have classified themselves as did Johnstone's respondents if the question had been the same. I should add that both Johnstone and Barton define the elite media rather more broadly than I have. Furthermore, both of them limited their sample to a relatively small proportion of those working for the media involved. My reanalysis of Johnstone's data was limited to the elite media as defined in this paper.

46. Allen H. Barton, "Consensus and Conflict Among American Leaders," *Public Opinion Quarterly* 38 (Winter 1974): 530.

47. Barry Sussman, *Elites in America* (Washington, D.C.: The *Washington Post,* 1976), p. 10. The publication is a pamphlet reprinting five articles printed in the *Washington Post,* September 26–30, 1976.

48. (New York: Knopf, 1946).

49. See Edward J. Epstein, *Between Fact and Fiction: The Problem of Journalism* (New York: Random House, 1975), p. 206, and Theodore White, "America's Two Cultures."

50. B.H. Bagdikian, *The Effete Conspiracy* (New York: Harper and Row, 1973).

51. B.H. Bagdikian, "Newspaper Mergers: The Final Phase," *Columbia Journalism Review* 15 (March–April 1977): 17–22.

52. See Nick Kotz, "What the *Times* and the *Post* are Missing," *Washington Monthly,* March, 1977, pp. 45–49. Of course both the *Times* and the *Post* are gaining control of other media outlets, as are some television networks. The *Washington Post,* for example, owns *Newsweek,* and five television stations; The *New York Times* owns six daily newspapers and four weekly newspapers in Florida and three daily newspapers in North Carolina. It also owns three publishing houses. CBS owns five TV stations and four publishing houses. This may be one of the reasons that more conservative critics of the media, such as Kevin Phillips, have now joined Bagdikian in decrying media concentration. See Kevin Phillips, "Busting the Media Trusts," *Harper's* 255 (July 1977): 23–34.

53. Rodney W. Stark, "Policy and the Pros: An Organizational Analysis of Metropolitan Newspapers," *Berkeley Journal of Sociology* 7 (Spring 1962): 30.

54. For a review of some of the literature on the issue of objectivity and bias in news reporting see Ithiel de Sola Pool, "Government and the Media," *American Political Science Review* 70 (December 1976): 1234–41.

55. Thomas S. Kuhn, *The Structure of Scientific Revolutions,* 2nd ed. (Chicago: University of Chicago Press, 1970). For a detailed discussion of some of the issues as they apply to the social sciences see Stanley Rothman, "Mainstream Political Science and Its Discontents," in Vernon Van Dyke, ed., *Political Science: The Teacher and the Polity* (New York: Humanities Press, 1977), pp. 1–33.

56. See Gay Talese, *The Kingdom and the Power* (New York: World, 1969), and Epstein, *News From Nowhere.*

57. Epstein, *News From Nowhere;* Michael J. Robinson, "American Political Legitimacy in an Era of Electronic Journalism: Reflections on the Evening News," in Richard Adler, ed., *Television as a Social Force* (New York: Praeger, 1975), pp. 409–32; Michael J. Robinson, "Public Affairs Television and the Growth of Political Malaise," *American Political Science Review* 70 (June 1976): 409–32, and Paul H. Weaver, "Captives of Melodrama," *New York Times Magazine* (August 29, 1976), pp. 48ff.

58. In Ruth Adler, ed., *The Working Press: Special to the* New York Times (New York: Putnam, 1966), p. 28.

59. Jeremy Tunstall, ed., *Communication and Society: The Manufacture of News* (Beverly Hills, Ca.: Sage Publications, 1973), p. 19.

60. "Interview with Walter Cronkite: A Candid Conversation with America's Most Trusted Newsman," *Playboy,* June 1973, p. 76. The paradigm is (not surprisingly) characteristic of much writing in contemporary American mainstream social science. See Rothman, "Mainstream Political Science," and Peter B. Clark, "Newspaper Credibility: What Needs to be Done," in John C. Merrill

and Ralph D. Barney, eds., *Ethics and the Press: Readings in Mass Media Morality* (New York: Hastings House, 1975), pp. 172–73.

61. The essay is reprinted in Epstein, *Between Fact and Fiction*, pp. 33–77.

62. (Boston: Houghton Mifflin, 1976).

63. Quoted in Barry Goldwater, "The Networks and The News," Merrill and Barney, *Ethics and the Press*, p. 229.

64. Daniel Schorr, *Clearing the Air* (Boston: Houghton Mifflin, 1977), p. 11.

65. See Epstein, *Between Fact and Fiction*, pp. 78–100.

66. *America in Vietnam* (New York: Oxford University Press, 1978), pp. 39–41.

67. Ibid., p. 322.

68. Ibid., pp. 321–22.

69. Ibid., pp. 52–53.

70. Peter Braestrup, *Big Story* (Boulder, Colo.: The Westview Press, 1977).

71. Eric Sevareid, *Not So Wild A Dream*. Sevareid describes a number of occasions on the Italian Front when prisoners were maltreated or killed, as well as other occasions when the lives of Italian civilians were sacrificed in order to reduce American casualties. As he admits, he never reported these events.

72. See the discussion in Lewy, *America in Vietnam*, pp. 322–24.

73. A comparison of the original report and the *New York Times's* treatment of it is quite instructive. The original *Times* story appeared on February 21, 1974. It was given a front-page spread. For the actual report see Committee on Foreign Affairs of The House of Representatives: Subcommittee on National Security Policy and Scientific Developments, *U.S. Chemical Warfare Policy* (Hearings, 93rd Congress, 2nd Session, May 1, 2, 7, 9 and 14, 1974), pp. 251–93.

74. Bernard Rubin, *Media, Politics and Democracy* (New York: Oxford University Press, 1977), p. 8.

75. My discussion of the role of NBC and the *Washington Post* is taken from *Accuracy in Media* (March 1974), a conservative newsletter which monitors newspapers and television. I have not seen the original NBC script, but, within certain limits, I have found *Accuracy in Media* to be reasonably accurate in its summaries.

76. This is an old tactic, which liberal critics of the media have often noted, although they rarely see the other side. See, for example, Gaye Tuchman, "Objectivity as Strategic Ritual: An Examination of Newsmen's Notions of Objectivity," *American Journal of Sociology* 4 (January, 1972): 660–79. Almost any report on a reasonably controversial issue, even in supposedly "scientific" areas, will involve some dissent, leaving reporters a considerable amount of leeway to follow the dictates of their common sense (paradigms).

77. George Crile, III, "A Good Word for the CIA," *Harper's,* January 1976, pp. 28–32.

78. *New York Times, The Week in Review,* January 2, 1977, p. 8.

79. *New York Times,* June 17, 1977, p. 1ff.

80. For a good discussion of the coverage see the articles by George Feaver in *Encounter,* especially, "An Indian Melodrama" (May, 1975, pp. 23–34), and "The True Adventure," pp. 25–32.

81. David G. Yellen, *Special: Fred Freed and the Television Documentary* (New York: Macmillan, 1973), p. 238.

82. *New York Times,* Sunday, July 17, 1977, *The Week in Review,* p. 1; Sunday, July 25, p. 1. For a summary of television reporting, see Edith Efron's discussion in *TV News,* August 20–26, 1977, pp. A5–A6.

83. Edward Banfield, *The Unheavenly City Revisited* (Boston: Little, Brown, 1974), pp. 20–21.

84. Computed from *Statistical Abstract of the United States: 1977* (98th ed.), (Washington, D.C., 1977), p. 59, and *Social Indicators, 1976* (Washington: U.S. Department of Commerce, 1977), p. 29. Social welfare expenditures include housing, vocational rehabilitation, institutional care, child nutrition, child welfare, etc. They do not include income maintenance.

85. *U.S. News and World Report,* August 8, 1977, p. 48.

86. Preliminary reports of the characteristics of some of those arrested for looting estimated that some 45 percent had jobs. See *The Christian Science Monitor,* August 15, 1977, p. lf.

87. *New York Times,* Sunday, July 31, 1977, *The Week in Review,* p. 17.

88. One could offer a rather large number of citations, but see Banfield, *Unheavenly City,* passim; William Gorham and Nathan Glazer, eds., *The Urban Predicament* (Washington: The Urban Institute, 1976), and Stanley Lebergott, *The American Economy* (Princeton: Princeton University Press, 1976).

89. Edith Efron, *The Newstwisters* (Los Angeles: Nash Publishing, 1971). For comments see Michael Robinson, "Public Affairs Television and the Growth of Political Malaise: The Case of the Selling of the Pentagon," *The American Political Science Review* 70 (June 1976): 429, and Ithiel de Sola Pool, "Government and the Media." Robinson suggests that Efron has captured an "anti-institutional" and "disestablishment bias" rather than a particular paradigm. I agree that the set is partly anti-establishment, but, as I think the evidence suggests (and more will be offered) that is hardly the whole story. Incidentally, Efron's book was never reviewed by the *New York Times, Time,* or *Newsweek.* It was belatedly reviewed by the *Washington Post.*

90. Ernest Lefever, *TV and National Defense* (I.A.S. Press: Boston, Va., 1974).

91. The American Institute for Political Communication, *Liberal Bias As a Factor in Television News Reporting* (Washington, 1972). On the other hand, C. Richard Hofstetter's study of the 1972 election indicates that, on the whole, little or no consistent bias was displayed. See *Bias in the News* (Columbus, Ohio: Ohio State University Press, 1976).

92. T.J. Madden, "Editor Authoritarianism and Its Effect on News Display," *Journalism Quarterly* 48 (Winter 1971): 887–96.

93. For a discussion, see Stanley Rothman et al., "Ethnic Variations in Student Radicalism," in Seweryn Bialer and Sophia Sluzar, ed., *Radicalism in the Contemporary Age,* vol. 1, *Sources of Contemporary Radicalism* (Boulder: Co.: Westview Press, 1977), pp. 151–211 and the literature cited therein.

94. Quoted in Epstein, *Between Fact and Fiction,* pp. 195–96.

95. Fred W. Friendly, "What's Fair on the Air?" *New York Times Magazine,* March 30, 1975, pp. llff.

96. (New York: Random House, 1976), pp. 150–53.

97. For examples see Ben Bagdikian, *The Effete Conspiracy,* and Robert Cirino, *Don't Blame the People* (New York: Random House, 1971).

98. Bob Shanks, *The Cool Fire: How to Make It in Television* (New York: Vintage,

1976), pp. 99–104; Michael J. Robinson, "Television and American Politics," *Public Interest,* Summer 1977, pp. 3–39.

99. Shanks, *Cool Fire,* p. 101.

100. *Citizen Nader* (New York: Saturday Review Press, 1972), p. 110.

101. The report and Nader's charges are to be found in U.S. Congress, *Senate, Congressional Record,* 93rd Congress, 1st session, March 27, 1973, S.5870–S5903; March 27, 1973, S.6013–S.6099.

102. David Sanford, a disillusioned ex-member of Nader's staff, offers a number of instances in his (not very adequate) book *Me and Ralph* (Washington, D.C.: The New Republic Book Company, 1976). Very often "Nader's Raiders" consisted of young people who knew little about what they were investigating, and really did not try to learn. Yet in the 1960s their reports were given wide attention, even by those who should have known better. For a horror story which strikes one as not untypical see Gene V. Glass, "Nadir is to Nader as Lowest is to. , , ," *National Review,* July 8, 1977, pp. 776–77. Glass describes a Nader investigation of the Educational Testing Service.

103. For an excellent discussion of some of the issues involved in such calculation, see William W. Lowrance, *Of Acceptable Risk* (Los Altos, Ca.: William Kaufman, 1976).

104. Lippmann's classic work was *Public Opinion* (New York: Macmillan, 1922). For examples of the conventional wisdom which underplay the role of the mass media, see William J. McGuire, "The Nature of Attitudes and Attitude Change," in Gardner Lindzey and Elliot Aronson, eds., *The Handbook of Social Psychology,* 2nd ed., vol. 3 (Reading, Mass.: Addison-Wesley 1969), and the references cited therein. See also Bernard Berelson and Gary A. Steiner, *Human Behavior: An Inventory of Scientific Findings* (New York: Harcourt Brace and World, 1964), and the references therein.

105. See the various essays by Robinson cited above and Richard Adler and Douglas Cater, eds., *Television as a Cultural Force* (New York: Praeger, 1976).

106. Alex Inkeles and Raymond A. Bauer, *The Soviet Citizen* (Cambridge, Mass.: Harvard University Press, 1959), pp. 159–88.

107. For a study of the effects of television on middle-class attitudes toward the Vietnam War, see James D. Wright, "Life, Time and the Fortunes of War," *Transaction* 9 (1972): 42–48.

108. See the articles by Robinson and Wright cited above. See also Colin Seymour-Ure, *The Political Impact of the Mass Media* (Beverly Hills, Ca.: Sage Publication, 1974); Gary L. Wamsley and Richard A. Pride, "Television and Network News: Re-thinking the Iceberg Problem," *Western Political Quarterly,* vol. 25 (September 1969): 334–50, and the citations in both studies.

109. This is fairly clear from the Barton and Weiss studies cited in footnotes 46 and 37, respectively.

110. Nathan Glazer, *Affirmative Discrimination* (New York: Basic Books, 1975), pp. 218–19.

111. One of the few sources of television criticism which could not be ignored by those in the industry was "Newswatch," a column printed for a number of years in the mass circulation *TV Guide.* The column consisted of commentaries on television by critics of a variety of non liberal-cosmopolitan persuasions. Of these Edith Efron was, as even many of those opposed to her perspective admitted, the most trenchant.

112. They are Thomas Sowell, *Black Education: Myths and Tragedies* (New York: McKay, 1972) and *Race and Economics* (New York: McKay, 1975).

113. To name just a few, Benjamin J. Cohen, *The Question of Imperialism* (New York: Basic Books, 1973); Edward J. Mitchell, ed., *Vertical Integration in the Oil Industry* (Washington: AEI, 1976); Neal Jacoby, *Multinational Oil* (New York: Macmillan, 1976); Robert B. Krueger, *The United States and International Oil* (New York: Praeger, 1975), and Thomas D. Duchesneau, *Competition in the U.S. Energy Industry* (Cambridge, Mass.: Ballinger, 1975).

114. For an overall discussion see Barbara Hobbie, *Oil Company Divestiture and The Press: Economic vs. Journalistic Perceptions* (New York: Praeger Publishers, 1977); for the Ford study see Duchesneau, *Competition in the U.S. Energy Industy.*

115. The council's full statement will be found in Herbert Schmertz, *The Energy Crisis and the Media: Some Case Histories* (Mobil Oil Company, n.d.). I suspect that, as usual, those responsible for the program were convinced that they had produced a balanced primer. One additonal note: given all the media publicity of threats of oil spills and their supposed dangers to marine life, it may come as a surprise that at least some reputable scientists regard the danger as minimal. See the letter by Jeremiah F. Payne of the Newfoundland Biological Station Fisheries and Marine Service in *Science,* April 1, 1977.

116. The volumes are cited in Professor Lewy's study, *America in Vietnam.*

117. John S. Turner, *The Chemical Feast* (New York: Grossman, 1970). The review by John Leonard in the daily *Times* of July 24, 1970, was quite favorable. The review in the *Sunday Book Review Section* was somewhat more cautious but basically quite favorable.

118. Lowrance, *Of Acceptable Risk,* pp. 64–70, reviews some of the problems of extrapolating from animals to humans in testing.

119. Two relatively popular books are Dr. Elizabeth M. Whalen, Sc.D., and Dr. Frederick J. Stare, M.D., *Panic in the Pantry* (New York: Atheneum, 1975), and Dr. Melvin A. Benarde, *The Chemicals We Eat* (New York: McGraw Hill, 1971) Fergus S. Clydesdale and Frederick J. Francis have written a more technical study, *Food Nutrition and You* (Englewood Cliffs, N.J., 1977). See also Theodore P. Labuza, *Food and Your Well-Being* (Boulder, Co.: West Publishing Company, 1977). Dr. Whalen is a research associate at Harvard and Dr. Stare is chairman of the Department of Nutrition at the Harvard School of Public Health.

120. See Dr. Whalen's discussion of NBC and CBS documentaries on this issue in the November 15, 1976, issue of *Barron's.* By 1978 (after this paper had been completed) the consensus of knowledgeable scientists had become sufficiently great that the *Times* was beginning to include stories which make just these points. See *New York Times,* June 30, 1978, and July 12, 1978. However, the data had, in fact, been available for some time. See, for example, the studies in Joseph Fraumeni, ed., *Persons at High Risk of Cancer* (New York: Academic Press, 1975) and Ernst L. Wynder, M.D., and Gro B. Gori, Ph.D., "Contribution of the Environment to Cancer Incidence: An Epidemiologic Exercise," *Journal of the National Cancer Institute* 58 (April 1977): 825–32.E121

121. Some evidence for this can be found in Kadushin, *American Intellectual Elite.*

122. Elizabeth Noelle-Neumann, "Return to the Concept of Powerful Mass Media,"

in *Studies of Broadcasting* (Radio and T.V. Culture Research Institute: Japan, Nippon Hoso Kyokai, March 1973, No. 9), pp. 67–112.

123. Gabriel Almond and G. Bingham Powell, Jr., *Comparative Politics* (Boston: Little, Brown, 1966), p. 53.

124. Ralph Levine, "Left Behind in Brooklyn," in Peter Rose, ed., *Nation of Nations* (New York: Random House, 1972). See also the essays by Welks and Rothman in Peter I. Rose, Stanley Rothman, and William J. Wilson, eds., *Through Different Eyes* (New York: Oxford University Press, 1973), pp. 166–84, 410–29, and Ben Wattenberg, *The Real America*, rev. ed. (New York: Putnam, 1976).

125. NBC News Presents, *Danger: Radioactive Waste* (National Broadcasting Company, January 26, 1977). The overwhelming impression of the script is that there is no way to manage radioactive waste, and that it poses a growing danger so long as we rely on nuclear power.

126. For a few of those who argue that such management can be accomplished with reasonable safety, whatever criticisms they may have of present policies, see: The Nuclear Energy Policy Study Group, *Nuclear Power: Issues and Choices* (Cambridge, Mass.: Ballinger, 1977) (sponsored by the Ford Foundation); Bernard L. Cohen, "High Level Radioactive Waste from Light-Water Reactors," *Review of Modern Physics*, January 1977, summarized in the *Wilson Quarterly*, Summer 1977, pp. 37–38; R.P. Hammond, "Nuclear Power Risks," *American Scientist* 62 (1974): 155–60, and Arthur S. Kubo and David J. Rose, "Disposal of Nuclear Wastes," *Science* 182 (December 21, 1973): 1205–11.

127. Network personnel have all but admitted that during the 1960s emphasis on crime was considered racist. See *TV Guide*, August 20–26, 1977, pp. 5–10.

128. It is extraordinarily difficult to obtain data on either of these questions. Scholars tend not to investigate them. On the financing of schools, Coleman had already documented that *overall* predominantly black schools were not inferior to predominantly white schools in terms of plant, etc. as early as 1966. See James M. Coleman, *Equality of Educational Opportunity* (Washington: Department of Health, Education and Welfare, 1966). For per capita expenses in various districts in New York, see W. Norton Grub and Stephan Michelson, *States and Schools* (Lexington: Mass.: Lexington Books, 1974), p. 66. In 1972, the New York City Administrator's office published a study of per capita city expenditures per planning district. Parts of it were printed in the *New York Times* on November 13. (To anyone who knows New York, it was clear that predominantly white working and lower middle-class districts were, so to speak, getting the short end of the stick. Efforts to obtain a full copy of the report from the *Times* and various city offices were unsuccessful.) A very good case can be made for allocating additional funds to ghetto schools. However, this is not the issue.

129. See Lynn A. Curtis, *Violence, Race, and Culture* (Lexington, Mass.: D.C. Heath, 1975); Nathan Glazer, *Affirmative Discrimination*; the chapter by Coleman (on education) in Gorham and Glazer, *Urban Predicament;* Michael Lalli and Leonard D. Savitz, "The Fear of Crime in The School Enterprise and its Consequences," *Education and Urban Society* 8 (August 1974): 401–16; and James S. Coleman, "Can We Revitalize Our Cities?" *Challenge*, November/December, 1977, pp. 23–34.

130. *People Magazine,* April 28, 1975, p. 42.

131. For some sketchy evidence on this, see Curtis, *Violence, Race, and Culture.*

132. "Extra-Legal Attributes and Criminal Sentencing: An Assessment of a Sociological Viewpoint," *Law and Society Review* 8 (Spring 1974): 357–83.

133. Ernest F. Martin, Jr., "The 'Hunger in America' Controversy," *Journal of Broadcasting* 16 (1971/72): 185–93.

134. Subcommittee of the Committee on Appropriations, House of Representatives, *Hearings, Department of Agriculture Appropriations for 1970,* 91st Congress 1st session, 1969. See also Lebergott, *American Economy,* pp. 77–87.

135. Kenneth W. Clarkson, *Food Stamps and Nutrition* (Washington: American Enterprise Institute, 1975).

136. For evidence of a decline in faith in traditional institutions, see Michael J. Crozier, Samuel P. Huntington, and Joji Watanuki, *The Crisis of Democracy* (New York: New York University Press, 1975), pp. 59–118.

137. For further discussion see Stanley Rothman, "Intellectuals and The Political System," in S.M. Lipset, *Emerging Coalitions in American Politics* (San Francisco, Ca.: Institute for Contemporary Studies), pp. 325–49.

138. Bell, *The Cultural Contradictions.*

139. For further discussion see Rothman, "Intellectuals and the Political System."

CHAPTER 16/Inkeles

1. Harriet Martineau, *Society in America,* vols. I and III (London: Sanders and Otley, 1837) pp. v–vi.

2. See, for example, Seymour Martin Lipset, "A Changing American Character?" reprinted from *Culture and Social Change* (1961), in Michael McGiffert, ed., *The Character of Americans* (Homewood, Ill.: The Dorsey Press, 1964), pp. 302–30; Lee Coleman, "What Is American? A Study of Alleged American Traits," *Social Forces* 19 (May): 492–99; Gabriel A. Almond, *The American People and Foreign Policy* (New York: Praeger, 1965).

3. Alex Inkeles and Daniel J. Levinson, "National Character: The Study of Modal Personality and Sociocultural Systems," in G. Lindzey and E. Aronson, eds., *The Handbook of Social Psychology,* 2nd ed., vol. 4 (Reading, Mass.: Addison-Wesley, 1969), p. 428. In my review of the American character I have taken a broader and more eclectic approach to personality than Inkeles and Levinson did. According to some technical conceptions of personality many of the characteristics considered in the sketch I give below would be considered too "superficial" or ephemeral to qualify as true attributes of personality.

4. Alexis de Tocqueville, *Democracy in America,* ed. Henry Steele Commager (New York: Oxford University Press, 1947), pp. 212–13. Hereafter referred to as de Tocqueville (1835a).

5. Ibid., p. 410.

6. Burkhard Strumpel, ed., *Economic Means for Human Needs: Social Indicators of Well-Being and Discontent* (Ann Arbor: Survey Research Center, Institute for Social Research, University of Michigan, 1976), pp. 292–93.

7. The statement about blacks should be understood to apply only to fundamental values and basic dispositions. Questions about one's objective situation elicit distinctive responses from blacks, which reflect their objective disadvantaged

situation and their experience of racial prejudice. For example, twice as many blacks as whites report that the local police "fail to show respect for people." Some of the relevant evidence is presented and interpreted in Alex Inkeles, "Rising Expectations: Revolution, Evolution, or Devolution?" in Howard R. Bowen, ed., *Freedom and Control in a Democratic Society, A Report on the 1976 Arden House Conference*, pp. 25–37.

8. de Tocqueville (1835a), pp. 212–13.

9. J. Hector Saint John de Crèvecoeur, "What Is An American?" reprinted from *Letters from an American Farmer* (1782), in McGiffert, ed., *The Character of Americans*. pp. 36–37.

10. de Tocqueville (1835a), p. 413.

11. Ibid.

12. Ibid., p. 414.

13. Martineau, *Society in America,* vol. III, p. 390.

14. Angus Campbell, Philip E. Converse, and Willard L. Rodgers, *The Quality of American Life* (New York: Russell Sage Foundation, 1976), pp. 281–85.

15. Gabriel A. Almond and Sidney Verba, *The Civic Culture: Political Attitudes and Democracy in Five Nations* (Boston: Little, Brown, 1965), pp. 64–65.

16. de Tocqueville (1835a), p. 44.

17. James Bryce, "The American Character in the 1880's," reprinted from *The American Commonwealth* (1910), in McGiffert, ed., *The Character of Americans,* p. 70.

18. James N. Morgan, Ismail Sirageldin, and Nancy Baerwaldt, *Productive Americans: A Study of How Individuals Contribute to Economic Progress,* Survey Research Center Monograph no. 43, p. 438. Institute for Social Research (Ann Arbor: University of Michigan).

19. The question was, however, precoded, with alternatives describing different degrees of emphasis on luck or fate vs. "one's own efforts." The question used by Morgan was open-ended, and God's will or fate had to be thought of by the respondent himself. It is possible that if the question used in the developing countries had also been open-ended, fewer might have mentioned "fate" so explicitly.

20. Strumpel, *Economic Means for Human Needs,* pp. 290–91.

21. Morgan, Sirageldin, and Baerwaldt, *Productive Americans,* p. 438.

22. Strumpel, *Economic Means for Human Needs,* p. 290.

23. Alexis de Tocqueville, "Democracy in America" reprinted from *Democracy in America,* 1835, in McGiffert, ed., *The Character of Americans,* p. 44. Hereafter referred to as de Tocqueville (1835b).

24. George Katona, Burkhard Strumpel, and Ernest Zahn, *Aspirations and Affluence; Comparative Studies in the United States and Western Europe* (New York: McGraw-Hill 1971), pp. 53–59; and Strumpel, *Economic Means for Human Needs,* p. 92.

25. de Tocqueville (1835b), pp. 45–46.

26. Benjamin T. Franklin, *The Autobiography of Benjamin Franklin,* ed. John Bigelow (New York: G.P. Putnam's Sons, 1909), p. 182.

27. Although it does not bear on the issue of voluntarism, we cannot omit noting Franklin's view of the effect which the spread of such libraries had on American

sensitivity about the preservation of individual freedom. He said: "These libraries have improved the general conversation of the Americans, made the common tradesmen and farmers as intelligent as most gentlemen from other countries, and perhaps have contributed in some degree to the stand so generally made throughout the colonies in defense of their privileges" (ibid., pp. 171–72).

28. Ibid., p. 220.

29. Almond and Verba, *The Civic Culture*, pp. 133, 257.

30. Manning Nash, *Machine Age Maya: The Industrialization of a Guatemalan Community* (Chicago: University of Chicago Press, 1973), pp. 97–105.

31. Franklin, *Autobiography*, p. 190.

32. Martineau, *Society in America*, vol. I, p. 39; vol. III., pp. 55, 63, 300.

33. Almond and Verba, *The Civic Culture*, p. 213. The American propensity to say most people can be trusted is documented by public opinion polls going back to 1942. It seems a stable American characteristic for about two-thirds of the population to affirm such trust. See Robert E. Lane, "The Politics of Consensus in an Age of Affluence," *American Political Science Review* 59 (1965): 879.

34. Calculated from Almond and Verba, *The Civic Culture*, Table IX-5, p. 229.

35. Obviously with such a question it makes a great deal of difference what is meant by the "opposition" party. Almond and Verba report that their analysis is based on "attitudes toward party intermarriage among the supporters of the two largest parties in each nation: in America, Republicans' attitudes toward marriage of a child with a Democrat; in Britain, Conservatives toward Labour; in Germany, CDU toward SPD; in Mexico, PRI toward PAN; and vice versa in each case. In Italy three parties are involved. Table IX-15 reports the attitudes of CD supporters toward marriage with a Communist supporter, and the attitudes of PCI and PSI supporters toward marriage with a Christian Democrat" (ibid., pp. 234–35).

36. The countries included in this study were United States, Costa Rica, Colombia, Peru, England, Holland, France, Yugoslavia, Denmark, Japan. (See John E. Jordan, *Attitudes Toward Education and Physically Disabled Persons in Eleven Nations*. Research Report No. 1, Latin American Studies Center (East Lansing, Mich.: Michigan State University, 1968), Tables A2, A4, A7; and Leonard V. Gordon, "Q-Typing of Oriental and American Youth: Initial and Clarifying Studies," *Journal of Social Psychology* 71 (1967): 185–95.

37. The response to this question from a Gallup poll highlights the contrast between sentiments which are basic and steady, and short-term judgments which are highly specific and therefore more unstable. In 1974, in more or less the same period in which the more positive *general* estimate was being given, the American public expressed extreme pessimism about the *immediate* prospects for the economy. For example, an overwhelming 85 percent expected unemployment to rise, and a comparable proportion expected 1974 to be a year of economic difficulties. Despite these gloomy short-term, and more or less "objective," estimates, the general level of confidence was, as noted, quite high. To have cited the short-term assessments as indicators of general optimism or pessimism would have been quite misleading. (See *New York Times,* January 3, 1974, p. 30; May 19, 1974, p. 44.)

38. Katona, Strumpel, and Zahn, *Aspirations and Affluence*, p. 201.

39. de Tocqueville (1835a), p. 378. De Tocqueville wrote "In the United States

citizens have no sort of preeminence over each other, they owe each other no mutual obedience or respect." He also said, at another point, the Americans "appear never to have foreseen that it might be possible *not* to apply with strict uniformity the same laws to every part and to all the inhabitants" (de Tocqueville, 1835a, pp. 403–4; 467).

40. U.S. Department of Commerce, Bureau of the Census, *Historical Statistics of the U.S.: Colonial Times to 1970.* Parts 1 and 2 (Washington, D.C.: U.S. Government Printing Office, 1975).

41. Among the traits which Turner saw as characteristic of the frontier personality were: coarseness and strength; acuteness and acquisitiveness; a practical inventive turn of mind; grasp of material things; lack of the artistic; restless nervous energy; dominant individualism; buoyancy and exuberance (Frederick Jackson Turner, "The Frontier Experience," reprinted from *The Frontier in American History* [1920], in McGiffert, ed., *The Character of Americans,* pp. 96–101).

42. David M. Potter, *People of Plenty* (Chicago: University of Chicago Press, 1954).

43. David B. Tyack, *The One Best System: A History of American Urban Education* (Cambridge, Mass.: Harvard University Press, 1974), pp. 230–31.

44. For a parallel but more detailed exploration of these themes, compare Richard Suzman, "Social Changes in America and the Modernization of Personality," in Gordon DiRenzo, ed., *We The People* (Westport, Conn.: Greenwood Press, 1977).

45. de Tocqueville (1835b), p. 51.

46. Martineau, *Society in America,* vol. III, pp. 300, 226–27.

47. Lee Coleman subjected "a large number" of books and articles on America and Americanism to what he called a "lexicographic analysis." The traits mentioned in those sources were grouped under 27 headings on which there was widespread agreement, and another 13 which were less often mentioned and seemed less agreed on. Neither the longer nor the shorter list contains the term *tolerance.* Indeed, there is no category I would identify as even approximately representing that social characteristic! (See Coleman, "What Is American?")

48. Lipset, "A Changing American Character?" p. 314.

49. Tyack, *The One Best System,* p. 75.

50. Robert Chandler, *Public Opinion: Changing Attitudes on Contemporary Political and Social Issues* (New York: R.R. Bowker Co., 1972), pp. 6–7.

51. Lane, "The Politics of Consensus," cites surveys showing a steady increase from 1939 to 1963 in the proportion who declared themselves ready to vote for a Catholic or a Jew to be president of the United States.

52. Otis Dudley Duncan, Howard Schuman, and Beverly Duncan, *Social Change in a Metropolitan Community* (New York: Russell Sage Foundation, 1973), pp. 66, 100, 106.

53. Ibid., p. 40.

54. In the national survey conducted by the Response Analysis Corporation, Princeton, N.J., the question was asked: "Should people be allowed to publish books which attack our system of government?" The percent saying "yes" was only 35 in 1970, rose to 43 in 1971, and reached 62 percent in 1975. Response Analysis Corp., *The Sampler,* no. 8 (Princeton, N.J., Spring 1977), p. 4.

55. Max Weber, *The Protestant Ethic and the Spirit of Capitalism,* trans. Talcott Parsons (New York: Scribner's, 1958), esp. pp. 47–78.

56. Franklin, *Autobiography,* p. 189.

57. Arthur M. Schlesinger, "What Then Is the American, This New Man?" reprinted from *Paths to the Present* (1949), in McGiffert, ed., *The Character of Americans,* pp. 106–7.

58. Franklin, *Autobiography,* pp. 188–90.

59. Ibid., p. 185.

60. Duncan, Schuman, and Duncan *Social Change,* p. 73.

61. Morgan, Sirageldin, and Baerwaldt, *Productive Americans,* p. 431.

62. de Crèvecoeur, "What Is an American?" p. 35.

63. Katona, Strumpel, and Zahn, *Aspirations and Affluence,* pp. 89–99.

64. Ibid., pp. 89–100, 171–72.

65. Franklin, *Autobiography,* p. 191.

66. Morgan, Sirageldin, and Baerwaldt, *Productive Americans,* p. 451.

67. The figures were given by the Harris Survey in *The Herald Tribune* published in Paris on March 24, 1976, page 3. The fuller account with commentary may be found in Everett C. Ladd, Jr., "The Polls: The Question of Confidence," *Public Opinion Quarterly* 40 (Winter): 544–52. Different statistics based on the Gallup survey leading to "a markedly less alarming conclusion" are offered by Francis Rourke, Lloyd A. Free, and William Watts, *Trust and Confidence in the American System* (Washington, D.C.: Potomac Associates, 1976).

68. Although the general trend is unmistakable, the exact percent of the people judged to feel the government is no longer listening depends somewhat on how one asks the question. The statement in the text is based on data, from Wayne County only, as reported in Duncan, *Social Change.* The subject was "Public officials really care what people like me think." In 1957, 21 percent disagreed, in 1971, up to 57 percent. Trends over time relating to this type of question will be found in Angus Campbell and Philip E. Converse, eds., *The Human Meaning of Social Change* (New York: Russell Sage Foundation, 1972), and Ladd, "The Polls." The latter reports a Harris survey taken in March 1976 in which 64 percent of a national sample said they feel that what they think "doesn't count anymore."

69. William Watts and Lloyd A. Free, eds., *State of the Nation* (New York: Universe Books, 1973), p. 348. Here again we are faced by the persistent difficulty that when some questions are asked a different way, the evidence may point in a different direction. Thus, as noted above, even at the time of the severe recession in 1974, 68 percent of all Americans said they had "quite a lot" of confidence in the future of the United States.

70. As the authors of the report on *The State of the Nation* put it, "Americans appear. . . to hold a common system of values, goals, and social outlooks against which the national situation is judged. And this is true of Americans of almost all income groups, races, and religions, no matter what their ideological persuasion or where they live—East, West, South, North, in cities, towns, villages or rural areas" (ibid., p. 269).

71. See Inkeles, "Rising Expectations."

72. For comparable data on Europe see R. Inglehart, *The Silent Revolution: Politi-*

cal Change Among Western Publics (Princeton: Princeton University Press, 1977).

73. In 1977 there was a slight upturn in the percent expressing confidence in American institutions. Only time can tell whether this is the beginning of a new cycle. Certainly these sentiments have waxed and waned in the past. Thus, the proportion of American citizens who seemed alienated from government fell noticeably between 1952 and 1960, only to rise again by 1964 (Lane, "The Politics of Consensus," p. 893). And, as we have seen, alienation rose still further in the next decade. The population would, therefore, have to go a very long way to get back to the levels of confidence in the working of our institutions which it expressed in earlier periods.

74. Despite all their complaints about the workings of government and other institutions, 80 percent of the American people affirmed in 1975 that "the American way of life is superior to that of any other country." Indeed 60 percent said they "strongly believed" that statement. It seems, therefore, that the Garden of Eden complex is still pervasive among the American people. Whether the proportion holding this view has declined over time cannot be judged because we lack an earlier poll using the same question. The figures given are from a Yankelovich poll reported by Ladd, "The Polls," p. 551.

75. See especially his statement in *The Cultural Contradictions of Capitalism* (New York: Basic Books, 1976).

Contributors

PETER BERGER. Sociologist. Author of *Pyramids of Sacrifice, The Sacred Canopy*, and *Facing up to Modernity*. Coauthor of *The Social Construction of Reality*. Associate editor, *Worldview* magazine. Formerly with the New School for Social Research (New York City), Brooklyn College, and Rutgers University. Professor of sociology, Boston College.

KINGSLEY DAVIS. Demographer. Author of *World Urbanization 1950—1970*, vols. I and II, *Cities: Their Origin, Growth and Human Impact*, and others. Former Ford Professor of Sociology, Comparative Studies, and Chairman of the International Population and Urban Research Center at the University of California, Berkeley. Professor, Population Research Laboratory and Department of Sociology, University of Southern California.

JOHN T. DUNLOP. Economist. Author of *Wage Determination under Trade Unions, Collective Bargaining: Principles and Cases*, and coauthor of *Labor and the American Community*. Former Dean of the Faculty, Harvard University. Former Secretary of Labor and director, Cost of Living Council, and Lamont University Professor of Economics, Harvard University.

DANIEL ELAZAR. Political scientist. Author of *American Federalism: A View from the States* and *The American System: A New View of Government in the U.S.* Former professor at the Jerusalem Institute for Federal Studies. Currently, Director, Center for the Study of Federalism, and professor of political science, Temple University, and at the Bar Ilan University, Israel.

NATHAN GLAZER. Sociologist. Author or coauthor of many books, including *The Lonely Crowd, The Social Basis of American Communism, Beyond the Melting Pot*, and *Affirmative Discrimination*. Former editor, *Commentary*, Doubleday and Random House, and current coeditor of *Pub-*

lic Interest. Former professor of sociology, University of California, Berkeley. Professor of education and sociology, Harvard University.

ANDREW GREELEY. Sociologist. Author of books and other writings on ethnicity, Catholicism, and the church in America, including *Ethnicity in the United States, The American Catholic: A Social Portrait*, and *The Making of the Popes, 1978*. Editor of *Ethnicity*. Former director, Center for Pluralism, the National Opinion Research Center and lecturer at the University of Chicago. Professor of sociology, the University of Arizona.

ALEX INKELES. Social psychologist. Specialist in comparative studies of civilizations and analysis of national character. Writings include *What is Sociology* and *Becoming Modern*. From 1948 to 1970 taught at Harvard and conducted research at the Russian Research Center and the Center for International Affairs. Currently, professor of sociology and Senior Fellow at the Hoover Institution, Stanford University.

SHEILA JOHNSON. Social anthropologist and freelance writer. Author of *Idle Haven: Community-Building Among the Working-Class Retired* and *American Attitudes Toward Japan, 1941–1975*. Sometime faculty member at California State universities of Hayward, San Francisco, and Sonoma.

IRVING KRISTOL. Social critic and editor. Author of *On the Democractic Idea in America, The American Revolution as a Successful Revolution*, and *Two Cheers for Capitalism*. Coeditor of *Public Interest*. Contributor to the *Wall Street Journal* and other publications. Former Resident Scholar of the American Enterprise Institute. Henry R. Luce Professor of Urban Values at New York University.

EVERETT CARLL LADD, JR. Political scientist. Author or coauthor of many works including *Negro Political Leadership in the South, The Divided Academy: Professors and Politics*, and *Transformations of the American Party System*. Professor of political science at the University of Connecticut, Director of its Social Science Data Center, and Director of the Roper Center.

SEYMOUR MARTIN LIPSET. Sociologist. Author of *Agrarian Socialism, Political Man, The First New Nation*, and *Revolution and Counterrevolution*. Coauthor of *The Politics of Unreason, The Divided Academy, Dialogues on American Politics*, and others. Coeditor, *Public Opinion* and *Political Psychology*. Formerly at Berkeley, Columbia, and George D.

Markham Professor of Government and Sociology, Harvard. Professor of political science and sociology, and Senior Fellow at the Hoover Institution, Stanford University.

ROBERT NISBET. Sociologist. Author of *Social Change and History*, *Twilight of Authority*, *Sociology as an Art Form*, and others. Board of editors, *The American Scholar*. Former professor at the University of California (Riverside and Berkeley), the University of Arizona, and formerly Albert Schweitzer Professor in Humanities at Columbia University. Resident Scholar, the American Enterprise Institute.

ORLANDO PATTERSON. Sociologist. Author of *The Sociology of Slavery*, *Ethnic Chauvinism*, and others. Adviser to the prime minister and government in Jamaica. Former lecturer at the London School of Economics and the University of the West Indies. Currently, professor of sociology, Harvard University.

STANLEY ROTHMAN. Political scientist. Coauthor of *European Society and Politics*, *Through Different Eyes*, and *Soviet Society and Politics*. Professor of government, Smith College.

MARTIN SHAPIRO. Political scientist. Author of *Law and Politics in the Supreme Court*, and coauthor of *American National Government*, *The Politics of Constitutional Law*, and *Dynamics of American Politics*, among others. Formerly professor at the University of California (Irvine and San Diego), and at Harvard. Professor of law, University of California, Berkeley.

SANFORD WEINER. Political scientist. Author of *The Competition for Certainty: The Polls and the Press in Britain*, and others. Currently, Ph.D. candidate, department of political science, Massachusetts Institute of Technology.

AARON WILDAVSKY. Political scientist. Author or coauthor of *The Revolt Against the Masses*, *The Politics of the Budgetary Process*, *Implementation*, *Presidential Elections*, and many other works. Former professor at Oberlin. Former dean, Graduate School of Public Policy, Berkeley. Former president, Russell Sage Foundation. Professor of political science, University of California, Berkeley.

Index